Publishers, Censors and Collectors in the European Book Trade, 1650–1750

Library of the Written Word

VOLUME 126

The Handpress World

Editors-in-Chief

Andrew Pettegree (*University of St Andrews*)
Arthur der Weduwen (*University of St Andrews*)

Editorial Board

Trude Dijkstra (*University of Amsterdam*)
Falk Eisermann (*Staatsbibliothek zu Berlin – Preußischer Kulturbesitz*)
Shanti Graheli (*University of Glasgow*)
Katherine Halsey (*University of Stirling*)
Earle Havens (*Johns Hopkins University*)
Ian Maclean (*All Souls College, Oxford*)
Angela Nuovo (*University of Milan*)
Malcolm Walsby (*ENSSIB, Lyon*)
Alexander Wilkinson (*University College Dublin*)

VOLUME 103

The titles published in this series are listed at *brill.com/lww*

Publishers, Censors and Collectors in the European Book Trade, 1650–1750

Edited by

Ann-Marie Hansen
Arthur der Weduwen

BRILL

LEIDEN | BOSTON

Cover illustration: Interior of the library of the University of Leiden, *c.* 1650–1700. Rijksmuseum, Amsterdam: RP-P-2019-1218

Library of Congress Cataloging-in-Publication Data

Names: Hansen, Ann-Marie, editor. | Weduwen, Arthur der, editor.
Title: Publishers, censors and collectors in the European book trade, 1650–1750 / edited by Ann-Marie Hansen, Arthur der Weduwen.
Description: Leiden ; Boston : Brill, 2024. | Series: Library of the written word, 1874–4834 ; volume 126 | Includes bibliographical references and index.
Identifiers: LCCN 2023056079 (print) | LCCN 2023056080 (ebook) | ISBN 9789004691933 (hardback) | ISBN 9789004691940 (ebook)
Subjects: LCSH: Book industries and trade—Europe—History—17th century. | Book industries and trade—Europe—History—18th century. | Publishers and publishing—Europe—History—17th century. | Publishers and publishing—Europe—History—18th century. | Censorship—Europe—History—17th century. | Censorship—Europe—History—18th century. | Libraries—Europe—History—17th century. | Libraries—Europe—History—18th century. | Book collecting—Europe—History—17th century. | Book collecting—Europe—History—18th century. | LCGFT: Essays.
Classification: LCC Z291.3 .P83 2024 (print) | LCC Z291.3 (ebook) | DDC 381/.45002094—dc23/eng/20231220
LC record available at https://lccn.loc.gov/2023056079
LC ebook record available at https://lccn.loc.gov/2023056080

Typeface for the Latin, Greek, and Cyrillic scripts: "Brill". See and download: brill.com/brill-typeface.

ISSN 1874-4834
ISBN 978-90-04-69193-3 (hardback)
ISBN 978-90-04-69194-0 (e-book)
DOI 10.1163/9789004691940

Copyright 2024 by Koninklijke Brill NV, Leiden, The Netherlands.
Koninklijke Brill NV incorporates the imprints Brill, Brill Nijhoff, Brill Schöningh, Brill Fink, Brill mentis, Brill Wageningen Academic, Vandenhoeck & Ruprecht, Böhlau and V&R unipress.
All rights reserved. No part of this publication may be reproduced, translated, stored in a retrieval system, or transmitted in any form or by any means, electronic, mechanical, photocopying, recording or otherwise, without prior written permission from the publisher. Requests for re-use and/or translations must be addressed to Koninklijke Brill NV via brill.com or copyright.com.

This book is printed on acid-free paper and produced in a sustainable manner.

Contents

Preface VII
List of Figures and Tables X
Notes on Contributors XIII

PART 1
Publishing Strategies

1 Practitioners, Pills and the Press: Publishing Strategies in the Dutch Medical Market (*c.*1660–*c.*1770)   3
   Jeroen Salman

2 School Books, Public Education and the State of Literacy in Early Modern Catalonia   21
   Xevi Camprubí

3 The Cometary Apparition of 1743/44: Periodical Journals in the Holy Roman Empire and Their Communicative Role   44
   Doris Gruber

PART 2
Censorship and Evasion

4 A Peculiar Case of Entrepreneurial Bravery: The First Edition of Galileo Galilei's Collected Works in the Context of Mid-seventeenth-century Publishing and Censorship   71
   Leonardo Anatrini

5 Persecuted in the Spanish Colonies: Inquisitorial Censorship and the Circulation of Medical and Scientific Books in New Spain and New Granada   106
   Alberto José Campillo Pardo and Idalia García

6 The Troubles of a Protestant Bookseller in a Catholic Market: The Nuremberg Bookseller Johann Friedrich Rüdiger (1686–1751) and the Prague Book Trade   127
   Mona Garloff

7 Disclosing False Imprints: a New Look at Eighteenth-Century French Printed Production   161
   Dominique Varry

PART 3
Auctions, Collectors and Catalogues

8 Early Modern English Parish Libraries: Collecting and Collections in the Francis Trigge Chained Library and the Gorton Chest Parish Library   189
   Jessica G. Purdy

9 'Libri Anglici': English Books in Danish and Dutch Library Collections, c.1650–1720   210
   Hanna de Lange

10 The Government at Auction: Urban Policy and the Market for Books in Eighteenth-Century Lübeck   238
    Philippe Bernhard Schmid

11 *Philosophie* or *Commerce*? Classification Systems in Eighteenth-Century French Private Library Catalogues   263
    Helwi Blom

12 Sir Hans Sloane's Collection of Books and Manuscripts: an Enlightenment Library?   290
    Alexandra Ortolja-Baird

Index   319

Preface

This volume of essays derives from the 12th annual book history conference held at the University of St Andrews, hosted by the *Universal Short Title Catalogue* project group. In 2019, we welcomed scholars at St Andrews to discuss *Crisis or Enlightenment? Developments in the book trade, 1650–1750*. The conference was partially inspired by the planned extension of the USTC project's from 1650 to 1700, an extension that is now happily concluded, and makes available to the global community of print scholars more than 1.5 million records of editions printed with moveable type, surviving in over 6 million copies worldwide.

Our conference was also prompted by a broader sense that the period between the end of Thirty Years' War and the middle of the eighteenth century represented an era that has never enjoyed particular attention in the book historical profession. It is a period that is far removed from the heydays of incunabula and the formative development of the print trade in the sixteenth century, a period which has understandably garnered much interest. But the century between 1650 and 1750 is also generally too early for the dynamic crowd of book historians who occupy themselves with the era of European revolutions.

To intellectual historians, this might seem baffling: the second half of the seventeenth century and the opening decades of the eighteenth century are the critical years in Paul Hazard's defining *Crisis of the European Mind, 1680–1715* (first published 1935), and they also occupy centre stage in accounts of the Early Enlightenment. This was the age of Baruch de Spinoza, Isaac Newton and Gottfried Leibniz, an era of momentous scientific and philosophical experimentation that would ultimately reshape fundamentally the European intellectual world. What we wanted to test at our conference, was the extent to which the European book trade engaged with this 'Crisis of the European Mind', and whether the Enlightenment itself affected the book trade in any major way.

Over the course of our conference, it became clear that, in the book trade, the impact of Enlightenment was extremely limited, and that Enlightenment ideals only very gradually infused the practices of what remained a conservative trade. This was not because book professionals themselves were necessarily a reactionary crowd, but because European society as a whole remained far more hesitant to radical intellectual change. Instead, the staples of the print trade, the Bible, bestselling devotional prayer-books, almanacs, news books, political pamphlets, poems and song books remained at the heart of the book business throughout the century between 1650 and 1750.

What our contributors did demonstrate, is that there were specific areas of development and change in the book trade that were worthy of note, and worthy of expansion upon. There was a general geographical shift in the balance of production, which saw European printed output gravitate towards Britain, the Netherlands and northern Germany, from earlier heartlands in southern Germany and Italy. The conference highlighted too that regional or national output could regress as much as progress; political and religious factors, in Catalonia, Poland-Lithuania, Czechia and the Southern Netherlands saw regression instead of growth. As Xevi Camprubí's contribution in this volume highlights, the era of 'Enlightenment' could in fact also mean an absolute decline in terms of education, literacy and the consumption of books.

Change manifested itself in other ways between 1650 and 1750. The rise of vernacular publishing came at the expense of Latin, but the persistence of universities, and the numerous opportunities for occasional publications at academic institutions (funeral orations, congratulatory poetry, wedding pamphlets, invitations to public events) ensured that printing in Latin declined far less than is commonly presumed. The rise of periodicals and serial publishing, most of which were printed in vernacular languages, did ensure that the splintering of the international book trade was mediated through frequent translations and imitations. While the French language increasingly challenged Latin to the status as the polite pan-European language, contributors to this volume (in particular Hanna de Lange and Alexandra Ortolja-Baird) demonstrate that European readers and collectors continued to build varied libraries, richly populated by books in diverse languages, vernacular and scholarly alike.

The twelve following contributions in this volume all expand on the issue of change or development in the European book world between 1650 and 1750. They comment in particular on three notable areas: publishing strategies; practices of censorship; and the circulation of second-hand books and the building of libraries. They demonstrate that the era of Early Enlightenment saw formative changes in each of these realms: book trade practices, sales and advertising, the modus operandi of censors, and collecting habits. They also show that these changes took place in tandem with the activities of Enlightenment luminaries, but that they were rarely connected closely to their intellectual priorities.

Ultimately, this volume emphasises that the century between 1650 and 1750 is a period of book history which deserves our close attention, and we hope that this collection of essays might serve as a launching platform for future research and publications.

We wish to express our gratitude to our contributors for their pieces, and for their patience with the development of this volume since our conference in St Andrews.

Ann-Marie Hansen and Arthur der Weduwen
September 2023

Figures and Tables

Figures

1.1 Advertising booksellers per city, 1669–1770 12
1.2 Booksellers and titles in the STCN 12
1.3 Portrait by Pieter van Gunst of the medical doctor and publicist Steven Blankaart when he was fifty years old. Engraving, between 1700–1731 (Rijksmuseum Amsterdam, RP-P-OB-55.762) 16
1.4 Title page of Leonardus Stocke, *Berichten Wegens De Keelziekten En Scorbut of Blauwschuit. Dienende Tot Bewys Der Ontdekkingen Van Veele Heilzaame Genees-middelen* (Utrecht: Gijsbert Tieme Van Paddenburg, 1759) (copy UL Leiden 626 F 2) 18
2.1 *Alphabet* (beceroles) (Barcelona: Vicenç Surià, 1676). Axiu Historic de la Ciutat de Barcelona 28
2.2 *Seven Penitential Salms* (Barcelona: Vicenç Surià, 1677). Axiu Historic de la Ciutat de Barcelona 29
2.3 *Llibre de bons amonestaments* (Barcelona: Pere Malo, 1584). Collecció Domènech-Ballester 30
2.4 *Peregrinació del venturós pelegrí* (Barcelona: Sebastià i Jaume Mathevat, 1634). New York Public Library 31
2.5 Aelii Antonii Nebrissensis, *Grammaticae Latinae* (Barcelona: Jaume Cendrat, 1590). Biblioteca de Catalunya 33
2.6 Marcus Tullius Cicero, *Epistolarum* (Barcelona: Antoni Lacavalleria, 1666). Biblioteca de Montserrat 35
3.1 Printed works on the cometary apparition of 1743/44 (including new editions, N = 164) 49
3.2 Numbers of articles in periodical journals on the cometary apparition of 1743/44 in relation to the titles of periodical journals (N = 87) 50
3.3 Media types of the publications reviewed within the collected articles in periodical journals on the cometary apparition of 1743/44 (N = 74) 55
3.4 Geographical origins of the reviewed publications in the collected articles in periodical journals on the cometary apparition of 1743/44 (N = 74) 56
3.5 Numbers of collected reviews in periodical journals on the cometary apparition of 1743/44 (N = 74) in relation to the number of independent publications (N = 40) 58
3.6 *Göttingische Zeitungen von Gelehrten Sachen auf das Jahr MDCCXLIV* (Göttingen: Johann Peter Schmid, 1744), title-page, VD18 10945385 61

FIGURES AND TABLES   XI

3.7   Christian Gottlieb Guttmann, *Vernünftige Gedancken über die neue Cometenlehre* (Leipzig: Bernhard Christoph Breitkopf, 1744), title-page, VD18 11508167   61
3.8   Johann Heyn, *Gesamlete Briefe von den Cometen, der Sündflut, und dem Vorspiel des jüngsten Gerichts, etc.* (Berlin: Ambrosius Haude, 1745), VD18 10945385   62
3.9   *Freye Urtheile und Nachrichten zum Aufnehmen der Wissenschaften und Historie überhaupt* (Hamburg: Georg Christian Grund, 1744), title page, VD18 90151410   65
6.1   Portrait of Johann Friedrich Rüdiger (1686–1743). Austrian National Library (PORT_00142196_01)   136
6.2   Title-page of Johann Friedrich Rüdiger's *Catalogus oder Verzeichnuß aller Büchern* (1748). Národní muzeum Praha [National Museum], 57 F 8   156
7.1   Title-page of the original 1639 edition of *La Charge des gouverneurs des places*   170
7.2   Title-page of the counterfeit 1640 edition of *La Charge des gouverneurs des places*   171
7.3   Title-page of the original 1770 edition of *Soirées hélvétiennes, alsaciennes et fran-comtoises*   173
7.4   Title-page of the counterfeit 1772 edition of *Soirées hélvétiennes, alsaciennes et fran-comtoises*   174
7.5   '*Londres*' editions published in the eighteenth century   178
7.6   '*Londres*' editions published with tacit permission in the eighteenth century   178
8.1   The list of books sent to Gorton Chapel for the Parish Library   202
9.1   Page 758 of the *Catalogi Bibliothecæ Gerstorffianæ*, volume 3   211
9.2   Page from the index of the *Bibliotheca Furliana*   219
9.3   The total number of books in the Danish and Dutch catalogues surveyed for this chapter   221
9.4   Pages 99 and 98 of *Introductio ad lectionem linguarum orientalium* by Brian Walton (London: Tho. Roycroft, 1655)   230
9.5   Subdivision of Danish catalogues by language   232
9.6   Subdivision of Dutch catalogues by language   232
10.1 Petition of Jasper Köneken (1629–1715) to the city council in 1679; Lübeck, AHL: ASA Interna, Nr. 02263, fol. 1r   244
10.2 Front of St Catherine's Church in Lübeck (Katharinenkirche Lübeck). Book auctions took place in the auditorium on the premises of the old St Catherine's Monastery (Katharinenkloster)   252
10.3 Interior of St Catherine's Church in Lübeck (Katharinenkirche Lübeck) with Epitaph of Johann Heinrich von Seelen (1687–1762)   261
11.1 Private library catalogues published in France (1701–1800)   269

11.2 Classification systems in eighteenth-century private library catalogues printed in France   271
11.3 Catalogue titles 1751–1800   273
11.4 Catalogue Perrot 1776, Bibliothèque nationale de France, department of Littérature and Arts, Q-8300, title page   278
11.5 Catalogue Mirabeau 1791, Bibliothèque nationale de France, Arsenal library, 8-H-25167, table of divisions   282
12.1 Two folios from Sloane's catalogue of books. Sloane MS 3972C, vol. 6, fols. 6v, 7r. British Library (Public Domain in most countries except the UK)   298
12.2 Floorplan showing the arrangement of the foundational collections of the British Museum and the separation of Hans Sloane's books and manuscripts from the other objects in his collection. BMCA, (uncatalogued, Flitcroft and Brazier Plans of Montague House 1740–1779)   314

Tables

1.1 Booksellers in medical advertisements   10
5.1 Scientific and medical books in the Dominican Index   111
9.1 Percentage of English imprints found in the collections surveyed   221
9.2 The composition of the four catalogues by date of publication   233

Notes on Contributors

Leonardo Anatrini
PhD, is a research fellow and adjunct professor in the History of Science and Technology at the University of Florence. His research topics concern the evolution of the relations between science and belief from the 16th to the 20th century, with a particular interest in the history of alchemy and chemistry, the history of censorship and scientific communication.

Helwi Blom
is a literary historian whose research focuses on early modern France. Her scholarly interests include popular print (the *Bibliothèque bleue*), library history, the Huguenot diaspora and reception studies. She is currently lecturer in French at Radboud University (Nijmegen). She also holds a Postdoctoral Fellowship at the Université Lumière Lyon 2. Recent publications comprise articles on narrative fiction in the *Bibliothèque bleue de Normandie*, a newly discovered sixteenth-century edition of *Robert le Diable*, and sale catalogues of seventeenth-century Huguenot book collections. She is co-editor of *Private Libraries and their Documentation 1665–1830. Studying and interpreting sources* (Brill, 2023); *Top Ten Fictional Narratives in Early Modern Europe. Translation, Dissemination and Mediality* (De Gruyter, 2023), and *Du* Calendrier des Bergers *au* Pantagruel; *l'atelier Nourry à Lyon au début du XVIe siècle* (Droz, forthcoming).

Alberto José Campillo Pardo
holds a PhD in History from the Universidad de Sevilla. His research focus has been in two main areas: the circulation of knowledge between Spain and New Granada in the Early Modern Period and the inquisitorial and gubernamental censorship in the Hispanic Monarchy. He has published several works on these subjects with high impact publishers, such as Brill, Palgrave MacMillan, Comares, and the Universidad de Sevilla. He is currently a member of the ERC project 'Before Copyright' at the University of Oslo.

Xevi Camprubí
is Associate Professor of Early Modern History and the History of Journalism at the Universitat Autònoma de Barcelona. He obtained his PhD in 2014 with the thesis *L'impressor Rafael Figueró (1642–1726) i la premsa a la Catalunya del seu temps* (Fundació Noguera, 2018). He has also published *La premsa a Catalunya*

durant la Guerra de Successió (PUV, 2016), *La revolució de la imprenta. La contribució de la tipografia al desenvolupament de la Catalunya moderna* (Afers, 2020) and *Els mestres de minyons i l'ensenyament públic a la Catalunya Moderna (segles XVI–XVIII)* (Fundació Noguera, 2023). His research is focused on the study of the printing industry, the circulation of information, the origins of the periodical press and literacy in the early modern period.

Idalia García

is a researcher at the Library Science and Information Research Institute in the National Autonomous University of Mexico (UNAM). She received her PhD in Scientific Documentation from the University of Granada (1999). She is the author of numerous articles dedicated to book production, the inquisitorial control of books and the history of libraries in New Spain. She has research in progress on "The Witnesses of Book's Culture: Bibliographical Canon and Circulation of Knowledge in Colonial Mexico (2021–2024)" and she is studying for a doctorate in History at the Universidad Nacional de Educación a Distancia in Spain (UNED).

Mona Garloff

is assistant professor at the Institute of History, University of Innsbruck. From 2013–2020 she was assistant professor at the University of Stuttgart. She studied history, philosophy and politics in Munich and Paris and completed her PhD in Frankfurt and Trento in 2013 (*Irenik, Gelehrsamkeit und Politik. Jean Hotman und der europäische Religionskonflikt um 1600*. Göttingen: Vandenhoeck & Ruprecht, 2014). Her current research projects are a second book project on the Central European book trade in the Early Modern Period ("Foreign Booksellers in Vienna and Prague, 1680–1750") and a research project on "Historical and Philosophical Perspectives on Academic Failure". Her research interests are the History of the Book in the 17th–18th Centuries; Early Modern History of the Habsburg Monarchy, Central Europe and France; Cultural History of Early Modern Commerce; Political Theory and Intellectual History 1500–1800; and Reformation History and Religious Conciliation in Early Modern Europe.

Doris Gruber

is a historian and art historian, currently based at the Austrian Academy of Sciences in Vienna. Her research revolves around the question of the relationship between media and knowledge change in the early modern period and explores how new digital methods may stimulate new findings. She authored *Frühneuzeitlicher Wissenswandel: Kometenerscheinungen in der Druckpublizistik des Heiligen Römischen Reiches* (Bremen: edition lumière 2020) that discusses early modern comet apparitions and their perceptions in the Holy Roman Empire and was awarded the *Frances Stephen Award* and the *Jubiläumspreis des Böhlau Verlages Wien*. She also publishes on digital humanities, travel writing, and Ottoman–European relations.

Hanna de Lange

completed her Universal Short Title Catalogue (USTC) PhD at the University of St Andrews in 2023. Her doctoral research studied the dissemination of English and Irish books on the early modern northern European book market. She graduated from the University of Amsterdam with a degree in Early Modern History. Her thesis explored the news consumption of a seventeenth-century Dutch militiaman, as related in his diary. She contributed to various editions for the research project 'Correspondence of Johan de Witt (1625–1672)' at the Huygens Institute in the Netherlands. She co-authored an article with Andrew Pettegree for *The Oxford Handbook of the History of the Book in Early Modern England* (Oxford, 2023), edited by Adam Smyth.

Alexandra Ortolja-Baird

is a Lecturer in Digital History and Culture at the University of Portsmouth and a Visiting Researcher at The British Museum.

Jessica G. Purdy

is Associate Lecturer in Early Modern History at the University of St Andrews. She is the co-editor of *Communities of Print: Books and their Readers in Early Modern Europe* (Brill, 2021). She is also the author of *Reading Between the Lines: Parish Libraries and their Readers in Early Modern England, 1558–1709* (Brill, 2023), which explores the foundation and use of parish libraries and examines marginalia in surviving parish library books. Her research focuses on the social history of early modern England and Scotland, particularly the history of the book and reading, education and identity.

Jeroen Salman

is a senior researcher at the Faculty of Humanities of the University of Utrecht. His main research interests include early modern book history, cultural history, the history of science and popular culture. He recently published an edited volume (co-edited by Massimo Rospocher and Hanu Salmi) entitled *Crossing Borders, Crossing Cultures. Popular Print in Europe (1450–1900)* (De Gruyter Oldenbourg, 2019). In 2014 he published his monograph *Pedlars and the popular press. Itinerant distribution networks in England and the Netherlands (1600–1850)* (Brill, 2014). From 2016–2018 he led the project 'The European dimensions of popular print culture' (EDPOP). Dr Salman is a member of the 'Descartes Centre of History and Philosophy of the Sciences and the Humanities' (Utrecht University) and board member of the book historical association the Dr. P.A. Tielestichting.

Philippe Bernhard Schmid
is a Postdoctoral Research Fellow at the University of Basel funded by the Swiss National Science Foundation (SNSF). He completed his PhD in Modern History at the University of St Andrews in 2022. His research focuses on the early modern history of knowledge, the history of science, material culture and the history of collecting. In 2020 and 2021 he was a visiting fellow at Freie Universität Berlin and Harvard University. In 2023 he was a Centre for Research Collections Fellow at the *Institute for Advanced Studies in the Humanities* (IASH) at the University of Edinburgh.

Dominique Varry
is professor emeritus at the *École nationale supérieure des sciences de l'information et des bibliothèques*, part of the University of Lyon. He is an expert on the history of the French book in the *Ancien Régime*, and is the author of numerous monographs and articles in that field.

PART 1

Publishing Strategies

CHAPTER 1

Practitioners, Pills and the Press: Publishing Strategies in the Dutch Medical Market (*c*.1660–*c*.1770)

Jeroen Salman

Medical care in the early modern Dutch Republic was often inadequate in its practice. As a trade, it was also obscure, complex and competitive. In this unstructured world, medical practitioners had to rely on effective forms of communication to promote, explain and legitimise their medical knowledge and skills. For the patient, on the other hand, it was difficult to find reliable information, and if available, to judge the quality and credibility of a very heterogeneous group of practitioners. In general, sick people showed little interest in the social or scientific status of these doctors, but more in successful and affordable treatment. Without a doubt publishers and booksellers played a crucial role in facilitating this communication, in establishing and maintaining reputations and in bringing medical supply and demand together.

An often used and productive concept in this field of study is the 'medical market', because it interconnects the relevant disciplines of medical history and book history and draws attention to the intellectual as well as commercial dimensions of medical communication. In medical history this concept is also inclusive, as it encompasses official scientific knowledge and university-trained practitioners, as well as 'alternative medicine', irregular practitioners and quacks.[1]

---

[1] About the early modern medical market, see David Gentilcore, *Medical Charlatanism in Early Modern Italy* (Oxford: Oxford University Press, 2006); Margaret Pelling, *Medical conflicts in early modern London: patronage, physicians, and irregular practitioners 1550–1640* (Oxford: Oxford University Press, 2003), pp. 225–274; Ann Digby, *Making a medical living. Doctors and patients in the English market for medicine, 1720–1911* (Cambridge: Cambridge University Press, 1994); Roy Porter and Dorothy Porter, *Patient's Progress. Sickness, Health and Medical Care in England, 1650–1850* (London: Polity Press, 1989); Mary E. Fissell, *Patients, Power and the Poor in Eighteenth Century Bristol* (Cambridge: Cambridge University Press, 1991); Lauren Kassel, *Medicine and Magic in Elizabethan London. Simon Forman: Astrologer, Alchemist, and Physician* (Oxford: Oxford University Press, 2005); Andrew Wear, *Knowledge and Practice in English Medicine 1550–1680* (Cambridge: Cambridge University Press, 2000); Charles Webster, *Paracelsus. Medicine, magic and mission at the end of time* (New Haven/London: Yale University Press, 2008); Mark Jenner and Patrick Wallis (eds.), *Medicine and the market in England and its colonies c. 1450–c. 1800* (New York: Palgrave Macmillan, 2007).

From a book historical perspective this concept directs us to the exploration of the logistical and commercial aspects of printed medical communication. Books, pamphlets, flyers, posters and advertisements enabled professional communication among practitioners and scientists, but also functioned as educative and promotional tools to inform patients about medical practices and remedies. The insertion of a book historical approach into medical research finds strong support amongst prominent scholars in the field such as Andrew Wear, Roy Porter and Mary Fissell. Among other things, they have stressed the importance of self-help books, recipe books and almanacs to understand the medical mindset of practitioners and patients in early modern Europe.[2] Another expert, Deborah Harkness, has convincingly demonstrated the impact of a Paracelsian 'battle of the books' in late sixteenth-century London.[3] Others have argued that print was vital in the early modern period to establish and maintain medical authority and to pursue a public identity.[4]

In this chapter, two book historical questions related to the Dutch medical market will be discussed. First, to what extent and how did regular and irregular practitioners use newspaper advertisements and other forms of print to disseminate their practices and medications and to establish and enhance their reputation on the medical market?[5] Second, were medicines a marginal by-product or a crucial source of income for booksellers, and, was this sale of remedies a generic phenomenon or confined to a specific category of booksellers? In my search for answers I relied heavily on newspaper advertisements, and, due to the availability of data, focused mainly on the medical market in Amsterdam. As a source, advertisements have proven to be extremely valuable in tracing long-term features of medical marketing strategies, knowledge dissemination and changes within the book industry.[6] Additionally, I studied

---

2 Wear, *Knowledge and practice*; Roy Porter, 'Introduction', in Roy Porter (ed.), *The popularisation of medicine, 1650–1850* (London and New York: Routledge, 1992), pp. 1–16; Mary. E. Fissell, 'Popular medical writing', in Joad Raymond (ed.), *The Oxford History of Popular Print Culture. Vol. 1: Cheap Print in Britain and Ireland to 1660* (Oxford, Oxford University Press, 2011), pp. 398–430.
3 Deborah E. Harkness, *The Jewel House. Elizabethan London and the scientific revolution* (New Haven/London: Yale University Press, 2007), pp. 75–96.
4 William H. Helfand (ed.), *Quack, quack, quack. The sellers of nostrums in prints, posters, books & ephemera. An exhibition on the frequently excessive and flamboyant seller of nostrums as shown in prints, posters, caricatures, books, pamphlets, advertisements, and other graphic arts over the last five centuries* (New York: Grolier Club Winterhouse, 2002), p. 44.
5 See also some previous work on this: Jeroen Salman, 'The battle of medical books. Publishing strategies and the medical market in the Dutch Republic (1650–1750)', in Daniel Bellingradt, Paul Nelles and Jeroen Salman (eds.), *Books in Motion in Early Modern Europe. Beyond Production, Circulation and Consumption* (New York: Palgrave Macmillan, 2017), pp. 168–192.
6 On the value of newspaper advertisements see among others: Arthur der Weduwen and Andrew Pettegree, *The Dutch Republic and the Birth of Modern Advertising* (Leiden: Brill,

a selection of medical authors and their works, and perused bibliographical data, guild records and other archival sources. To contextualise and explain the different strategies of practitioners and booksellers, I will first sketch the features of the Dutch medical market.

1   Features of the Medical Market

In order to determine how regular and irregular practitioners used print to establish their position in the medical market, we must elaborate on the diffuse structure of healthcare in the Dutch Republic. In general, we can distinguish three categories of medical practitioners. First came the university-trained and officially licensed physicians and the surgeons and apothecaries who were trained and supervised by their guilds; second, non-regular specialists such as dentists, oculists, stonecutters and midwives; third, a mixture of irregular practitioners such as astrologers, quacks, magical healers, herbalists, empirics and alchemists.[7]

To get a sense of the quantities and density of local practitioners, Amsterdam in the seventeenth and eighteenth centuries is an instructive example. Around 1640, two regular practitioners were available in Amsterdam for every 1,000 inhabitants. In the 1680s, Amsterdam counted 80 physicians and in 1688 the guild of surgeons included 243 members.[8] This means that in the 1680s at least one surgeon per 800 inhabitants and one physician per 2,687 inhabitants were available.[9] This ratio remained the same during the eighteenth century.[10]

2020); Hannie van Goinga, *Alom te bekomen. veranderingen in de boekdistributie in de Republiek 1720–1800* (Amsterdam: De Buitenkant, 1999); Arianne Baggerman, 'Excitement and sensation on a postage stamp. Dutch book advertisements as a go-between in the eighteenth century', *Quaerendo*, 42 (2012) pp. 274–285.

7   Empirics were disqualified by the medical establishment because they based their treatment exclusively on experience and observation, devoid of any scientific knowledge. Pelling, *Medical Conflicts in Early Modern Europe*, pp. 136–188; Mary Lindemann, *Medicine and Society in Early Modern Europe* (Cambridge: Cambridge University Press, 2010), pp. 261–262; Matthew Ramsey, *Professional and Popular Medicine in France, 1770–1830* (Cambridge: Cambridge University Press, 1988), pp. 129–175; M.A. van Andel, *Volksgeneeskunst in Nederland* (Leiden: University of Leiden, 1909).

8   Harold J. Cook, *Matters of Exchange. Commerce, medicine, and science in the Dutch Golden Age* (New Haven/London: Yale University Press, 2007), p. 145.

9   Willem Frijhoff and Maarten Prak (eds.), *Geschiedenis van Amsterdam. Zelfbewuste stadstaat, 1650–1813* (Amsterdam: SUN, 2005), vol. 2.2, pp. 90–92; Cook, *Matters of Exchange*, pp. 145, 153–154.

10 Frijhoff and Prak, *Geschiedenis van Amsterdam*, Vol 2.2, pp. 121–122. In 2017, the Netherlands counted 5,000 medical practices (with often more than one GP) for about

The status of the different medical professionals varied, however, due to the fact that the magistrates of Amsterdam organised privileged medical care. They selected, appointed and employed a group of approved city practitioners. In the period 1682–1802 there were annually on average 130 medical practitioners active in the city, including surgeons, city doctors, obstetricians, midwives, plague masters, fracture masters, inspectors of the medical college, and professors or lecturers.[11] This privileged group hardly ever appears in the newspaper advertisements, because their income was guaranteed and their reputation established.

These official numbers do not paint the whole picture though, since specialists, irregular and unauthorised practitioners are ignored. Although not registered by the local authorities, we can assume, on the basis of indirect sources such as newspaper advertisements, that this group was indeed substantial.[12] Taking all this into account, we can deduce that the coverage of medical caretakers was robust in Amsterdam and competition between practitioners of different stripes likely to be rather fierce. To make a proper living and foster their reputation, practitioners must have felt the need to institutionalise, advertise and promote – be it in oral, written or printed form – their medical knowledge, products and skills, on a frequent and persistent basis.

The first and most efficient strategy to achieve this in Amsterdam was to acquire an official status via local institutions and professional organisations, such as the Collegicum Medicum (established in 1638) and the guilds of apothecaries and surgeons.[13] If membership of these organisations remained out of reach, an alternative option was to acquire separate licenses and other forms of protection.[14]

---

17 million people. This means a ratio of one medical practice for c.3,400 people. See the NIVEL medical care registration, www.nivel.nl.

[11] City Archive Amsterdam, 'Archief van de Burgemeesters: stukken betreffende ambten en officiën', inv. nr. 54–57: 'Ambtenboek. Registers van ambten en officiën met de namen van de bezitters, data van hun aanstelling, mutaties en andere gegevens, 1682–1815'. See also 'Ambtenboek van Amsterdam 1682–1868', Boerhaave Museum Leiden (BOERH a inst 51). The population in Amsterdam stabilised in the eighteenth century. Around 1680, Amsterdam counted between 210,000 and 220,000 inhabitants and in 1795 this was more or less the same (221,000 inhabitants). Frijhoff, and Prak, *Geschiedenis van Amsterdam*, pp. 9, 219.

[12] See Salman, 'The battle of medical books' and D. Kranen, *Advertenties van kwakzalvers en meesters in de Oprechte Haerlemse Courant uit de periode 1656–1733* (Ede: D. Kranen, 2008).

[13] See Cook, *Matters of Exchange*, pp. 158–163; Frijhoff and Prak, *Geschiedenis van Amsterdam*, pp. 117–119.

[14] In the last decades of the eighteenth century, several 'quacks' received permission from the local authorities to perform medical activities in Amsterdam. City Archive Amsterdam, 'Quohier van de gepreviligeerde quakzalvers'. Register van contributiebetaling door

Patients not only faced professional and logistic difficulties (where and when can I find a good, qualified doctor?), but a financial threshold as well. Medical care had a price. Summoning a university-trained doctor to your bedside was costly and therefore only obtainable for the well-to-do.[15] Poor people in urban centres on the other hand, were often served by institutionalised and state or church supported health care. So, remarkably enough, it was people in the countryside and the urban middle classes who usually had a problem finding affordable medical care.[16] Is it indeed the case that farmers and the middling sort predominantly frequented non-university and non-guild trained specialists and irregular practitioners? Did they also form the dominant group of buyers of (cheaper) medical genres in the vernacular such as self-help books, recipe books and almanacs?[17] I will come back to these issues later in this chapter.

2   Forms of (Printed) Communication: Practitioners and Patients

In this section I want to explore the modes of communication that practitioners employed to endorse their goods, services and reputation. One of the obvious tactics was to advertise in well-known and widely disseminated newspapers, such as the *Oprechte Haarlemsche Courant* (Authentic Haarlem Newspaper; henceforth OHC). This newspaper, initially published by Abraham Casteleyn in Haarlem, appeared weekly from 1656 onwards and was the most well-known and widely read newspaper in the Dutch Republic in this period.[18]

The circulation of this newspaper was impressive, considering the limited forms of transport and communication. In 1742, the OHC was published three times a week in a print run of around 4,600 copies, for a total of 13,800 copies per week. The newspaper was distributed to around twenty-seven cities, including some cities abroad. The price was relatively low: approximately half a stuiver per copy.[19] The low price and substantial print run ensured that the OHC

---

toegelaten kwakzalvers', 1785 [Register of subscription fees for admitted quacks]. Archief van de Gilden en het Brouwerscollege, inv.nr. 293.

15   In seventeenth-century Amsterdam a doctor's visit would cost about one guilder (Frijhoff and Prak, *Geschiedenis van Amsterdam*, p. 132).
16   Frijhoff and Prak, *Geschiedenis van Amsterdam*, p. 133.
17   Cook, *Matters of exchange*, p. 138; Jeroen Salman, *Populair drukwerk in de Gouden Eeuw. De almanak als lectuur en handelswaar* (Zutphen: Walburg Pers, 1999), pp. 103–134.
18   From 1737 onwards the Haarlem publishing firm Enschedé continued the production.
19   D.H. Couvée, 'The administration of the 'Oprechte Haarlemsche Courant' 1738–1742', *Gazette. International Journal of the Science of the Press*, 4 (1958), pp. 91–110.

was an influential newspaper, one that probably reached a widely-dispersed audience. What is more, the content of specific advertisements reached further than just one newspaper title. Several other weekly newspapers in the Dutch Republic ran the same advertisements as the OHC.[20]

The advertisements were sent directly to the newspaper or passed on via the retailers of the newspaper or specific intermediaries. In 1738–1740, such intermediaries included the bookseller Potgieter and notary A.D. Marolles in Amsterdam and G. Callenfels in The Hague. In these years the total turnover of these advertisements in the OHC rose from 1,233.88 guilders in 1738 to 2,083.55 guilders in 1740.[21] The costs of advertising were substantial, so the expected turnover of these products must have been high. In the period 1738–1740, the first four lines of an advertisement cost 1 guilder and 4 stuivers, and five lines and over cost 5 stuivers per line.[22] In 1778, regular advertisers paid 1 guilder and 10 stuivers for the first three lines, and 9 stuivers for four lines and over. Booksellers paid a reduced price of 1 guilder for the first three lines and 6 stuivers for five lines and more. Even if they advertised other goods (like medicinal products) booksellers paid less than other advertisers: 1 guilder and 4 stuivers for three lines, and 7 stuivers per line for more.[23]

For my survey of the OHC, I included all advertisements that mentioned medical practitioners, medicine or medical books. For the period 1669–1733, I could rely on the impressive work done by D. Kranen, who perused all the medical advertisements in that period. In total he found 333 medical advertisements, of which 119 were repeat advertisements.[24] For the period 1730–1770 I did not examine every single year but excerpted two years in every decade. In order to make a sound quantification, I only entered the Kranen advertisements of two years in every decade between 1669 and 1730. Together this resulted in a database of 222 medical advertisements for the period 1669 to 1770, without repeat advertisements (see Table 1.1).

On the basis of this sample we can discern some interesting patterns and changes in the content of the OHC advertisements. Unsurprisingly, most practitioners opened their advertisement by showcasing their specialisations, previous successful treatments and effective medications. To enhance their credibility, practitioners asserted that their therapies and drugs were approved

---

20 Van Goinga, *Alom te bekomen*, pp. 35–52.
21 Couvée, 'The administration', pp. 102–103.
22 Idem.
23 'Notitie der pryzen volgens welke de advertentien, die men begeert in de Haarlemsche Courant te plaatsen, na den eersten january 1779 zullen berekend worden.' *Prospectus* 1778. Enschede archief, NH archief Haarlem, Inv.nr: HBA 04891, Doos E 066/27.
24 Kranen, *Advertenties van kwakzalvers*.

by the local or provincial authorities, or that they had a royal or aristocratic seal of approval. It was also common to refer to written testimonials and to witnesses of people who were cured by this treatment.[25]

Specialists, irregulars and itinerant practitioners, more specifically, tended to highlight the many gaps in medical care. They offered help for complaints that regular doctors considered too risky to treat, such as cataracts, bladder stones and hernias. What also stood out was that these irregulars offered medication often as an alternative for painful operations. In terms of transparency, they not only praised and priced their pills, salves and potions, but also provided information about the ingredients, the effects and the ways to administer them. Their remedies could be multifunctional, but also very specific. In general, they were based on the old tradition of humoral pathology and were therefore not very 'enlightened', but this does not mean that they were not innovative or creative.[26] The practitioners themselves often presented them as a scientific breakthrough and a panacea. Margaretha van Kamp, a midwife in Amsterdam, announced in the OHC of 30 August 1759 that she had invented a definitive (daily) remedy for women who suffered from their 'monthly disease': namely 28 cookies! The price was just 24 stuivers, including an instruction.[27]

Aside from the remedies, information about the spatial and temporal whereabouts of the practitioners in these advertisements, was equally valuable for patients. Many quacks, empirics and travelling specialists did not have a permanent address and therefore instructed readers where, when and how long they were available. The widow Allouëll, who advertised in 1699 with a medicinal water against freckles and facial spots, was very specific and detailed: people could find her on the Raamgracht, behind the Zuiderkerk in the 'Queen of Portugal', in the house of the French baker.[28] The licensed quack Samuel Lehmans was available for his skills in dental surgery in Haarlem and for his treatment of venereal diseases in Amsterdam.[29]

As stated above, booksellers had, due to their special discounts, a lower financial threshold to publish newspaper advertisements. The growing impact of booksellers' advertisements in the eighteenth century can easily be demonstrated by the rising numbers: in 1720 the OHC published 203 advertisements

---

25 Frank Huisman, 'Itinerant medical practitioners in the Dutch Republic. The case of Groningen', *Tractrix*, 1 (1989), pp. 78–81.
26 Huisman, 'Itinerant medical practitioners', pp. 67, 78–80; Frank Huisman, 'Shaping the Medical Market. On the Construction of Quackery and Folk Medicine in Dutch Historiography', *Medical History* 43 (1999), p. 369.
27 OHC, 30 August 1759.
28 OHC, 25 January 1699.
29 OHC, 15 June 1779.

TABLE 1.1   Booksellers in medical advertisements

Year	Total med. ads	Med. ads with booksellers	% booksellers adv in med adv	Total no. different booksellers in ads	Books	Medication, instruments and treatment
1669/70	6	0	0	0	No	Yes
1679/80	3	0	0	0	No	Yes
1689/90	5	1	20%	1	No	Yes
1699/1700	3	1	7.5%	2	No	Yes
1709/10	9	1	11%	1	No	Yes
1719/20	11	1	9%	4	No	Yes
1729/30	16	4	25%	6	No	Yes
1739/40	21	14	66.6%	20	Yes: 1	Yes
1749/50	33	15	45.5%	33	No	Yes
1759/60	42	18	43%	42	Yes: 8	Yes
1769/70	63	41	65%	45	Yes: 17	Yes
Total	222	96	43%	154	26	

by booksellers, in 1740 this number rose to 409, in 1760 to 661 and in 1770 to 1,304.[30] So, for practitioners who wanted to use this medium for their promotion, collaboration with booksellers saved time and costs. Table 1.1 shows the total number of medical advertisements per two years and the (growing) number of advertisements that involved booksellers in the period 1669–1770.

What one notices in these statistics is an increase of the share of booksellers in medical advertising from the 1730s onwards, ranging from 25% to sometimes 65% of the total number of medical advertisements. What we also observe is a growing number of booksellers per medical advertisement from the 1730s onwards. It is important to note here, that these numbers do not even include the (frequent) repetitions of the same advertisements, which would make their presence even more dominant. It is telling that the large share of booksellers in the medical advertisements occurs in a period that we associate with a decline in the Dutch international book trade, and a focus on the domestic market. With that in mind, it makes sense that more and more booksellers considered selling pills and potions as an additional source of income. Mutual

---

30   Van Goinga, *Alom te bekomen*, pp. 41–42.

collaboration was equally beneficial for medical practitioners. In a commercial sense it augmented their points of sale, and from a social perspective the name of a (respectable) bookshop amplified the status and respectability of their products and practices.

The overlap between books and pills was certainly not hailed by everyone. Commentators of the *Nederlandsche Spectator* (Dutch Spectator) were irritated by the fact that around 1750 the majority of the Dutch booksellers sold – in their eyes – all kinds of dubious medicines.[31] And some authors in a philosophical journal complained that around 1760 booksellers were selling hardly any new books, but instead more second-hand books and pills, elixirs and oils.[32]

Bookshops selling medicines is not a unique Dutch phenomenon in early modern Europe. The idea that selling pharmaceuticals added to the income of booksellers is generally accepted as a valid explanation. A question without a satisfying answer is what kind of bookshops included or even relied on these non-book items? Was it a general phenomenon, or only visible in a specific segment of the market? For the late seventeenth-century English market it was suggested that only the smaller, neighbourhood booksellers had to resort to this practice.[33] In the Dutch Republic the group represented in the advertisements in the eighteenth century, however, did not appear to be as marginal as assumed here, albeit that we do see a division between the kind of activities of larger and smaller bookshops.

I would like to provide some more specific data to elaborate on this. In my survey of medical advertisements, I counted 129 different Dutch booksellers who were represented in 222 advertisements, distributed between 21 cities.

Most of the advertising booksellers were based in Amsterdam, followed at a large distance by The Hague, Utrecht, Leiden, Haarlem, Rotterdam, Middelburg and Dordrecht. The diagram below shows the number of booksellers and publishing houses based on the number of titles they produced (figure 1.2). Of course these figures, based on the Dutch Short Title Catalogue (STCN), do not represent the whole book and print production of the Dutch Republic, due to the acknowledged omissions in this retrospective bibliography, but for the

---

31   *De Nederlandsche Spectator*, 2 (1750), p. 30.
32   José de Kruif refers in her book on reading culture in The Hague to this quote from the journal *De philosooph* (The Philosopher) from 1766 (*Liefhebbers en gewoontelezers. Leescultuur in Den Haag in de achttiende eeuw*. Zutphen: Walburg Pers, 1999, p. 133). She also confirms that many booksellers in this period sold medicines.
33   John Alden, 'Pills and Publishing. Some notes on the English Book Trade, 1660–1715', *The Library*, 5 (1952), pp. 21–22.

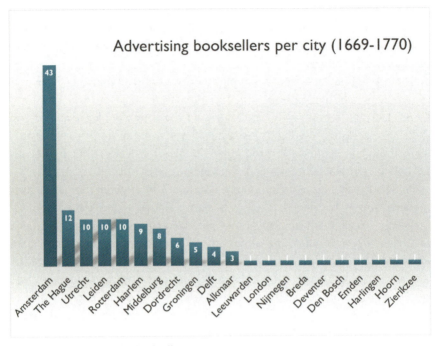

FIGURE 1.1   Advertising booksellers per city, 1669–1770

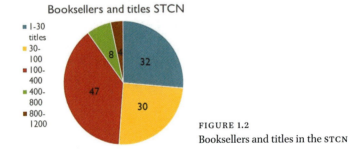

FIGURE 1.2
Booksellers and titles in the STCN

purpose of this chapter they give a good indication.[34] What becomes clear is that a large number of booksellers in my corpus, more than 60, had a known list of less than 100 titles (blue and yellow). A considerable group of 47 booksellers produced at least between 100 to 400 titles (red). Eight booksellers belonged to

---

34   See Andrew Pettegree and Arthur der Weduwen, 'What was published in the seventeenth-century Dutch Republic?', *Livre. Revue Historique* (2018), pp. 1–22; Andrew Pettegree, 'The Legion of the Lost. Recovering the Lost Books of Early Modern Europe', in Flavia Bruni and Andrew Pettegree (eds.), *Lost Books. Reconstructing the Print World of Pre-Industrial Europe* (Leiden: Brill, 2016), pp. 1–27.

the category of a minimum of 400-800 titles (green), and 12 to the top segment of at least 800 to 1200 titles (brown).

Although the twenty prominent booksellers with more than 400 titles are indeed represented in the medical advertisements, they almost always sold medical books, and not pharmaceuticals. The twenty-six books on offer aimed to diffuse scientific knowledge in the vernacular among professionals. They comprised works on surgery, dentistry, obstetrics, anatomy, healthcare and sometimes chemical medicines. The large group of advertising booksellers (1 to 400 books) who sold potions, ointments, herbal baths and other remedies and treatments, hardly sold medical books. Apparently, the landscape of retailers was divided in two different branches of booksellers: a large one aiming mainly at the patients, and a small, more exclusive one aiming at professional readers and buyers.

When we delve deeper into the content and rhetoric of the medical bookseller advertisements, a few observations catch the eye. Medicines were often sold on commission, meaning that the bookshop merely served as an additional point of sale for practitioners or medical institutions, without running a commercial risk. This does not exclude bookshops who did act independently from a supplier or medical experts. They offered drugs and drops from 'foreign doctors', stressing the exclusiveness and scarcity of this product. An example is the widow of the Amsterdam bookseller Jean Francois Jolly, who stated in an advertisement in 1759:

> The flying spirit of Amber Gris, developed and prepared by Thomas Greenough, chemist and apothecary in London, will be sold exclusively by the Widow J.F. Jolly, bookseller at the Rokin in Amsterdam. This spirit is well-known among the French and English nobility and is much more potent than other English essences.[35]

This advertisement exemplifies another observation, namely that the Dutch audience took great interest in English remedies, often intermediated by an English bookseller in the Dutch Republic. A famous example of such a broker is Mercy Browning, the widow of Joseph Bruyning, who sold an English potion based on 'scurvy grass'.[36] Mercy continued to sell this (lucrative) remedy even after she had sold her bookshop to Rest Fenner in 1685.[37] An apprentice of

---

35 OHC, 6 January 1759.
36 Paul Hoftijzer, *Engelse boekverkopers bij de Beurs. De geschiedenis van de Amsterdamse boekhandels Bruyning en Swart, 1637-1724* (Amsterdam-Maarsen: APA, 1987). See also Paul Hoftijzer, 'Het Elixer Salutatis. Verkoop en voorbereiding van een Engels medicijn in Amsterdam', *Maandblad Amstelodamum*, 72 (1985), pp. 73-78.
37 Hoftijzer, *Engelse boekverkopers*, pp. 38-48.

Joseph Bruyning, the bookseller Jacob van de Velde, sold the same medicine from 1683 onwards. And the widow (Abigael May) and son of another English bookseller, Steven Swart, not only advertised scurvy grass in 1699, but also breast cookies, eye lotion (from Doctor Russel), *Elixer Salutatis* (from Anthony Duffy) and a liquid to expel stones (from W. Tippings).[38] Especially the English products, scurvy grass and the *Elixir Salutatis*, remained 'steady sellers' during the whole eighteenth (and nineteenth) century.[39]

'Englishness' became such an asset that it was used in proper names for medicines. From the late 1730s onwards the booksellers Hendrik I Walpot (in Dordrecht) and Adam Meerkamp (in Amsterdam) advertised their 'Tinctura Stomachica Anglicana' (for 16 stuivers) and an 'English ointment against gout'.[40] The Middelburg bookseller Nathan Bollaerdt (or Bollart) offered English lung and breast cookies in 1769 (for 15 stuivers per box), developed by 'Sr. Carel Archbald'. He claimed that they cured hoarseness, as well as shortness of breath and consumption (tuberculosis).[41] He also sold 'English court plasters' that cured wounds and would really stick to the skin.[42]

Always popular were all sorts of dental remedies and treatments, English ones in particular.[43] From the 1730s onwards, booksellers such as Samuel Schoonwald, Dirk Jemans (in Amsterdam), Adam Meerkamp (in Amsterdam and Middelburg) and Hermanus Besseling (in Utrecht) advertised the 'Dentifricium Anglicanum' or 'English toothpaste' (for 14 stuivers per jar). According to the text this remedy whitens the tooth, prevents decay and produces a fresh breath.[44]

The English apothecary Thomas Greenough was not only the inventor of 'Amber Gris', but developed several dental tinctures as well. Initially he gave the English booksellers John Newbery (in Reading and London) the exclusive right of sale in 1744, but over time this monopoly disintegrated.[45] From the

---

38 In the OHC we find the Amsterdam bookseller Jacob Claus selling the same potion (OHC, 7 July 1693). Kranen, *Advertenties van kwakzalvers*, p. 105. Already in the 1670s, the Elixer was sold in the coffeehouse of Benjamin Swart and Elizabeth Ainsworth. They bought the Elixer directly from Duffy (Hoftijzer, *Engelse boekverkopers*, p. 62; Hoftijzer, 'Het Elixer Salutatis', p. 74).

39 Hoftijzer, 'Het Elixer Salutatis', pp. 73–78. Apothecaries and doctors also advertised (e.g. in 1707) in the OHC with scurvy grass and the Elixer (Kranen, *Advertenties van Kwakzalvers*, pp. 190–191).

40 OHC, 11 August 1739 (and often repeated until 1780).

41 OHC, 11 March 1769.

42 OHC, 25 April 1769.

43 An interesting Dutch case is described by Anna de Haas, 'De Weduwe Vrombout, voor witte en regelmatige tanden', *Mededelingen van de Stichting Jacob Campo Weyerman*, 41 (2018), pp. 56–68.

44 OHC, 21 February 1739 (repeated until 1780).

45 Anne Hargreaves, 'Dentistry in the British Isles', in Christine Hillam (ed.), *Dental Practice in Europe at the End of the 18th Century* (Amsterdam/Atlanta: Rodopi, 2003), p. 210.

1750s onwards, these tinctures were available in Amsterdam at the bookshop of the widow of Jean Francois Jolly where the Amber Gris was also sold.[46]

Alongside the direct sale of pills, potions and remedies, booksellers functioned as intermediaries and information brokers between medical practitioners and their potential clients. This indirect form of communication took place for instance when the medical disorder was delicate or shameful. The Amsterdam bookseller Jacobus II van Egmont stated in an advertisement of 1 July 1749 that letters for the anonymous doctor and physician who made a medicine against impotency and infertility, could be sent to his bookshop. Van Egmont would take care of all discrete communication.[47] Bookshops also seem to have functioned as centres of medical advice and consultation. Patients could not only buy medication, self-help books, recipe books and almanacs in the bookshop, but could also meet the doctors themselves or arrange indirect consultations. This was the case with the Cartesian chemical doctor and publicist Steven Blankaart (1650–1704), who was active in the second half of the seventeenth century and who worked in close collaboration with the publishing house of Jan ten Hoorn. Ten Hoorn facilitated doctor visits to specific patients and now and then patients came to the bookshop to consult Blankaart.[48]

Due to their prominent local and public function, bookshops even functioned as brokers for the sale of apothecaries and surgeons' shops. The bookseller Gerardus Lequien Jr announced in 1760 that a surgeon's shop in Amsterdam was for sale and that people could come to him or to the apprentice of the surgeon's guild for further information.[49] This type of message implies that there was no institutional animosity or rivalry between surgeons, apothecaries and booksellers, despite the fact that they tried to profit from the same market. They probably saw more benefits than downsides to collaboration.

Some booksellers were more entangled with the medical world than only through the sale of medication and medical books. In previous publications, I discussed the close collaboration between medical practitioners and booksellers considering medical publications and the dissemination of medical knowledge. One of the strategies we can discern is the production of medical journals, especially in the vernacular, trying to provide larger groups in society with access to medical knowledge. Steven Blankaart and Jan ten Hoorn published many medical works and also started one of the first Dutch medical journals: the *Collectanea Medico-physica* (1680), which was published until

---

46   OHC, 6 January 1759; 9 May 1769; 29 December 1770.
47   OHC, 1 July 1749.
48   See more about Blankaart and his collaboration with the bookseller Ten Hoorn: Salman, 'The battle of medical books', p. 179.
49   OHC, 27 March 1760.

FIGURE 1.3   Portrait by Pieter van Gunst of the medical doctor and publicist Steven Blankaart when he was fifty years old. Engraving, between 1700–1731 (Rijksmuseum Amsterdam, RP-P-OB-55.762)

1686.[50] Blankaart and Ten Hoorn probably had difficulties in maintaining a regular correspondence with medical colleagues, or perhaps overestimated the market for popularised medical science. Similar failures occurred in the late eighteenth century. Together with the Rotterdam bookseller Abraham Bothall, the medical doctor Albertus Lentfrinck (1738–1778) initiated the *Geneeskundig tijdschrift of verzameling van ontleed-, heel-, artzenij- en natuurkundige waarnemingen en nieuwe ontdekkingen* (Medical journal or collection of anatomical, healing, surgical and physical observations and new discoveries). This journal started with high expectations but was also short-lived, from 1768 until 1771. Lentfrinck, who edited this journal, noted that it had wide distribution, but was unpleasantly surprised by the immense workload of compiling the issues. He collected medical cases from many fellow doctors, and often had to translate contributions from foreign colleagues. Around 90% of the contributions were translated into Dutch. The other editorial work was also too time-consuming. Time and again, for instance, he had to reject contributions he considered too polemical.[51]

The collaboration between medical publicists and booksellers also concerned editorial work. Blankaart assisted Ten Hoorn in editing medical works from others, such as Thomas Fienus' *De twaalf voornaamste handgrepen der heelkonst* (The twelve most important treatments in surgery), published by Jan ten Hoorn in 1685. In one of his comments, Blankaart demonstrated his rather 'modern' view on medical treatment, disapproving of certain passages on bloodletting. In his opinion this would not cure but harm the patient.[52]

Despite the restraint of practitioners like Lentfrinck, sometimes doctors and booksellers did become involved in medical polemics. This was the case with the legacy of the medical doctor and pamphleteer Leonardus Stocke (1710–1775).[53] During his life, Stocke was famous for his specialism in and remedies against throat afflictions, which he often advertised in newspapers. In 1759, Gijsbert van Paddenburgh in Utrecht published his

---

50   Blankaart, *Collectanea medico-physica* (copy consulted: John Rylands Library Medical (pre-1701) Printed Collection (298), Manchester).

51   *Geneeskundig tijdschrift of verzameling van ontleed-, heel-, artzenij- en natuurkundige waarnemingen en nieuwe ontdekkingen* (Rotterdam: Abraham Bothall, 1768–1771). See also an OHC advertisement placed in the issue of 27 January 1770. See also Constant Charles Delprat, *De geschiedenis der Nederlandsche geneeskundige tijdschriften van 1680–1857* (Amsterdam: Ellerman, Harms en Co, 1927), pp. 43–48 and the online resource 'Encyclopedie Nederlandstalige Tijdschriften, www.ent1815.nl/.

52   Thomas Fienus, *De twaalf voornaamste hand-grepen der heelkonst* [...] *met noten verciert, door S. Blankaart* (Amsterdam: Jan ten Hoorn, 1685) (copy consulted: Bijzondere Collecties UvA, OK 63–64:1), p. 75.

53   See P.H. Kramer, 'Leven, werken en geheimmiddelen van Dr. L. Stocke in Rotterdam', *Rotterdam Jaarboek* (1934), pp. 1–28.

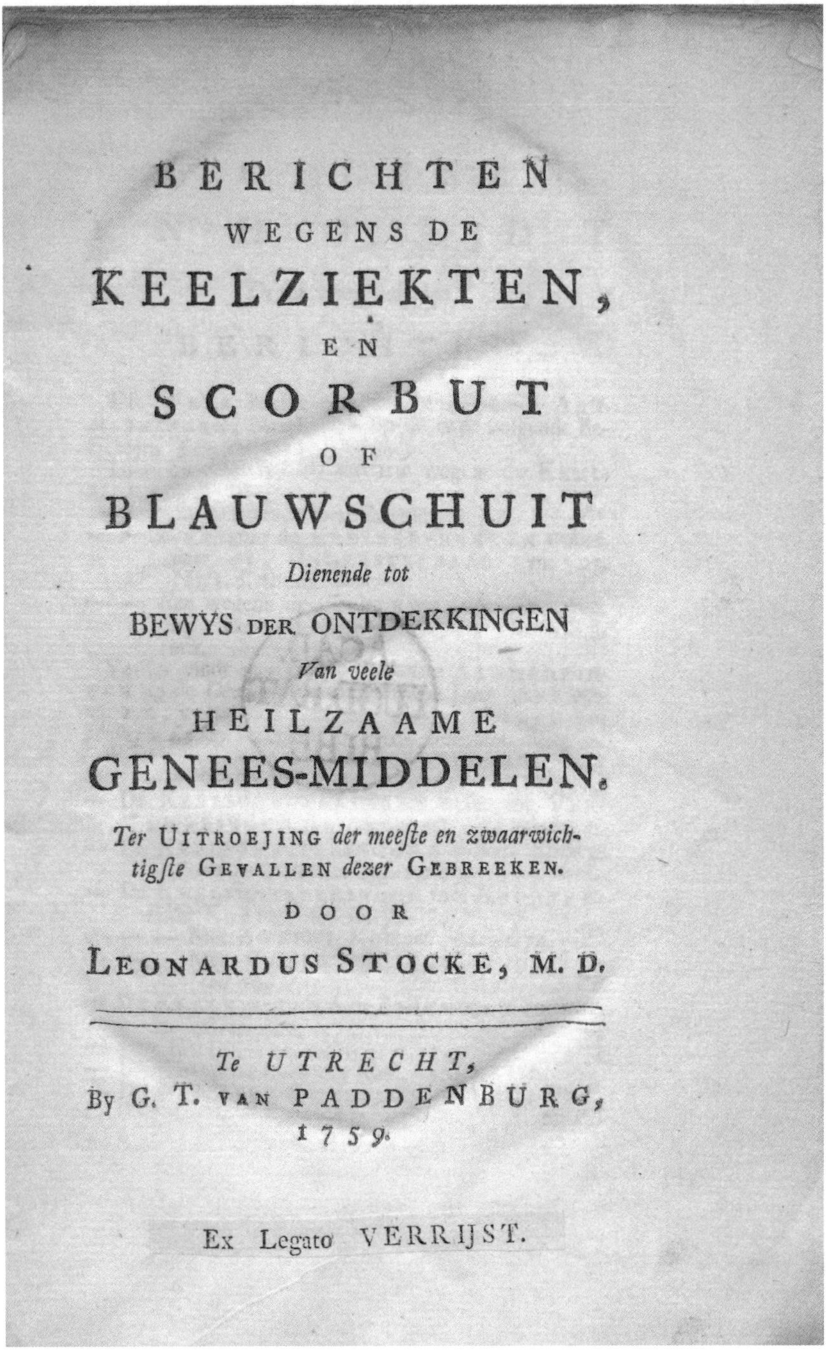

BERICHTEN
WEGENS DE
KEELZIEKTEN,
EN
SCORBUT
OF
BLAUWSCHUIT

Dienende tot

BEWYS DER ONTDEKKINGEN

Van veele

HEILZAAME
GENEES-MIDDELEN.

Ter UITROEJING *der meeste en zwaarwichtigste* GEVALLEN *dezer* GEBREEKEN.

DOOR

LEONARDUS STOCKE, M. D.

Te UTRECHT,
By G. T. VAN PADDENBURG,
1759.

Ex Legato VERRIJST.

FIGURE 1.4 Title page of Leonardus Stocke, *Berichten Wegens De Keelziekten En Scorbut of Blauwschuit. Dienende Tot Bewys Der Ontdekkingen Van Veele Heilzaame Genees-middelen* (Utrecht: Gijsbert Tieme Van Paddenburg, 1759) (copy UL Leiden 626 F 2)

Berichten Wegens De Keelziekten En Scorbut of Blauwschuit (Report on throat afflictions and scurvy).[54]

Like many other practitioners, Stocke kept the compound of his throat remedies secret, to the detriment of his fellow doctors. After Stocke died in 1775, however, his widow announced in the Rotterdam newspaper that the recipe of his famous medicine was now in the hands of another local medical doctor: Johannes van Noorden. The remedy was still available at her address. Their son-in-law, doctor Abraham Heemskerk, with whom the Van Noordens were on bad terms, also claimed that he owned the recipe and had the right to sell it. To ensure his position on the medical market, he published a response in the Rotterdam newspaper of 11 May 1775. Soon after, others ran off with the recipe or pretended they had it in their possession. In 1779, B. Rigagneau in Amsterdam, who had a perfumery on the Rokin, announced that he sold the remedy on commission.[55] Because they often found their expression in pamphlets and advertisements, the many quarrels and medical conflicts affected the publishing industry directly. Booksellers profited commercially from the sale of pamphlets for and against certain medical ideas and from the extra publicity pamphlets and advertisements offered for other works from the same authors.[56]

3   Conclusion

It has become clear that newspaper advertisements, especially in the eighteenth century, proved to be a crucial medium to facilitate communication between medical practitioners and patients in the need of healthcare. Especially specialists, itinerant and irregular practitioners were dependent on advertisements to inform people about the exclusiveness of their products and the time and place of their activities. In general, medical advertisements do not seem to have disseminated new scientific insights, but they do demonstrate creative and sometimes innovative solutions to medical problems. An example is the import or imitation of foreign (notably English) pills and potions.

From the 1730s onwards, booksellers increasingly started to intermediate between patient and doctor. There are several explanations for this new

---

54   *Berichten Wegens De Keelziekten En Scorbut of Blauwschuit. Dienende Tot Bewys Der Ontdekkingen Van Veele Heilzaame Genees-middelen* (Utrecht: Gijsbert Tieme Van Paddenburg, 1759) (copy consulted: UL Leiden 626 F 2).
55   See OHC, 13 July 1779.
56   See also Salman, 'The Battle of medical books', p. 179.

phenomenon. The growing group of practitioners profited financially (with lower prices for advertisements, more patients and additional points of sale) and socially (a boost to their reputation) from this collaboration. Small and medium-sized booksellers, on the other hand, could use the sale of medicines as a source of additional income, especially in an era of economic stagnation. These goods also attracted more customers to their bookshops and strengthened their medical network. The fact that they acted as brokers for the sale of apothecaries and surgeon's shops, is a manifestation of this interaction between doctors and booksellers. Patients, for their part, considered the bookshop as a convenient, additional medical hub, where they could find medication, buy self-help books and sometimes also receive medical advice. The partnership between medical practitioners and booksellers also led to collaborative publications, editorial activities and initiatives such as new medical journals. The latter appeared to be rather unsuccessful, due to general inexperience, lack of (international) collaboration and an overestimated market. Collaboration with the polemic medical world had another downside for booksellers: they could easily become involved in medical conflicts and animosities. But if these polemics would lead to pamphlet wars or advertisement battles, there was no reason to complain in the end.

CHAPTER 2

School Books, Public Education and the State of Literacy in Early Modern Catalonia

Xevi Camprubí

In 1556, the council of Mataró, a Catalan village with less than 1,000 inhabitants, approved the decision to employ a teacher to instruct children how to read and write. The argument was clear: the teacher was needed, in the words of the council members, 'for the benefits provided by knowledge and for the detriment that comes from ignorance'. The council provided an annual wage to the teacher and also lodging in exchange for teaching the sons of the poor families at no charge.[1]

A similar example comes from the village of Olot, with 1,700 inhabitants, located in the countryside 75 miles north of Barcelona. In 1565, the council's members reached an agreement with some local friars to open a school for children. Among the conditions, the friars were required to teach, free of charge, all the poor boys in town. In 1581, the council of Olot hired a new teacher for the public school. The conditions, however, did not change. The teacher was asked to teach the sons of all poor families of the village for free.[2]

Provisions of this sort were common in early modern Catalonia. Although grammar schools existed before, mainly for aspirant clergymen, from the sixteenth century onwards education was extended to the laity, even in the rural areas, and also to the poor. One reason that explains this development is the influence of humanism across Europe. The spread of humanist ideas on education prompted local authorities to promote learning to read and write among children. As we will see below, the books of important humanists, like Erasmus

---

[1] Arxiu de la Corona d'Aragó (Archive of the Crown of Aragon. Hereafter, ACA), Notarials, Mataró, 1556–1558, C-3, June 29th, 1556. The subject of this article has been previously developed in the framework of research that I have been doing as an independent researcher since 2014. See: Xevi Camprubí, *Els mestres de minyons i l'ensenyament públic a la Catalunya Moderna (segles XVI–XVIII)* (Barcelona: Fundació Noguera, 2023). I wish to thank professor Paul Freedman, from Yale University, for ensuring the accuracy of my written English in this article.

[2] Arxiu Comarcal de la Garrotxa (Archive of Garrotxa County. Hereafter, ACGAX), Ajuntament d'Olot, Llibre de deliberacions, 1564–1578, fol. 59v, July 6th, 1565; ibid, 1578–1588, fol. 195v, August 20th, 1581.

of Rotterdam, Antonio de Nebrija or Lluís Vives, were well known across the country, even in small villages. The works of classical authors like Cicero or Virgil were also used in the public grammar schools. This was nothing new in Europe. According to Lawrence Stone, in the sixteenth century some sectors of English upper classes were influenced by Vives' optimism about education as a mean to improve society.[3]

There were, however, practical reasons as well. Geoffrey Parker has pointed out that both religious and civil authorities desired that ordinances and proclamations were understood by the common people. In 1588, the Bishop of Barcelona, Joan Dimas Lloris, reminded the school teachers of his diocese of the importance of teaching children to read all kind of legal papers: 'He [the teacher] will take care that children are capable of reading notarial deeds, legal proceedings, letters and other difficult documents, in order to be good readers of all kinds of writing'. It was common for ecclesiastical and secular authorities to post decrees in public spaces to inform people about important occurrences. In 1599, for example, the Bishop of Barcelona had a note affixed at the main door of the cathedral, so that it could be 'easily read by everyone', as he pointed out.[4]

In early seventeenth-century Catalonia, access to public jobs, which required a basic level of education, was open to peasants and artisans. Many became jurors or councillors in municipal governments in cities, towns and villages of the region. In Barcelona, artisans were granted the sixth councillor's seat in 1641, a political achievement that had been demanded for years. Artisans also worked in a large variety of civic posts which required education, such as guards of the city gates (supervising passports and bills of health), or controlling the weight of some of the products that entered into towns. Finally, to read, write and count was also important for the trade of many artisans, mainly for business accountancy.[5]

The aim of this paper is to show that in Catalonia, from the sixteenth to eighteenth centuries, there was an effective public education system, provided by the local councils, that gave a basic education to children from lower and middle classes, including the sons of the poorest families, in most cases for

---

3 Lawrence Stone, 'Literacy and Education in England, 1640–1900', *Past and Present*, 42 (1969), p. 90.
4 Geoffrey Parker, *Europa en crisis, 1598–1648* (Madrid: Siglo XXI, 1981), pp. 372–373. Arxiu Diocesà de Barcelona (Archive of the Diocese of Barcelona. Hereafter, ADB) Comú, 1591–1594, Llibre 69, fol. 173. February 13th, 1588; ibid, Comú, 1597–1599, Llibre 71, fol. 189v, July 6th, 1599.
5 An explanation of the social structure of early modern Catalonia can be seen in English in: James A. Amelang, *Honored citizens of Barcelona: patrician culture and class relations, 1490–1714* (Princeton: Princeton University Press, 1986).

free. In the towns and villages where education was not completely free, it was affordable for most of the families because the local authorities paid a substantial part of the teacher's wages. This public system was complementary to the private education reserved for the families with higher economic means. Education, as we will see, also benefited greatly from the local print trade, which supplied the schools with a great quantity of books. School books, in fact, were produced on a large scale and they became an important part of the income of Catalan printers and booksellers in this period.

From 1714 onwards, coinciding with the establishment of the absolutist Bourbon regime of King Philip V of Spain, education in Catalonia entered into a period of decline, mainly because both the state and the local authorities (financially curtailed by new taxes) were unable to improve the school system and to provide it with the necessary funds to face the growth of the population. In relative terms, the number of children that attended school decreased, and this situation affected mainly the sons of the poor families.

1 The Benefits of Public Education

The importance of primary education for the public good can be seen in the decision taken in 1570 by the council of La Seu d'Urgell, a city of 2,500 inhabitants in the Pyrenees. The members of the council decided to employ a teacher, 'due to the importance of the literacy of the youth for any republic'. With the word 'republic' they referred to the public interest, from the Latin *res publica*. For the same reason, the council of Vilanova i la Geltrú, a village of 1,000 inhabitants, decided in 1591, after being informed that the teacher of the public school had resigned, to immediately look for a replacement. The council considered that the lack of a teacher would bring great damage to the town, because in the opinion of its members, education was very useful and profitable for the sons of all families.[6]

There is evidence of the existence of free public schools for boys in many Catalan towns and villages throughout the seventeenth century. For example, in Vilanova i la Geltrú in 1650, the council increased the teacher's wage on the condition that he teach for free all the boys who wanted to attend the public school. The same took place in Sabadell in 1670, a village of 1,000 inhabitants;

---

[6] Arxiu Comarcal de l'Alt Urgell (Archive of Urgell County. Hereafter, ACAU), Ajuntament de la Seu d'Urgell, Llibre de Consells, 1513–1578, fol. 625, August 27th, 1570. Arxiu Comarcal del Garraf (Archive of Garraf County. Hereafter, ACGAF), Ajuntament de Vilanova i la Geltrú, Acords del Consell, 1576–1593, fol. 206v, September 15th, 1591.

and in 1693 in Verdú, a village of only 500 inhabitants. It is important to point out that public education was available to male children only. In Igualada, the 115 pupils who attended public school in 1570 were, according to the list of names, all boys. There is evidence that some local councils paid female teachers to educate girls in domestic crafts and skills. This was the case, for example, with the agreement reached in 1666 between the councilors of La Seu d'Urgell and a woman called Elionor Vilella, who received some quantity of wheat every year in exchange for teaching the daughters of the poor families to sew.[7]

Free public education was often intended specifically to educate poor children. In 1700, the council of Sitges, a village of 1,500 inhabitants, dismissed the school teacher, because he did not accept the sons of the poor families. The teacher argued that those families were not able to pay him. Afterwards, the council employed another teacher for the public school, giving him a higher salary, but with the stipulation that he teach all the boys in town for free.[8]

It is also important to note that during the early modern period, education was not compulsory. Nevertheless, a great number of parents decided to send their children to school. In 1574, for example, in Sant Boi de Llobregat, a small village near Barcelona, 35 out of 38 families signed an agreement with a teacher named Marc Biscarro to provide basic education to their sons. In Igualada, a village with 179 families, one hundred boys attended the local public school in 1566. By 1570, this had increased to 115. The reason for the increase was the order given by the council to the parents, asking them to bring their children to the public school, instead of sending them to the school of other private teachers.[9]

The city councils usually paid the teachers' wages with the revenue from the excise duties on basic foodstuffs such as meat, bread and wine. In 1555, the

---

7 ACGAF, Ajuntament de Vilanova i la Geltrú, Acords del Consell, 1625–1650, fol. 232, February 20th, 1650. Arxiu Historic de Sabadell (Historical Archive of Sabadell. Hereafter, AHS), Ajuntament de Sabadell, Llibre d'actes del Ple, 1657–1677, fol. 113, March 2th, 1670. Arxiu Municipal de Verdú (Municipal Archive of Verdú. Hereafter, AMVe), Ajuntament de Verdú, Llibre de determinacions, 1692–1733, fol. 1v, March 19th, 1693. Arxiu Comarcal de l'Anoia (Archive of Anoia County. Hereafter, ACAN), Ajuntament d'Igualada, Llibre d'actes de la Universitat, 1570, fol. 72, October 18th, 1570. ACAU, Ajuntament de la Seu d'Urgell, Llibre de Consells, 1661–1707, f. 51v, January 6th, 1666.
8 Arxiu Històric Municipal de Sitges (Municipal Historical Archive of Sitges. Hereafter, AHMSi), Ajuntament de Sitges, Llibre del Consell, 1693–1705, fol. 100v, January 24th, 1700.
9 Arxiu Històric de Protocols de Barcelona (Historical Archive of the Notaries of Barcelona. Hereafter, AHPB), Bartomeu Bofill, Quadern d'aprísies de 1574, 441/6, June 27th, 1574. ACAN, Ajuntament d'Igualada, Llibre d'actes de la Universitat, 1566, fol. 53; ibid, Llibre d'actes de la Universitat, 1570, fol. 72, October 18th, 1570.

council of Vic, an important city in the countryside, with some 3,000 inhabitants, approved to pay the salary of the teacher – eight pounds per year – with money obtained from the duty on the sale of fruit in the marketplace. Four years later, the council increased the teacher's wage by another eight pounds, this time taking the money from the toll on the city bridge. In La Seu d'Urgell, in 1617, the councillors proposed to the council assembly to offer a higher salary to the grammar school teacher, taking 40 pounds that the city obtained each year from the tax on the wood collected in nearby forests. In doing so, said the councillors, they would be able to find a better teacher. In a similar way, in 1658 in Sallent, a village with 1,000 inhabitants, the teacher was paid with the proceeds of the duty on the meat that came from the slaughterhouse.[10]

In 1677, the council of Terrassa, a village of some 1,500 inhabitants, paid the teacher of the public school with money obtained from the taxes on the sales of tobacco and on *aiguardent* (firewater). In this case, the education provided had to be free of charge for all boys. Moreover, in 1699, the council promised 180 pounds per year to a grammar teacher, 44 pounds of which were taken from the duty on the sale of salted fish. The last example of this practice comes from Arbúcies, a village in the countryside, with about 1,000 inhabitants at the beginning of the eighteenth century, many of them living in isolated cottages. In 1711, during the War of the Spanish Succession, the local council approved to pay the school teacher from the revenue of all the public excise duties, and it also did the same in 1714.[11]

It is interesting to observe that the existence of public schools in Catalonia during the early modern period was regular, in spite of the economic difficulties caused by the calamities of the time, such as wars (which caused civilian casualties, but also implied recruitment and billeting of soldiers), plague or natural disasters. These events did not prove an impediment for most of the towns to pay the teacher's wages, which reinforces our notion of the importance attached to education in this period. The capacity of the towns and

---

10   Arxiu Municipal de Vic (Municipal Archive of Vic. Hereafter, AMV), Ajuntament de Vic, Acords, 1547–1570, Llibre 6, fol. 82v, April 29th, 1555; ibid, fol. 135, April 22th, 1559. ACAU, Ajuntament de la Seu d'Urgell, Llibre de Consells, 1617–1657, fol. 2v, July 30th, 1617. Arxiu Municipal de Sallent (Municipal Archive of Sallent. Hereafter, AMS), Ajuntament de Sallent, Actes del Ple, 1657–1726, May 26th, 1658.

11   Arxiu Comarcal del Vallès Occidental (Archive of Occidental Vallès County. Hereafter, ACVOC), Ajuntament de Terrassa, Llibre de consells, 1658–1678, 7/1, fol. 254, April 25th, 1677; ibid, 1678–1715, 8/1, fol. 194v, December 6th, 1699. Arxiu Històric Municipal d'Arbúcies (Municipal Historical Archive of Arbúcies. Hereafter, AHMA), Ajuntament d'Arbúcies, Llibre d'actes del comú, 1680–1740, fol. 173–174, March 8th, 1711; ibid, fol. 199–200, November 1th, 1714.

villages to raise their own duties and to pay their teachers' wages can only be fully understood if we take into account that Catalonia was, until 1700, an autonomous state within the composite monarchy of the Spanish Habsburg. Until this time, the bond between the King and the Catalan *Corts* (Parliament) was based on a mutual compromise of loyalty and respect. After his coronation, the King would travel to Barcelona and swear to uphold the Catalan laws, the *Constitucions*. After doing so, the *Corts* recognised him as the new monarch and, in response, he might agree to concede more laws and privileges (political rights) to his subjects. The deputies sent to the *Corts* by many towns requested the right to raise some duties, like those on basic foodstuffs. In exchange for some of these new privileges, the King would receive a sum of money, agreed upon by the *Corts* and the King's advisors after a negotiation. This money, called the 'donatiu' (donation), was provided during the following years by all the cities, towns and villages and was usually used by the King to finance the army.[12]

The ample provision of public funds even made it possible for some towns to hire more than one teacher, if this was necessary. In the larger towns, there could be two teachers, who divided the responsibilities to teach reading and writing. In 1677, the councillors of Mataró put a teacher in charge of the boys who learned to read and another one for those who learned to write and count. The decision was taken due to an increase in the number of children attending the municipal public school. In most large towns there was also a third teacher in charge of the Latin grammar studies, attended only by the oldest boys.[13]

In such cases that the salary provided by the councillors was not enough for the teacher to live on, he was allowed to collect money from the parents. In 1562, the council of Olot was able to offer no more than 18 pounds per year to the school teacher, and therefore he was authorised to take one sou per month from the boys who learned to read, two sous from those who learned to write and three sous from the students of grammar. In a similar way, in 1569, the councillors of Cardona, a village of some 1,100 inhabitants, located 60 miles northwest of Barcelona, promised 12 pounds per year to the school teacher, and allowed him to ask for four sous from the reading students, 10 sous from the writing students and 26 from the grammar students. In 1655, the viceroy of Catalonia, Juan José de Austria, took measures to reduce inflation, including the establishment of a price ceiling for various products and services. The

---

12   See an approach to the Catalan political system, in English, in: Joaquim Albareda & Manuel Herrero Sánchez (eds.), *Political representation in the ancien régime* (New York and London: Routledge, 2019).
13   ACA, Notarials, Mataró, 1675–1678, C-17, s.f., August 1st, 1677.

money that parents might give to school teachers was established at a rate of two sous per month for the beginners in reading, four sous for those who had an advanced level in reading, six sous for the writing students and eight sous for those who also learned counting. According to the rates implemented by the viceroy, at that time a manual worker's daily wage was between eight and ten sous, which means that the cost of the education of a single son was the equivalent to 2.5% of the monthly income of a working family.[14]

2   Print and Education

Public education in Catalonia benefited greatly from the print trade, thanks to the substantial production of short school books. The first book used to teach reading was the alphabet book, popularly known in Catalonia as 'beceroles' (see figure 2.1) and 'cartillas' in Castile. Another popular school book for beginners were the 'salms', that is to say the *Seven Penitential Psalms* (figure 2.2). These books were certainly small and short. Based on the copies that have survived, in the seventeenth century the 'beceroles' commonly had 16 pages and the 'salms' had 32, both printed in 16mo format.[15]

After progressing on from the alphabet, pupils continued with a book called 'franselm', which was a compendium of moral advice. In fact, the book bore the formal title *Llibre de bons amonestaments* (The book of good warnings) and was written at the end of the fourteenth century by the Majorcan friar Anselm Turmeda (fra Anselm), who has been considered a forerunner of Renaissance humanism (figure 2.3). Another book of this kind was *La Peregrinació del venturós pelegrí* (The pilgrimage of the good pilgrim), popularly known as

---

14   ACGAX, Ajuntament d'Olot, Llibres del consell, 1546–1564, f. 365, April 28th, 1562; Biblioteca de Catalunya (National Library of Catalonia. Hereafter, BC), Batllia de Cardona, Llibre dels Cònsols, 1564–1610, Bat Car 7/4, s.f., October 26th, 1569. See the viceroy price rate in 'Tarifa y postura de preus de les coses infrascrites', in: Ramon Alberch [et al.], *Gremis i oficis a Girona. Treball i societat a l'època pre-industrial*, (Girona: Ajuntament de Girona, 1984), pp. 252 and 263.

15   See the use of the 'cartillas' in: Jaime Moll, 'La cartilla et sa distribution au XVIIème siecle', in *De l'alphabétisation aux circuits du livre en Espagne, XVI–XIX siècles* (Paris: CNRS, 1987), pp. 311–322; Augustin Redondo, 'Les livrets de lecture (cartillas para enseñar a leer) au XVIe siecle: lecture et message doctrinal', in Augustin Redondo (ed.), *La formation de l'enfant en Espagne aux XVIe et XVIIe siècles* (Paris: Publications de la Sorbonne, 1996), pp. 71–91. The oldest 'beceroles' and 'salms' printed in Catalonia that I have seen date from 1676 and 1677. They have been preserved inside notarial and judiciary documents and are not catalogued. Arxiu Historic de la Ciutat de Barcelona (Historical Archive of the City of Barcelona. Hereafter, AHCB), Notarial, IX-4; ACA, Reial Audència, Plets civils, 23921.

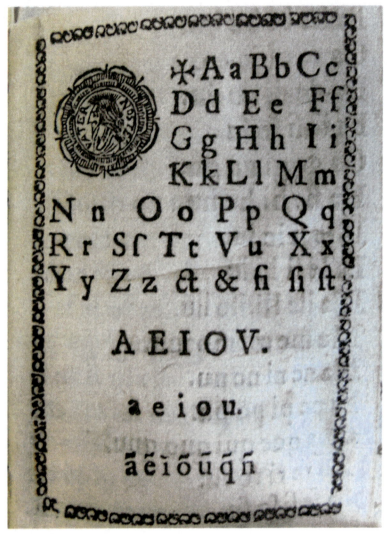

FIGURE 2.1   *Alphabet* (beceroles) (Barcelona: Vicenç Surià, 1676). Arxiu Històric de la Ciutat de Barcelona

'pelegrins' (figure 2.4). The 'franselms' were commonly composed of 32 pages and the 'pelegrins' of 48, both printed in an octavo format.[16]

---

16   The oldest copy of Turmeda's book printed in Catalan that I have seen dates from 1584 and belongs to the private collection of the family Domenèch, to whom I am grateful for the digital reproduction given to me. The oldest copy preserved in the Catalan public archives and libraries dates from 1667. Biblioteca Pública Episcopal de Barcelona (Library of the Bishopric of Barcelona. Hereafter, BPEP), 243 = 499 Tur. A copy of the *Peregrinació del venturós pelegrí* printed in Barcelona in 1635 has been preserved in the

FIGURE 2.2   *Seven Penitential Salms* (Barcelona: Vicenç Surià, 1677)
Arxiu Històric de la Ciutat de Barcelona

There is evidence of the production and trade of these books soon after the arrival of the printing press in Catalonia. Among the books that master printer Pere Posa sold in 1498 to Gaspar Mir and Antoni Vernet, booksellers of Barcelona, were several copies of alphabets, salms and 'franselms'. In 1503, Joan Rosembach, a German printer by then established in Perpinyà (Perpignan) – the

New York Public Library. Universal Short Title Catalogue (hereafter, USTC), 5034165. The oldest copy preserved in Catalan archives dates from 1677. BC, 6-1-7/1.

FIGURE 2.3
Llibre de bons amonestaments
(Barcelona: Pere Malo, 1584). Col·lecció Domènech-Ballester

second largest city in Catalonia at that time – signed an agreement with Joan Trinxer, bookseller of Barcelona, to print several works, among which were 550 alphabets printed on parchment, and also two reams of alphabets and salms printed on paper. According to an inventory from 1507, 200 'beceroles', 400 psalms and 500 'franselms' were stocked in Pere Posa's office. Unfortunately, not a single copy of these books is known to have survived.[17]

These kind of school books were not only used in urban schools, but also in small villages in the countryside. In 1569, the council of Cardona employed Joan Torrabadella as a teacher for the public school. Under the conditions of his employment, it was agreed that he should teach the beginners using 'beseroles y sept salms', that is to say, alphabets and the *Seven Penitential Salms*.[18]

In 1588 the bishop of Barcelona, Joan Dimas Lloris, drew up a list of instructions addressed to all school teachers of his diocese, mentioning in one instruction a list of books that boys might read:

> Regarding the books they use to learn to read, he [the teacher] is ordered that after the alphabets they must read the seven psalms and litanies (…).

---

17 Jordi Rubió i Balaguer and Josep Maria Madurell i Marimon, *Documentos para la historia de la imprenta y librería en Barcelona, 1474–1553* (Barcelona: Gremio de Editores y Libreros, 1955), pp. 272, 361 and 456.

18 BC, Batllia de Cardona, Llibre dels Cònsols (1564–1610), Bat Car 7/4, October 26th, 1569.

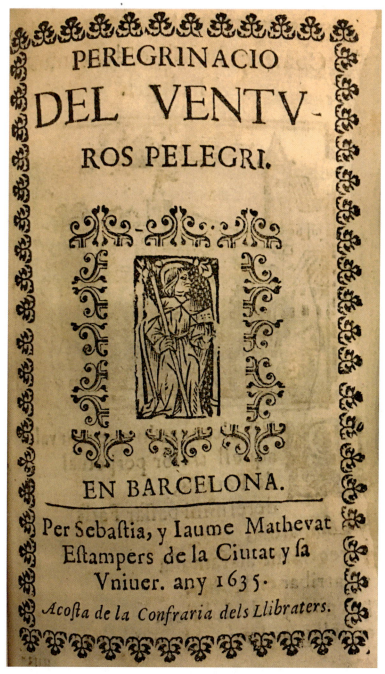

FIGURE 2.4　*Peregrinació del venturós pelegrí* (Barcelona: Sebastià and Jaume Mathevat, 1634). New York Public Library

And he has to assure they read the *franselm*, newly printed and approved, because it contains several examples of good moral advice. And he has to take care that the rest of books they read, either in vernacular language or in Latin, must reflect good and approved doctrine.[19]

As we can see, children were taught in both Latin and Catalan, and for this reason school books were printed mainly in these two languages. The knowledge of Latin was important because it was the language of religious services. However, the main tenets of the Christian doctrine – the catechism – was taught in Catalan as instructed by the bishops, who considered that the best way for children to learn Christian principles was in their mother tongue. In 1608, Rafael de Rovirola, Bishop of Barcelona, ordered teachers to use 'the Catalan doctrine of father Ledesma'. It was the book titled *Doctrina Christiana a manera de diàlogo entre lo mestre y lo dexeble*, written by the Jesuit Diego de Ledesma. This book was originally written in Latin but was soon after translated into many languages, including Italian, English, Castilian and Catalan.[20]

Grammar books, on the other hand, were always printed in Latin, because the knowledge of this language was considered critical to unlock other faculties of higher learning. The most important grammar books used in Catalan schools were the works of the Sevillian linguist Antonio de Nebrija, now considered the most representative author of Spanish humanism (figure 2.5). In 1497, the master printer Joan Rosembach, by then established in Barcelona, printed 500 copies of Nebrija's grammar, commissioned by the bookseller Nicolau Mazà. Again, in 1523, Rosembach and a conglomerate of booksellers agreed to print and sell 1,100 copies of this grammar book.[21]

Antonio de Nebrija's Latin grammar, popularly known as 'antonis', was produced for Castilian and Catalan audiences and reissued many times during the seventeenth and eighteenth centuries. In 1625, for example, the booksellers' guild of Barcelona ordered 2,500 copies of this grammar from Esteve Liberós,

---

19   ADB, Comú, 1591–1594, Llibre 69, fol. 173, February 13th, 1588.
20   ADB, Comú, 1604–1609, Llibre 74, fol. 123, February 4th, 1068. The oldest translation of Ledesma's doctrine that figures in the USTC was published in Italian in Ferrara in 1569. *Dottrina christiana per interrogazioni a modo di dialogo, del maestro & discepolo per insegnar alli fanciulli*, USTC 763172. The oldest printed copy in Catalan that has been preserved in Catalan archives and libraries, according to the Catàleg Col·lectiu de les Universitats Catalanes (Catalan Universities Collective Catalogue. Hereafter, CCUC), dates from 1692. *Doctrina Christiana a manera de diàlogo entre lo mestre y lo dexeble*, BC, 9-II-6, USTC 5101322.
21   Rubió; Madurell, *Documentos para la historia*, pp. 254 and 645. The edition of 1523 by Rosembach: *Aelii Antonii Nebrissensis in latinam grammaticen introductiones*, BC, Mar. 133-Fol (USTC 343613). On the grammar books and other classic works used in Catalan schools in the fifteenth century, see: Josep Hernando, 'El llibre escolar i la presència dels autors clàssics i dels humanistes en l'ensenyament del segle XV', *Estudis Històrics i Documents dels Arxius de Protocols*, 29 (2011), pp. 7–42.

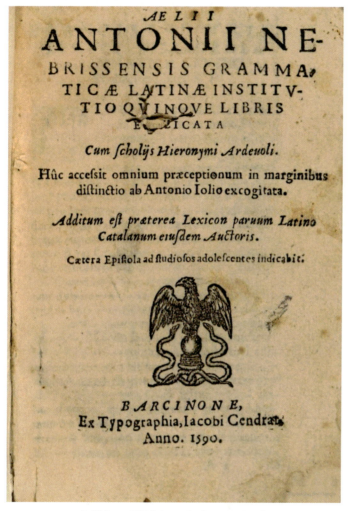

FIGURE 2.5   Aelii Antonii Nebrissensis, *Grammaticae Latinae*
(Barcelona: Jaume Cendrat, 1590). Biblioteca de Catalunya

a local printer. Another piece of evidence is the agreement between a master printer Martí Gelabert and the bookseller Miquel Planella signed in 1677 to print 18 reams of 'antonis'. This translated to a total of some 600 copies, because Nebrija's grammar was usually printed as an octavo of 240 pages. In 1723, the master printer Rafael Figueró, in Barcelona, printed 57 reams of the Nebrija's grammar – nearly 1,900 copies – on order of a conglomerate of booksellers.[22]

---

22   AHPB, Maties Amell, Dotzè manual, 613/26, September 24th, 1625. *Aelii Antonii Nebrissensis Grammaticarvm institvtionum*, Barcelona, Esteve Liberós, 1625. Biblioteca Universitària de Barcelona (University of Barcelona Library. Hereafter, BUB), B-62/5/33; AHPB, Joan Alomar, Quart manual, 814/4, fol. 229v–230v, November 23th, 1677. There is an earlier

Among the grammar books, is it also important to point out the importance of the works of Erasmus of Rotterdam, the most distinguished humanist in Europe. Despite the efforts of the Spanish Inquisition, Erasmus' book on syntax, popularly known as 'erasmes', was tolerated and widely used in Catalan grammar schools. In 1570, for example, 2,000 copies of this book were sold in Barcelona by the master printer Claudi Bornat to the merchants Tomàs and Jeroni Lucia. In 1677, Martí Gelabert printed 1,400 'erasmes' by order of multiple booksellers. Not a single copy of Erasmus' syntax printed in Barcelona before the eighteenth century has been preserved in the Catalan public archives and libraries.[23]

Another classic work used in public schools were Cicero's letters (figure 2.6). This book was commonly used by the local councils in order to elect the school grammar teacher, organising competitive examinations. The candidates' knowledge of Latin was evaluated by examining them on one of Cicero's letters, chosen at random by the examiners by sticking a needle on the fore edge of a closed book to mark the pages that contained the letters that would be used in the test. This method of selection appears in the minutes of the council of Mataró in regard to a competitive examination that took place in 1710.

> [The examiners] nailed three needles on the fore edge. After opening the book at the points where those needles were, they found that the first needle pointed to Cicero's seventh letter, book four; the second to the eleventh letter, book eleven, and the third touched the first letter, book fifteen, which starts *Si vos bene valets bene est, etc.* And this last letter was finally given for the exam.[24]

All of these school books were affordable for Catalans of any social background. According to a price list ordered by the Viceroy of Catalonia in 1655, alphabets should be sold at the price of two deniers each, salms at three deniers, and franselms at nine. Pelegrins, on the other hand, had to be sold for one sou, Nebrija's grammar and Erasmus' syntax for three sous each and Cicero's letters

---

edition of Nebrija's grammar printed by Gelabert by order of the bookseller Francesc Llopis, which includes Catalan comments. *Aelii Antonii Nebrissensis Grammaticarum institutionum libri quatuor*, Barcelona, Martí Gelabert, 1676. BUB, 195/3/3, USTC 5077088. The agreement between Figueró and the booksellers Jaume Roig, Anton March i Josep Pi, in: AHPB, Isidre Famades i Morell, Desè manual, 916/11, fol. 289r–289v, November 13th, 1723.

23 AHPB, Miquel Boera, Vintè manual, 396/4, January 9th, 1570; AHPB, Joan Alomar, Quart manual, 814/4, fol. 130v–132, 3 August 1677. On the use of the Erasmus' syntax at the University of Barcelona, see: Antonio Fernández Luzón, *La Universidad de Barcelona en el siglo XVI* (Barcelona: Publicacions de la Universitat de Barcelona, 2005), pp. 129–132.

24 Arxiu Municipal de Mataró (Municipal Archive of Mataró. Hereafter, ACM), Ajuntament de Mataró, Libres d'acords, 1705–1712, 7/C, fol. 52, October 21th, 1710.

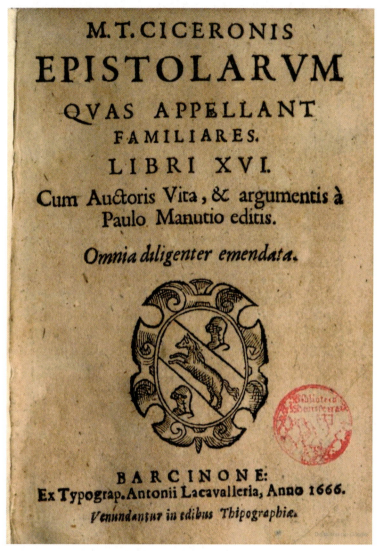

FIGURE 2.6 Marcus Tullius Cicero, *Epistolarum* (Barcelona: Antoni Lacavalleria, 1666). Biblioteca de Montserrat

for six sous. According to the same list, a worker's daily wage was ten sous, which means that the cost of an alphabet was the equivalent of less than two per cent of this daily wage.[25]

---

25 See the Viceroy's price list in: Alberch, *Gremis i oficis a Girona*, p. 303. During the Middle Ages and the early modern period the Catalan currency was based on the Carolingian system, created by Charlemagne in the eighth century. It consisted of *lliures*, *sous* and *diners*.

The use of grammar books was made compulsory in most Catalan public schools. In 1616, the council of Mataró established the rules for the local grammar teacher, asking him to teach Latin to all his students using the works of Nebrija and Erasmus. Some other classical authors, like Cicero, Virgil and Terence, were left to the teacher's choice. In 1633, the council of Vic employed a grammar teacher for the public school, with clear instructions to read Virgil to his pupils from 7 to 9 AM, Erasmus from 9 to 10 AM, and Cicero from 2 to 3 PM. In a similar way, in 1636 the council of La Bisbal d'Empordà – a village of 1,500 inhabitants – ordered the grammar teacher to give three daily lessons to his students, that is to say: Nebrija, Erasmus and Cicero.[26]

3   The Trade and Distribution of School Books

In 1553, the booksellers' guild of Barcelona obtained a privilege from Emperor Charles V that gave them a monopoly on the sale of books within the limits of the city. Thanks to this privilege, the booksellers' guild, to which all booksellers were compelled to belong, was able to prevent printers from selling books, or even to exhibit them publicly at the door of their printing offices. They were allowed, however, to sell books wholesale and unbound. This would prove the beginning of several conflicts between printers and booksellers during the sixteenth and seventeenth centuries, because the production and trade in school books had become an important part of the general income of both printers and booksellers. In 1623, the booksellers' guild received another privilege, this time from the city council, that allowed it to compel all booksellers to buy the school books wholesale from the guild, prior to selling them in their respective shops.[27]

One *lliura* was equivalent to 20 *sous* and to 240 *diners*. One *sou* was equivalent to 12 *diners*. This system was also used in France (*livre*, *sou* and *denier*) and in England (pound, shilling and pence).

26   ACA, Notarials, Mataró, C-9, 1608–1618, September 21th, 1616. AMV, Ajuntament de Vic, Acords, 1630–1638, Llibre 16, fol. 334, November 11th, 1634. Arxiu Comarcal del Baix Empordà (Archive of Baix Empordà County. Hereafter, ACBE), Ajuntament de la Bisbal d'Empordà, Llibre d'acords i resolucions, 1608-1652, p. 512, June 29th, 1636.

27   BC, Manuscrits, Ms.1903, fol. 9 and 23–24. These documents are reproduced in: Miquel González Sugrañes, *Història dels antichs gremis dels arts i oficis de la ciutat de Barcelona*, vol. 2 Llibreters-estampers (Barcelona: Impremta d'Henrich i cia., 1918), pp. 47–62. See a full explanation of the dispute between printers and booksellers for the book trade in: Xevi Camprubí, 'Llibres i lliure comerç a la Barcelona moderna: els conflictes entre l'impressor Rafael Figueró i la confraria dels llibreters (1671–1711)', *Recerques*, 65 (2012),

In order to control the distribution of alphabets, psalms and other school books, the guild designated one of its members to deliver the books to the shops of the rest of booksellers. The account books of this distribution that have been preserved are exceptional documents that make it possible to know the quantities of school books produced by the printing offices of Barcelona in the seventeenth century. From 1623 to 1636, the booksellers' guild delivered to the bookshops of the city up to 1,341 reams of printed alphabets and psalms, at an average of almost 96 reams per year.[28]

The alphabets and psalms printed in the seventeenth and eighteenth centuries were usually produced in a 16mo format, but while the alphabets had 16 pages, the psalms had 32. This means that with a single ream of paper – consisting of 500 sheets of printing paper – it was possible to print 500 psalms or 1,000 alphabets. The problem of converting the 96 annual reams into single copies is that alphabets and psalms are sometimes counted together in the guild account books. The total quantity of each, therefore, can only be estimated. If the 96 reams were of psalms only, the number of printed copies would have been 48,000, but if it were of alphabets, then it would have been 96,000. Considering, as I presume, that both books were consumed in approximately equal quantities, the estimated production can be established in a 2:1 proportion. So, 64 reams out of 96 would be psalms and the remaining 32 would be alphabets, which means that the estimated total number of alphabets and psalms delivered by the guild each year was approximately 32,000 alphabets and a similar number of psalm books.

It is important to consider that the quantity of books delivered to the bookshops was not necessarily the same as the books actually sold during the year, because some of them could have been stored in warehouses for months. However, I think that the estimated annual average of 32,000 copies indicates that the trade in those books was remarkably high. The explanation of such sales figures year after year must be partly due to the fragility of the books themselves. In 1592, the Castilian courts asked permission of the King to regulate the price of the alphabets, because it had been increased excessively. The argument was that the boys damaged the books, so that the copies could not be passed down amongst families, and those who were worst affected by the price hikes were the sons of poor families.[29]

---

pp. 75–107. See also: Xevi Camprubí, *L'impressor Rafael Figueró (1642–1726) i la premsa a la Catalunya del seu temps* (Barcelona: Fundació Noguera, 2018).

28 BC, Manuscrits, Llibre de la administració dels salms, misses i beceroles de la confraria dels llibreters, 1623–1637, MSS. Bergnes-Confraria dels Llibreters, 3.

29 Luis Resines Llorente, *La catedral de papel. Historia de las cartillas de Valladolid* (Valladolid: Diputación de Valladolid, 2007), p. 41.

The sale of school books was the cause of a bitter conflict between printers and booksellers over many years, which is further evidence of the importance of this segment for the book trade. Booksellers used their royal privilege to prevent printers from selling all kind of books to the public, including school books. Royal officials often visited printers' offices and confiscated all their publications, if they had suspicions that they had been selling them. In 1677, for example, as a result of an inspection carried out in Rafael Figueró printing office, the councillors of the booksellers' guild, assisted by the King's officials, found 1,248 alphabets and salms hidden in the warehouse. This affair was brought to court in the same year. During the case, another printer, named Vicenç Surià, claimed to have printed two bales of psalms in 1674 (10,000 copies), and one bale of psalms and alphabets each (5,000 and 10,000 copies, respectively) two years later. After a long judiciary struggle, the booksellers managed to maintain their privilege and, consequently, the monopoly over the retail of books.[30]

Despite the restrictions imposed by booksellers, printers were crucially aware of the importance of printed books for education, and their own role in producing them. In 1676, during one of these disputes with the booksellers, the printers' guild stated specifically to the city council of Barcelona the value of their work: 'How it would be possible to learn to read without the psalms, 'beceroles', 'franselms' and other books that regularly are being printed for this purpose, if they were hand-written?', asked the printers.[31]

The school books printed in Barcelona were delivered all throughout Catalonia. In 1678, the master printer Rafael Figueró sent 720 copies of salms and alphabets to a fair that took place in the village of Olot, located 60 miles away from Barcelona. Some years later, the book merchant Antoni Lacavalleria sent a cargo of alphabets, 'franselms' and 'antonis' to be sold in the city of Girona. Another example comes from the town of Reus, in the south of Catalonia. There is evidence that in those years a street vendor sold alphabets in the public market.[32]

---

30 The details of the inspection in Figuero's office were recorded by a notary. See: AHPB, Francesc Cortés, Setè manual, 807/7, fol. 211v–212v, November 12th, 1677. The explanation given by Vicenç Surià to the judge in: ACA, Reial Audiència, Plets Civils, 23921, November 9th, 1677. One bale of paper contained 10 reams. See also: Camprubí, 'Llibres i lliure comerç a la Barcelona moderna, pp. 75–107.

31 AHCB, Consell de Cent, Registre de Deliberacions de 1676, fol. 169v–170, July 27th, 1676.

32 The information on Figueró and Lacavalleria's activities comes from the statements of some witnesses during two different trails, which can be seen in: ACA, Reial Audiència, Plets Civils, 23921, April 25th, 1678; and: ibid, 18523, July 22th, 1686. The reference to the Reus street dealer appears in: Arxiu Comarcal del Baix Camp (Archive of Baix Camp County. Hereafter, ACBC), Ajuntament de Reus, Llibre d'actes, 1693–1710, p. 67, August 29th, 1694.

The trade in grammar books was also substantial. From 1635 until 1650 the booksellers' guild of Barcelona delivered up to 18,934 copies of Nebrija's grammar to the city's bookshops, which represents an annual average of 1,183. In the same period, 3,825 copies of Erasmus' syntax were delivered, that is to say, 239 per year, and also 1,289 copies of Cicero's letters, at an average of 80 per year.[33]

But the most important document to demonstrate the volume of the school books trade in Catalonia is an inventory made in 1726 that contains the stock of all the printing offices and bookshops in Barcelona at that moment. This inventory was made in order to confiscate all these books by order of the University of Cervera, which some years before obtained the exclusive privilege from King Philip V to print and sell school books. The University of Cervera was created in 1717 by order of the king with the aim to replace all other universities in Catalonia, including those of Barcelona, Lleida and Girona, which were abolished as a punishment after the Catalan defeat in 1714, which ended the War of the Spanish Succession (1701–1714). The assets of these universities were all pooled for the benefit of the new University of Cervera. In 1718, King Philip V also gave the University of Cervera the monopoly of the printing of school books, as a means to improve its finances. This was the reason why printers and booksellers were compelled by the university rector to gather all their school books and send them to Cervera.[34]

The inventory of 1726 showed that the stock of books stored in the printing offices and bookshops of Barcelona was as follows: 222,192 alphabets; 127,205 psalms; 41,882 'franselms'; 57,082 'pelegrins'; 12,842 copies of Nebrija's grammar; 2,192 copies of Cicero's letters and 2,066 copies of Erasmus' syntax. These and other school books – like catechisms, rosaries, Torrelles' grammar, and others – comprised a total amount of 550,000 books.[35]

Nevertheless, three years later it was necessary to make a new inventory, because the books had not yet been collected. The recount made in 1729 showed that the total amount of school books stored had been reduced to only 45,000 copies. The explanation given by the booksellers was that the missing books had been sold. The difference between these two inventories gives further evidence of the extraordinary volume of trade of school books that

---

33 Arxiu Nacional de Catalunya (National Archive of Catalonia. Hereafter, ANC), Col·lecció de Manuscrits, Companyia dels llibreters. Subministrament als agremiats, 1635–1662, ANC1-25-T-64.

34 See an explanation of this privilege in: Javier Burgos Rincon, 'Privilegios de imprenta y crisis gremial. La imprenta y librería barcelonesa ante el privilegio de impresión de los libros de enseñanza de la Universidad de Cervera', *Estudis Històrics i Documents dels Arxiusde Protocols*, XV (1997), pp. 257–298.

35 AHPB, Agustí Güell, Manual de 1726, 960/1, fol. 84v–91v, April 1st, 1726.

existed in the early eighteenth century. Surprisingly, very few copies of these books have survived, due to their popularity and fragility.[36]

4 The Decline of Public Education

The Catalan defeat of 1714 ensured the definitive establishment of the Bourbon King Philip V and an absolutist regime in Catalonia. One of his first decisions was to impose substantial taxes on Catalan cities, towns and villages, in order to acquire the financial means to maintain the army deployed across the country. It was, in fact, an imposition of martial law. In 1716, the tax was formally incorporated under the name of 'Cadastre'. The consequences were devastating, because the ordinary economic contribution of the country was multiplied almost eight times. From this point onwards, many local councils could not assure free education for poor boys anymore. This was, in my opinion, the starting point of a regression of the education levels in Catalonia.[37]

Another decision of Philip V that had negative consequences on education was the suppression of all Catalan universities. In some cities, like Barcelona, Girona or Vic, children's free public education had taken place within the institutional framework of the University, so the abolition left the poor boys literally on the street. Furthermore, the decision taken in 1717 by the king to give the University of Cervera the privilege to print and sell all the school books in Catalonia caused a major disruption in the book trade. In 1731, the booksellers' guild of Barcelona sent a petition to the King, asking for the abolition of the privilege. The booksellers argued that the lack of the income provided by the selling of school books was forcing them to close their shops and was reducing their families to poverty. The petition, however, was not accepted. The number of shops that were forced to close is unknown.[38]

The situation was further exacerbated by the fact that the printing office of Cervera was a complete failure. In 1740, the rector of the university, Miquel

---

36   AHPB, Agustí Güell, Manual de 1729, 960/2, fol. 51–57, July 25th, 1729; ACA, Reial Audiència, Consultas, 1729, Registres, 143, fol. 15–17v, June 19th, 1729. According to the CCUC, not a single copy of 'beceroles' or 'salms' published before 1700 has been preserved. The editions showed in this article do not figure in this catalogue. On the other hand, the CUCC contains two editions of the 'franselm' printed in Barcelona (1667 and c.1700), and two 'pelegrins', published in 1677 and 1683. The copies of 1584 (franselm) and 1635 (pelegrí) showed above does not figure in the CCUC.
37   Agustí Alcoberro, 'El cadastre de Catalunya (1713–1845): de la imposició a la fossilització', *Pedralbes*, 25 (2005), pp. 231–257.
38   ACA, Reial Audiència, Cartas Acordadas, 1731, Registres, 14, fol. 91–95, April 28th, 1731.

Gonser, complained that the printing office had to sell the school books at too high price. The rector blamed the booksellers of Cervera, who were in charge of the binding, because they demanded too much money for their work. As a result of the high prices a black market for school books appeared. Some years later, Gonser complained that the books printed by the University were piled up in the office's warehouse 'as if they were in a swamp'. In 1753, the printing office of Cervera had a debt of more than a thousand pounds, and ended finally in bankruptcy.[39]

The regression of education was also caused by the loss of the importance that the lower classes had ascribed to education in the previous centuries. The Bourbon regime abolished the ancient electing system, the *insaculació*, that had allowed artisans and peasants to intervene in local politics in all towns and to take civic jobs requiring a basic level of education. So, from that point onwards, the capacity to read and write was no longer relevant for many people.

But the most detrimental factor of the decline of education was the growth of the population, mainly from the mid-eighteenth century onwards. Due to the economic difficulties caused by the high taxes, as it has been pointed out above, many local councils could pay the wage of one teacher only – the same number as two hundred years earlier – while in most towns the population had tripled. The increase in the number of pupils brought the education system to its knees. The most severely affected were the children of the poor families, because the economic difficulties made it impossible for the councils to maintain free education.

The grammar schools were permitted to exist in the largest cities only, in order to prevent the councils of the small towns and villages from spending money on something that the Bourbon administration considered worthless. This is, in fact, the idea that Pablo de Olavide had in mind when he worked as a consultant of the Duke of Aranda, Secretary of State of King Charles III. When in 1767 a reform of the universities was ordered, Olavide proposed the suppression of all grammar colleges, because he considered that higher education should be reserved for noblemen and wealthy citizens. In his opinion, the place of the poor was agriculture and industry. It is therefore surprising that

---

39   ACA, Reial Audiència, Consultas, 1753, 474, fol. 291v, August 23th, 1753. See the failure of the printing office of the University of Cervera in: Marina Ruíz Fargas, 'El privilegio de privativa de libros de común enseñanza de la Universidad de Cervera en tiempos de Manuel Ibarra (1735–1749, 1754–1757)', in: Pedro Rueda Ramírez; Lluís Agustí, *La publicidad del libro en el mundo hispánico (siglos XVII–XX): los catálogos de venta de libreros y editores* (Barcelona, Calambur, 2016), pp. 129–159.

Charles III of Bourbon has been considered by many historians as an 'enlightened' king.[40]

The Industrial Revolution, in fact, converted peasants, craftsmen and artisans into workers and sent them to the factory, along with a lot of young poor boys who were obliged to abandon school. The capacity to read, write and count was no longer required for them anymore. As Lawrence Stone and Raymond Williams have pointed out in the case of England, industrialisation was among the factors contributing to a general regression in education.[41]

According to a survey made in 1772 by the Reial Audiència – the effective government of the king's administration in Catalonia after 1714 – the number of boys attending the schools of Barcelona had decreased by nearly 200 in the previous years, from 2,549 to 2,351. The explanation given was that those missing boys were actually working at the city chintz factories and, for this reason, they did not go to school. In the following years, the number of boys who did not attend school increased dramatically, to the point that in 1786 the Bishop of Barcelona, Gavino de Valladares, ordered the publication of a catechism book for the boys who worked at the chintz factories. The main concern of the bishop was that the boys were not instructed in the Christian doctrine properly.[42] The worries of the bishop were not unfounded. A survey made by the Trade Council of Barcelona in 1784 showed that there were 80 textile factories in the city, at which there worked 4,607 men, 1,740 women and, finally, 2,291 boys, representing 25% of the total workforce.[43]

Due to all these circumstances, while the number of children attending school decreased, the number of public schools did the same. Some villages that are known to have had a school in the seventeenth century had lost it at the beginning of the nineteenth century. According to a survey made in 1797 by order of Spanish prime minister Manuel de Godoy, only 38% of Catalan cities, towns and villages had a public school.[44]

---

40 Antonio Álvarez de Morales, *La Ilustración y la reforma de la universidad en la España del siglo XVIII* (Madrid: Pegaso, 1979), pp. 57–69.

41 Stone, 'Literacy and Education in England', p. 76; Raymond Williams, *The Long Revolution* (Peterborough: Broadview Press, 2001), p. 157.

42 ACA, Reial Audiència, Consultas, 1772, 812, fol. 144–170v, September 25th, 1772. See also: Isabel de Azcárate Ristori, 'La enseñanza primaria en Barcelona desde 1600 a 1772', *Cuadernos de Arqueologia e Historia de la ciudad*, 5, 1964, pp. 150–151. The bishop's book was: *Promptuari de la doctrina christiana*, Barcelona, Francisco Surià Burgada, 1786.

43 BC, Junta de Comerç, 53, 71, doc.29, 1784. See also: James Thomson, *Els orígens de la industrialització a Catalunya. El cotó a Barcelona, 1728–1832* (Barcelona: Edicions 62, 1994), pp. 214–215.

44 Censo de Godoy de 1797, Instituto Nacional de Estadística.

5   Conclusions

It is widely accepted among historians that the levels of literacy in the early modern period were extremely low. Some authors have pointed out that in this time Catalan society was 'massively' illiterate.[45] The existence of a public school system allows me to suggest that in Catalonia the levels of literacy in the early modern period must be considered higher than previously estimated. The presence of schools in small towns and villages in the countryside contradicts the idea that the rural areas were less culturally developed than the urban ones. From the sixteenth century onwards the presence of teachers in many Catalan towns and villages increased, in most cases paid for by public funds. The local authorities attached great importance to education, even during times of war. Although school attendance was not compulsory, some examples show that it was quite high. Schooling was possible because the local councils paid the teacher's wages, fully or in part. In some cases, payments were enough to allow free education for all boys. Along with this, the publication and sale of a massive number of cheap school books reinforces the idea that the level of schooling was high.

At the beginning of the eighteenth century, however, at the time of the installation of the Bourbon monarchy, public education in Catalonia started to decline. The main reasons were the growth of the population and the lack of teachers to handle the increase in the number of pupils. The excessive taxes prevented the local authorities from paying the teachers that were needed. This was also an important cause of the end of free education. The situation further worsened at the outbreak of the Industrial Revolution, because for many families, mainly for the poorest, it was more useful to send their sons to the factory than to school.

---

45   See: Ricardo García Cárcel, *Historia de Cataluña, siglos XVI–XVII. Los carácteres de la historia de Cataluña*, (Barcelona: Ariel, 1985), p. 388. Robert Darnton also uses the concept of illiterate masses to qualify the peasants in modern French rural areas. Robert Darnton, *La gran matança de gats i altres episodis de la història cultural francesa* (València: Publicacions de la Universitat de València, 2006), p. 30.

CHAPTER 3

The Cometary Apparition of 1743/44: Periodical Journals in the Holy Roman Empire and Their Communicative Role

Doris Gruber

In the winter of 1743/44, an unusual phenomenon attracted worldwide attention: the apparition of an uncommonly bright comet, visible to the naked eye and at times even during the day. From autumn 1743 until spring 1744, people around the world observed the comet's apparition and discussed its origin, nature and especially its supposed, mostly theological meaning.[1] This reaction was nothing new. Cometary apparitions have led to intense discussions for millennia. In Europe, several theories about their origin, physical nature and meaning had existed since antiquity. In the following centuries, people handed down these theories, modifying and adjusting them and in the process changing what people believed to be true about comets and accepted as knowledge.[2]

This multi-faceted process has not stopped to this day, but knowledge regarding comets was transformed most fundamentally during the early modern period. In the late sixteenth century, the great majority of people believed comets to be harbingers of doom, like famine, disease and death. These interpretations built upon several conceptual frameworks that had been accepted

---

1 This article presents and expands upon findings of a PhD thesis entitled *Frühneuzeitlicher Wissenswandel. Kometenerscheinungen in der Druckpublizistik des Heiligen Römischen Reiches* (Knowledge in Transition. Early Modern Cometary apparitions in the Printing Culture of the Holy Roman Empire) published in German as part of the series *Presse und Geschichte – Neue Beiträge* (Bremen: edition lumière, 2020). In the thesis, the cometary apparitions of 1577/78 and 1680/81 are analysed and compared to that of 1743/44. The project took place at the University of Graz (Austria) and was funded by a grant of the Gerda Henkel Foundation (Düsseldorf, Germany). For further reading on the discovery and observation of this cometary apparition see Gary W. Kronk, *Cometography. A Catalog of Comets. Vol. 1. Ancient – 1799* (Cambridge: Cambridge University Press, 1999), pp. 408–411; David Seargent, *The Greatest Comets in History. Broom Stars and Celestial Scimitars* (New York: Springer, 2009), p. 116; Ronald Stoyan, *Atlas der großen Kometen. Die 30 größten Kometen in Wissenschaft, Kultur und Kunst* (Erlangen: Oculum, 2013), pp. 96–98.
2 This paper uses a socially determined concept of knowledge, for which see Peter Burke, *What Is the History of Knowledge?* (Cambridge: Polity Press, 2016); Philipp Sarasin, 'Was ist Wissensgeschichte?', *Internationales Archiv für Sozialgeschichte der deutschen Literatur*, 36 (2011), pp. 159–172.

as knowledge for centuries or millennia. People regarded comets as portents sent by God to warn of divine punishments and to remind people to atone for their sins. At the same time, astrological interpretations of comets flourished, and several physical theories supported the assumptions of negative consequences of comets. Additionally, people tended to refer to examples of historical cometary apparitions that seemed to prove these mostly negative consequences. By the mid-eighteenth century, these interpretations had become rarer, and people predominantly regarded comets as natural celestial bodies, built of solid material, following calculable orbits. This process was by no means teleological: older interpretations had not diminished completely, and some people still believed in comets as negative portents.[3] Simultaneously with changes in the knowledge regarding comets, the media setting changed considerably, as

---

3 There is a vast body of literature on the subject of early modern cometary apparitions, and there is not enough room to mention all relevant titles here. To date, Volker Fritz Brüning has created the most extensive bibliography on the subject, see Volker Fritz Brüning, *Bibliographie der Kometenliteratur* (Stuttgart: Hiersemann, 2000). Further reading: Marion Gindhart, *Das Kometenjahr 1618. Antikes und zeitgenössisches Wissen in der frühneuzeitlichen Kometenliteratur des deutschsprachigen Raumes* (Wiesbaden: Reichert, 2006); Doris Gruber, 'Der Komet von 1680 und die Kalenderpublizistik im Alten Reich. Eine exemplarische Annäherung', in Klaus-Dieter Herbst and Werner Greiling (eds.), *Schreibkalender und ihre Autoren in Mittel-, Ost- und Ostmitteleuropa (1540–1850)* (Bremen: edition lumière, 2018), pp. 77–96; Doris Gruber, 'Text, Bild und Intermaterialität. Die frühneuzeitliche Kometenpublizistik im Heiligen Römischen Reich', *Jahrbuch für Kommunikationsgeschichte*, 21 (2019), pp. 85–114; Tofigh Heidarzadeh, *A History of Physical Theories of Comets, from Aristotle to Whipple* (Berlin: Springer, 2008); Clarisse D. Hellman, *The Comet of 1577. Its Place in the History of Astronomy* (New York: Columbia University Press, 1971); Anna Jerratsch, 'Celestial Phenomena in Early Modernity: The Integrated Image of Comets', in Pietro Daniel Omodeo and Volkhard Wels (eds.), *Natural Knowledge and Aristotelianism at Early Modern Protestant Universities* (Wiesbaden: Harrassowitz, 2019), pp. 187–208; Anna Jerratsch, *Der frühneuzeitliche Kometendiskurs im Spiegel deutschsprachiger Flugschriften* (Stuttgart: Franz Steiner, 2020); Christoph Meinel, *Grenzgänger zwischen Himmel und Erde. Kometen in der frühen Neuzeit* (Regensburg: Universitätsverlag Regensburg, 2009); Barbara Mahlmann-Bauer, 'William Whiston, Newtonianer und Antitrinitarier, und seine deutschsprachige Rezeption', in Philipp Auchter, et al. (eds.), *Des Sirius goldne Küsten – Astronomie und Weltraumfiktion* (Leiden: Brill, 2019), pp. 116–152; Adam Mosley, 'The History and Historiography of Early Modern Comets', in Miguel A. Granada, Adam Mosley and Nicholas Jardine (eds.), *Christoph Rothmann's Discourse on the Comet of 1585. An Edition and Translation with Accompanying Essays* (Leiden: Brill, 2014), pp. 282–325; Tabitta van Nouhuys, *The Age of Two-Faced Janus. The Comets of 1577 and 1618 and the Decline of the Aristotelian World View in the Netherlands* (Leiden: Brill, 1998); James Howard Robinson, *The Great Comet of 1680. A Study in the History of Rationalism* (Northfield: Northfield News, 1916); Sara J. Schechner, *Comets, Popular Culture, and the Birth of Modern Cosmology* (Princeton: Princeton University Press, 1997); Michael Weichenhan, *"Ergo perit coelum ...". Die Supernova des Jahres 1572 und die Überwindung der aristotelischen Kosmologie* (Stuttgart: Steiner, 2004).

evident especially in the expansion of periodicals and a continuously growing rate of printed communication. Assuming that knowledge needs material forms – media – to be able to circulate and change, these changes in the media environment played their part in accelerating changes in what people accepted as valid information regarding comets.[4]

This article reflects upon one specific aspect of this manifold process: the communicative role of periodical journals and their relation to other types of media in the Holy Roman Empire. The discussion of this topic sheds new light on the subject by responding to the need to compare different types of early modern media to analyse their intermedial relations, instead of the predominantly practiced focus on one specific media type (e.g. periodical journals, newspapers, pamphlets or broadsheets).[5] Concerning periodical journals in the Holy Roman Empire, this article also responds to the lack of research on the mid-eighteenth century, as previous research usually focuses either on the earliest days of periodical journals in the late seventeenth century, or on periods when periodical journals were already established forms of media, by the end of or after the late eighteenth century.[6] In this respect, the question arises whether periodical journals really were the '*Schlüsselwerke* (key works) of the Enlightenment' (in the words of Paul Raabe); whether, as Jürgen Habermas suggested, they really reconfigured the discussion and circulation of knowledge; and, as Anna Jerratsch proposed recently, they became the main media

---

4 This paper uses an event-orientated concept of media, for which see Julia Genz and Paul Gévaudan, *Medialität, Materialität, Kodierung: Grundzüge einer allgemeinen Theorie der Medien* (Bielefeld: transcript, 2016). On the circulation and change of knowledge see e.g. Frank Grunert and Anette Syndikus (eds.), *Wissensspeicher der Frühen Neuzeit. Formen und Funktionen* (Berlin: De Gruyter, 2015); David Gugerli and Daniel Speich Chassé, 'Wissensgeschichte. Eine Standortbestimmung', *Traverse. Zeitschrift für Geschichte*, 1 (2012), pp. 85–100; Sarasin, 'Wissensgeschichte', pp. 159–172.

5 E.g. Daniel Bellingradt, 'Periodische Zeitung und Akzidentielle Flugpublizistik. Zu den intertextuellen, interdependenten und intermedialen Momenten des frühneuzeitlichen Medienverbundes', in Volker Bauer and Holger Böning (eds.), *Die Entstehung des Zeitungswesens im 17. Jahrhundert. Ein neues Medium und seine Folgen für das Kommunikationssystem der Frühen Neuzeit* (Bremen: edition lumière, 2011), pp. 57–78; Daniel Bellingradt, Paul Nelles and Jeroen Salman (eds.), *Books in Motion in Early Modern Europe. Beyond Production, Circulation and Consumption* (Cham: Springer International Publishing, 2017); Burke, *History of Knowledge*, pp. 41–43.

6 E.g. Bauer and Böning (eds.), *Entstehung des Zeitungswesens*; Daniel Bellingradt, 'Forschungsbericht. Periodische Presse im deutschen Sprachraum der Frühen Neuzeit', *Archiv für Geschichte des Buchwesens*, 69 (2014), pp. 235–248; Gruber, *Wissenswandel*, pp. 95–106; Katrin Löffler (ed.), *Wissen in Bewegung. Gelehrte Journale, Debatten und der Buchhandel der Aufklärung* (Stuttgart: Franz Steiner, 2020); Flemming Schock, *Die Text-Kunstkammer. Populäre Wissenssammlungen des Barock am Beispiel der 'Relationes Curiosae' von E.W. Happel* (Köln: Böhlau, 2011).

platform for learned discussions on comets.[7] This article will show that the impact of periodical journals was not as great or distinctive as has previously been assumed.

1   The Cometary Apparition of 1743/44 and the Printing Press

During the early modern period, many printed works included discussions of comets. The publication of such works was especially pronounced during or shortly after the apparition of 'Great Comets' – remarkably bright comets that were visible for an exceptionally long time. The apparition of 1743/44, in the designation system of the International Astronomical Union officially known as *C/1743 X1*, was the greatest comet of the eighteenth century. Although in the summer and autumn of 1769 another 'Great Comet', officially known as *C/1769 P1 (Messier)*, came into view, the comet of 1743/44 was visible for a longer period, shined brighter and inspired a larger number of publications.[8] This cometary apparition was a media event, and the substantial number of printed works reflects the greater intensity of the discussion of comets during and shortly after this occurrence.[9]

The following arguments build on the analysis of a corpus of over five hundred printed works, systematically collected during a PhD project. This project was dedicated to three 'Great Comets', those of 1577/78, 1680/81 and 1743/44. A full bibliography of this corpus, including references to over 3,200 copies in over three hundred libraries and archives around the world is included in the published thesis.[10] All of the publications gathered for this research originate

---

7   Jürgen Habermas, *Strukturwandel der Öffentlichkeit. Untersuchungen zu einer Kategorie der bürgerlichen Gesellschaft* (Neuwied: Luchterhand, 1962); Jerratsch, *Kometendiskurs*, pp. 487–488, 509, 525, 528; Katrin Löffer, 'Wissen braucht einen Träger. Gelehrte Blätter als zentrales Medium der Aufklärung', in Löffler (ed.), *Wissen*, pp. 9–27; Paul Raabe, 'Die Zeitschrift als Medium der Aufklärung', *Wolfenbütteler Studien zur Aufklärung*, 1 (1974), pp. 99–136, p. 104.

8   At least according to the usual quantity of text produced during the early modern period (Brüning, *Bibliographie*; Meinel, *Grenzgänger*, pp. 122–123). For the seventeenth century, Anna Jerratsch's evaluations lead to similar results (Jerratsch, 'Phenomena', p. 187).

9   Christoph Meinel came to a similar conclusion concerning other cometary apparitions (Meinel, *Grenzgänger*, pp. 121–122). Further reading on 'media events': Daniel Dayan and Elihu Katz, *Media Events. The Live Broadcasting of History* (Cambridge, MA: Harvard University Press, 1994); Horst Carl, Herbert Schneider and Christine Vogel (eds.), *Medienereignisse im 18. und 19. Jahrhundert. Beiträge einer interdisziplinären Tagung aus Anlass des 65. Geburtstages von Rolf Reichardt* (München: R. Oldenbourg, 2009).

10 See Gruber, *Wissenswandel*.

in the Holy Roman Empire, the region where the largest number of publications on comets appeared during the early modern period.[11] The bibliography includes 111 editions on the cometary apparition of 1577/78, 305 on the apparition of 1680/81 and 164 on the apparition of 1743/44.[12]

Of course, these publications did not appear independently of other media. Information originating in oral communication, physical artefacts or manuscripts influenced the content of printed works and vice versa. Manuscripts could also circulate in similar ways to printed works.[13] In this article, however, the focus lies on the printed publications, as they enjoyed the widest circulation, and they were the easiest to collect and to analyse due to the current state of research.[14]

On the cometary apparition of 1743/44, a systematic search led to a collection of 164 printed works that were published during this apparition or within the following five years. This corpus includes two major types of publications: non-serial publications (broadsheets, pamphlets and books) and serial publications (almanacs [*Schreibkalenders*], *Messrelationen* [prints related to the

---

11   Following the most extensive bibliographies so far (Brüning, *Bibliographie*; Gindhart, *Kometenjahr*; Hellman, *Comet*; Robinson, *Great Comet*; Schechner, *Comets*).

12   The number before the brackets refers here and in the following to the amount excluding new editions of the same title; the number in brackets includes reprinted editions. Comet 1577/78: This number decreases to 84 if one does not include reprinted editions of the same title: 9 (12) broadsheets, 48 (67) pamphlets, 12 (16) books, 15 (16) almanacs. On the Comet 1680/81: 247 without including reprinted editions of the same title: 45 (56) broadsheets, 135 (179) pamphlets, 27 (30) books, 17 (17) almanacs, 3 (3) *Messrelationen*, 20 (20) articles in periodical journals. On Comet 1743/44: 159 without including reprinted editions of the same title: 3 (3) broadsheets, 44 (46) pamphlets, 13 (16) books, 11 (11) almanacs, 1 (1) *Messrelation*, 87 (87) articles in periodical journals. Since the finalisation of my PhD thesis, one more article has been discovered (Hermann Wahn, 'Hamburg vom 29 Febr.', *Hamburgische Berichte von den neuesten Gelehrten Sachen*, Tomus 13 (1744), pp. 145–149). An advertisement of a medallion commemorating the comet was not counted in this evaluation (*Hamburgische Berichte*, Tomus 13 (1744), p. 516). Here and in the following no differentiation is made between new editions and those editions that differ only due to corrections or *corruptelae* within one production process. The latter divergences unambiguously concern only one pamphlet on the cometary apparition of 1577/78, three pamphlets on the apparition of 1680/81 and no publication on the apparition of 1743/44. On the identification of such divergences see: Martin Boghardt, *Archäologie des gedruckten Buches* (Wiesbaden: Harrassowitz, 2008), pp. 285–340.

13   E.g. Adam Fox, *Oral and Literate Culture in England, 1500–1700* (Oxford: Clarendon Press, 2000); Paula McDowell, *The Invention of the Oral. Print Commerce and Fugitive Voices in Eighteenth-Century Britain* (Chicago: The University of Chicago Press, 2017); Katrin Keller and Marion Romberg, 'The Tagzettel and diaries of Cardinal Ernst Adalbert von Harrach: A source for 17th century central European history', *The Medieval History Journal*, 13 (2010), pp. 287–314; Noah Millstone, *Manuscript Circulation and the Invention of Politics in Early Stuart England* (Cambridge: Cambridge University Press, 2016).

14   Gruber, *Wissenswandel*, pp. 26–29.

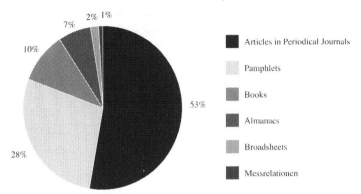

FIGURE 3.1   Printed works on the cometary apparition of 1743/44 (including new editions, N = 164)

German book fairs] and articles in periodical journals). At first glance, the constituent parts of this corpus (Figure 3.1) might suggest that periodical journals played the most important role, representing more than half of the works (eighty-seven articles). Pamphlets (forty-six) and books (sixteen) are prominent as well, but they seem to have played a lesser role.

By analysing this corpus on a deeper contextual level, the contrary seems to be the case. When differentiating between 'independent articles' that promote arguments of their own and 'reviews' that summarise and judge previous publications on the topic, a clear pattern is visible in the coverage of the periodical journals. Only thirteen articles include 'independent' findings, while the great majority, seventy-four, are reviews. These results put the role of periodical journals in perspective and show that they were not the preferred media type for publishing new findings on comets around 1744. The older media formats, especially pamphlets and books, continued to play the leading role, as all of the evaluated pamphlets and books were original publications and usually included independent arguments and new findings.[15]

The limited impact of journals becomes even more obvious if we count journal titles with coverage of the cometary apparition instead of single journal articles. This reduces the number from eighty-seven to only sixteen. By focusing on the seventy-four journal reviews, the number of journal titles further decreases to eleven, while the majority (fifty) appeared in just three journal titles. Most journals contained either reviews or independent articles, which probably reflected the editorial strategies of the individual titles (Figure 3.2).[16]

---

15   The 'independent' publications are discussed in detail in Gruber, *Wissenswandel*, pp. 332–447.
16   For a full list of the articles described here see Gruber, *Wissenswandel*, pp. 775–782.

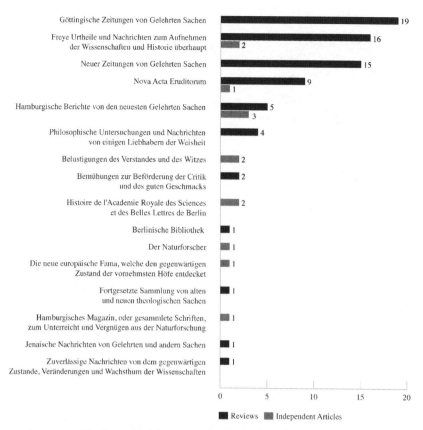

FIGURE 3.2 Numbers of articles in periodical journals on the cometary apparition of 1743/44 in relation to the titles of periodical journals (N = 87)

The thirteen 'independent' articles may be categorised in two groups: the first group comprises six articles that appeared in 'moral weeklies' (*Moralische Wochenschriften*) that aimed at larger audiences and were based on British predecessors like the *Tatler* (1708–1711), *Spectator* (1711–1712) and *Guardian* (1713).[17] The articles on the cometary apparition of 1743/44 in the moral weeklies either discussed the supposed theological meaning and the physical nature of the comet or represented didactic poems meant to educate and entertain their audience. The second group comprises seven articles that mainly deal with

---

17   See e.g. Helga Brandes, 'Moralische Wochenschrift', in Ernst Fischer et al. (eds.), *Von Almanach bis Zeitung. Ein Handbuch der Medien in Deutschland 1700–1800* (München: Beck, 1999), pp. 225–232; Gruber, *Wissenswandel*, pp. 100–101; Wolfgang Martens, *Die Botschaft der Tugend. Die Aufklärung im Spiegel der deutschen Moralischen Wochenschriften* (Stuttgart: Metzler, 1968).

new empirical findings and communicate data from empirical observations, some of which are re-editions or translations, but a few, especially those by the mathematician Leonhard Euler (1707–1783), disclose new findings.[18]

The second group and all of the seventy-four reviews, meaning the vast majority of all articles published in periodical journals on the cometary apparition of 1743/44, appeared in 'learned journals' (*Gelehrte Journale*) that, around 1750, usually reached a relatively small, highly-educated and wealthy segment of society, as can be assumed due to their high prices, relatively small print runs, and scholarly contents. Learned journals were common across Europe: the first titles were printed in Paris (*Journal des Sçavans*) and London (*Philosophical Transactions*), both from 1665 onwards. In Rome the *Giornale de' Letterati* was founded in 1668, and the *Acta Eruditorum* was the first learned journal in the Holy Roman Empire, published in Leipzig from 1682 to 1782. The *Acta* were also exceptional due to the long time-span of their apparition; most of the other learned journals in the Holy Roman Empire lasted only for one or two years, while in other parts of Europe, on average, learned journals seem to have survived a bit longer.[19] In the Holy Roman Empire, the prices of the learned journals were relatively high and probably ranged between two and four *Groschen* per issue during the eighteenth century.[20]

Previous scholarship has provided estimates on print runs of journals, and it is assumed that they were relatively small, with a minimum of 200 to 250 copies per issue and comprising in average 500 to 700 copies. Larger print runs between 1,000 and 2,000 copies were exceptional, and rare cases of up to 5,000 copies have been found.[21] The estimates on print runs of other media types in the Holy Roman Empire, although based on even less evidence and

18   These 'independent articles' are discussed in detail in Gruber, *Wissenswandel*, pp. 333–448, esp. pp. 437–442.

19   Thomas Munck, 'Eighteenth-Century Review Journals and the Internationalization of the European Book Market', *The International History Review*, 32/3 (2010), pp. 415–435, pp. 416–417.

20   Thomas Habel, *Gelehrte Journale und Zeitungen der Aufklärung. Zur Entstehung, Entwicklung und Erschließung deutschsprachiger Rezensionszeitschriften des 18. Jahrhunderts* (Bremen: edition lumière, 2007), pp. 106–107.

21   The details on this are discussed in Gruber, *Wissenswandel*, 57–58, 98–106. C.f. Habel, *Gelehrte Journale*, pp. 103–113; Holger Böning (ed.), *Deutsche Presse. Biobibliographische Handbücher zur Geschichte der deutschsprachigen periodischen Presse von den Anfängen bis 1815* (7 vols., Stuttgart: Frommann-Holzboog, 1996–2003); Joachim Kirchner, *Die Grundlagen des deutschen Zeitschriftenwesens. Mit einer Gesamtbibliographie der deutschen Zeitschriften bis zum Jahre 1790* (2 vols., Leipzig: Karl W. Hiersemann 1928–1931); Joachim Kirchner, *Die Zeitschriften des deutschen Sprachgebietes von den Anfängen bis 1830* (Stuttgart: Anton Hiersemann, 1969); David A. Kronick, *Scientific and Technical Periodicals of the Seventeenth and Eighteenth Centuries. A Guide* (Metuchen, N.J.: The Scarecrow

usually referring to the sixteenth and seventeenth centuries, most likely varied even more and were on average considerably larger. The print runs of broadsheets and pamphlets varied probably between 100 and 10,000 copies. The print runs of almanacs enlarged considerably over the centuries, around 1600, print runs probably varied between 600 and 1,000 copies, around 1800, the average encompassed presumably 10,000 and in rare exceptions up to 50,000 copies per title.[22]

From a material point of view, it should be noted that not a single article on the cometary apparition of 1743/44 in periodical journals contains illustrations regarding the comet, neither the 'independent articles' nor the reviews. While the lack of images is generally characteristic of learned journals in the Holy Roman Empire and probably rooted in the higher costs associated with printing illustrations, it still seems surprising given that this concerned a comet.[23] Most other media types frequently include images related to the comet. All broadsheets on the cometary apparition of 1743/44 do, as well as about two thirds of the books, and about one third of the pamphlets. While all evaluated *Messrelationen* and more than three-quarters of the almanacs include images as well, these do not always relate to the cometary apparition either.[24]

The large number of reviews, however, may not be that surprising, as Thomas Habel has already shown that, in the Holy Roman Empire, learned journals predominantly comprised reviews.[25] This also applies to similar journals across Europe.[26] Still, it needs to be noted that the survival rates and accessibility of periodical journals further distorts our data, as one will never know what was printed but did not survive. Although the numbers will probably always

---

Press, 1991); Jürgen Wilke, *Grundzüge der Medien- und Kommunikationsgeschichte* (Köln: Böhlau, 2008), pp. 98–99, 105–106.

22 For more details on this and further literature on the topic see Gruber, *Wissenswandel*, pp. 78, 93.

23 For more details on images in learned journals see Habel, *Gelehrte Journale*, pp. 190–204.

24 Gruber, *Wissenswandel*, esp. pp. 402–404, 468 (*Diagramm 7*).

25 Habel, *Gelehrte Journale*; Thomas Habel, 'Das Neueste aus der Respublica Litteraria. Zur Genese der deutschen "Gelehrten Blätter" im ausgehenden 17. und beginnenden 18. Jahrhundert', in Volker Bauer and Holger Böning (eds.), *Die Entstehung des Zeitungswesens im 17. Jahrhundert. Ein neues Medium und seine Folgen für das Kommunikationssystem der Frühen Neuzeit* (Bremen: edition lumière, 2011), pp. 303–340.

26 E.g. Ellen Kefting, Aina Nøding and Mona Ringvej (eds.), *Eighteenth-Century Periodicals as Agents of Change: Perspectives on Northern Enlightenment* (Leiden: Brill, 2015); Munck, 'Eighteenth-Century Review Journals', pp. 415–435; Jeanne Peiffer and Jean-Pierre Vittu, 'Les journaux savants, formes de la communication et agents de la construction des savoirs (17e–18e siècles)', *Dix-Huitième Siècle* 40 (2008), pp. 281–300, esp. pp. 283–285, 294–296; Jeanne Peiffer, Maria Conforti and Patrizia Delpiano (eds.), *Les Journaux savants dans l'Europe moderne. Communication et construction des savoirs* (Brepols: Turnhout, 2013).

remain estimates, it is very likely that a far larger percentage of the periodical journals survived to this day than of other media types, especially broadsheets, pamphlets and almanacs. Thanks to a more traditional scholarly interest in periodical journals, they are also relatively easily accessible. Although a comprehensive bibliography of eighteenth-century periodical journals originating in the Holy Roman Empire is still missing, to date at least ninety titles are known that appeared in the Empire between 1743 and 1748 alone.[27]

What has also escaped scholarly attention thus far, is the question of how learned journals and especially the reviews therein interacted with and related to other publication types in the mid-eighteenth century. The most obvious functions that periodicals fulfilled were as filters and multipliers. The reviews represented a form of preselection to help their readers decide whether to read the reviewed publications or not. Similar to today, the reviews gave insights into what people considered readable and relevant, as well as offering an opportunity to the authors of books or pamphlets to advertise their findings. Due to the increasing number of publications and the relatively high prices of books, the reviews also made it possible to access the most important arguments of a publication without having to read or buy the reviewed title. Therefore, reviews could also expand the audience of a title, which helped to accelerate the circulation of knowledge.

That people of the mid-eighteenth century were aware of the central functions of reviews as filters and multipliers is reflected in a statement by Martin Knutzen (1713–1751), professor of philosophy at Königsberg (present-day Kaliningrad) and teacher of Immanuel Kant (1724–1804). In 1744, he published a book on comets entitled *Vernünftige Gedanken von den Cometen* (Reasonable Thoughts on Comets).[28] In April 1744, he sent a copy of this book to Johann Christoph Gottsched (1700–1766) in Leipzig, who, among many other activities, edited several periodical journals. Along with this copy, Knutzen sent a letter in which he stated the following:

---

27   This number was determined in the course of the PhD-project. For an overview on this and the current state of bibliography of periodical journals in the Holy Roman Empire see Gruber, *Wissenswandel*, pp. 57–58, 101–103; Andreas Würgler, '"Popular Print in German" (1400–1800). Problems and Projects', in Massimo Rospocher, Jeroen Salman and Hannu Salmi (eds.), *Crossing Borders, Crossing Cultures. Popular Print in Europe (1450–1900)* (Berlin: De Gruyter, 2019), pp. 53–68.

28   Martin Knutzen, *Vernünftige Gedanken von den Cometen, zugleich eine kurze Beschreibung von dem merkwürdigen Cometen des jetztlauffenden Jahres mitgetheilet wird* (Frankfurt [am Main], Leipzig: s.n., 1744), VD18 13041290. In the same year, Johann Heinrich Hartung (1699–1756) printed another edition in Königsberg (VD18 10945393).

Concerning my thoughts about comets, they are full of typographical errors ... I kindly ask you to forgive them. Your Noble Magnificence [Gottsched] has to decide whether these thoughts deserve to be announced, for instance, in the *'Leipziger Journalen'*.[29]

Knutzen considered it an honour to receive a review in a journal. Even if this was just a rhetorical trope to please Gottsched, Knutzen was aware that his publication could reach a larger audience thanks to a review, as he explicitly used the words *'bekandt gemacht'* (announced). The importance of the reviews is additionally underlined by the fact that Knutzen sent a free copy to Gottsched without even knowing whether it would be reviewed.

The reviews themselves therefore deserve greater attention, as well as what they 'announced'. A differentiation between the media types of the reviewed publications, for instance, shows that books were the most likely media type to receive a review, representing sixty-seven per cent of all of the evaluated reviews (Figure 3.3). Pamphlets also made up an important part of reviewed materials (twenty-six per cent), as did two journal articles and two volumes of periodical journals.[30] No broadsheets, almanacs or *Messrelationen* were reviewed, which, given the nature of these media types, seems little surprising.

Equally unsurprising is the fact that the reviews appeared in a small geographical area. Of the seventy-four reviews most appeared in Leipzig (30), Hamburg (21) and Göttingen (19), and a few more in Halle (2), Berlin (1) and Jena (1). All these places are situated in north-eastern Germany, and were generally the main publication centres of learned journals in the Holy Roman Empire, although the journals themselves reached audiences across the empire and beyond.[31]

---

29 '*Was meine Gedancken von denen Cometen betrifft, so sind sie auch voller Druckfehler ...; bitte dieselbe gütig zu entschuldigen. Ob sie verdienen, etwa in den Leipziger Journalen bekandt gemacht zu werden; stelle Ew HochEdelg. Magnificence [Gottsched] anheim.*' Letter from Martin Knutzen to Johann Christoph Gottsched, Königsberg 12 April 1744, printed in Detlef Döring et al. (eds.), *Johann Christoph Gottsched. Briefwechsel. Unter Einschluß des Briefwechsels von Luise Adelgunde Victorie Gottsched* (11 vols., Berlin: de Gruyter, 2007–2017), X, p. 73. All translations in this article are mine.

30 Leonhard Euler, 'Recherches physiques sur la cause de la queue des cometes, de la lumiere boreale, et de la lumiere zodiacale', *Histoire de l'Académie Royale*, 2 (1746), pp. 117–140. Reviewed in *Berlinische Bibliothek: worinnen von neu heraus gekommenen Schriften und andern zur Gelahrtheit gehörigen Sachen kurze Aufsätze und Nachrichten mitgetheilet werden*, 2 (1748), pp. 377–383; *Nova Acta Eruditorum*, 69 (1750), pp. 600–601.

Heinrich Kühn, 'Unvorgreifliche Gedancken von dem wahren Ursprung des Cometen=Schweifes', *Versuche und Abhandlungen der Naturforschenden Gesellschaft in Danzig*, 1 (1747), pp. 546–600. Reviewed in *Neuer Zeitungen von Gelehrten Sachen*, 32 (1746), pp. 649–650; and 33 (1747), pp. 827–829; *Nova Acta Eruditorum*, 62 (1743), pp. 131–139.

31 E.g. Habel, *Gelehrte Journale*, pp. 110–126.

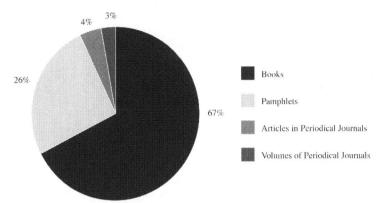

FIGURE 3.3   Media types of the publications reviewed within the collected articles in periodical journals on the cometary apparition of 1743/44 (N = 74)

A bit more surprising, however, is that a comparison of the numbers of reviews with the composition of the corpus (Figure 3.1 and Figure 3.3) reveals that while the number of books was relatively small, they received about two-thirds of all reviews. This result, of course, depends on the definitions of a pamphlet and a book. Within the evaluations of this study, this differentiation mostly responds to the assumed price of each publication – a factor that strongly depended on the amount of leaves as well as the inclusion of images – and the corresponding audience that could afford and access the publications.[32] Following these assumptions, the reviews either aimed at a wealthy and highly educated audience that could afford to buy books or at audiences that could not afford to buy books and therefore needed reviews to access the content of the books, or, most likely, a combination of both.

Another relevant question is whether German periodical journals helped to internationalise knowledge about comets. The analysis of the geographical origins of the reviewed publications indicates that they did, but only to a limited

32   Pamphlets are defined as independent publications that appeared in response to current incidents or discourses (*akzidentiell*), were originally published without bindings and stretched between two and generally up to twenty-five but sometimes to a maximum of forty-eight leaves. The differentiation between pamphlet and book and the prices of the publications are discussed in detail in Gruber, *Wissenswandel*, pp. 65–69, 425–427. These categories build on Daniel Bellingradt, 'Die vergessenen Quellen des Alten Reiches. Ein Forschungsüberblick zu frühneuzeitlicher Flugpublizistik im Heiligen Römischen Reich deutscher Nation', in Astrid Blome and Holger Böning (eds.), *Presse und Geschichte. Leistungen und Perspektiven der historischen Presseforschung* (Bremen: edition lumière, 2008); Daniel Bellingradt and Michael Schilling, 'Flugpublizistik', in Natalie Binczek, Till Dembeck and Jörgen Schäfer (eds.), *Handbuch Medien der Literatur* (Berlin: de Gruyter, 2013), pp. 273–289, p. 273.

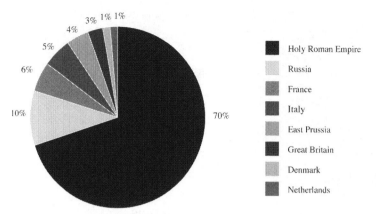

FIGURE 3.4 Geographical origins of the reviewed publications in the collected articles in periodical journals on the cometary apparition of 1743/44 (N = 74)

degree (Figure 3.4). The majority of the reviewed publications originated in the Holy Roman Empire: seventy per cent (fifty-two reviews). Reviews of publications that appeared in Russia occupy second place, but all seven of these reviews concerned a single publication: a book by Gottfried Heinsius (1709–1769).[33] Heinsius was German, as was the language of his publication. In 1744, he was a professor of astronomy in St. Petersburg, where his book appeared.[34] His origins in and ties to German-speaking scholarship were most likely the reason for his prominent treatment in the reviews. Nonetheless, some reviews concerned publications from geographical areas outside the Holy Roman Empire, from France, Italy, East Prussia, Britain, Denmark and the Netherlands, but this ultimately concerned only a relatively small number of them (fifteen in total). These findings correspond to the results of Thomas Munck who evaluated three late eighteenth-century titles of learned journals from different European areas, all of

---

33 Gottfried Heinsius, *Beschreibung des im Anfang des Jahrs 1744 erschienenen Cometen nebst einigen darüber angestellten Betrachtungen* (St. Petersburg: Akademie der Wissenschaften, 1744), VD18 11411368.

34 On the biography of Gottfried Heinsius see Samuel Baur, *Neues Historisch=Biographisch= Literarisches Handwörterbuch von der Schöpfung der Welt bis zum Schlusse des achtzehnten* (5 vols., Ulm: Stettinische Buchhandlung, 1807–1810), I (1807), p. 695; Christian Bruhns, 'Heinsius, Gottfried', in *Allgemeine Deutsche Biographie* (56 vols., Leipzig: Duncker & Humblot, 1875–1912), XI (1880), p. 656; Johann Samuel Ersch and Johann Gottfried Gruber (eds.), *Allgemeine Encyklopädie der Wissenschaften und Künste* (Leipzig: F. A. Brockhaus, Johann Friedrich Gleditsch, 1818–1889), Section 2, Part 5 (1829), pp. 17–18; Johann Georg Meusel, *Lexikon der vom Jahr 1750 bis 1800 verstorbenen teutschen Schriftsteller* (15 vols., Leipzig: Gerhard Fleischer d. J., 1802–1816), V (1805), pp. 308–310.

which seem to prefer to review publications in their 'native' languages, although the proportion differed from title to title.[35]

By taking a closer look at the content of the reviews, one might ask how they judged the reviewed works. An evaluation of the reviews shows that many of them did not offer a judgement at all, which seems to have been a common practice, as it was not until the second half of the eighteenth century that judgements became an integrative part of reviews.[36] In the case of the cometary apparition of 1743/44, thirty of the seventy-four reviews represented excerpts or short summaries without judgements about the content of the reviewed publications. If the reviewers judged the content, the majority highlighted only positive (twenty-five) or positive and negative aspects (eight). Eleven reviews were solely negative. The large number of excerpts from the reviewed works suggests that many 'reviews' were meant to function as alternative means of consulting the works. If judgements were included, then they could range from praise and criticism on the quality of the writing and the inclusion or neglect of relevant literature, to the quality of illustrations or the reputation of the author, and encompassed at times even personal conflicts between the author and reviewer.

In addition, the reviews concentrated on only a few publications. While forty of the sixty-seven books and pamphlets were reviewed, only seven publications led to almost half of the reviews in total, and all seven of these publications were books (Figure 3.5). Besides the aforementioned Gottfried Heinsius in St. Petersburg, five men were responsible for these publications: Johann Bernhard Wiedeburg (1687–1766), a university professor in Jena; the Berlin-based mathematician Leonhard Euler; Christian Gottlieb Guttmann (1699–1747), a school principal in Bernstadt; as well as the self-educated astronomer Eberhard Christian Kindermann (born c.1715), who, in 1744, was based in Dresden; and Johann Heyn (1709–1746), a preacher and school principal in Netzen in Old-Brandenburg.[37] To expand upon the style and content

---

35 Munck, 'Eighteenth-Century Review Journals', pp. 432–433 (endnote 11).
36 Johannes Arndt, 'Die historisch-politischen Zeitschriften innerhalb der zirkulären Struktur des Mediensystems der politischen Publizistik', in Johannes Arndt and Esther-Beate Körber (eds.), *Das Mediensystem im Alten Reich der Frühen Neuzeit (1600–1750)* (Göttingen: Vandenhoeck & Ruprecht, 2010), pp. 139–171, esp. p. 167; Bellingradt, 'Forschungsbericht', p. 240; Habel, *Gelehrte Journale*, pp. 218–295; Flemming Schock, 'Wissen im neuen Takt – Die Zeitung und ihre Bedeutung für die Entstehung erster populärwissenschaftlicher "Zeitschriften"', in Bauer and Böning (eds.), *Entstehung Des Zeitungswesens*, pp. 281–302, esp. 285–286.
37 Two of Johann Bernhard Wiedeburg's publications were reviewed multiple times. Six reviews exist for: Johann Bernhard Wiedeburg, *Astronomisches Bedenken Ueber die Frage Ob der bevorstehende Untergang der Welt natürlicher Weise entstehen Jns besondere Durch Annäherung eines Cometen zur Erden werde befördert werden. Nebst einer Anzeige des*

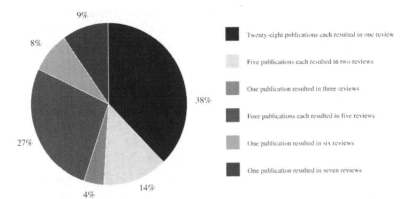

FIGURE 3.5   Numbers of collected reviews in periodical journals on the cometary apparition of 1743/44 (N = 74) in relation to the number of independent publications (N = 40)

of these reviews, the next section is dedicated to one of these men, whose publications led to intense debates in the German scholarly world.

2   Reviews of Johann Heyn's Theories on Comets

Johann Heyn was born on 23 February 1709 in Westheim in Franken. After studying pedagogy and theology in Halle and Jena, he became the co-principal of a

---

Cometen, welcher von December des 1743sten Jahres an noch ietzo erscheinet (Jena: Johann Adam Melchior, 1744), not listed in the VD18, but copies survive in the British Library [8561.aaaa.16.(2.)] and in other collections. In the same year, Johann Adam Melchior († 1745?) in Jena published two further editions (VD18 11841886 (?), VD18 11961554). Three reviews exist for: Johann Bernhard Wiedeburg, *Joh. Bernhardt Wiedeburgs Anmerkungen. Zur Erläuterung Seines Astronomischen Bedenkens über die Frage Ob der bevorstehende Untergang der Welt natürlicher Weise entstehen Und besonders Durch Annäherung Eines Cometen zur Erden werde befördert werden. Nebst einer Vorrede und vollständigen Nachricht von den leztern Cometen, der im Jahr 1744. erschienen* (Jena: Johann Adam Melchior, 1746), VD18 11007206. Five reviews exist for: Leonhard Euler, *Theorie motuum planetarum et cometarum* (Berlin: Ambrosius Haude, 1744), VD18 10755063. Five reviews exist for: Eberhard Christian Kindermann, *Vollständige Astronomie, Oder: Sonderbare Betrachtungen derer vornehmsten an dem Firmament befindlichen Planeten und Sternen. Ferner: Woher alle Phænomena, Cometen und dergleichen ungewöhnliche Himmels=Zeichen ihren Ursprung nehmen, oder was selbige nach sich ziehen können; ingleichen, wie das gantze Himmels=Heer von einer unermößlichen Allmacht des Schöpffers zeuget* (Rudolstadt: Wolfgang Deer, 1744), VD18 90220730. Five reviews exist for: Johann Heyn, *Gesamlete Briefe von den Cometen, der Sündflut, und dem Vorspiel des jüngsten Gerichts, etc.* (Berlin, Leipzig: Ambrosius Haude, 1745), VD18 10945385.

school in Halle, and in 1736 the principal of the Salders' School in Brandenburg. Four years later, he married Johanna Sophie Mathesius. From 13 December 1743 onwards, he was a preacher, at first in the village of Netzen, near the town of Brandenburg, and from 1745 on in Werder, near Potsdam.[38]

During the early 1740s, Heyn published several books and pamphlets on comets.[39] In them, he argued for a special interpretation that connected traditional interpretations of comets as portents sent by God with new physical findings. Following Isaac Newton (1643–1727), Heyn believed that comets consisted of solid material and followed calculable orbits. In consequence, he argued, comets could also affect the earth in a negative way, especially due to the possibility of an impact or collision. Additionally, and this was the more controversial aspect of his arguments, he believed that the natural consequences of comets would shed new light on some parts of the Bible. By building on the physico-theological theories of William Whiston (1667–1752) and

---

38 Johann Gottlob Wilhelm Dunkel, *Historisch-Critische Nachrichten von verstorbenen Gelehrten und deren Schriften* (3 vols., Cöthen: Cörnerische Buchhandlung, 1753–1757), I (1753), pp. 643–659, not listed in the VD18, but held by the New York Public Library [811228A] and in other collections; Ferdinand Josef Schneider, 'Kometenwunder und Seelenschlaf (Johann Heyn als Wegbereiter Lessings)', *Deutsche Vierteljahresschrift für Literaturwissenschaft und Geistesgeschichte*, 18 (1940), pp. 201–232, 203–205; Erwin Thyssen, *Christlob Mylius. Sein Leben und Wirken. Ein Beitrag zur Kenntnis der Entwicklung der deutschen Kultur, besonders aber der deutschen Literatur in der Mitte des 18. Jh.* (Marburg: Universitäts-Buchdruckerei, Koch, 1912), pp. 24–31.

39 Johann Heyn and Johann Christoph Gottsched, *Versuch einer Betrachtung über die Cometen, des Sünd=flut und das Vorspiel des jüngsten Gerichts, mit* HERRN *Johann Christoph Gottscheds, berühmten Lehrers der Weltweisheit zu Leipzig, Vorrede begleitet* (Berlin: Ambrosius Haude, 1742), not listed in the VD18, but extant in the Bavarian State Library Munich [Astr.p. 66] and in other collections. Johann Heyn and Balthasar Friedrich Kunstmann, *Dissertatio Scholastica De Diluvio Orbi Terrarum Per Cometam Inducto* (Brandenburg: s.n., 1742), VD18 11647655. Johann Heyn, *Sendschreiben An des Hrn. Magister Semlers, worinnen einige unmaßgebliche Vorschläge gethan werden, wie dessen vollständige Beschreibung des Sterns der Weisen noch etwas vollständiger gemacht werden könte* (Berlin: Ambrosius Haude, 1743), not listed in the VD18, extant in the Herzogin Anna Amalia Bibliothek, Weimar [79066 – A; 19 A 21345] and in other collections. Johann Heyn and Pierre Louis Moreau de Maupertuis, *Eines Parisischen Astronomi Sendschreiben von den Cometen. Aus dem Französischen übersetzet, Und Mit einem Brief eines Schlesischen Freyherrn nebst Dessen Beantwortung von eben dieser Sache begleitet* (s.l.: s.n., 1743), VD18 10811419. Ambrosius Haude (1690–1748) published a second edition of this pamphlet in the following year (Leipzig: Haude, 1744): VD18 10738606. Heyn, *Gesamlete Briefe*. Two biographical entries from the eighteenth century describe these publications in more detail: *Beyträge zu den Actis Historico-ecclesiasticis, Oder zu den neuesten Kirchengeschichten gesamlete Nachrichten von dem Leben, merkwürdiger Männer* (3 vols., Weimar: Siegmund Heinrich Hoffmann, 1746), VD18 90290232, I, pp. 409–441; Dunkel, *Historisch-Critische Nachrichten*, I, pp. 643–659.

Thomas Burnet (around 1635–1715), he argued, for instance, that the creation of the earth, the Genesis flood, the last judgement and even the solar eclipse and earthquakes that followed the passion of Christ were the results of comets approaching the earth.[40]

Throughout the following years, people discussed these theories intensively, including in several reviews in periodical journals. Eight reviews, a tenth of all reviews on the cometary apparition of 1743/44 collected in the course of this study, concern Heyn's publications. On three of his first publications, the reviews, all of them published in the *Göttingische Zeitungen von Gelehrten Sachen*, were relatively neutral; the articles mostly summarised the content of Heyn's works (Figure 3.6).[41] In pamphlets and books, people criticised Heyn more harshly, especially for his ideas that the advent of the last judgement would occur in 1748, ushered in by the approach of a comet. Martin Knutzen, for instance, described Heyn's theories as '*bloße Muthmaßungen*' (sheer conjectures) and Christian Gottlieb Guttmann even referenced Heyn in the title of his publication, in which he argued against Heyn's theories (Figure 3.7).[42] Johann Bernhard Wiedeburg most strongly opposed Heyn, claiming that he wrote his book mainly because Heyn and others had introduced these physico-theological theories about comets to the German-speaking world. Wiedeburg's arguments against these interpretations that he described as '*falsche Vorurteile*' (false prejudices) stretched over more than two hundred pages.[43] In response, a reviewer of Wiedeburg's book commented on this dispute and mentioned that the author was looking forward to what Heyn would have to say in response.[44]

---

40 Barbara Mahlmann-Bauer recently described the circulation of these ideas inspired by William Whiston and Thomas Burnet in the German-speaking world in more detail: Mahlmann-Bauer, 'William Whiston'. On William Whiston's *Theory of the Earth* see: Maureen Farrell, *William Whiston* (New York: Arno Press, 1981); James E. Force, *William Whiston. Honest Newtonian* (Cambridge: Cambridge University Press, 1985); Heidarzadeh, *History*, pp. 129–133. See also Thomas Burnet, *Telluris Theoria Sacra: Orbis Nostri Originem & Mutationes Generales* (London: R.N. Impensis Gualt. Kettilby, 1681), held by the State Library of Passau [S nv/Ri (b) 50–1] and in other collections.

41 *Göttingische Zeitungen von Gelehrten Sachen*, 5 (1743), pp. 117–119; 620–621; 621–622.

42 Knutzen, *Vernünftige Gedanken*, pp. 97–98. Guttmann, *Vernünftige Gedanken*. For other examples of criticism of Heyn's theories see Dunkel, *Historisch-Critische Nachrichten*, I, 645–655; Martin Mulsow, *Freigeister im Gottsched-Kreis. Wolffianismus, studentische Aktivitäten und Religionskritik in Leipzig, 1740–1745* (Göttingen: Wallstein, 2007), pp. 41–47.

43 Wiedeburg, *Astronomisches Bedenken*, ff. AIIv–BIir, pp. 73–76.

44 *Freye Urtheile und Nachrichten zum Aufnehmen der Wissenschaften und Historie überhaupt*, 1 (1744), pp. 115–118, 125–127.

FIGURE 3.6
Göttingische Zeitungen von Gelehrten Sachen auf das Jahr MDCCXLIV (Göttingen: Johann Peter Schmid, 1744), title-page, VD18 10945385
SOURCE: STATE AND UNIVERSITY LIBRARY GÖTTINGEN [8 EPH LIT 148/7], RESOLVER.SUB.UNI-GOETTINGEN.DE/PURL?PPN319732576_1744

FIGURE 3.7
Christian Gottlieb Guttmann, *Vernünftige Gedancken über die neue Cometenlehre* (Leipzig: Bernhard Christoph Breitkopf, 1744), title-page, VD18 11508167
SOURCE: SAXON STATE AND UNIVERSITY LIBRARY DRESDEN [ASTRON.873.M,MISC.1], DIGITAL.SLUB-DRESDEN.DE/ID344543250, PUBLIC DOMAIN MARK 1.0

FIGURE 3.8
Johann Heyn, *Gesamlete Briefe von den Cometen, der Sündflut, und dem Vorspiel des jüngsten Gerichts, etc.* (Berlin: Ambrosius Haude, 1745), VD18 10945385
SOURCE: STATE AND UNIVERSITY LIBRARY GÖTTINGEN [8 ASTR II, 4595], RESOLVER.SUB.UNI-GOETTINGEN.DE /PURL?PPN654189684

Heyn did have a response to Wiedeburg. On 20 April 1744, he wrote a letter to Johann Christoph Gottsched in Leipzig, in which he referred to Wiedeburg's arguments. Heyn believed that this dispute would more likely support his theories than refute them, and announced that, in God's name, he would put his pen to paper on this topic again.[45] In 1745, he published a book entitled *Gesamlete Briefe von den Cometen, der Sündtflut, und dem Vorspiel des jüngsten Gerichts, etc.* (Collected Letters on Comets, the Deluge and the Advent of the Last Judgment), a collection of twenty-eight letters from and to Heyn (Figure 3.8). The text filled more than 800 pages in octavo, by far the most extensive of all known publications on comets of that time. Heyn tried to defend his theories against his adversaries, like Knutzen, Guttmann and Wiedeburg, mainly by repeating what he had published before.[46]

This collection of letters led to even more criticism. A review in the *Göttingische Zeitungen von Gelehrten Sachen* claimed, for instance, that 'The preacher Heine … is now no longer using playful but ludicrous imagination',

---

[45] Letter from Johann Heyn to Johann Christoph Gottsched, 20 April 1744 (printed in Döring, *Gottsched*, X, pp. 99–101).
[46] Heyn, *Gesamlete Briefe*.

going on to call some of his arguments 'intrinsic errors and paradoxical phrases'.[47] In response, Heyn published a letter in a newspaper in Berlin, in which he condemned this review:

> Gentlemen! Although I offer my collection of letters to the freest of judgments of the public, and I do not ask for leniency or any favours on behalf of my errors, if I have committed any, I do believe I have a legitimate claim to complain about the treatment of my book ... I believe that an honest man wishing to rail against a paper should have read it beforehand ... As Mr. Reviewer has deceived the audience and is striving to harm me ... I, Gentlemen, seek my refuge in you and ask you, in the interest of truth, to contradict this unknown man publicly.[48]

Shortly after these reproaches, the authors of the *Göttingische Zeitungen von Gelehrten Sachen* responded. In their journal, they affirmed that the reviewer had indeed read Heyn's *Gesamlete Briefe*, but they did not argue extensively against Heyn. They also declared that this journal was not the place for scholarly disputes and that the impartial public should judge the review on Heyn themselves. In response to the supposed personal affront to Heyn, they added:

> Mr. Heyn may rest assured that we seek only to contradict mistakes and in no way the learned man who is mistaken. Our soul hates the terrible, and our journal is dedicated to the truth, and in no way to the whitewashing of errors. We display both, as and where we find them.[49]

---

47 'Der Hr. Pastor Heine verfällt nunmehro aus der spielenden in die überwitzige Einbildungskraft' and 'würkliche Jrthümer und paradoxe Sätze', *Göttingische Zeitungen von Gelehrten Sachen*, 7 (1745), pp. 668–669.

48 'Meine Herren! Ob ich gleich die Samlung meiner Briefe vom freyesten Urtheil des Publice überlasse, und mir für meine Jrrthümer, wenn ich einige begangen habe, keine Nachsicht und Gefälligkeit ausbitte; so glaube ich doch berechtiget zu seyn, mich über die Erzehlung meines Buchs ... beschweren zu können. Jch bin nemlich der Meynung, daß ein ehrlicher Mann, welcher wieder eine Schrift eifern will, dieselbe gelesen haben sollte ... Da nun der ... Herr Recensent das Publicum hintergangen, und mir zu schaden trachtet ....: so nehme ich, meine Herren, zu Jhnen meine Zuflucht und bitte, daß Sie, zu Steuer der Wahrheit, diesem unbekanten Herrn öffentlich wiedersprechen wollen.' *Berlinische Nachrichten von Staats und Gelehrten Sachen*, CXXXVI (13 November 1745), pp. A II r–v.

49 'Allein Hr. Heyn kann versichert seyn, daß wir nur den Jrrthum, keines weges dem gelehrten irrenden Mann, zu schaden trachten. Unsere Seele haßet nur das Arge, und unsere Blätter sind der Wahrheit, keines weges der Beschönigung des Jrthums gewidmet. Wir zeigen beides so an, wie und wo wir es finden.' *Göttingische Zeitungen von Gelehrten Sachen*, 7 (1745), pp. 782–784.

If Heyn formulated a response to these arguments, none could be found. Other reviews of Heyn's *Gesamlete Briefe* took a more neutral tone; one reviewer even hoped for Heyn to approve of his review and admitted that he had, purposely, passed over several points at which he had differed in his opinion, probably to avoid an escalation.[50] Nevertheless, Heyn's conflict with the authors of the *Göttingische Zeitungen von Gelehrten Sachen* was not singular. Johann Bernhard Wiedeburg, for instance, also reacted to Heyn's *Gesamlete Briefe*. He did not write a review, but a whole book that appeared in 1746. Wiedeburg insisted that he had felt forced to write this book because of Heyn's response.[51] Wiedeburg's arguments were very much the same as in his previous book on the topic, but this time he proclaimed that he would not be willing to add anything else to the dispute with Heyn, as he thought that Heyn held his opinions excessively dear and that it would be impossible to 'convert' him.[52]

This response, again, did not go unnoticed. A reviewer in *Freye Urtheile und Nachrichten* (Figure 3.9) asked for this controversy to end:

> It seems to be time to end the whole dispute. The sensitivity that can be felt in several comments shows clearly enough that it has come to the extreme, and that not everybody who can teach is also skilful at refutation.[53]

Wiedeburg's book did mark the end of the dispute, but this was most likely not an intentional decision, as Johann Heyn died of unknown causes on 12 August 1746.[54] Nevertheless, the discussion and criticism in the aftermath of Heyn's publications on comets shows the intensity and emotionality of the discussions on knowledge regarding comets in the Holy Roman Empire by the mid-eighteenth century. A learned public paid close attention to new publications on the topic, their reception and responses to them. The authors of these works were well aware of each other and often closely connected. This network and associated critical exchanges manifested in various types of publications, from periodical journals to books, pamphlets and newspapers, but were, of course, also present in personal correspondences.

---

50   *Neuer Zeitungen von Gelehrten Sachen*, 31 (1745), 919–920. *Zuverlässige Nachrichten von dem gegenwärtigen Zustande, Veränderungen und Wachsthum der Wissenschaften*, 7 (1746), pp. 516–541, pp. 540–541.
51   Wiedeburg, *Anmerkungen*, preface, pp. 3–5.
52   Ibid, pp. 51–52.
53   'Allein, es scheinet Zeit zu seyn, daß der ganze Streit geendigt werde. Denn die Empfindlichkeit, so in einigen Anmerkungen angemahlt stehet, zeiget deutlich genug, daß es aufs höchste gekommen, und daß nicht alle, welche lehren können, auch zu widerlegen geschickt sind.' *Freye Urtheile und Nachrichten zum Aufnehmen der Wissenschaften und Historie überhaupt*, 3 (1746), pp. 358–359.
54   Dunkel, *Historisch-Critische Nachrichten*, I, p. 644.

FIGURE 3.9
Freye Urtheile und Nachrichten zum Aufnehmen der Wissenschaften und Historie überhaupt (Hamburg: Georg Christian Grund, 1744), title page, VD18 90151410
SOURCE: SAXON STATE AND UNIVERSITY LIBRARY DRESDEN [EPH.LIT.786-1.1744], DIGITAL.SLUB-DRESDEN.DE /ID37067202X-17440000, PUBLIC DOMAIN MARK 1.0

This documentation shows that periodical journals were by far not the only media type to include critical thoughts on comets. On the contrary, the strongest criticism were voiced in older types of media, books and pamphlets, whereas the reviews and responses in the periodical journals remained, at first, relatively neutral. Only after the conflict intensified, could stronger arguments also be found in the reviews, though still hesitantly so.

3 Conclusion

In contrast to previous assumptions, the findings of this article show that, by the 1740s, periodical journals in the Holy Roman Empire were not the preferred media type to discuss the nature and meaning of comets, and new findings and controversial arguments were still preferably published in older media types, especially in pamphlets and books.[55] The questions of whether periodical journals really were the '*Schlüsselwerke* of the Enlightenment' and if they

---

55 Such previous assumptions were recently repeated by Anna Jerratsch (*Kometendiskurs*, pp. 487–488, 509, 525, 528).

really reconfigured the discussion and circulation of knowledges require more complex answers and cannot be determined within a single case study.[56]

The analysis presented above, however, sheds new light on these questions and suggests that in the 1740s, periodical journals were one manifestation out of many, rather than 'the key works' of Enlightenment, as reflected in their materiality, reach, content and media reverberations. Most of the journal coverage of comets appeared in learned journals (*Gelehrte Journale*) that had relatively small print runs and targeted a highly-educated and wealthy audience. Only six out of eighty-seven articles were aimed at a relatively large audience, those that were published in the moral weeklies (*Moralische Wochenschriften*). Although such types of periodical journals became more popular in later periods, by the 1740s such a diverse audience was therefore still more likely to be targeted through older media types such as broadsheets, pamphlets or almanacs, at least with regards to comets. The content of the articles also limits their impact, since the majority represented excerpts of previously published books and pamphlets, whereas critical judgements, more controversial arguments and new findings were, at this time, more likely expressed in other types of media, again, preferably in books and pamphlets.

The main communicative roles of periodical journals on the cometary apparition of 1743/44 therefore were those of multipliers and filters, and to a limited degree they helped to internationalise information. By doing so, the periodical journals contributed to the acceleration of the circulation and change of knowledge, since they suggested, prevented or replicated the consultation of a title and thereby helped their audiences to save both time and money. Their impact, however, was mostly limited to a small segment of society.

Future studies need to determine whether these findings regarding the cometary apparition of 1743/44 represent the exception or the rule, and whether, or more likely when, this changed, within the Holy Roman Empire and beyond. In either case, this case study illustrates that the media system was always dynamic and continued to adapt to new communicative realities. By the 1740s in the Holy Roman Empire, periodical journals were a relatively young media type and in a two-fold transition zone. On the one hand, they filled a gap in the media system, as they responded to the increasing number of publications, and learned journals offered a time-saving option to access the contents of reviewed titles without having to buy or borrow them.[57]

---

56   Habermas, *Strukturwandel*; Raabe, 'Die Zeitschrift', p. 104.
57   Contemporaries reckoned with around 750 new publications per year around 1750, and 5,000 in the 1780s and 1790s. Reinhard Wittmann, *Geschichte des deutschen Buchhandels* (München: Beck, 1999), p. 122.

To do so, they built on widened infrastructural networks and audiences that had emerged in connection to older media types. Learned journals therefore did not 'create' these audiences as previously suggested; the audiences were already there and they continued to expand.[58] On the other hand, the periodical journals themselves helped to change the media system that they were born in. They started to diversify and reach out to larger audiences. In the case of learned journals, they also began to incorporate new findings on their own as well as more critical judgements of reviewed titles. Thus, periodical journals were slowly taking over functions traditionally tied to older media types like broadsheets, pamphlets, and books, and thereby changing them.

---

58   Katrin Löffler recently described such an assumption as a 'commonplace' (*Gemeinplatz*) in research: Löffler, 'Wissen braucht einen Träger', p. 9. See also Peiffer and Vittu, 'Les journaux savants', pp. 281–282.

PART 2

Censorship and Evasion

∴

CHAPTER 4

A Peculiar Case of Entrepreneurial Bravery

The First Edition of Galileo Galilei's Collected Works in the Context of Mid-seventeenth-century Publishing and Censorship

Leonardo Anatrini

In many studies dedicated to Catholic censorship in the early modern period, emphasis is given to the dynamics with which the ecclesiastical authorities enforced preventive control over printed books and implemented a stable regulation concerning the trade routes used to import all kinds of goods within the boundaries of the Catholic Ecumene.[1] This attitude has often led to generalizations only partially confirmed by primary sources. By virtue of the resulting interpretations, the existence has often been taken for granted, on the one hand, of a tendency towards increasing centralization of powers by the Roman Curia and, on the other hand, of the widespread inability showed by the local officers to apply adequately the relevant provisions. The resulting risk is to ignore political and commercial dynamics that, since the first half of the seventeenth century, were often opposed to Counter-Reformation interests and objectives.

In this article, I outline the most relevant aspects of an emblematic case, the first collected edition of the works of Galileo Galilei (1564–1642), representing one of the rare cases of posthumous publication in Italy of works by an author condemned by the Church. Reconstructing its long gestation, the intricate editorial history and the salient moments of its commercial distribution, I try to show how what is remembered as one of the first cases of programmatic scientific dissemination was above all a display of political power and a bold entrepreneurial move, made possible thanks to the intellectual and economic efforts of individuals who acted as cultural mediators, such as editors, diplomats and lay censors.

---

1 Cf. Gigliola Fragnito (ed.), *Church, Censorship and Culture in Early Modern Italy* (Cambridge: Cambridge University Press, 2001); Vittorio Frajese, *Nascita dell'Indice. La censura ecclesiastica dal Rinascimento alla Controriforma* (Brescia: Morcelliana, 2006); Elisa Rebellato, *La fabbrica dei divieti. Gli indici dei libri proibiti da Clemente VIII a Benedetto XIV* (Milan: Sylvestre Bonnard, 2008).

1 Selling Galileo Abroad

Despite his role in the Scientific Revolution, for a long time, Galileo showed little interest in making his work known internationally. Thanks to recent and in-depth studies concerning his intermediaries and foreign correspondents, we can affirm with certainty that the latter originally took care of the dissemination of the Pisan scientist's discoveries and achievements abroad.[2] Modern historiography has often lingered over representations of Galileo as extraordinarily self-confident and adamant of the veracity of his hypotheses, as well as sometimes excessively critical of the work of his colleagues, and even choleric. It has been rightly pointed out that his attacks *ad hominem* denote an attitude devoted more to dogmatism than to scientific rigour, a typical feature of that principle of *auctoritas* repeatedly rejected and pilloried in favour of quantifiable data in works such as The Essayer (1623) and the Dialogue Concerning the Two Chief World Systems (1632).[3] Concerning the editorial agenda followed by Galileo, political motivations guided some of his choices. In general, in the intellectual battle between *Germanitas* and *Romanitas* it is easy to recognise the scientist's nationalism, aimed not only at giving prestige to the Italian scientific panorama but mainly at recovering Copernicanism from protestant circles, naturally considered as heretical.[4]

To achieve proper guidance relating to the diffusion of Galileo's work in Europe, it was necessary to wait for the appearance of the Swiss jurist and lawyer Elia Diodati (1576–1661), who needed years, from the beginning of an epistolary exchange (1620) up to the first meeting (1626), to overcome the diffidence of the Tuscan scientist. The collaboration that arose was extraordinarily fruitful and Diodati proved to be a formidable mediator, gradually succeeding, among other things, in bringing Galileo into contact with many of the most prominent European scientists of the time.

---

[2] Cf. Stéphane Garcia, *Élie Diodati et Galilée. Naissance d'un réseau scientifique dans l'Europe du XVIIe siècle* (Florence: Leo S. Olschki, 2004), pp. 231–363.

[3] One of the first scholars to highlight this specific aspect of Galileo's *forma mentis* was William R. Shea, in *Galileo's Intellectual Revolution* (London: MacMillan, 1972), esp. pp. 85–87. The phrase that ends the book is extremely famous, referring to Galileo's theory of tides and pointing out how his speculations were more 'a Platonic gamble' than 'an experimental game' (p. 186).

[4] As reported in Garcia, *Élie Diodati et Galilée*, p. 260. Cf. Isabelle Pantin, 'New philosophy and old prejudices: Aspects of the reception of Copernicanism in a divided Europe', *Studies in History and Philosophy of Science*, 30 (1999), pp. 237–262; Idem, *'Dissiper les ténèbres qui restent encore à percer*. Galilée, l'Eglise conquérante et la République des philosophes', in Alain Mothu (ed.), *Révolution scientifique et libertinage* (Turnhout: Brepols, 2000), pp. 11–34.

The success and interest aroused by Galileo's work, especially in academic circles, was unquestionable, as underlined by secondary projects aimed at further disseminating his works. In this regard, it will suffice to quote the emblematic case of the first edition of the *Mechanics* and the paraphrase of the *Two New Sciences*, edited in French by Marin Mersenne (1588–1648).[5] Mersenne also proposed to draw up a French paraphrase of the *Dialogue*, but this idea was plausibly discarded due to the criticisms by the Sorbonne theologians, in the face of the possibility of discussing theses condemned in Rome.[6] After the notorious trial, it did not take long for someone to propose to the scientist to finally do justice to his work by producing a collected edition of his writings, but unfortunately, the curtain fell on Galileo's life on 8 January 1642, before this undertaking was completed.[7]

However, the problem of safeguarding the role he played in the Scientific Revolution remained (becoming even more pressing after his death), for two interdependent political-cultural reasons. Firstly, it was necessary to show the historical precedence of the Galilean project of a reform aimed at converting both Academia and the Church to *libertas philosophandi*.[8] A second motivation was to consolidate Galileo's authority as an exceptional discoverer and inventor, as well as a pioneer of a new tradition, finally free from the constraints of Aristotelian-scholastic epistemology and, in general, from textual authority, in favour of the experimental method. Consequently, to disseminate the Galilean *methodus* and to renew the prestige of his patrons, the House of Medici (who had suffered a political debacle as a result of the inability to spare their protégé the humiliation of the trial and abjuration) the best option was to publish a complete edition of his works. Such an undertaking was impossible in Catholic countries and impractical for one of the few European publishers able to take on the related investment, the Elzeviers. Their interest in the dissemination of the complete Galilean works had rapidly waned in the face

---

5   Marin Mersenne (ed.), *Les méchaniques de Galilée* (Paris: chez Henri Guenon, 1634); *Les nouvelles pensées de Galilée* (Paris: chez Henri Guenon, 1639). Cf. John Lewis, *Galileo in France: French Reactions to the Theories and Trial of Galileo* (New York: Peter Lang, 2007), pp. 113–140.

6   Project drafted in chapters 44–45 of his *Questions théologiques, physiques, morales et mathématiques* (Paris: chez Henry Guenon, ruë sainct Iacques, prés les Iacobins, à l'image sainct Bernard, 1634), pp. 201–228. On the controversy raised by this project, cf. Cornélis de Waard and Armand Beaulieu (eds.), *Marin Mersenne. Correspondance* (17 vols.; Paris: PUF-CNRS, 1932–88), IV, pp. 267–268, 403–407 (letters to Nicolas-Claude Fabri de Peiresc, 28 July and 4 December 1634).

7   For a succinct reconstruction of the attempts at a collected edition during Galileo's lifetime, cf. Garcia, *Élie Diodati et Galilée*, pp. 315–317.

8   On Galileo's politico-cultural programme, see Ludovico Geymonat, *Galileo Galilei: A Biography and Inquiry into his Philosophy of Science* (New York: McGraw-Hill, 1965), pp. 111–155.

of the apparent failure to sell the two works funded and printed by them, the *Letter to the Grand Duchess Christina* and the *Two New Sciences*.[9] Engaging in this adventure in any Catholic country meant to incur voluntarily the undesirable attentions of the Inquisition, not exactly a financially and politically enlightened move (at least in theory).

Furthermore, in the aftermath of Galileo's death, the need was felt to collect the memory of his exploits and discoveries, and the most immediate method was to recover all the Galilean manuscripts, from the treatises to the correspondence, with a particular interest in the unpublished papers. A tireless advocate of this mission, carried out for decades, was the last and youngest of the Pisan scientist's pupils, Vincenzo Viviani (1622–1703).[10] As his correspondence already suggests, Viviani is to be considered the heir of the *opera omnia* editorial project. The first reference to Viviani as the collector of his master's manuscripts can be read in a reply letter sent to him by Vincenzo Renieri (1606–1647) on 12 November 1642.[11]

The quest for the Galilean papers, carried out with vivacity and passion by Viviani, as we know, never materialised in a comprehensive edition of the *maestro*'s work, and most of the pupil's documents concerning this venture remain unpublished today.[12] Such an enterprise became fundamentally impossible with the demise of the great patron of Galilean studies and founder of the *Accademia del Cimento*, Prince Leopoldo de' Medici (1617–1675). In fact, from the end of the 1670s, the references to the preparation of this edition decrease, disappearing from Viviani's correspondence at the end of the

---

9 *Nov-antiqua sanctissimorum patrum, & probatorum theologorum doctrina, de sacrae Scripturae testimoniis, in conclusionibus mere naturalibus, quae sensata experientia, & necessariis demonstrationibus evinci possunt, temere non usurpandis* (Augustae Treboc[orum].: impensis Elzeviriorum, typis Davidis Hautti, 1635); *Discorsi e dimostrazioni matematiche, intorno a due nuove scienze attenenti alla mecanica & i movimenti locali* (Leida: appresso gli Elsevirii, 1638).

10 A court mathematician since 1647, Viviani is remembered as one of the most prominent geometers and engineers of his generation; cf. Luciano Boschiero, 'Post-Galilean thought and experiment in seventeenth-century Italy: the life and work of Vincenzio Viviani', *Hsitory of Science*, 43 (2005), pp. 77–100.

11 Published in: Paolo Galluzzi and Maurizio Torrini (eds.), *Le opere dei discepoli di Galileo. Carteggio, 1642–1656* (hereafter ODG *Carteggio*; 2 vols.; Florence: Giunti-Barbera, 1975–84), I, p. 31.

12 Draft plans for Galileo's *opera omnia*, mentioning a biography, indices and the Latin translations of those works originally written in vernacular, have come down to us; see Antonio Fàvaro, 'Documenti inediti per la storia dei manoscritti galileiani nella Biblioteca Nazionale di Firenze', *Bullettino di bibliografia e di storia delle scienze matematiche e fisiche*, 18 (1885), pp. 1–112, 151–230: 20–22.

century.[13] Nevertheless, he continued the painstaking work of searching for the Galilean sources until the end of his days.

2 An Almost Forgotten Protagonist of the Mid-seventeenth-century Bolognese Publishing Environment

What is the story of the 1655–56 *opera omnia* of Galileo?[14] How was it possible that the first collected edition of the writings of one of the fathers of New Science was produced by a publisher, Carlo Manolessi (1613/4–1661), devoid of scientific knowledge and an editor, Carlo Rinaldini (1615–1698), who was in those years a professor at the University of Pisa and a founding member of the *Accademia del Cimento*, but also and above all an eclectic Aristotelian, loathed by Galileo's heirs and disciples? Moreover, this edition was published in the city of Bologna, which was a Papal legation for centuries, historically linked to the study of astrology and natural philosophy according to the Aristotelian canon. Finally, how much is it necessary to downplay Viviani's contribution to this edition, despite his conspicuous epistolary exchange with the publisher in the years of publication?[15]

This is a story in which economic interests intertwine with delicate diplomatic games and, although the result certainly did not allow the Galilean *programme* to be reintroduced in Italy in its entirety, the Bolognese edition of the Pisan scientist's works offered a singular opportunity to reiterate implicitly the authoritativeness of New Science, in a certain way also reaffirming the political prestige of the Grand Ducal family. Extraordinarily, the main promoter of this editorial project dictated by audacity and occasion, together with Prince Leopoldo, patron of science, letters and arts of the House of Medici, was the publisher himself, whose professional life and affairs we can now reconstruct thanks to unpublished documents, scattered throughout the collections of libraries and archives in central Italy (and beyond).

---

13   Cf. A. Fàvaro, 'Sulla pubblicazione della sentenza contro Galileo e sopra alcuni tentativi del Viviani per far rivocare la condanna dei dialoghi galileiani', Idem, *Miscellanea galileiana inedita: studi e ricerche* (Venice: Tip. di Giuseppe Antonelli, 1887), pp. 97–156: 116–121, 128–156.

14   *Opere di Galileo Galilei Linceo Nobile Fiorentino. Già Lettore delle Matematiche nelle Università di Pisa, e di Padova, di poi Sopraordinario nello Studio di Pisa* (hereafter OGM; 2 vols.; Bologna: per gli HH. del Dozza, 1655–56), USTC 1742422, 1750033-4.

15   Viviani's lack of interest in this edition and the unconcealed annoyance in ascertaining his own authority as depositary of the Galilean legacy usurped, is evident immediately after the publication, for which he reserved severe criticism; see *ODG Carteggio*, II, pp. 305, 321 (letters to Elia Diodati, 23 February and to Cosimo Galilei, 21 March 1656).

Carlo Manolessi is undoubtedly one of the most mysterious personalities in the history of seventeenth-century Bolognese publishing, whose entrepreneurial skills were surpassed only by an inexhaustible desire for success, in an extremely competitive commercial environment.[16] A native of Ancona, Carlo was the second son of Diana Salvioni and Francesco, a bookseller of Venetian origin remembered as mediator and financier of some works published between 1608 and 1623 by his brothers-in-law, also of Venetian origin, Marco and Pietro Salvioni. They were both printer-publishers, and while Pietro operated mainly in Macerata from 1611 to 1632, Marco worked in Ancona up to 1648.[17]

The young Carlo moved to Bologna around 1636, following in the footsteps of his older brother Giovanni Cesare (1609/10–1662), who worked in the same city as a notary from 1631 until his death.[18] The oldest dedicatory letter signed by Manolessi dates to this year. It was composed for the first edition of the correspondence of Prospero Bonarelli (1580–1659), a courtier, writer and theatrical impresario widely known at the time.[19] In his letter, Manolessi tells how he had obtained the autograph directly from the author (plausibly brought to Bologna from Ancona, the city where Bonarelli had already resided for many years) and promised to release further unpublished works. This dedication demonstrates Manolessi's skills as a refined intermediary, being the result of personal knowledge and a taste for letters and the arts aimed at commerce and at establishing an editorial offer suited to the demands of a mundane yet sophisticated audience. As can be seen in this first publication, while Niccolò Tebaldini was the typographer, the financiers were the Dozza brothers, for the publishing company of which Manolessi, in a few years, became chief editor

---

16   The dates of birth and death are taken from late eighteenth-century transcriptions of the original parish registers, kept at the Archiginnasio Public Library in Bologna (BCABo), B 914, p. 43. The only biographical profile of Manolessi is: Davide Ruggerini, 'Carlo Manolessi', *Dizionario biografico degli italiani* (100 vols., Rome: Istituto della enciclopedia italiana, 1960–2020), LXIX, pp. 138–140, from which we deviate on several occasions due to its numerous inaccuracies and shortcomings.

17   For the little information available concerning the commercial activities of Francesco Manolessi and the Salvioni brothers, see Filippo M. Giochi and Alessandro Mordenti, *Gli Annali della Tipografia in Ancona* (Rome: Edizioni di storia e letteratura, 1980), pp. LII–LVII.

18   BCABo, *Ridolfi*, 18, 120; B 911, p. 408.

19   *Lettere in varij generi a prencipi, e ad altri del S. Co. Prospero Bonarelli della Rovere con alcune discorsive intorno al primo libro de gl'An. di Cor. Tac. all'ellezione de gl'ambasciadori, al modo di vivere in corte, et altre* (Bologna: appresso Nicolò Thebaldini; ad istanzia delli eredi di Evangelista Dozza, 1636), USTC 4011562.

and funder.[20] Although the information and documents on the matter are particularly limited, the beginning of Manolessi's *bibliopola* activity dates back to these years. It was always accompanied by the signing of dedicatory letters of works published by other printers, for which, in many cases, Carlo is to be identified as the funder. By reading these testimonies it is possible to reconstruct the network of contacts established by this cunning bookseller, including members of the city patriciate, as well as noblemen of his native land. Thus, for example, in 1637 Manolessi paid Clemente Ferroni to print a new edition of the panegyric offered to Louis XIII (1601–1643) on the occasion of the defeat of the Huguenots at the end of the siege of La Rochelle by the Jesuit Étienne Petiot (1602–1675), an encomiastic writer, biographer and theologian.[21] As specified in the dedicatory letter, the idea for this reprint was suggested to Manolessi by another prominent writer of the time, a protégé of several powerful men of the Church and member of a noble Bolognese family, Giovanni Battista Manzini (1599–1664). The dedicatee of the edition was another man of letters, Jacopo Gaddi (d. 1668), founder of a literary academy in Florence which promulgated its own statutes precisely at the beginning of 1637.[22]

Manolessi's letters clearly express the intention to signal his presence in the circles of the noble *amateurs* of letters, science and arts, with a constant desire to create synergies and contacts for his editorial projects. Moreover, the will to establish links abroad was, most likely, a symptom of a deeper urge to set himself free from the sphere of influence of the Church, within which Manolessi

---

20   We have very little data on the Dozza brothers. Their use of the expression *Dozza Heirs* and *Heirs of Evangelista Dozza* throughout their whole career as publisher-printers (1630–1672), makes it impossible to clarify even if they were two or more. The name of only one of them is known, Bernardino, quoted in a 1644 act of the local Inquisition (BCABo, B 1875 – *Liber expeditorum a die 23 ianuarij 1635 usque ad diem 3 mensis decembris 1660* –, leaves 49ʳ–50ʳ) since pardoned, together with Manolessi, following a public abjuration carried out to annul a punishment imposed for the possession and sale of an anti-papal libel. The Dozza brothers inherited the job from their father Evangelista (d. 1630, see BCABo, B 911, p. 85), who worked mainly as publisher and bookseller, first together with his brother, also called Bernardino, between 1619 and 1620, and then on his own until 1629, often funding the publications of Tebaldini and another Bolognese printer-publisher, Clemente Ferroni.

21   *Panegyricus Ludovico XIII. Vindici rebellionis, domitori Elementorum, aeterno triumphatori: Pro fracta Britannia, pro subiugato Oceano, pro triumphata Rupella* (Burdegalae, & Bononiae typis Clementis Ferronij, 1637), USTC 4014295. Originally published in Bordeaux in 1628, a further edition of this work was released by Manolessi and the Dozza brothers in 1649.

22   For further details concerning Gaddi's academy, see Michele Maylender, *Storia delle Accademie d'Italia* (5 vols.; Bologna: L. Cappelli, 1926–30), v, pp. 287–289.

continued to dwell, despite having moved from Ancona to Bologna.[23] The search for a powerful patron, free from the constraints that in Bologna affected the senatorial class as well (factually subject to the control of the Cardinal Legate) was the dream of every entrepreneur. Thus, maintaining relations with noble families and powerful people, Manolessi, around 1641, established a relationship particularly important for the history of Bolognese publishing.

The ambassador of the Grand Duchy in Bologna since 1624, the Marquis Ferdinando Cospi (1606–1686) was an art collector, as well as the owner of the most important Bolognese Wunderkammer of the period. Besides, he acted as an agent and intermediary on behalf of Prince Leopoldo for the purchase of works of art and, more generally, as a mediator between the Bolognese and Tuscan authorities favouring all types of exchange.[24]

We can easily speculate that Manolessi turned to Cospi with the declared intent to establish commercial contacts within the Grand Duchy. This dynamic can be confirmed thanks to an important archival document, at the origin of the long-term partnership between Manolessi and the House of Medici. This is the late seventeenth-century copy of a letter (allegedly dating to 1641) which Cospi presented to the secretary of the *Accademia della Crusca*, Benedetto Buonmattei (1581–1647). It included Manolessi's offer to reprint at his own expense a new edition of the *Vocabolario*, the first vocabulary of the Italian language, originally published in 1612.[25] After a break of several years, the work

---

23 Being a territory under the direct control of the Church, Bologna often served as a laboratory for experimenting the repressive policies of the Holy Office in the field of editorial production and circulation of texts. For example, a 1603 edict presented the rules, still valid at mid-century, which printers and booksellers had to follow, including, among other things: an annual oath in the presence of the Archbishop or the members of the local Inquisition with which professionals committed themselves not to print or sell books without imprimatur; the absolute prohibition on holding or selling books for which the imprimatur had been denied in Bologna but granted elsewhere; the obligation for booksellers to provide the local Inquisition with a list of all the books held for sale, no later than three days after their purchase. The text of this edict can be found in Albano Sorbelli, *Storia della Stampa in Bologna* (Bologna: Nicola Zanichelli Editore, 1929), pp. 129–130.

24 For the relationships between Cospi and the House of Medici, see Riccardo Carapelli, 'Un importante collezionista Bolognese del Seicento: Ferdinando Cospi e i suoi rapporti con la Firenze Medicea', *Il Carrobbio*, 14 (1988), pp. 99–114.

25 Harry Ransom Center (Austin, TX), Ranuzzi Family Archive, Ph. 12735.34 (*Offerta del Manolesi Libraro di Bolog.ᵃ fatta a Firenze per stampare il Nuovo Vocabolario della Crusca nell'Anno* [omissis]). The document is part of a volume of *copialettere* made at the time of Annibale Ranuzzi (1625–1697), son-in-law of Ferdinando Cospi. This transcription presents neither dates nor the recipient's name. These details are assumed based on the content of the document. Furthermore, it seems that Manolessi asked Cospi not to divulge

of the *Accademia della Crusca* restarted with the meeting of 25 November 1640, during which the new secretary was also appointed. In a subsequent meeting (7 April 1641), he asked the other members to resume the revision of the *Vocabolario*.[26] Reading this letter, we can observe how up to date Manolessi was concerning the issues related to literary academies operating outside Bologna. Such information could only come from his network of contacts. In the same letter it is specified that, if necessary, the recipient could forward the plea of the publisher to Prince Leopoldo, referred to as *Mecenate di questo secolo* (the Maecenas of this century). Prince Leopoldo had coincidentally during the meeting of 17 April 1641 been elected member by acclamation, becoming the *de facto* protector of the academy.[27]

The hypothesis of tracing this letter back to 1641 is based on data obtained from other dedicatory letters signed by Manolessi, the only other surviving documents useful to reconstruct his affairs during this period. For instance, the second edition of *Il guerriero politico e prudente* by the historian and man of arms Galeazzo Gualdo Priorato (1606–1678) dates back to this year. It was dedicated by Manolessi to Cospi on the occasion of the Marquis' appointment to the office of *Balì* (Bailiff) of Arezzo. This edition (published a few months after the first) is defined in the dedicatory letter as proof of *devota servitù* (devoted servitude) and *riverente affetto* (reverential affection) of the publisher towards his new protector.[28] As we know, Manolessi did not obtain this important commission (since the third edition of the Crusca's *Vocabolario* was published only in 1691, in Florence), but around 1641 he managed to get another one. In this case, unfortunately, the total lack of archival documentation does not allow us to substantiate any hypothesis, although the options are limited. It is plausible that, in the face of the *Accademia*'s refusal, Manolessi raised the stakes, extending through Cospi a new plea to Prince Leopoldo, or that Leopoldo, eager to test the resourcefulness of the entrepreneur, entrusted him with a commission even more suited to his tastes. The fact remains that six years later, in 1647, there was published a new edition of the *Lives of the Most Excellent Painters, Sculptors, and Architects* by Giorgio Vasari (1511–1574), edited by Manolessi and printed by the Dozza brothers. This is the first major work edited by the

---

his name, plausibly desiring to be known by the *Crusca*'s academics through his own work and not thanks to mere recommendation.

26 Giovanni Battista Zannoni, *Storia della Accademia della Crusca e rapporti ed elogi editi ed inediti detti in varie adunanze solenni della medesima* (Florence: Tipografia del Giglio, 1848), p. 14.

27 *Ibid.*

28 Galeazzo Gualdo Priorato, *Il guerriero prudente, e politico* (In Venetia, & in Bologna: Presso Gio. Battista Ferroni, 1641), USTC 4017081, leaf a²ᵛ.

publisher and the first one dedicated to the House of Medici, specifically to the Grand Duke himself, Ferdinando II (1610–1670).[29]

The long hiatus between the first contacts with Florence and the publication of Vasari's work is not surprising. It is explained in the *Note to the Readers*, signed by Manolessi, as usual:

> Some years ago, I decided to undertake this difficult venture, with the only impediment being the desire to publish these *Lives* in the same form as the original edition, that is, with the same portraits and ornaments with which they were printed in Florence by Giunti in 1568. But Fortune has been favourable to my plans and (after six years of searching) has finally brought the aforesaid portraits and ornaments into my possession. Therefore, having overcome such an important difficulty, I have spared no effort or expense to perfect the edition I now present to you.[30]

Furthermore, the fact that the dedicatee of the work was not Prince Leopoldo, but his older brother, can be easily explained. Despite Leopoldo's consolidated reputation as a patron of the arts and a great collector, he was a man of the Church, so the choice of not appearing as the dedicatee of a work of such a profane topic was part of the dictates of Counter-Reformist sobriety. Moreover, something similar happened with Galileo's works, since, despite the role of primary importance played by Leopoldo in their publication (as evidenced by numerous archival documents), they were dedicated to the Grand Duke, by virtue of his power and position, and to emphasise the importance of letters, arts and sciences in the Medici's political agenda.

Confirming the consolidation of the business relationship between the Dozza brothers, increasingly relegated to the role of mere printers, and Carlo Manolessi, the undisputed manager of the editorial and commercial activities, is the purchase, made by Manolessi on 24 March 1646, of part of the typographic equipment previously owned by Niccolò Tebaldini.[31] This purchase

---

29 G. Vasari, *Le Vite de' più Eccellenti Pittori, Scultori et Architetti* (3 pts. in 2 vols.; Bologna: per gli Heredi di Evangelista Dozza, 1647), USTC 4020626.

30 *Ibid*, I, leaf ††1r: 'Sono alcuni anni, che m'invogliai di questa, per altro sì difficile impresa, ne altro m'impediva, che il desiderio di pubblicar queste Vite nella stessa forma in tutto col primo Originale, cioè co' Ritratti medesimi, & ornamenti, con cui furon stampate in Firenze da i Giunti l'anno 1568. Ma la Fortuna favorevole a i miei disegni (dopo sei anni di traccia) m'ha finalmente portati i sudetti ornamenti, e Ritratti nelle mani; ond'io, superata sì importante difficoltà non ho perdonato a fatiche, né a spese per ridur l'opera alla perfezione, con la quale ora ve la presento'.

31 Bologna State Archive (ASB), *Notarile, Rogiti di Lorenzo Mariani*, prot. S, leaves 99v–101r. This document has been published in Pierangelo Bellettini, 'Il torchio e i caratteri:

was plausibly made in view of the printing of more complex and expensive publications than those produced up to that moment, like Vasari's *Lives*.

For the period following the beginning of Cospi's brokerage in favour of Manolessi, we find traces of financial activities carried out by the publisher, relating to purchases and the signing of lease contracts. It is thus possible to discern a complex scheme from which it can be assumed that Manolessi conducted a second activity, parallel to that of publisher-bookseller, as administrator and tenant of real estate properties, possibly with the specific intent of obtaining a personal credit line to finance his editorial projects.[32] This aspect completes the profile of the businessman and humanities aficionado with that of the self-made entrepreneur, capable of understanding good business models, also thanks to the information that his brother, as a notary, could provide him, and obtaining, within ten years from his arrival in Bologna, an economically stable position.

Thanks to his extensive network, precisely in 1647, Manolessi achieved a new, important result. From this year onwards the Dozza brothers began to print 'scientific' works, in the broadest sense of the term. The first result of this new editorial policy was the *Discorso dell'anno astrologico 1647* by Artemisio Tebano, *nom de plume* of Marquis Cornelio Malvasia (1603–1664).[33] This *Discorso* was nothing more than an annual astrological prediction, the product

---

l'attrezzatura tipografica a Bologna in Età Moderna', A. Ganda, E. Grigani and A. Petrucciani (eds.), *Libri, tipografi, biblioteche. Ricerche storiche dedicate a Luigi Balsamo* (2 vols.; Florence: Leo S. Olschki, 1997), I, pp. 241–276: 275–276. Among the other expedients adopted by Manolessi to consolidate his relationship with the Dozza brothers it seems possible to speculate that he married a relative of theirs. His wife, Orsola Veli (1615/6–1693), in her death record (BCABo, B 911, p. 67) is named Orsola Visconti Veli Dozza Manolessi. We can hypothesise that she was the daughter of a sister of the Dozza brothers, who married a man named Veli (possibly a descendant of a branch of the noble Visconti family). If that were the case, Orsola's mother would have been the daughter of Evangelista and his wife, Orsola Dozza (d.1626; see BCABo, B 911, p. 83).

32 Cf. ASB, *Notarile, Rogiti di Francesco Sabbatini*, prot. I, leaves, 46, 47, 86; *Rogiti di Orazio Scavazzoni*, prot. M, leaf 84; prot. P, leaf 93; prot. R, leaf 68; prot. S, leaf 20.

33 On Cornelio Malvasia, see Giovanni Fantuzzi, *Notizie degli Scrittori Bolognesi* (9 vols, Bologna, nella stamperia di San Tommaso d'Aquino, 1781–94), V, pp. 159–162; Gian Luigi Betti, 'Ogn'huom per natura è obligato a procacciarsi la sua fortuna. Esempi di pratica cortigiana in una famiglia del Seicento', *L'Archiginnasio. Bollettino della Biblioteca Comunale di Bologna*, 104 (2009), pp. 257–414: 328–329. For further information concerning his role in the astronomical and astrological research in seventeenth-century Bologna, see Rodolfo Calanca, 'Aspetti dell'astronomia del Seicento: Le "Ephemerides novissimae" di Cornelio Malvasia, Giovan Domenico Cassini e Geminiano Montanari', *Atti e Memorie dell'Accademia Nazionale di Scienze, Lettere e Arti di Modena*, 4, VIII series (2002), pp. 497–607; Andrea Gualandi, *Teoria delle Comete. Da Galileo a Newton* (Milan: Franco Angeli, 2009), pp. 61–69.

of a literary genre that in Bologna, a city traditionally devoted to the study of astrology, enjoyed great success until the end of the eighteenth century.[34] At the time, despite the growing diffusion of New Science, it was not uncommon for experimental research enthusiasts to be passionate about astrology, and Malvasia was a shining example of this way of thinking. A man of arms, member of the senatorial nobility and appreciated poet, he was above all an *amateur* and scholar of mathematics and astronomy, so much so as to erect an observatory in his residence in Panzano (near Modena). He was also a patron of science and protector of Geminiano Montanari (1633–1687) and Giovanni Domenico Cassini (1625–1712), whom he invited in 1649 and for whom he obtained, in 1651, the chair of Mathematics at the University formerly held by Bonaventura Cavalieri (1598–1647), member of the order of the Jesuits, disciple of Castelli and correspondent of Galileo. Among the other personalities of the Bolognese scientific *milieu* of the second half of the seventeenth century for which Manolessi published several works in the period 1647–1653, we find the astrologer Lorenzo Grimaldi (1623–1696) and Carlo Antonio Manzini (1600–1677), among the best scholars of astronomy and optics of his time, as well as the younger brother of Giovanni Battista.[35] Precisely Malvasia, Grimaldi and Manzini are remembered by Cassini in his memoirs as the only three astronomy *amateurs* operating at the time of his arrival in Bologna outside of the university setting.[36]

Towards the middle of the century, a tripartition of scientific research was emerging in the city. On the one side, we find the University, linked to the Aristotelian-scholastic tradition and enforcing largely obsolete teaching models. It was an institution in crisis, in which it systematically chose not to allocate funds for scientific research.[37] On the other side, we find the college of Santa Lucia, the headquarters of the Jesuits, who moved permanently to Bologna

---

34   On the tradition concerning the study of astrology in Italy during the modern period, see Elide Casali, *Le spie del cielo. Oroscopi, lunari e almanacchi nell'Italia moderna* (Turin: Einaudi, 2003).

35   Manolessi published Grimaldi's annual astrological predictions, together with those of two other Bolognese astrologers: Carlo Guglielmo Ingegneri and Lucrezio Gessi. By Carlo Antonio Manzini, he published instead a letter on magnetic declination in 1650 (*Della sicura incertezza nella declinatione dell'ago magnetico dal meridiano*), and a treatise concerning geodetic measurements in 1654 (*Stella Gonzaga sive geographica ad terrarum orbis ambitum, et meridianorum differentias*).

36   Jean-Dominique Cassini IV, 'Anecdotes de la vie de J.-D. Cassini rapportés par lui-même', Idem, *Mémoires pour servir à l'Histoire des Sciences et à celle de l'Observatoire Royal de Paris* (Paris: Chez Bleuet, successeur de Jombert, 1810), pp. 255–312: 263–264.

37   Cf. Enrica Baiada and Marta Cavazza, 'Le discipline matematico-astronomiche tra Seicento e Settecento', G.P. Brizzi, L. Marini and P. Pombeni (eds.), *L'Università a Bologna. Maestri, studenti e luoghi dal XVI al XX secolo* (Bologna: Silvana editoriale, 1988), pp. 153–164.

from Parma in 1635 due to the political-military conjuncture that, shortly thereafter, would trigger the Wars of Castro, an Italian episode of the Thirty Years' War.[38] Unlike the University administration, the Jesuits could count on substantial funds, becoming the real engine of experimental research in Bologna in the second half of the seventeenth century, thanks to the work of scientists of the likes of Giovanni Battista Riccioli (1598–1671) and Francesco Maria Grimaldi (1618–1663).[39] In addition to these two distinct groups, we find that of the aristocratic *amateurs*, who, with their initiatives and bestowals, worked both as patrons for scholars dissatisfied of the academic situation, and as a link between the lay representatives of scientific research and the Jesuits, to which they made conspicuous donations.[40] In recent years, research has contributed to diminishing the idea of conflict underlying the relationship between these three groups and, in particular, already from the reading of Cassini's memoirs it appears that, in many cases, lay and Jesuit scholars made common cause, although adhering to irreconcilable epistemological models. Furthermore, each group was not always clearly definable. In the case of University professors, there were both attempts to update the study programs, like those proposed by Cavalieri, and applications to projects of private academies, in the face of a rigorous attachment to tradition in the context of academic teaching, as in the case of Ovidio Montalbani (1601–1671).[41]

38 Fought between 1641 and 1649, these wars had enormous consequences for the cultural life of seventeenth-century Italy; cf. Giovanni Tocci, 'Il Ducato di Parma e Piacenza', Lino Marini (ed.), *I ducati padani, Trento e Trieste* (Turin: UTET, 1979), pp. 215–356: 268–270; Lorenzo Paliotto, 'Castro – I Farnese – Ferrara: Reportage di guerra', *Analecta Pomposiana*, 30 (2005), pp. 271–323; Ugo Baldini, 'La scuola scientifica emiliana della Compagnia di Gesù, 1600–1660: linee di una ricostruzione archivistica', *Università e cultura a Ferrara e Bologna* (Florence: Leo S. Olschki, 1989), pp. 109–178; Idem, 'San Rocco e la scuola scientifica della provincia veneta: il quadro storico (1600–1773)', Gian Paolo Brizzi, Roberto Greci (eds.), *Gesuiti e Università in Europa (secoli XVI–XVIII)* (Bologna: CLUEB, 2002), pp. 283–323.
39 Faced with the progressive academic autonomy of the Jesuits, the University tried, from the late sixteenth century, to safeguard the monopoly of higher education. Thus, for example, in 1641 the Senate of Bologna obtained from Pope Urban VIII (1568–1644) the issuance of a brief with which the Jesuits were ordered not to teach subjects for which a university chair was foreseen; cf. Andrea Battistini, 'La Scienza dei Gesuiti a Bologna', *Galileo e i Gesuiti. Miti letterari e retorica della Scienza* (Milan: Vita e Pensiero, 2000), pp. 239–281: 253–254.
40 Cf. *Ibid*, pp. 245–247; Marta Cavazza, 'La scienza, lo Studio, i Gesuiti a Bologna nella metà del Seicento', *Giornale di Astronomia: rivista di informazione, cultura e didattica della Società Astronomica Italiana*, 32 (2006), pp. 11–19.
41 On the updating of study programs put forward by Cavalieri, see John L. Russell, 'Catholic Astronomers and the Copernican System after the Condemnation of Galileo', *Annals of Science*, 46 (1989), pp. 365–386: 380–381; Fabrizio Bònoli, 'Cassini e la tradizione

An illustrious representative of Aristotelian tradition and Baroque encyclopedism, Montalbani held a chair for the teaching of mathematics from 1633 to 1650 and, in his classes, only the standardised programs were discussed, based on the study of Euclid and Ptolemy. He had also been a professor of Theoretical Medicine from 1628 to 1632, while from 1651 he became a professor of Moral Philosophy and a Law professor from 1654. During his long career, he held an impressive series of public offices, thanks also to uncommon political skills. For example, he was the writer and editor (for over thirty years from the end of the 1620s) of the *Tacuinus astrologicus* (astrological booklet), a yearbook of astrological forecasts, highly appreciated by physicians and widespread among all social strata. But most importantly, he was a censorial consultant, at the local Inquisition, for all the works concerning scientific subjects, for more than twenty years.[42] Montalbani, however, was also an eclectic science scholar and a convinced supporter of the dissemination of knowledge through academic partnerships. His own house was the gathering venue of the *Accademia dei Vespertini*, founded in 1624 by Carlo Antonio Manzini and dedicated to the study of mathematics and experimental research.[43] Once again with Manzini, Montalbani was a member of other important institutions dedicated to the study of science, letters and arts, like the Florentine *Accademia degli Apatisti*, founded in 1632 by the scholar Agostino Coltellini (1613–1693), a supporter of Galilean philosophy.[44]

The broad picture of the cultural and academic life of Bologna in the mid-century is complex and multifaceted. In it, we find at the same time reactionary attempts to preserve tradition, openings towards experimentalism and curious commingling between astrological beliefs and the quantitative methods of New Science. Consequently, it is not difficult to understand how the three groups were driven by different projects, but which at times could provide points of contact. In the same way, printing was a formidable weapon for the most varied scientific and political-cultural aims, as evidenced by the

---

astronomica galileiana a Bologna', Luigi Pepe (ed.), *Galileo e la scuola galileiana nelle Università del Seicento* (Bologna: CLUEB, 2011), pp. 171–190: 173–174.

42 For the most updated profile of Montalbani, see Linda Bisello, 'Ovidio Montalbani: scienza e curiositas. Nota bio-bibliografica', Ovidio Montalbani, *Del vento e delle comete: speculazioni accademiche* (Florence: Leo S. Olschki, 2017), pp. v–xxv.

43 Cf. Carlo Antonio Manzini, *Tabulae primi mobilis, quibus nova dirigendi ars, et praecipue circuli positionis inventio non minus facilis, quam exacta ostenditur* (Bononiae: Typis Thebaldini, 1626), leaf Q^{3v}. On the Bolognese academies founded during the first half of the seventeenth century, see Gian Luigi Betti, 'Tra Università e accademie. Note sulla cultura Bolognese del primo Seicento', *Strenna Storica Bolognese*, 37 (1987), pp. 81–98.

44 For the *Accademia degli Apatisti*, see Alessandro Lazzeri, *Intellettuali e consenso nella Toscana del Seicento. L'Accademia degli Apatisti* (Milan: Giuffrè, 1983).

progressive involvement of Manolessi as a publisher for the works of astronomy and astrology scholars since 1647. Furthermore, the noble *amateurs* certainly had to be enticed by the privileged channel with the House of Medici established by the publisher, as demonstrated by the fact that, for example, Malvasia decided to dedicate his *Discorso* to the man who received the title of *First Mathematician of the Grand Duke* after Galileo's death, Evangelista Torricelli (1608-1647).[45] However, both Torricelli and Cavalieri, the last representative of the Galilean school operating outside Tuscany in Academia, disappeared that same year, with the consequent risk that the management of scientific research would end up entirely in the hands of the Jesuits. Such a prospect was undesirable for the other two groups for both political and epistemological reasons. The University, in the aftermath of Cavalieri's death, attempted to consolidate its institutional role on traditionalist positions, with the specific aim of avoiding new controversies that the assignment of chairs to scholars adhering to the methods of New Science would have entailed. Thus, the vacant chair of Mathematics was assigned to Cassini only in 1651 and thanks to the intermediation of Cornelio Malvasia.[46] On the other hand, the group of *amateurs* headed by Malvasia, Manzini and Grimaldi, held positions incompatible with those of the Jesuits. Although these two groups were united by an impulse towards the experimental study of natural phenomena and their potential mathematization, for the Jesuits, the study of the causes of these phenomena was part of the dictates of a qualitative physics of Aristotelian inspiration, which, together with metaphysics, remained subordinate to theology.

The substantial differences between the reformed Aristotelianism of the Jesuits and a peculiar adherence to the experimental method that left room for attempts to quantify astrology represent the distant echoes of that struggle aimed at establishing a clear boundary between scientific knowledge and religious belief – one of the key features of Galileo's work. Less than fifteen years after his condemnation, with the disappearance of his last disciple operating within Academia and with the consequent protectionist closures implemented

---

[45] The relationships of cultural exchange between Bolognese and Tuscan scientists date back to the late sixteenth century, and although extensive research has not yet been attempted, there are several important studies dedicated to individual characters, such as: Denise Aricò, 'Giovanni Antonio Roffeni: un astrologo bolognese amico di Galileo', *Il Carrobbio*, 24 (1998), pp. 67–96; Gian Luigi Betti, 'Lettere di argomento scientifico conservate nell'Archivio della famiglia Manzini presso l'Archivio di Stato di Bologna', *Nuncius*, 10 (1995), pp. 691–714; Idem, 'Giovan Ludovico Ramponi: un arciprete 'copernicano' e l'*esquisita dottrina* di Galileo', *Galilaeana. Journal of Galilean Studies*, 9 (2012), pp. 161–179.

[46] Not to mention that, according to Cassini's memoirs, he was invited to Bologna by Malvasia because the Marquis erroneously believed him the author of some inspired astrological predictions (Cassini IV, *Anecdotes de la vie de J.-D. Cassini*, pp. 261–262).

by the University of Bologna, Galileo's legacy was safeguarded also through editorial initiatives of an eminently political nature, like the republication of his works.

3 Between Source Retrieval and Editorial Issues

The dynamics that led to the preparation of the 1655–56 edition, especially in the period before 1652, are difficult to reconstruct, due to the almost complete loss of the correspondence of Carlo Manolessi. Understanding the situation of Bolognese intellectual life in the mid-seventeenth century, it is nevertheless possible to make some hypotheses. At least since 1647, Manolessi began to cooperate with the group of noble *amateurs* dedicated to astrological and mathematical studies, going as far as to reprint two of the most important works by Cavalieri.[47] Except for very few original editions for which no editing was necessary, the scientific publications produced by Manolessi were reprints of celebrated works, a detail which, besides underlining the publisher's meagre scientific knowledge, denotes how he followed the requests of the market and his clients in the establishment of an editorial agenda. The particular case of Galileo's works could, therefore, be explained as follows. It is plausible to believe, in my opinion, that it was precisely the noble amateurs who suggested to Manolessi this undertaking which, if on the one hand it would have signalled his courage and devotion to the House of Medici, on the other would have represented a political stand in favour of those who recognised themselves in the stances of Galilean *libertas philosophandi* and New Science. This move emphasised the sentiment that some historians call *desiderio di un principe* (longing for a Prince), which is, the search for a political power capable of promoting cultural and scientific enterprise and defending free thinkers. This was a characteristic that, in cities like Bologna, certainly brought together both entrepreneurs and members of the aristocracy.[48]

---

47 *Lo specchio ustorio* (Bologna: per gli HH. del Dozza, 1650), USTC 4021174, republished a few months earlier by Ferroni as well; *Geometria indivisibilibus continuorum nova quadam ratione promota* (Bononiae: ex Typographia de Ducijs, 1653), USTC 1750118.

48 Cf. Marta Cavazza, *Settecento Inquieto. Alle origini dell'Istituto delle Scienze di Bologna* (Bologna: Il Mulino, 1990), p. 176; Cesare S. Maffioli, *Out of Galileo: The Science of Waters, 1628–1718* (Rotterdam: Erasmus Publishing, 1994), pp. 34–35. Over and above this hypothesis, it cannot be excluded that Manolessi led a multi-phased editorial project entrusted to him by the House of Medici since about 1641; cf. Leonardo Anatrini, 'Primacy, Prestige & Authority. The Bolognese Edition of the *Opere* at the Dawn of Galilean Mythology', in Massimo Bucciantini (ed.), *The Science and Myth of Galileo between the Seventeenth and*

We come now to analyse the schedule followed for the preparation of this edition of Galileo's works, as well as the dynamics that led to the choice of those who dealt with the editing process. A document, often ignored, allows for the inception of the editorial project to be backdated by a few years.[49] It is a letter from 6 August 1650, in which Prince Leopoldo asked Virgilio Spada (1596–1662) which path could be taken to try and obtain a new imprimatur for the *Dialogue Concerning the Two Chief World Systems*, put on the Index after Galileo's condemnation.[50] Many questions are raised by such a document, especially related to the recipient of the letter.

Virgilio Spada, the Oratorian father working as Papal Almoner for Innocent X (1574–1655), was, like Leopoldo, a renowned art collector. The origins of their relationship are unknown, although it can be speculated that the two met during the stay in Rome of Leopoldo and his brother Mattias (1613–1667) at the beginning of 1650 on the occasion of the Jubilee.[51] To make Spada's choice as an interlocutor for so a delicate matter even more mysterious, let us point

---

Nineteenth Centuries in Europe. Proceedings of the International Conference of Florence – 29-31 January 2020 (Florence: Leo S. Olschki, 2021), pp. 53–68: 60–62.

49 The few pages dedicated so far to the circumstances that led to the 1655–56 collected edition of Galileo's works, are: Antonio Fàvaro, 'XXIX. Vincenzo Viviani', *Amici e corrispondenti di Galileo* (3 vols.; Florence: Salimbeni, 1983²), III, pp. 1009–1163: 1106–1108; *ODG Carteggio*, II, pp. VIII–XII; Michael Segre, *In the wake of Galileo* (New Brunswick: Rutgers University Press, 1991), pp. 104–106; Battistini, *Galileo e i Gesuiti*, pp. 257–259; Cavazza, *La scienza, lo Studio, i Gesuiti*, pp. 17–18; Idem, 'Bologna e Galileo. Da Cesare Marsili agli Inquieti', *Galileo e la scuola galileiana nelle Università del Seicento*, pp. 155–170: 166–168. More pages have been dedicated to the iconography of the frontispiece that adorns this edition: Erwin Panofsky, 'More on Galileo and the Arts', *Isis*, 47 (1956), pp. 182–185; Pietro Redondi, 'La nave di Bruno e la pallottola di Galileo: uno studio di iconografia della fisica', A. Prosperi, M. Donattini and G.P. Brizzi (eds.), *Il piacere del testo. Saggi e studi per Albano Biondi* (2 vols.; Rome: Bulzoni, 2001), I, pp. 285–363: 343–351; Jaco Rutgers, 'A Frontispiece for Galileo's "Opere". Pietro Anichini and Stefano Della Bella', *Print Quarterly*, 29 (2012), pp. 3–12; Klaus Zittel, 'Zeichenkunst und Wissenschaft: Stefano della Bellas Frontispize zu Werken Galileo Galileis', in A. Albrecht, G. Cordibella and V.R. Remmert (eds.), *Tintenfass und Teleskop. Galileo Galilei im Schnittpunkt issenschaftlicher, literarischer und visueller Kulturen im 17. Jahrhundert* (Berlin: De Gruyter, 2014), pp. 369–403: 396–403.

50 Both the draft and the actual letter are preserved. The first is held at the National Library of Florence (BNCF), *Galileiano*, 282, leaf 1ʳ and published in *ODG Carteggio*, II, pp. 38–39. The second can be found at the Rome State Archive (ASR), *Spada-Veralli*, vol. 235, p. 163 and published in Leonardo Anatrini, 'The Theologian's Endgame: On the Recently Discovered Censorial Report on Galileo's *Dialogue* and Related Documents', *Galilaeana. Studies in Renaissance and Early Modern Science*, 17 (2020), pp. 219–288: 258, 282.

51 An account of the sojourn in Rome of Leopoldo and Mattias is contained in an unpublished travel journal and related letters sent by them to Grand Duke Ferdinando II, kept conserved in the State Archive of Florence (ASF), *Miscellanea Medicea*, 94, 5; *Mediceo del principato*, 5508, leaves 50–67.

out that no other letters are known which could suggest a correspondence between him and the Prince. Among the reasons that led Leopoldo to turn to Spada, there was perhaps a common sensibility towards arts and sciences, as suggested, for example, by the fact that the Oratorian father, in 1645, purchased the painting *The Astronomers* by Niccolò Tornioli (1598–1651), in which is depicted a heated cosmological debate being conducted by several personages, including a figure in the background whom some have identified as Galileo himself.[52] Leopoldo also knew that Virgilio was the younger brother of Cardinal Bernardino Spada (1594–1661), who in those years held the position of Prefect of the Congregation of the Index, the only institutional body, other than the Congregation of the Holy Office, empowered to review the condemnation of Galileo's work and to grant a new imprimatur.[53]

Still, the question remains: why did Leopoldo decide to expose himself with this request? The motivation given in the letter simply indicates that a new publication of Galileo's works would have brought *non poco profitto* (no small benefit) to scholars. The political motivations are evident, but what occasion led Leopoldo to formulate such a bold request? At that time, no one in the restricted circle of scholars who enjoyed the protection of the Medici had a position or the power to promote the undertaking. Galileo's pupils had all disappeared, except for Viviani, who was in those years still very young and at the beginning of his career. Everything would suggest that the project may have been conceived by both Manolessi – building on the success and favour obtained with the publication of Vasari's *Lives* – and Leopoldo himself, not as a man of the Church but as a prominent member of the Tuscan ruling family. The circumstances were as peculiar as they were politically favourable. The House of Medici finally had the opportunity to reaffirm its prestige in the cultural and scientific field, reaffirming the role of patronage of the man who, with his work, had forever changed the course of science. The point was not really about endorsing the methods of New Science, but reaffirming the primacy and authority of one of its greatest protagonists and, consequently, of his patrons. The fact that the Medici were interested in this venture highlights the desire for redemption after the political defeat represented by Galileo's 1633 condemnation. In this sense, the political significance inherent in the

---

52   Cf. Federico Tognoni (ed.), *Iconografia galileiana* (Florence: Giunti, 2013), pp. 75–76; Giulia Martina Weston, 'After Galileo: The Image of Science in Niccolò Tornioli's *Astronomers*', *Art History*, 39 (2016), pp. 302–317.

53   On the role of Bernardino Spada in the Roman Congregations, see Arne Karsten, *Kardinal Bernardino Spada: eine Karriere im barocken Rom* (Göttingen: Vandenhoeck & Ruprecht, 2001); Herman H. Schwedt, *Die römische Inquisition: Kardinäle und Konsultoren 1600 bis 1700* (Freiburg, Basel, Wien: Verlag Herder, 2017), pp. 572–573.

possibility of republishing his works in the heart of the Church's domains is even more evident.

Judging by the known archival documents, the first reliable information concerning the preparation of the Bolognese edition of Galileo's works date back to the end of 1652, as shown in a letter sent by Carlo Roberto Dati (1619–1676), a philologist, historian, *Crusca* academician and personal librarian of Prince Leopoldo, to one of Galileo's correspondents, the art collector and man of letters Cassiano dal Pozzo (1588–1657).[54] As for the editorial progress, the first detailed mention comes from an exchange of letters between Rinaldini and Viviani (November-December 1654), from which we learn that the scientific editing was about to be completed and the professor reached out for the help of Galileo's last pupil to obtain a copy of some works that were extremely hard to find, together with an unpublished demonstration to be added to the third day of *Two New Sciences*.[55] At this point in history, the dynamics relating to the composition of the editorial committee were already well-delineated. Similarly, the discontent of at least one of its members can be observed quite clearly. Thus, for example, in the letter of 5 December 1654, Viviani peremptorily asks Rinaldini to inform Manolessi that he did not want any mention of his name to be made in the introduction to this new edition.[56] Viviani's reasons, as proven by the subsequent correspondence, do not imply a formal refusal or an exercise in modesty, but a sincere disinterest in an editorial project that he did not approve of and which was in competition with the one he spent his whole life trying to complete. Furthermore, the short biography of Galileo that his pupil composed at Leopoldo's behest, completed in April 1654, should have been included in the new edition, but this did not happen.[57]

---

54 Alfonso Mirto, 'Rapporti epistolari fra Cassiano dal Pozzo e Carlo Roberto Dati', *Nouvelles de la République des Lettres*, 2 (2001), pp. 7–102: 37–38 (12 October).
55 *ODG Carteggio*, II, pp. 158–162.
56 *Ibid*, II, p. 160.
57 Antonio Fàvaro et al. (eds.), *Le opere di Galileo Galilei. Edizione nazionale sotto gli auspicii di Sua Maestà il re d'Italia* (hereafter *OG*, 20 vols.; Florence, Tip. di G. Barbèra, 1890–1909), XIX, pp. 597–632. On Viviani's biography of Galileo, see Michael Segre, 'Viviani's Life of Galileo', *Isis*, 80 (1989), pp. 207–231; Maurizio Torrini, 'La *Vita di Galileo* di Vincenzo Viviani', Idem (ed.), *Scelta de' migliori opuscoli* (Napoli: Istituto universitario suor Orsola Benincasa, 2002), pp. 115–129; Lucrezia Ruospo, 'La biografia galileiana di Vincenzio Viviani', Mauro di Giandomenico and Pasquale Guaragnella (eds.), *La prosa di Galileo: la lingua, la retorica, la storia* (Lecce: Argo, 2006), pp. 281–296; Paula Findlen, 'Rethinking 1633: Writing about Galileo after the Trial', in Mario Biagioli and Jessica Riskin (eds.), *Nature Engaged: Science in Practice from the Renaissance to the Present* (New York, Palgrave Macmillan, 2012), pp. 205–226; Stefano Gattei (ed.), *On the Life of Galileo. Viviani's Historical Account and other Early Biographies* (Princeton: Princeton University Press, 2019), pp. XII–XXVIII, 1–93; Anatrini, *Primacy, Prestige & Authority*.

As further confirmation of the complexity and time necessary to complete this undertaking, we can quote another unpublished letter, dated 11 November 1652, sent by Rinaldini to Dati. In it, we read that Manolessi was already carrying out printing tests and that, to complete the edition, he needed the short treatise written by Baldassarre Capra against Galileo on the invention of the geometric compass.[58] The fact that the editing was at an advanced stage already at the end of 1652, as well as the nature of the requests expressed in this letter, allow us to present some conjectures.

Regardless of who may have advised Manolessi to devote himself to the publication of Galileo's works, it is plausible to hypothesise that Manolessi sought the constant blessing of Leopoldo in order to preserve the political protection that the Prince could offer. Dealing with Galileo's works meant, first and foremost, to incur the attention of the Inquisition, an indispensable interlocutor for obtaining a printing licence. Moreover, the presence of Rinaldini as a scientific editor can only be the consequence of a choice made by the House of Medici.

An heir of a noble family of Ancona, Carlo Rinaldini, after having studied philosophy and theology at the University of Macerata, moved to Rome in the 1640s, where he was a pupil of the mathematician Antonio Santini (1577–1662), a correspondent of Galileo and among the first men of science to deal with the dissemination of the new algebra of François Viète (1540–1603) and Cartesian geometry in Italy.[59] Rinaldini, at least since 1643, held the role of personal assistant to the general of the Papal Army, Taddeo Barberini (1603–1647), nephew of Pope Urban VIII. This position led him to become a tutor to the children of Barberini and a military engineer during the Wars of Castro. He managed to maintain this last role even after the Barberini family fell out of favour and went into exile in Paris in 1646. During the fortification works of the Ferrara borders, commissioned to him in 1648 by Federico Savelli (1583–1649), commander of the Papal Army and lieutenant of Pope Innocent X, Rinaldini obtained the chair of Mathematics at the local university, which he held for only a few weeks, since, at the invitation of Grand Duke Ferdinando II, he

---

58 BNCF, *Carteggi vari*, 60, 1. The mentioned work by Capra is *Usus et frabrica circini cuiusdam proportionis, per quem omnia fere tum Euclidis, tum mathematicorum omnium problemata facili negotio resolvuntur* (Patavij: apud Petrum Paulum Tozzium, 1607).

59 Gino Arrighi, 'P. Antonio Santini da Lucca discepolo di Galileo (1577–1662)', *Lucca. Rassegna del Comune*, 9 (1965), pp. 3–21; Federica Favino, 'Mathematics and Mathematicians at Sapienza University in Rome (XVII–XVIII Century)', *Science & Education*, 15 (2006), pp. 357–392: 361–362. The correspondence between Manolessi and Viviani shows also that Santini helped the publisher in authenticating unpublished Galilean material, cf. ODG *Carteggio* II, p. 216 (Manolessi to Viviani, 8 May 1655).

joined the University of Pisa at the end of 1649 to receive the chair of Natural Philosophy. In Tuscany, he soon stood out for his abilities and skills, as can be seen from the surviving correspondence, from which we know that he became the tutor of the future Grand Duke Cosimo III (1642–1723) and that already at the beginning of the 1650s he offered his services as a scientific consultant to Ferdinando II.[60]

As far as Rinaldini's philosophical-scientific thought is concerned, he can be counted among the so-called eclectic Aristotelians. Strongly convinced of the potential and necessity of experimentalism, interested in mathematical investigation and the use of geometric demonstrations, at the same time he oriented his research towards a broad project of renewal and updating of the Aristotelian tradition. This peculiarity kept him safe from the criticism of the University's traditionalist teaching, yet often made him detestable in the eyes of those who, following Galileo, had rejected textual authority in favour of free research, and were almost completely devoted to experimentation. These opposing positions frequently led to methodological clashes, especially within the *Accademia del Cimento*.[61]

It is not difficult to understand the reasons behind the decision made by the House of Medici to entrust Rinaldini with the scientific editing of the new edition of Galileo's works. Compared to Viviani (although they were just seven years apart), Rinaldini was already a renowned scholar, a war veteran and a man with undeniable diplomatic skills, with important connections in the papal court, who could be extremely useful in this venture. Viviani, being interested above all else in rehabilitating the name of his master and in reiterating the primacy of his discoveries in the events relating to the Scientific

---

60 Until the beginning of the 1670s, Rinaldini focused his research on the development and dissemination of algebra and Cartesian geometry, then dedicating himself to the formulation of his own philosophical system, designing an enormous work (of which he managed to complete and publish only a part, between 1681 and 1694) organised according to the university teaching program. Cf. Aldo Brigaglia '*Algèbre et géométrie dans l'œuvre de Carlo Rinaldini*', E. Festa, V. Jullien and M. Torrini (eds.), *Géométrie, atomisme et vide dans l'école de Galilée* (Fontenay-aux-Roses: ENS, 1999), pp. 79–96; Antonio Poppi, 'Le vie del filosofare nell'aristotelismo seicentesco di Carlo Rinaldini', Sandro Ciurlia (ed.), *Filosofia e storiografia: studi in onore di Giovanni Papuli. II. L'Età Moderna* (Galatina: Congedo, 2008), pp. 335–356; Ugo Baldini, 'Tra due paradigmi? La *Naturalis Philosophia* di Carlo Rinaldini', *Galileo e la scuola galileiana nelle Università del Seicento*, pp. 189–222.

61 On Rinaldini and the Aristotelian-scholastic reactions within the Grand Ducal environments dedicated to experimental research, see Paolo Galluzzi, 'L'Accademia del Cimento: "gusti" del principe, filosofia e ideologia dell'esperimento', *Quaderni storici*, 16 (1981), pp. 788–844: 798–823; Luciano Boschiero, *Experiment and Natural Philosophy in Seventeenth-Century Tuscany: The History of the Accademia del Cimento* (Dordrecht: Springer, 2007), pp. 94–98.

Revolution, would have hardly understood the political value of Manolessi's undertaking.

At this point, the publisher had a privileged double-channel in the Florentine court. On the one side, there was the political intermediary, represented by Ambassador Cospi, who, by virtue of his role, could supervise the progress of the edition, intervening, if necessary (as it would be) at the local offices that could stonewall, namely the Inquisition. On the other side, there was the scientific intermediary, Rinaldini, who certainly would have been able to lend his help to Manolessi, recovering the necessary material and directing the editorial agenda in compliance with a precise conduct that was necessary to maintain. However, the obstacles that hindered the accomplishment of this quest were not few, compounded by the attitude of Manolessi who, particularly after Rinaldini was forced, for essentially technical reasons, to pass the torch to Viviani, often oscillated between excessive gumption and out-and-out recklessness.

Regardless of his limited diplomatic skills, Manolessi, in these years, kept performing his second job as a prudent investor and administrator, which allowed him to deepen his business relationships with the members of the Bolognese aristocracy. Thus, for example, he became so close to Cornelio Malvasia that the Marquis, in 1655, signed a fideicommissary substitution with which he chose Manolessi as the trustee of his assets in favour of his firstborn son, Giovanni Battista.[62] Similarly, Malvasia treasured the contacts made by Manolessi with the House of Medici, so much so that, at the beginning of 1653, he sent Leopoldo the report of the comet's observations of December 1652, conducted together with his protégé Giovanni Domenico Cassini.[63] The reason was clear and openly stated by Malvasia: precede the Jesuits. If on the one hand, the choice of the nobleman underlined the consolidated role of Leopoldo as the patron of science, on the other, it would seem to represent a gesture of esteem and thanksgiving addressed to the one who, even in Bologna, was bestowing favour on New Science's scholars and enthusiasts through granting the commission of Galileo's collected edition to Manolessi.

---

62   ASB, *Notarile, Rogiti di Bartolomeo Buchini*, 11, 327 (7 September 1655). Malvasia's motives remain unknown. He probably feared for his life in a period when he was struggling with financial problems resulting from the mismanagement of the family pawnbrokers; cf. BCABo, B 3666 (*Cronica di Bologna, 1642–1737*), p. 17. Thus, in order to avoid seizures that could have affected his heir in case of his death, the Marquis appointed Manolessi *fideicommissum*.

63   ODG *Carteggio*, 11, p. 82 (11 January 1653). With the letter, Malvasia sent the Prince a copy of G. D. Cassini, *De cometa anni 1652 & 1653* (Mutinae: apud Bartolomeum Sulianum, 1653).

As for the choice of the works to be included in the edition, it is obvious that the editorial plan was established at the beginning of the enterprise and, even if Manolessi solicited the advice of local experts in the absence of personal scientific knowledge, he must have proposed some sort of project to the Florentine court, through Cospi, in order to receive the necessary approval and the help of Rinaldini as well. Rinaldini, in addition to his role of scientific editor, as we know from the letter of November 1652, also took care of providing the publisher with the necessary material, calling on the help of Carlo Dati, who served as librarian and antiquarian consultant for Prince Leopoldo.[64] However, the difficulties encountered in the search for some of the works led Rinaldini to request the help of other experts. It should also be noted that he only turned to Viviani towards the end of 1654, perhaps out of personal pride or because, as editor, he became a competitor of Viviani and his parallel editorial project. Thus, from the surviving correspondence, we know that Rinaldini asked one of his students to help him find some of the material. This was Cosimo Galilei (1636–1672), grandson of the scientist and a student of the University of Pisa since 1653. Nevertheless, from this period and for the rest of his life, Cosimo had a constant epistolary exchange with Viviani, also by virtue of the friendship that bound him to Vincenzo's younger brother, Francesco (fl. 1652–1696).[65]

Manolessi, for his part, did not know (and perhaps never discovered) that Viviani, put forward to the Prince his own editorial concept.[66] Moreover, to complicate further an already delicate situation, Viviani interposed various delays to the completion of the Bolognese edition, inferable by reading the long correspondence between him and Manolessi (March 1655–February 1656). Viviani's ambivalent attitude, in all likelihood, was also caused by the political motivations underlying the publisher's design, which Galileo's last pupil

---

64 Unfortunately, there are still no extensive studies on Dati and his fundamental role as a supplier of books and cultural mediator between the various men of science and letters who centred around the House of Medici. Of his enormous correspondence, preserved in the National Library of Florence, only a few dozen letters have been published: Mirto, *Rapporti epistolari fra Cassiano dal Pozzo e Carlo Roberto Dati*; Idem, 'Antonio Magliabechi e Carlo Dati: lettere', *Studi secenteschi*, 42 (2001), pp. 382–433; Idem, 'Carlo Roberto Dati e Vincenzo Viviani: carteggio (1659–1672)', *Studi secenteschi*, 51 (2010), pp. 291–346.
65 ODG *Carteggio*, II, pp. 147, 176, 182 (Cosimo Galilei to Viviani, 6 May 1654, 15 February and 3 March 1655).
66 As evidenced by the correspondence between Prince Leopoldo, Giovanni Battista Barducci (d. 1661, resident minister of the Tuscan court in Paris), Elia Diodati and Viviani; see esp. ODG *Carteggio*, II, pp. 301–308 (Viviani to Diodati, 23 February 1656), 349–356 (Diodati to Viviani, 24 June 1656).

understood and endorsed only in part.[67] He wanted a proper *opera omnia*, published in a vernacular/Latin bilingual edition, which included Galileo's correspondence, all of the unpublished works and a comprehensive biography. As a result, it would have become necessary to turn to a publisher operating in a country outside the jurisdiction of the Inquisition. However, republishing Galileo outside Italy meant abandoning the battlefield, implicitly emphasizing the subservience of the House of Medici (and, in general, of all those intellectuals who shared the values of Galilean philosophy) to the policies of the Holy Office. It would also have been particularly difficult to dedicate such an edition to the Grand Duke without generating clashes with the Church, especially if the general editor had been a member of the courtesan intelligentsia. In this respect, to the House of Medici, Manolessi's plan represented the better bet.

One thing that Manolessi perhaps never fully realised, was the extent of the risks he ran and of which, in many cases, the cause was precisely his audacious behaviour. In the months of the printing of the *Opere*, Manolessi sent Viviani several versions of the index, sticking, as far as possible, to the requests of Galileo's last disciple, who also did not hesitate to provide the publisher with some unpublished letters from the Galilean correspondence.[68] In a clever entrepreneurial move, Manolessi proceeded with the printing of the individual works, providing each of them with a dedicated title page and numbering, and including the 'critical works' like Capra's *Fabrica* and the various 'defences' (consisting largely of letters of correspondents and disciples of Galileo), as appendices. In doing so, it was possible to market the individual works, providing them with an apparatus lacking in the original editions, with an explicitly propagandistic purpose, aimed at defending the authority of Galileo, the primacy of his discoveries and, implicitly, the prestige of his patrons. Besides, the possibility of selling individual works allowed the publisher to recoup more quickly the investment related to production costs, which, as we will see, led Manolessi to fix, for the complete edition, a high sales price.

---

67 *Ibid*, II, pp. 189–294: *passim*. Reading their correspondence, one has the clear impression that in many cases Viviani, despite his undoubted contribution, deliberately delayed his answers and, above all, the peroration of the publisher's requests addressed to Prince Leopoldo.

68 Albeit without mentioning to Manolessi the letters of Galileo – far more important – that he received, by the intercession of Prince Leopoldo, from Elia Diodati in March 1655, cf. ODG *Carteggio*, II, pp. 181, 189, 202–203 (Giovanni Battista Barducci to Prince Leopoldo, 3 March, 12 March and 9 April 1655).

4   Censorship as an Occasion for Intellectual and Political Confrontation

Even if endowed with natural commercial prudence and shrewdness, Manolessi showed occasional foolhardiness in his relations with the local inquisitorial office, which lasted until the end of August 1655 for the censorial review. Bologna's inquisitor, the Dominican friar Guglielmo Fuochi (d. 1660), enlisted two other censors to assist him in this delicate task, as proven by the *Opere*'s imprimatur.[69] One, as usual, was acting as a delegate of the highest ecclesiastical authority in the city, the archbishop of Bologna. He was the Barnabite father Invenzio Torti (fl. 1645–1665), who held the role of censor for works of scientific, political and literary subjects.[70] The other was the technical censor, Ovidio Montalbani. He embodied perfectly the brokerage functions attributed in Counter-Reformation Italy to the censors (especially the secular ones) in charge of carrying out difficult intermediations between the Church and the Republic of Letters. It seems that Montalbani always juggled, thanks to uncommon diplomatic skills, the difficult role of censor. Thus, while he was able to assert his authority in the establishment of an editorial standard aimed at safeguarding the tradition of which he was a shining example within the University, he could also plead the causes of his colleagues from the private academies of which he was a member, to favour the success of more innovative projects, whose implementation would have been far more complex without the involvement of a mediator embedded in the hierarchies of the ecclesiastical authority.[71]

---

69 General inquisitor of Bologna from 1652 to 1660, Fuochi taught philosophy and theology, and was appointed Prior Provincial of Lombardy, Bohemia and the Holy Land; see BCABo, B 1891, 1 (*De Inquisitione, Inquisitoribusque Bononiae*), p. 9: 'P. Mag.r F. Gulielmus Fochus de Como, dictus de Montecalvo 1652 prudentia dexteritate, ac doctrina inter primos Ord.is Pr[a]ed.rum cum omnium plausu publice Parisijs disputavit, Philosophiam, Theologiamque pluribus in locis docuit, studij Bononien[si]. S.ti Dom.ci Bacalaureus fuit, Provincialis Bohemiae, Terrae Sanctae, ac Lombardiae utriusque'.

70 In addition to the minimal information obtainable from the imprimaturs signed by him, the only certain fact concerning Torti is the date of his arrival in Bologna (16 May 1645), by order of his Superior General; cf. Giuseppe M. Cagni, 'Il p. Antonio Pagni, la Congregazione secolare dell'Annunziata di Pescia e i Barnabiti', *Barnabiti Studi*, 23 (2006), pp. 7–117: 112–113.

71 On the topic of cultural brokerage, see M. Keblusek and B.V. Noldus (eds.), *Double Agents. Cultural and Political Brokerage in Early Modern Europe* (Leiden: Brill, 2011), pp. 11–25, 95–110; concerning censors as mediators between the Church and the Republic of Letters in seventeenth-century Italy, see Marco Cavarzere, *La prassi della censura nell'Italia del Seicento. Tra repressione e mediazione* (Rome: Edizioni di Storia e Letteratura, 2011), pp. 135–171.

The necessary precautions were countered by the dangerous ventures of Manolessi, who, over the months became increasingly impatient with the restrictions imposed by the Inquisitor. Furthermore, Manolessi did not demonstrate a great knowledge of the events relating to Galileo's trial, as evidenced, for example, from the first prospectus sent to Viviani, in which he presented the possibility of reprinting the *Dialogue*, while in another letter the publisher informed Viviani that he had submitted to the Inquisitor's analysis no less than the three *Copernican letters*.[72] For his part, the Inquisitor, although certainly aware of the events of 1633, lacking comprehensive scientific knowledge, delegated the technical censorship to Montalbani, which Fuochi combined with a rigid observation of the standard dictates of censorial practice, seeking 'things contrary to the dogmas of faith, and good morals', intending to expunge them. Thus, for example, he denied Manolessi the reprinting of the pamphlet published in 1610 by Kepler in defence of the *Sidereus Nuncius*.[73] Even though the work had been reprinted in Florence in the same year of the *editio princeps*, Montalbani could object that in some parts it presented a defence of Copernican cosmology, while Fuochi, insisting merely on the fact that it was the production of a Protestant author, could have prohibited both its printing and circulation.

Manolessi, faced with the refusal of the Inquisitor, instead of consulting his mediator for issues of this nature, Ambassador Cospi, bypassed the local ecclesiastical authorities as well, directly addressing their highest superiors in Rome, the Master of the Sacred Palace and the General Commissioner of the Holy Office. The publisher completed his disputable initiative going so far as to ask Viviani to plead with Prince Leopoldo on his behalf so that he too wrote to Rome to try to obtain the permit to reprint Kepler's work.[74] Given that the exact content of the letter sent by Manolessi to Rome in the first days of May 1655 is unknown, we can assume that, in his display of audacity, he at least avoided mentioning the reprint of Galileo's works, simply asking for a generic printing licence for a work already published in Italy. From the documentation preserved in the Vatican Archives and at the Archiginnasio Public

---

72   ODG *Carteggio*, II, pp. 191, 218 (Manolessi to Viviani, 16 March and 18 May 1655). The letters concerning the defence of the Copernican cosmology and the importance of epistemological boundaries between science and religious belief can be found in OG, V, pp. 281–288 (Galileo to Benedetto Castelli, 21 December 1613); pp. 297–305 (Galileo to Piero Dini, 23 March 1615); pp. 309–348 (Galileo to the Grand Duchess Christina of Lorraine, Spring-Summer 1615).

73   *Ioannis Kepleri Mathematici Caesarei Dissertatio cum Nuncio Sidereo nuper ad mortales misso a Galilaeo Galilaeo Mathematico Patavino* (Pragae: Typis Danielis Sedesani, 1610), USTC 2106608.

74   ODG *Carteggio*, II, p. 216 (Manolessi to Viviani, 8 May 1655).

Library of Bologna, it would seem that neither Manolessi nor Fuochi received an answer. The reasons behind this silence can be attributed both to the censorial legislation in force at the time and the characters of this story. The General Commissioner of the Holy Office was the Dominican friar Vincenzo Preti (*c*.1587–1664), who, from 1647 to 1650, had been, like Fuochi, Bologna's General Inquisitor and, probably, to avoid wronging his successor, did not reply to Manolessi, possibly writing privately to his colleague (even if there is no evidence of a correspondence between the two). Manolessi's request was inconsistent with the role of Preti, whose duties, although including the mediation between the local courts and the Congregation of the Holy Office, essentially concerned the direction of trials and interrogations of defendants and witnesses. The General Commissioner also possessed censorial skills, but in theological subjects. As for the Master of the Sacred Palace, the censor par excellence within the Roman Curia, namely the Dominican friar Raimondo Capizucchi (1616–1691), he denied Manolessi a response for both regulatory and jurisdictional reasons. For one thing, his authority applied only within the boundaries of Rome, and furthermore the current censorial regulation, established with a decree of January 1640 and incompatible with Manolessi's request, indicated a precise practice, which at the same time underlined the will of the Roman Curia to centralise decision-making power and the desperate attempt to control the press. It established that for each work for which a licence was requested, the local inquisitors sent the Congregation of the Holy Office details on the author, title and printing place:

> To the Inquisitors of Italy:
> This Sacred Congregation has resolved that, for the sake of respect, of all the books that are printed in the district of this Inquisition, Your Reverence must send here a note of the title, the name of the author and the place of printing. To do this with greater care, you may send the title page of these books, where the mentioned details are shown. Your Reverence will also give this order to the Vicars of the Holy Office in your district.[75]

---

75 Vatican City, Archive of the Congregation for the Doctrine of the Faith (ACDF), S.O., *Tituli librorum, 1640–1658*, leaf 1r (28 January 1640): 'A gl'Inquisitori d'Italia. Ha risoluto questa Santa Cong.ne per degni rispetti che di tutti i libri, che si stampano nel distretto di codesta Inquisizione v.R. mandi qua nota del titolo, del nome dell'Autore, e del luogo della stampa e per ciò fare con maggior cautela potrà inviare il frontespizio dei med.i libri, ove sono notate le cose accennate. In tal conformità v.R. darà l'ordine a' Vicari del S. Off.o del suo distretto'. The original letter sent to Bologna containing the decree is preserved in BCABo, B 1868, 5, leaf 10r (Francesco Barberini to Paolo de Vicariis).

It was a rule that was difficult to apply and which, to a large extent, saw the power of the local inquisitorial offices greatly reduced. In fact, from the archival documentation preserved, we know that the decree remained largely unenforced.

Fuochi's non-observance of the decree was quite another matter. The Inquisitor forgot (or maybe was persuaded to forget) to send the Congregation of the Holy Office a printing permit request for Galileo's works, as indicated by the absence of references to this edition in the Vatican Archives collections. As proof of this, when the decree was reissued in June 1657, Fuochi seemed genuinely surprised and confused as to what to do.[76] Particularly, he asked the Holy Office for which works the indicated procedure was necessary since the decree implicitly involved any printed document. Given the impossibility of submitting such an immense production to the judgement of the Congregation, the General Secretary of the Holy Office, Francesco Barberini (1597–1679), reassured Fuochi that the new provisions concerned the same works of which the authorities in charge of censorship had always tried to prevent the printing and circulation, namely those 'contrarie alli dogmi della nostra S. Fede, e buoni costumi' (contrary to the dogmas of our Holy Faith, and good morals).[77] While remaining a rather vague indication, it nonetheless drastically reduced the number of works to be submitted to the judgement of the Congregation. Fuochi, well-aware of his new duties, applied them to the scientific works about which he could have doubts, perhaps also by virtue of his Galilean experience. Thus, he demonstrated commendable impartiality, by submitting to Rome printing permit requests for the works of leading members of the Bolognese scientific environment apparently above suspicion, like *Geographia et Hydrographia reformata* and *Astronomia reformata* by the Jesuit father Riccioli, or the *Dendrologia* by Ulisse Aldrovandi (1522–1605), edited by Montalbani.[78]

---

76   BCABo, B 1870, 88, leaf 183ʳ (Francesco Barberini to Fuochi, 30 June 1657). Fuochi's answer can be found in ACDF, S.O., *Tituli librorum, 1640–1658*, leaves 304, 305, 308 (7 July 1657).

77   BCABo, B 1870, 92, leaf 191ʳ (Francesco Barberini to Fuochi, 21 July 1657).

78   G.B. Riccioli, *Geographiae et hydrographiae reformatae libri duodecim quorum argumentum sequens pagina explicabit* (Bononiae: ex typographia haeredis Victorij Benatij, 1661), USTC 1730847; Idem, *Astronomiae reformatae tomi duo, quorum prior obseruationes, hypotheses, et fundamenta tabularum, posterior praecepta pro usu tabularum astronomicarum, et ipsas tabulas astronomicas CII. continet* (2 vols.; Bononiae: ex typographia haeredis Victorij Benatij, 1665), USTC 1723549; Ovidio Montalbani (ed.), *Ulyssis Aldrovandi Patricii Bononiensis Dendrologiae Naturalis scilicet Arborum Historiae libri duo* [...] (Bononiae: typis Io. Baptistae Ferronii, 1667-8), USTC 1750020. Imprimatur requests in ACDF, S.O., *Tituli librorum, 1658–1664*, leaves 132, 134 (8 October 1659), 237, 240 (24 April 1660); *Tituli librorum, 1640–1658*, leaves 644, 646 (14 May 1658).

As for the censorial editing of the *Opere*, although Fuochi ignored part of the current regulations, he proceeded with the utmost caution, even trying to prevent the printing of works that had not yet circulated in Bologna, like the *Mechanics* and *Bilancetta* (Galileo's early work on the hydrostatic balance), or of his unpublished correspondence.[79] Even more meaningful is Fuochi's refusal of the possibility of publishing texts containing criticisms addressed to the Jesuits, in order to maintain the difficult balance between them, the University and the *amateurs*. This was the case for a letter to be added to the *History and Demonstrations Concerning Sunspots and Their Properties*, chosen as proof of the Galilean paternity of the discovery of sunspots, in which the theologian and historian Fulgenzio Micanzio (1570–1654) reminded the scientist, among other things, of the bad faith that distinguished the Jesuits. Manolessi's requests to Viviani for the intervention of Leopoldo remained largely disregarded so far, for the simple reason that a man of the Church could not compromise by unduly relying on his political authority on issues relevant to the censorial legislation established by the Congregation of the Holy Office. Yet for those cases where the Inquisitor's decisions demanded a political will, the Prince guaranteed Manolessi his direct support.[80] Thus, in the summer of 1655, when the printing of the *Opere* had almost been completed, Leopoldo gave Ambassador Cospi the task of manifesting the wishes of the House of Medici to the Inquisitor. The only surviving evidence concerning this diplomatic mission is the incipit of a letter with which Cospi informed Leopoldo of the willingness expressed by Fuochi, surely intimidated by the interference of the Florentine court:

> In regard to the favoured order that Your Serene Highness has given me with his [letter] of [August] 7th, I paid a visit to the Right Reverend Father Inquisitor on behalf of Your Highness. Not only has he proved to be in favour of ensuring the printing of part of the letter of the Servite Friar Fulgenzio [...], but [he also said] that he will do as much as he can to allow [the printing of] the other works that the printer is submitting to him as well, to serve Your Highness, as he seems eager to do. For this I thanked him on your behalf, assuring him of the favour of Your Highness.[81]

---

79   ODG *Carteggio*, II, pp. 225–226 (Manolessi to Viviani, 29 May 1655).
80   However, from Manolessi's letters to Viviani of 15 and 22 June and 10 July 1655, we know that Leopoldo actually sought to circumvent the Inquisitor's prohibition of printing Kepler's *Dissertatio* (and other writings), resorting to Cardinal Giovan Carlo de' Medici (1611–1663) as a mediator between Bologna and the Roman Congregations (cf. ODG *Carteggio*, II, pp. 230, 232, 237), yet unsuccessfully so.
81   ASF, *Mediceo del Principato*, 5531, leaf 87ʳ (Cospi to Prince Leopoldo, 21 August 1655): 'In ordine al favoritissimo comando di v.a.s. con la sua de' sette del corrente, sono stato da

From this moment on, the printing of Galileo's works continued without the local inquisition placing further obstacles, but the problems were not over. The rest of the correspondence between Manolessi and Viviani concerns the completion of the allegorical frontispiece to be inserted at the beginning of the first volume.[82] After several technical issues and setbacks, the engraving was prepared by Stefano Della Bella (1610–1664), who had already made the frontispiece for the *Dialogue* in 1632, and the matrix was finally sent to Manolessi at the end of January 1656. Besides the direct involvement of Prince Leopoldo even in this frontispiece affair, two details are of particular interest for the role of this edition in the history of publishing and book trade, concerning its dissemination and price.

5   On the Marketability of the *Opere*

In a letter of early December 1655, Manolessi asked Viviani to encourage the completion of the frontispiece matrix since the pre-sales of this new edition had reached considerable numbers:

> last week I received a visit from an English merchant and another one from Amsterdam, on their way to Rome. They will come back in five weeks and have assured me that they intend to buy one hundred copies each.[83]

It is reasonable to think that this transaction was successful considering that today, Great Britain is the country with the largest number of complete copies of this edition preserved in public collections. The other important fact is derived from Viviani's reply to this last letter, in which he specifies that Della Bella guaranteed that the plate on which he had made the engraving could

---

questo Rev.mo P. Inquisitore per parte di V.A., et non solo egli si è contentato che si stampi il capitolo della lettera di fra Fulgentio servita [...] ma anco faciliterà tutte l'altre scritture che li va portando lo stampatore fin dove può per che l'A.V. resti servita come ne mostra gran desiderio, onde io per sua parte lo ho ringratiato et accertatolo del aggradimento che V.A. è per conservarli'. As specified by Cospi, only a part of Micanzio's letter was published (*OGM*, II.2, p. 155). The sections containing severe criticism of the Jesuits were censored (cf. *OG*, XIV, pp. 298–299 for the unabridged version).

82 The most accurate and detailed analysis of the frontispiece can be found in Redondi, *La nave di Bruno e la pallottola di Galileo*, pp. 343–351.

83 *ODG Carteggio*, II, p. 277 (Manolessi to Viviani, 7 December 1655): 'la settimana passata appunto furono da me un mercante Inglese, et uno d'Amsterdam, che vanno a Roma, e questi fra 5 settimane saranno di ritorno, e mi hanno detto levaranno 100 corpi di libri per ciascheduno [...]'.

be used to print at least 2,500–3,000 copies before deteriorating.[84] This detail allows us to hypothesise broadly the print run of the edition. Given that copies of the frontispiece with clear signs of wear and fading are unknown, and that only one state of it seems to exist, we can assume that between 1,000 and 2,000 complete copies were printed, although we will never know the print run of the individual works.

By the beginning of February 1656, the edition was finally completed.[85] Contrary to the requests made by Viviani to Rinaldini already over a year earlier, in the general preface Manolessi retraced the history of the enterprise, reserving great praise for Galileo's last pupil for his indispensable contribution and Prince Leopoldo for his constant protection. The content of this preface, and in particular the dedication to Grand Duke Ferdinando II, sanctioned the role of the Medici as patrons of science. Moreover, the events related to the edition had taken place in compliance with the provisions of the Church and censorial practices. It was a diplomatic and political victory for Florence and an affirmation of the Galilean *methodus* in the heart of the State of the Church.

Manolessi went to Florence during the second half of February, where he donated several copies to all those mentioned in the preface and to other prominent figures of the court, spending about ten days in the city for commercial purposes. Thanks to the transactions carried out there, we have an idea of the original sale price of the *Opere*. Once back in Bologna, Manolessi wrote to Viviani to collect revenue from the sale of five copies entrusted to him: 'The price for the five copies amounts to 48 lire for the three unbound and 36 lire for the two bound [...]'.[86]

From this letter, we learn that the *Opere* cost 16 (unbound copies) and 18 (bound copies) Bolognese lire. In the mid-1650s, this particular currency had a total weight of $c.6.35$ g with 91.7% silver ($c.5.82$ g), having value and weight slightly higher than that of the Florentine lira.[87] This then was a considerable price. In those same years, it was possible to rent houses in the city centre of Bologna for 5 to 6 lire per month, while for houses with an attached workshop near the city walls, the price went down to less than 4 lire per month.[88]

---

84   ODG *Carteggio*, II, p. 281 (Viviani to Manolessi, 21 December 1655).
85   *Ibid*, II, p. 288 (Manolessi to Viviani, 1 February 1656). The print run was allegedly completed on 17 February, the date of the dedicatory letter (OGM, I, leaf †1r).
86   ODG *Carteggio*, II, p. 310 (Manolessi to Viviani, 4 March 1656): 'Il prezzo de' cinque corpi di Galilei, che saranno lire 48 i tre sciolti, e lire 36 i due legati [...]'.
87   Giovanni Battista Salvioni, 'Il valore della lira bolognese dal 1626 al 1650', *Atti e Memorie della R. Deputazione di Storia Patria per le Provincie di Romagna*, 14, 4–6 (1924), pp. 197–228: 226–227; 15, 4–6 (1925), pp. 207–276: 263.
88   Historical Archive of the Dominican Order in Bologna (ASDBO), III.80502g (Fr. Antonio Ortolani da Venezia, *Annali del Convento di S. Domenica di Bologna*), II, pp. 1093, 1101 (rental agreements, 1655–57). This chronicle of the Dominican convent of Bologna was

As already mentioned, in all probability, the overall price of the edition was one of the reasons that led Manolessi to print Galileo's works so that they could be sold separately. Moreover, it was a collection of texts designed for specialised studies that would hardly have interested the common reader. The prohibitive price apparently also dissuaded many local institutions from purchasing a copy. For example, no mention is made of this edition in the eighteenth-century inventories of two of the major ecclesiastical libraries of Bologna (those of the Barnabites and the Dominicans). However, their interest in Galileo is demonstrated by the fact that the Barnabites owned the first, rare edition of the *Two New Sciences*, and the Dominicans had a copy of no less than the condemned *Dialogue*, while both purchased or received a copy of the second edition of Galileo's collected works, printed in Florence in 1718.[89] Individuals who were engaged in experimental research and those who held university chairs considering themselves followers of Galilean philosophy proved to be much more interested in purchasing. The international market, as we have seen, was no different. The extreme rarity of some of the original editions of Galileo's works made the *Opere* palatable and thus, already in mid-1656 this edition had arrived on the French market as well and, in the face of its success, the Lyonnais publisher Jean Antoine Huguetan (1619–1681) planned a new edition of the *Dialogue*, to complete the Bolognese edition (but unfortunately this never materialised).[90]

On the university front, the new availability of Galileo as a study text encouraged the possibility of instructing students in the propositions of New Science, causing mounting tensions between traditionalists and neoterics. At the heart of this dispute, we find the present edition of Galileo's works, mentioned in correspondences ascribable to the environments of the University of Pisa. Thus, for example, from Cosimo Galilei, we know that the prudent Rinaldini, in public followed the standard study programs, while in private he discussed the works of Galileo with his students.[91] The scientist Giovanni Alfonso Borelli (1608–1679) did not behave very differently. He was called to Pisa at the beginning of 1656 to hold the chair of Mathematics and, still in 1660, he took care to provide his colleagues with copies of the *Opere* through

---

written between 1737 and 1753, including a detailed account, based on the original registers, the bulk of which are lost, of the financial transactions carried out by this institution.

89 BCABo, B 2350, p. 148 and B 1952, pp. 16, 19–21. The state of preservation of the related archival documents does not allow for clarifying which works of Galileo were kept in the collections of the local Jesuit convent.

90 ODG *Carteggio*, II, pp. 360–361 (Rasmus Bartholin to Viviani, 26 July 1656).

91 BNCF, *Galileiano* 161, leaf 119 (Cosimo Galileo to Viviani, 3 January 1658).

Carlo Dati.[92] The controversies within the University went sour, up to the point where the *Provveditore* (University Administrator), Giovanni Battista Quaratesi (1601–1662) sought a solution, presenting the Grand Duke with the possibility of establishing a chair of Galilean Studies, to be entrusted to Rinaldini for the academic year 1662–63.[93] The suggestion had to be immediately abandoned, both because of the controversies it must have aroused and the untimely death of the administrator.[94] Nevertheless, further evidence of Galileo's transitory passage from the curricula of Pisan students of the second half of the seventeenth century can be found in an inventory of the library of one of the University Colleges, in which the *Opere* are mentioned.[95]

Manolessi had carried out an undertaking of rare difficulty, establishing himself as a reckless but loyal executor of the Medici political agenda. His success guaranteed him a third Florentine commission, which led him to publish in 1659 the third, ultimate edition of Benedetto Castelli's major work, dedicated to hydraulics and the regulation of river waters, which for the most part had remained unpublished until then.[96] This time, however, the control of the

---

92   BNCF, *Baldovinetti* 258, II, 31, 4 (Borelli to Dati, 6 January 1660), published in Luigi Guerrini, 'Matematica ed erudizione. Giovanni Alfonso Borelli e l'edizione fiorentina dei libri V, VI e VII delle *Coniche* di Apollonio di Perga', *Nuncius*, 14 (1999), pp. 505–568: 527–529.

93   For a profile of Giovanni Battista Quaratesi, see Danilo Marrara (ed.), *I priori della Chiesa conventuale dell'Ordine di Santo Stefano e provveditori dello Studio di Pisa, 1575–1808* (Pisa: ETS, 1999), pp. 143–149.

94   Pisa State Archive (ASP), *Università* 2, G. 78, leaves 85ʳ–90ᵛ (*Proposizioni per il Ruolo del 1662*): leaf 90ʳ; cf. Angelo Fabroni, *Historia Academiae Pisanae* (3 vols.; Pisis: Excudebat Cajetanus Mugnainius, 1791–95), III, pp. 395–399.

95   ASP, *Università* 2, F. III. 6 (*Indice della Libreria del Collegio R. di Sapienza*), leaf [33]ᵛ. The drafting of this inventory dates to the end of the eighteenth century, but we believe that the copy of the *Opere* must have been acquired in 1656 or shortly thereafter. The access to the College libraries of the University of Pisa was guaranteed only to collegiate students (chosen mainly on merit and limited economic possibilities) and the collections were enriched mostly thanks to Grand Ducal bestowals. Therefore, the sale of doubles and obsolete works could have represented a valid financing method. Nonetheless, mention is made in the inventory of the third edition of Galileo's collected writings as well (4 vols.; Padova: nella stamperia del Seminario, appresso Gio. Manfrè, 1744), more complete and more accurate. Consequently, it is possible that the copy of the *Opere* was preserved until the end of the eighteenth century in the library collections of the *Sapienza* college because it was a gift from the House of Medici or from one of the experts who worked on the edition, like Rinaldini. However, such a dynamic would have been almost impossible after the *Opere* were out of stock. On the Colleges' libraries of the University of Pisa, see Alessandro Volpi, 'La Biblioteca Universitaria', *Storia dell'Università di Pisa* (2 vols. in 5 tomes; Pisa: Edizioni Plus, 2000), II.3, pp. 1045–1107.

96   B. Castelli, *Della misura dell'acque correnti* (Bologna: per gli HH. Del Dozza, 1659). A second print run was released the following year.

Grand Ducal agents over the publisher was more stringent. Viviani was not part of this new venture, as he was probably uninterested in further editorial initiatives carried out by the man who, in his opinion, had not been able to do justice to Galileo's legacy.[97] From the few related letters preserved, the only intermediary between Bologna and Florence seems to have been Ambassador Cospi, who kept the Prince updated on the progress of the edition.[98] Unfortunately, it is not known whether Manolessi had made agreements with the House of Medici for further editorial projects after the success of the edition of Castelli's treatise, as he unexpectedly passed away on 14 September 1661.[99] However, from the surviving documents, we know how long Galileo's collected works remained available to the publisher. The last mention of a direct sale from Bologna can be found in a letter dated January 1662 sent to Carlo Dati by the Dozza brothers. From an attached autograph list by Dati (which constitutes part of the draft reply, now lost), it can be deduced that the subject of the transaction was an exchange of scientific books, including eight copies of the *Opere*.[100]

Although it can be reasonably hypothesised that in Bologna all the copies were sold out shortly after this last letter, the most important point is represented by the fact that this specific editorial enterprise constitutes a scientific and cultural manifesto. If it aimed at rehabilitating the political image of the Grand Duchy of Tuscany and to consolidate the role of patrons of the most prominent members of the ruling family, it also made it possible to convey those ideals of dialogue and shared knowledge at the core of the Republic of Letters.

6 Conclusions

The historical reconstruction of the events concerning the preservation of Galileo's legacy in the decades following his demise (of which this contribution

---

[97] See note 15.
[98] ASF, *Carteggio degli Artisti*, XVI, 337–338 (Cospi to Prince Leopoldo, 28 August 1659 and Manolessi to Cospi, 28 October 1659).
[99] ASB, *Notarile, Rogiti di Michele Tamburini*, 1, 274 (19 September 1661). In the absence of a will, a few days after the death of Carlo Manolessi, the notary Tamburini prepared a *cura* (testamentary care), a document with which the widow, Orsola Veli, was named universal heir in favour of their eight children. She held the share of the business founded by her husband with the Dozza brothers until the age of majority of their fifth- and sixth-born sons, Emilio Maria (1648/9–c.1690) and Evangelista (1650/1–1730), heirs of the publishing company. For Evangelista's date of death, see BCABo, B 911, p. 150.
[100] BNCF, *Baldovinetti*, 258, VI, 25 (Dozza brothers to Carlo Dati, 10 January 1662).

represents the preliminary reconstruction of one of its relevant episodes) constitutes a case study in the history of that European scientific and cultural dialogue of which the history of the book is a cornerstone.

The relationship between the dissemination of scientific knowledge and the controlling policies implemented by both ecclesiastical and secular authorities after the Galileo affair has in recent years received the attention of the academic community. Some of the most promising studies on related topics tend to resize the commonly accepted image of an intransigent and hyper-centralised ecclesiastical power less and less able to enforce stable and functional censorial mechanisms while emphasising how the structures of the Roman Inquisition played an active role in the new, Europe-wide cultural network.[101] This last aspect does not however lend itself to generalisations of any kind, nor to the elaboration of a historiographic category useful to analyse the history of the relationships between book market and censorship in the Republic of Letters, since it would automatically tend to shift the attention to interpretations almost exclusively focused on intellectual and cultural encounters and clashes, to the detriment of more clearly quantifiable and contextualised aspects of a political and economic nature. Lastly, as I have tried to show on this occasion, a rigorous study of such dynamics demands a thorough analysis dedicated to those experts (editors, censors, agents) that with their beliefs, affiliations, personal interests and contact networks substantially contributed to shaping the early modern book market and science communication.

Acknowledgements

The results presented in this contribution have been realised partly thanks to the advice and suggestions of scholars and archivists to whom I am sincerely grateful: Gian Luigi Betti, Elizabeth L. Garver (Austin, TX, Harry Ransom Center), Clara Maldini (Bologna, Archiginnasio Public Library), Daniel Ponziani (Vatican City, Archive of the Congregation for the Doctrine of the Faith), Isabella Truci (Florence, National Library) and Andrea Zanarini (Bologna, Historical Archive of the Dominican Order).

---

101 On this crucial topic, see Daniel Stolzenberg, 'The Holy Office in the Republic of Letters: Roman Censorship, Dutch Atlases, and the European Information Order, circa 1660', *Isis*, 110 (2019), pp. 1–23.

CHAPTER 5

Persecuted in the Spanish Colonies: Inquisitorial Censorship and the Circulation of Medical and Scientific Books in New Spain and New Granada

Alberto José Campillo Pardo and Idalia García

Printed books first arrived in the Americas in the early sixteenth century in the luggage of conquistadors and missionaries. Once the first cities had been founded, a dynamic book market was established, supported by a network of booksellers and merchants that had been operating in Europe since the fifteenth century. The book trade was a profitable business for many families in the New World, but it was also a risky trade, especially due to the imposition of high fines and the threat of expulsion from the trade if a bookman was found guilty of any offence. For the Spanish Crown, the book represented a potential vehicle for heresy and a danger to the Catholic Faith, and therefore the transatlantic market for books was strictly controlled until the second half of the eighteenth century. One part of this control was carried out by the Inquisition, and thanks to its proceedings we have a wealth of historical documents that inform us about the role of books in the Spanish colonial territories. Most of these inquisitorial sources date from the eighteenth century, but there is also important evidence from the sixteenth and seventeenth centuries, thanks to sources such as the 'memorias', inventories of book barrels or boxes that travelled through the Spanish Empire and included specific information about the books they contained.

In this article, we will use some of these sources to test the Inquisition's interest in and control over medical and scientific writing and publishing in New Spain and New Granada. A careful examination of the available sources suggests that, in contrast to traditional historiography, the Inquisition did not impede the circulation of medical and scientific books.[1]

---

1 For this traditional perspective, see: José Pardo Tomás, 'Censura inquisitorial y lectura de libros científicos. Una propuesta de replanteamiento', *Tiempos Modernos*, 4 (2003), pp. 1–18; Teresa Eleazar Serrano Espinosa and Jorge Arturo Talavera González, 'La obra de imprenta y la Inquisición en la Nueva España: los libros prohibidos', in Noemí Quesada, Martha Eugenia Rodríguez and Marcela Suárez (eds.), *Inquisición novohispana*, (Mexico: UNAM. Instituto de Investigaciones Antropológicas; Universidad Autónoma Metropolitana, 2009), vol. 2, pp. 393–403; Maria Pia Donato, *Medicine and the Inquisition in the Early Modern World*

1   The Spanish Inquisition and the New World

The Spanish Inquisition was established in 1480 as a tool of social and doctrinal control for the Catholic monarchy at the end of the process of unification of the Spanish kingdoms. This Inquisition was different from its medieval predecessors, as in addition to being a tool of religious control to fight heresy, it also had a clear political objective: to consolidate a unified Spanish kingdom under the cultural banner of Christianity. In America, the Tribunal of the Holy Office was originally established as an *ad hoc* episcopal tribunal, to be governed by bishops when it was required. However, in 1569 and 1570, King Philip II ordered that permanent inquisitorial tribunals be established in Peru and Mexico, with the mission to stop new heresies from entering and spreading in the American territories, and to fight against the heresies that were already corrupting orthodox belief in the empire. The new Kingdom of Granada's Inquisition was originally a lower court whose authority depended on the Peruvian Tribunal. However, in 1610 the Crown decided to establish a new Tribunal in the city of Cartagena (in present-day Colombia), given the importance of this port as the gateway for most of the goods that came from Spain to the Caribbean and the northern territories of South America, including the Viceroyalty of Peru.

In the Spanish Empire, censorship was present at all stages of the publication process, from printing to distribution. Yet the Inquisition's activities mostly took place during the distribution stage, when readers found their books. After a book was printed with the royal privilege or viceroyal authorisation, the work might be the subject of suspicion and denounced to the Inquisition. Only then did the inquisitorial 'calificadores' decide if the book was dangerous or not, and in those cases when it was deemed dangerous, they decided whether it needed expurgation or was forbidden *in totum*. This censorship was explicitly defined in the inquisitorial regulations, which included Indexes and Edicts. This meant that 'revisores' were only permitted to censor what was designated as potentially dangerous. In fact, after 1584, at the beginning of every Index, whether it was a list of *expurgatorum* or *prohibitorum*, there appeared a section under the heading 'Reglas y Mandatos' (rules and commandments) that included a series of instructions for the censors and qualifiers on how to censor.

The Inquisition developed a series of mechanisms to control the circulation of books, working hand in hand with the Crown. The process began in Spain, at the House of Trade, where, since 1550, every commodity that was destined to travel to or which had arrived from America had to be inspected, and where

---

(Leiden: Brill, 2019); William Eamon, 'Spanish Science in the Age of the New', in Hilarie Kallendorf (ed.), *A Companion to The Spanish Renaissance*. (Leiden: Brill, 2019), pp. 473–507.

the merchants were obliged to register all of their goods in the 'Registros de Navío' (ship registers).[2] In the case of books, they also had to have an inquisitorial license that was issued by the local inquisitorial officer who either sat on a local tribunal, as in the case of Seville, or was one of the port commissioners, as in the case of Cadiz. In both cases, the merchant presented a list of the books to be shipped, the commissioner designated by the local tribunal checked it and, if they were approved books, provided the merchant with a license that served as a passport for their circulation. If the list contained any books that were forbidden *in totum*, or that required expurgation, the officer was responsible for their seizure and either confiscated or expurgated them. On the other side of the ocean, another commissioner would recheck the books upon arrival in the destination port, to ensure that no contraband books had been included in the boxes during the voyage. Only when this verification was concluded, were the books freed.

In addition to this, there were other practices of censorship, such as visitations of libraries, where inquisitorial 'visitadores' visited bookshops or certain libraries. We have historical evidence that suggests these visits happened to libraries of religious orders when they were required by a local tribunal. Booksellers and institutional libraries were obligated to own a copy of the *Index*, to make sure that none of the books for sale or in their collection were forbidden. Furthermore, the Inquisition had ordered in the second half of the sixteenth century that every book owner had to maintain an inventory of their books so that inquisitors could search for problematic or heretical titles. This meant that readers were also under inquisitorial control. At least thirty extant Mexican 'memorias' serve as evidence that this requirement was fulfilled between 1585 and 1716. Many of these inquisitorial instructions were promulgated through the 'cartas acordadas' or specific instruction of the Council of the Supreme Inquisition. The 'acordada' was applicable for one or more territories and some decisions were a result of the initiatives of the regional inquisitors, as was the case in the Mexican example.

Finally, the Inquisition had the power, from 1632 onwards, to exercise a strict control over the books of deceased persons, which fell under a different process. The practice of selling the collection of books of the deceased, represented the reintroduction of these items onto the market, and thus potentially allowed for the circulation of forbidden texts. For that reason, the Inquisition established a specific rule for the heirs of book collections and any booksellers who wanted to appraise a private library after the owner died: they must deliver a list of its contents so that inquisitors could verify that the deceased

---

2   Carlos Alberto González Sánchez and Pedro Rueda Ramírez, 'Con recato y sin estruendo: puertos atlánticos y visita inquisitorial de navíos', *Annali della Classe di Lettere e Filosofia. Scuola Normale Superiore di Pisa*, 5 (2009), pp. 474–475.

had not owned any dangerous books. In addition to this procedure, civil law also ensured oversight through the requirement of an 'Inventario de Bienes de Difuntos', required when people from Spain or other foreign countries who had been living in the colonial territories did not have family in the territory where they died, while a different process was outlined for when Spaniards did have family in the cities or towns of their deaths.

All these practices left a significant amount of documentation on what was prohibited and what was acceptable to be transported to and circulate in the New World. As a result, we have precise information about many editions which circulated in the Viceroyalties of New Spain and New Granada and other territories of Spanish America. This allows us to demonstrate that many medical scientific books were considered to be common merchandise in these territories during the seventeenth and eighteenth centuries, and were not a target of inquisitorial institutions.

2   The Circulation of Medical and Scientific Books in Colonial Mexico

One of the largest territories of the Spanish Crown in the Americas was the Viceroyalty of New Spain, established after the destruction of the city of Mexico-Tenochtitlán in 1521. Soon after, religious orders began to establish monasteries in the new viceregal capital and in the rest of the territory. The first Order to arrive was that of the Franciscans and the last to arrive in the sixteenth century were the Jesuits. These religious orders all had libraries, and many documentary and bibliographical testimonies survive that allow us to study these collections: we have access to more than one hundred such inventories in three Mexican repositories.

Other sources that shed light on this subject were the inventories created after the Expulsion of the Jesuits in 1767. These documents are remarkable because they contain much information about individual books, including details of authors, titles, editions, year of publication, condition and binding.[3] Finally, there are other interesting testimonies, such as the General Index of

---

3   The testimonies of the expulsion are widely spread around the world, so there are some academic studies using these documents in several territories. See Bernabé Bartolomé M., 'Las librerías e imprentas de los jesuitas (1540–1767): una aportación notable a la cultura española', *Historia Sacra*, 40 (1988), pp. 315–388; María Dolores García Gómez, *Testigos de la memoria: los inventarios de las ibliotecas de la Compañía de Jesús en la expulsión de 1767* (San Vicente del Raspeig: Publicaciones de la Universidad de Alicante, 2010); Idalia García, 'Imprenta y librerías jesuitas en la Nueva España', in Idalia García Aguilar and Pedro Rueda Ramírez (eds.), *El libro en circulación en la América colonial: producción, circuitos de distribución y conformación de bibliotecas en los siglos XVI–XVIII* (Mexico: Quivira, 2014), pp. 205–237.

the Dominican Library or the Alphabetical Bibliographic Dictionary of the Franciscans, institutions that were based in Mexico City and founded at the end of the sixteenth century.[4] It is likely that the libraries of these monasteries were established at the same time of the construction of the buildings that house them. Other documents help us to understand the role of science in the Mexican Viceroyalty, especially those that give us some insight on how the religious orders acquired their books.[5]

In the case of the Dominicans, their book index began to be written in 1810. The bibliographic system to register books in this index was very simple: the texts were ordered by title or a combination of author and title because the index was an instrument that served to locate a book on the bookshelves of the library. This index represents the physical order of the books rather than all the bibliographic details. For that reason, it is difficult to identify which editions were in the library. However, we can identify certain older editions based on the author and the key words of the title. In addition, we have identified evidence of provenance that can help in the reconstruction of these colonial libraries.[6] The most important are the 'fire marks' (shelf marks made by branding the books with fire) used by all religious houses, secular and regular, and the manuscript notes that related a book to a specific institution.

Because of this, we can say that the Dominican Index offers a wealth of bibliographic information. Contrary to what one might expect, this institution had many books of natural philosophy, mathematics, medicine, biology, astronomy and other disciplines of scientific knowledge that the friars considered useful to their vocation and their daily life. The monastery was more than a religious centre, it was also a centre of studies and an infirmary – one that even appears to have served women, as the library's General Index shows that the Dominicans owned a book on obstetrics and other works dedicated to women's anatomy. The following list, a small selection of the 2,466 titles in 5,380 volumes that make up this library, gives us an idea of their scientific collection.[7]

---

4   Dominicans: 'Índice general de la Biblioteca del Imperial Convento de Nuestro Padre Santo Domingo de México, formado en el año de mil ochocientos diez por el Muy Reverendo Padre Fray Vicente de la Peña, quien fue nombrado bibliotecario el día 26 de Abril del citado año de 1810 por el Muy Reverendo Padre Maestro Fray Alexandro Fernandez actual Prior de este Imperial Convento y siendo Prior Provincial Nuestro Muy Reverendo Padre Maestro Fray Domingo Barrera'. National Library of Mexico, Ms. 1119; Franciscans: 'Diccionario bibliographico alphabetico e indice sylabo repertorial de quantos libros sencillos existen en esta libreria de este convento de Nuestro Santo Padre San Francisco de Mexico'. National Library of Mexico, MS.10266.
5   Idalia García, 'Para que les den libre paso en todas partes sin que los abran ni detengan: libros para las comunidades religiosas de la Nueva España', *Cuadernos de Historia Moderna*, 42 (2017), pp. 151–173.
6   Catálogo Colectivo de Marcas de Fuego, available at www.marcasdefuego.buap.mx.
7   All these books were registered in the 'Índice general'.

TABLE 5.1   Scientific and medical books in the Dominican Index

Scientific and medical books in the Dominican Index

Astruc. Enfermedades Venereas.	Irañeta. Enfermedad por el Veneno de la Tarantula	Spallanosa. Inoculacion de las Viruelas.
Adelantamientos de la medicina.	Iciar. Arismetica.	Sans. Medicina practica.
Armat. de Tabardillos.	Lemeri. Chimica.	Salgado. Cursos Medicus.
Armat. de viruelas	Luis Tessari. Elementa Chimiae.	Secretos de Artes Liberales.
Aforismos de Cirugia	Madama Fouquet. Medicina.	Siguenza. Libra Astronomica.
Arte de partear	Manual de la Salud.	Saa. de Navegatione.
Abadie. Enfermedades de la dentadura	Martinez. Enfermedades por el uso de las Cotillas.	Silecei. Arihmetica.
Curvo. Observaciones Medicas	Nomenclatura nueva Chimica.	Torre. de Medicina.
Chiaramonte. Polvos de Lacterre	Najer. Navegación.	Theatrum Chemicum.
Corral. Agua de Brea	Nonio. Para navegar.	Tratado de Navegación.
Cecio. de Minerabilis	Ortega. Curso elemental de Botanica.	Tacquet. Elementa Geometri.
Castronio. Mathematica	Ortega. Tablas de Botanica.	Taboada. Arithmetica.
Ciruelo. Aritmetica	Porras. Anatomia.	Vigilias del Sueño.
Castrillo. Magia natural	Piquer. Traduccion de Hipocrates.	Uvendlingen. Matematica.
Desterro. Falsas Anatomias	Piquer. de Calenturas.	
Foart. Sobre la Gonorrea, Hernia, Purgacion, Timosis	Polyanthea Medicinal.	
Guerrero. Tratado de Viruelas	Roca. Sanidad del Cavallo.	
Garcia. Regimiento de Navegacion	Reduccion de Doblones de oro.	
Horta. Sobre la epilepsia	Roix. Reloxes Solares.	
Higuera. Contra la Sangria	Rodriguez. Ensayo para las Ciencias.	

The selection includes some entries of medical books to show that certain books were more practical than others. For example, one book on obstetrics, listed under the title 'Arte de partear' (The art of giving birth), which can refer to one of three editions published in the eighteenth century, shows us what kind of medical information the friars had access to at their monastery.[8] Some of these books helped the friars treat diseases like smallpox, toothaches and sleeping problems, as is the case of the books: 'Armat. de viruelas' (Armat, About Smallpox), 'Guerrero. Tratado de Viruelas' (Guerrero, A treaty on Smallpox), or 'Abadie. Enfermedades de la dentadura' (Abadie, Illnesses of the teeth), 'Vigilias del Sueño' (Sleep vigils).[9] Other books gave testimony about the illnesses prevalent in this colonial society, such as 'Foart. Sobre la Gonorrea, Hernia, Purgacion, Timosis' (Foart, About Gonorrhea, Hernia, Purges and Thymus), 'Irañeta. Enfermedad por el Veneno de la Tarantula' (Irañeta, Illness caused by the Tarantula's venom), or 'Astruc. Enfermedades Venereas' (Astruc, Venereal diseases).[10] These books are the best proof of the existence of a Dominican nursing house.[11] Such a house likely provided services to a part of the local population, that can be described as playing a role as 'conversion

---

[8] 'Índice general', f. 2r. *Compendio de el arte de partear: compuesto para el uso de los Reales Colegios de Cirugia* (Barcelona: por Thomas Piferrer, 1765), CCPB000459689-7; Pedro Vidart, *El discipulo instruido en el arte de partear* (En Madrid: en la Imprenta Real, Se hallará casa de Copin, 1785), CCPB000489873-7; Juan de Navas, *Elementos del arte de partear* (Madrid: en la Imprenta Real, 1795), CCPB000301890-3.

[9] 'Índice general', ff. 2r., 33r. José Amar y Arguedas, *Instruccion curativa de las viruelas: dispuesta para los facultativos, y acomodada para todos* (Madrid: por D. Joachin Ibarra, impresor, 1774). We have not identified the book by Guerrero, CCPB000206078-7; 'Índice general', f. 2r. Pedro Abadie, *Tratado odontalgico en el que se exponen las enfermedades de la dentadura y los medios asi manuales como medicinales propios a corregir sus vicios y à conservar su limpieza* (En Madrid: en la imprenta de D. Antonio Muñoz del Valle, 1764). There is another edition published in 1842, CCPB000626843-9; 'Índice general', f. 85v. Pedro Álvarez de Lugo y Uso de Mar, *Primera y segunda parte de las vigilias del sueño: representadas en las tablas de la noche y dispuestas con varias flores del ingenio* (En Madrid: por Pablo del Val, a costa de Antonio de Riero y Tejada, 1664), USTC 5085636.

[10] 'Índice general', f. 29v. Samuel Foart Simons, *Observaciones sobre la curacion de la gonorrèa, hernia venèrea, purgaciones de garabatillo, fimosis, parafimosis, bubon, ulceras ... traducido del ingles al francés y al castellano por don Antonio Tenllado de Carbajál y Sandovál* (En Llerena: [s.n.], 1786), CCPB000238907-X; 'Índice general', f. 40r. Manuel Irañeta y Jauregui, *Tratado del tarantismo o enfermedad originada del veneno de la tarántula* (En Madrid: en la Imprenta Real, 1785), CCPB000488875-8; 'Índice general', f. 2r. Jean Astruc, *Tratado de las enfermedades venereas* (En Madrid: en la imprenta de Pedro Marin, se hallará en las librerias de Francisco Fernandez y de Miguel Copin, 1772).

[11] Guimel Hernández Garay, *La economía de los conventos mendicantes en Nueva España, Santo Domingo de México, 1748–1813* (Mexico: UNAM, 2016), p. 6.

medicine', assisting the evangelisation of the locality.[12] At the same time, other medicine books were more theoretical, such as manuals for the education of physicians, which included general advances in medicine, such as those written by Lázaro Rivero, and classics such as the works of Galen, Dioscorides and Hippocrates, present in different languages, including Spanish, French and Latin. The Dominican library also possessed a similar selection of works on other scientific subjects, including on arithmetic, geometry, mathematics, mineralogy and navigation.

The library of the Dominicans represents only one example of the circulation of medical and scientific works in the colonial period. Other evidence of the circulation of this knowledge can be found in private libraries.[13] One example is the library of Melchor Pérez de Soto, architect of the cathedral in Mexico City, that was visited by the Inquisition in 1655.[14] Another collection, described in 1774, belonged to Francisco González y Avendaño, author of a sermon written in honour of the Virgin of Guadalupe and a physician who participated in the embalming of the Viceroy Marquis of Amarillas.[15] Doctor González had one of the most interesting colonial libraries of medicine, containing 448 books, known to us thanks to their having been inventoried in a 'memoria', as required by the Inquisition.

At the beginning of the seventeenth century, the Holy Office recognised a problem in the inheritance process: the transmission of forbidden books. Some people had permission to read forbidden books, but when they died, these books were sometimes reintroduced into the book market without the proper

---

12 José Pardo Tomás, 'La medicina de la conversión: el convento como espacio de cultura médica novohispana', in José Pardo Tomás y Mauricio Sánchez Menchero (eds.), *Geografías médicas. Orillas y fronteras culturales de la medicina, siglos XVI y XVII* (Mexico: UNAM, 2014), p. 22.

13 Idalia García, *La vida privada de las bibliotecas: rastros de colecciones novohispanas, 1700–1800* (Universidad del Rosario and Universidad Autónoma Metropolitana-Cuajimalpa, 2020).

14 Manuel Romero de Terreros, *Un bibliófilo en el Santo Oficio* (Mexico: Librería de Pedro Robredo, 1920).

15 'Memoria y avaluó de los libros que quedaron por fallecimiento del doctor Francisco González Avendaño (1774)', AGN, Inquisición vol. 1168, exp. 1, ff. 18v.–34v. This library is part of the documental evidence provided in García, *La vida privada de las bibliotecas*. Franciscus González y Avendaño, *Parhelion Marianum, Mexici conspicuum suburbijs. Disertatio inauguralis, quam ad clepsydram dicebat arenariam, in archigimnasio regiae, ac Pontificiae Mexicanae Minervae* (Mexici: apud Haerederus Domine Maria de Rivera, 1757). Juan Lorenzo de la Garza-Villaseñor and Juan Pablo Pantoja, 'La España peninsular, la Nueva España y la autopsia de una malformación', *Revista de Investigación Clínica*, 60 (2008), p. 266.

permission or 'licencia'. To avoid this, the Inquisition ordered that anyone who possessed a library had to deliver a list of the books in their possession. The list was checked by the inquisitors and, if there were no dangerous books on it, they would authorise their sale. This process was formalised in 1632, when the Holy Office introduced, at the beginning of the Index of Forbidden Books, a rule to enforce this requirement. Thanks to this, in Mexico more than one hundred lists of books, or 'memorias', have been preserved. These documents fall into two categories: one records only basic information about the books, such as authors and titles, while the other contains more detailed information, enough to identify the editions in contemporary libraries or catalogues. Doctor González's 'memoria' is of the more detailed type, which allows us to analyse its content in detail. The space in this article does not permit us to transcribe the entire list, in which 448 books were registered, of which only 113 books (a quarter) were not scientific in subject.[16] Here we enumerate nine important examples from the 335 medical and scientific books listed in the library, to give a reasonable representation:

> 1 Fusquio (Leonardo) Historia de Plantas y estirpes. Basilia año de 1542 apolillado.[17]
> 1 Tholomeo (Claudio) Geografia restituida por Gerardo Mercator. En Amsterdan año de 1574 con poca polilla Pergamino.[18]
> 1 Dioscorides (Pedasio) comentado por Pedro Andres Mathiolo. Historia de Plantas. En Basilea año de 1676. Vitela.[19]
> 2 Gomez Pereyra (Margarita Antonia) Fisica Medica y Theologica. En Madrid año de 1749 Pasta.[20]

---

16 These books, and those of other private libraries, can be seen in *Kobino*, available at libant.kohasxvi.mx.

17 'Memoria y avalúo', f. 19r. Leonhard Fuchs, *De historia stirpivm commetarii insignes, maximis impensis et vigiliis elaborati* (Basileae: in Officina Isingriniana, 1542), USTC 602520.

18 'Memoria y avalúo', f. 19r. This edition was not located. This is a later edition: Claudio Tolomei, *Claudii Ptolemaei Alexandrini Geographiae libri octo Graeco-Latini Latine primum recogniti & emendati, cum tabulis geographicis ad mentem auctoris restitutis per Gerardum Mercatorem* (Amsterodami: sumptibus Cornelij Nicolai & Iudoci Hondij, 1605), USTC 1019310.

19 'Memoria y avalúo', f. 19v. This edition was not located, but the USTC does record sixteenth-century editions of this work of Pietro Andrea Mattioli, though none printed in Basel.

20 'Memoria y avalúo', f. 19v. Juan Gómez Pereira, *Antoniana Margarita, opus nempe physicis medicis ac theologis* (Matriti: ex typograhia Antonii Marin: se hallarà en la Libreria de Manuel Ignacio de Pinto, 1749), CCPB000182986-6.

1 Aguapendente (Geronimo Fabricio) Anatomia y Phisiologia, con un copiosissimo Yndice de los Verbos y cosas mas notables. en Lipcia año de 1687, poco maltratado y poca polilla Vitela[21]

1 Zepeda y Adrada (Don Alonso) Arbol de la Siencia de Reymundo Lulio. En Bruselas año de 1663, casi nuevo poca polilla Pergamino.[22]

1 Gorraes (Job) Definiciones de los medicamentos por Abecedario, con un Yndice grecolatino. En Francofurti año de 1601 apolillado.[23]

1 Gualterio Carleton de las diferencias y nombres de animales, y Anatomia. En Ocsonia año de 1677. bien tratado.[24]

1 Sabonarola (Juan Miguel) sobre todo genero de enfermedades. En Venecia año de 1547. En Pergamino.[25]

1 Carranza (Alfonzo) tratado de Partos en Madrid año de 1628. Viejo.[26]

1 Lopes de Leon (Pedro) theorica y practica de las Apostemas, Questiones de Cirugia sobre heridas etcétera. en Zaragoza año de 1699.[27]

1 Balverde (Juan) Historia de la composición de el Cuerpo humano. En Roma año de 1556. Viejo y apolillado.[28]

---

21 'Memoria y avalúo', f. 20r. Gerolamo Fabrici, *Hieronymi Fabricii ab Aquapendente ... Opera omnia anatomica & physiologica* (Lipsiae: sumptibus Johannis Friderici Gleditschii, excudebat Christianus Goezius, 1687), USTC 2666900.

22 'Memoria y avalúo', f. 20v. Ramón Llull, *Arbol de la ciencia de el iluminado maestro Raymundo Lulio, nuevamente traducido y explicado por ... Don Alonso de Zepeda y Adrada* (En Brusselas: por Francisco Foppens, impressor y mercader de libros, 1663), USTC 1554071.

23 'Memoria y avalúo', f. 21r. Jean de Gorris, *Definitionum medicarum libri 24, literis Graecis distincti* (Francofurti: typis Wechelianis apud claudium Marnium, & heredes Ioannis Aubrij, 1601), USTC 2065169.

24 'Memoria y avalúo', f. 21v. Walter Charleton, *Gualteri Charletoni Exercitationes de differentiis & nominibus animalium: Quibus accedunt mantissa anatomica, et quaedam de variis fossilium generibus, deque differentiis & nominibus colorum* (Oxoniae: E Theatro Sheldoniano, 1677), USTC 3096510.

25 'Memoria y avalúo', f. 21v. This edition was not located. This is a variant edition: *Johannes Michele Savonarola, Practica Ioannis Michaelis Sauonarole. Practica ad omnes egritudines vtilissima Ioannis Michaelis Sauonarole* (Impressum Venetijs: in edibus nobili viri Luceantonij de Giunta florentini, die 20. martij 1518), USTC 855317.

26 'Memoria y avalúo', f. 22r. Alonso Carranza, *Disputatio de vera humani partus naturalis et legitimi designatione* (Madridii: auctoris impensis, ex typographia Francisci Martinez, 1628), USTC 5027221.

27 'Memoria y avalúo', f. 22r. This edition was not located. This is a variant edition: Pedro López de León, *Pratica y teorica de las apostemas en general y particular; Questiones y praticas de cirugia de heridas, llagas y otras cosas nuevas y particulares, por el licenciado Pedro Lopez de Leon; primera parte [y segunda]* (Impresso en Sevilla: en la Oficina de Luys Estupiñan, 1628), USTC 5017767.

28 'Memoria y avalúo', f. 22v. Juan Valverde de Hamusco, *Historia de la composicion del cuerpo humano* (Roma: impressa por Antonio Salamanca y Antonio Lafrerij en Roma, 1556, en casa de Antonio Blado), USTC 340662.

1 Burgos (Frai Vicente) de las propiedades de todas las cosas. En Toledo año de 1529 de letra de Tortis mui Viejo, falto y apolillado.[29]

1 Nuñez de Acosta (Doctor Duarte) varios papeles sobre purgas, sangrías y demas año de 1674. Pergamino.[30]

1 Torre (Luis) de Tabardillos chichimecos. En Burgos año de 1574 viejo apolillado.[31]

In this collection there were editions from most prominent European cities of publication, and works by important scientific authors, such as Athanasius Kircher, Friedrich Hoffmann, Ramón Llull, Galen, Dioscorides, and noteworthy Spanish scholars, such as Juan Gómez Pereira. These works were all foundational texts in the medical training of the early modern period. In this sense, this library could be considered a professional collection because most of the books were devoted to the subject of medicine.[32] The specialised nature of this library is especially remarkable because Doctor González was also a writer of religious texts, as evidenced by his authorship of a sermon.

Like many other inventories of its kind, the document that lists the contents of González's library was drawn up by Ignacio Rodríguez Sandoval, a bookseller who specialised in the sale of used books. He described some of the volumes as old, worm-eaten and mistreated ('maltratado').[33] This provides good evidence of the existence of a second-hand book market in Colonial Mexico, where an important number of editions published in the sixteenth and seventeenth centuries were still in circulation by the end of the eighteenth century. In addition to these editions that were one or two centuries old, the Doctor's

---

29 'Memoria y avalúo', f. 22v. Bartholomaeus Anglicus, *Libro de proprietatibus rerum en romance: hystoria natural do se tratan las propiedades de todas las cosas* (Toledo: en casa de Gaspar de Auila ynpresor, 1529), USTC 334942.

30 'Memoria y avalúo', f. 27r. Duarte Nuñez de Acosta, *Luminar menor, que con luz participada de los mayores autores, resplandece a vista de tenebrosas calumnias: ventilanse nuevamente las dos questiones de purgar los humores, que hazen decubito arriba y la de sangrar del braço en los afectos superiores pendientes de fluxion* (S.l.: s.n., 1674), USTC 5105467.

31 'Memoria y avalúo', f. 31v. Luis de Toro, *De febris epidemicae et noue, quae Latine P⁻ucticularis, vulgo Tauardillo, et Pintas dictur, natura, cognitione, & medela* (Bvrgis: apud Philippum Iuntam, impresis Francisci Lopez iunoris, 1574), USTC 342082.

32 'Memoria y avalúo', f. 29v. Antonio de Peralta, *Dissertationes scholasticae de sacratissima Virgine Maria Genitrice Dei, nostraqve etiam dileectissima Madre, ac Domina* (Genova: Apud Ex Typographia. Matheo Garbizza, 1726). National Library of Mexico, BNMx RFO 232.91 PER.d. 1726.

33 In 1779, this bookseller also inventoried and valued the library of the Marquis of Jaral de Berrio.

collection also contained titles that were recently produced, and the condition of some books was highlighted by Sandoval as: 'one new and another old without title-page' or 'in vellum new'.[34]

The 'memorias' were different from formal library inventories, such as that of the Dominicans, because the 'memorias' did not require a notary's validation. However, both inventories and 'memorias' were used by the inquisitors to identify and censor editions that they considered dangerous. This censorship was more focused on religion and politics than on scientific and practical books, which it is evident on the documents thanks to the handwritten marks made by the censors next to the titles that they considered suspicious or dangerous. Thanks to the evidence that we have presented so far, we can say that several groups of medical and scientific books were not censored by the Inquisition, such as the following items present in one of the 'memorias': '40 small notebooks, small damaged old books of medicine, surgery, philosophy and other subjects, some of them ... moth-eaten. In Latin, Castilian Spanish and Italian printed in different places, made in parchment'.[35] This list, as incomplete as it is, is evidence of the unimpeded circulation of medical and scientific books.

3   The Circulation of Medical and Scientific Books in New Granada

In the case of New Granada, we also have examples of how scientific books circulated in both private and institutional libraries. There is the case of Juan de Ayllón, surgeon of the ship San Francisco de Paula, commanded by Captain Joseph de Arizon, who was also a book merchant and in whose home in Cartagena Juan de Ayllón died in 1750.[36] Since, as mentioned above, the libraries of deceased individuals were inspected to prevent the circulation of forbidden books, a list of the books Ayllón owned at the time of his death can be found in the 'Auto de Bienes de Difuntos'. Ayllón owned a small library composed of twenty-four books, of which twenty were medical books.[37]

---

34   'Memoria y avalúo', ff. 32r, 23r.
35   '40 Quadernos Chicos, libritos truncos de Medicina, Cirugia, Filosofia y otras materias, viejos, y algunos apolillados. En Latin, Castellano e Ytaliano impresos en distinta partes en pergamino.'. 'Memoria y avalúo', f. 27v.
36   'Auto de bienes de difuntos: Juan de Ayllon'. Archivo General de Indias, Contratacion, 5616, N.6, image No. 1.
37   'Auto de bienes de difuntos: Juan de Ayllon', images 14 and 15.

Un libro de a folio viejo de titulo Dioscorides[38]
Otro libro de a folio viejo, Zirujia Unibersal[39]
Un libro de a quartilla de titulo Mesue Defendido[40]
Otro libro, Epistola Satisfactoria[41]
Otro Clava de Arzides[42] = Otro Anatomia Completa[43]
Otro de a folio Lazari Riveri[44]
Otro el Abece de Galeno[45]
Otro Medicina y Zirujia Razional[46]
Otro dicho Arte Poetica
Otro Dudas de la aniquilacion y defensa de las Sangrias[47]
Otro papeles varios
Otro de media cuartilla Antigua y Moderna curazion[48]

---

38 Dioscórides, *Acerca de la materia medicinal y de los venenos mortíferos, Pedacio Dioscorides anazarbeo; traduzido de lengua griega en la vulgar castellana & illustrado con claras y substantiales annotations ... por el doctor Andrés de Laguna* (En Anuers: en casa de Iuan Latio, 1555), USTC 440099.

39 Juan Calvo, *Cirugía universal, Primera y segunda parte de la Cirugia vniuersal y particular del cuerpo humano: que trata de las cosas naturales, no naturales, y preternaturales* (En Madrid: por Diego Flamenco, a costa de Diego Logroño, 1626), USTC 5019561.

40 Jorge Basilio Flores, *Mesue defendido contra D. Felix Palacios: muy util para todos los profesores de la Medicina* (En Murcia: por Joseph Diaz Cayuelas, 1721), CCPB000062351-2.

41 Gonzalo de Aguilar, *Epistola satisfactoria a el doctor D. Gonzalo de Aguilar y Eslava, en que se le intima la verdad de las tres proposiciones contenidas en el parecer del Doctor Lucas de Gongora, sobre la mixtura del musgo con el tabaco* (S.l.: s.n., [c.1700]), Library of Sevilla University A 109/049(06).

42 Duarte Nuñez de Acosta, *Clava de Alcides con que se desbaratan propugnaculos tan ruidosos en la apariencia como vanos en la contextura ... escrivela Duarte Nuñez de Acosta* (Jerez de la Frontera: por Diego Perez de Estupiñan, 1660), USTC 5092834.

43 Martin Martinez, *Anatomia completa del hombre, con todos los hallazgos, nuevas doctrinas, y observaciones raras hasta el tiempo presente, y muchas advertencias necessarias para la cirugia* (En Madrid: En la Imprenta Real por Don Miguel Francisco Rodriguez, 1745), CCPB000230368-X.

44 Lazare Riviere, *Lazari Riverii ... Praxis medica cum theoria. Editio novissima cui accessit index rerum amplissimus* (Lugduni: sumpt. Ioannis-Ant. Huguetan., 1674), USTC 6154085.

45 Galen, *Galeni Ars medicinalis, comentarijs Francisci Vallesij Cobarrubiani ... illustrate* (Compluti: excudebat Andreas de Angulo, 1567), USTC 336412.

46 Juan de Vidos y Miro, *Medicina, y cirugia racional, y espargirica ... con su antidotario de rayces, yervas, flores, semillas, frutos, maderas, aguas, vinos, &c. medicinales que usa la medicina racional, y espargirica* (En Madrid: en la Imprenta Real de Musica, a costa de Pedro del Castillo, s.d.), CCPB000479834-1.

47 Alonso Granado, *Dudas a la aniquilación y defensa de las sangrias del touillo* (Impresso en Seuilla: por Iuan Lorenço Machado, 1653), USTC 5078376.

48 José Lopez, *Maravillosa curacion antigua y moderna de las heridas en comun y en particular* (En Madrid: por Alonso Balvás, 1730), CCPB000489140-6.

Otro Estilo de Cartas
Otro en Latin Spicileguium Anatomicum[49]
Otro Bibliopola Medicina[50]
Otros dos primero y segundo tomo, escritos en frances, sus titulus Trate de Maledies[51]
Otro dicho Tratado de Medicamentos[52]
Otro Practica de enfermedades agudas[53]
Otro dicho en frances de titulo Recuil
Un librito de Oficio parvo de la Virgen
Otro Semanero en Francés
Otro escripto en latin de titulo Guidonis.[54]

When we consider this list, we can draw several conclusions: first of all, that this library, like that of Doctor González Avendaño, was a professional library intended as a tool for the practice of medicine. This suggests that this kind of specialised collection circulated in the early modern colonial world, and that they bore no trace of censorship. Secondly, as in the Mexican collections, this library contained second-hand books, as indicated by the expression 'viejo' (old), describing the first two items on the list, again demonstrating the existence of a second-hand book market in the territories of the Spanish Empire.[55]

---

49 Theodor Kerckring, *Spicilegium anatomicum, continens observationum anatomicarum rariorum centuriam unam: nec non Osteogeniam foetuum, in qua quid quique ossiculo singulis accedat mensibus, quidve decedat, & in eoper per varia immutetur tempora, accuratissimè oculuis subjicitur* (Amstelodami: sumptibus Andreae Frisii, 1670), USTC 1807078.

50 Jérôme Tencke, *Instrumenta curationis morborum deprompta ex pharmacia Galenica & chymica, chirurgia & diæta. Opus in quo multa traduntur praxim ineuntibus utilissima, eòsque velut manu ducentia* (Lugduni: apud Caesarem Chappuis, 1681), USTC 6152851.

51 Jean-Adrien Helvetius, *Traite des maladies les plus frequentes, et des remedes specifiques pour les guerir, avec la methode de s'en servir pour l'utilite du public & le soulagement des pauvres par m. Helvetius* (A Paris: chez Laurent d'Houry, rue s. Severin, chez Pierre-Augustin Le Mercier, rue du Foin, 1703), IT\ICCU\LIAE\040898.

52 Herman Boerhaave, *Traité de la vertu des medicamens. Traduit du latin de m. Herman Boerhaave, par m. de Vaux maitre chirurgen juré à Paris, & ancien prevot de sa Compagnie* (A Paris: chez les freres Osmont, proche le Pont Saint Michel, au Soleil d'Or, 1729), IT\ICCU\MILE\025513.

53 Daniel Tauvry, *Pratique des maladies aigues et de toutes celles qui dependent de la fermentation des liqueurs, par M. Tauvry ... revûe, corrigée & beaucoup augmentée sur les memoires de l'auteur; tome premier* (A Paris: chez Laurent D'Houry, 1706), CCPB000246748-8.

54 Guy de Chauliac, *Guidonis de Cauliaco, In arte medica exercitatissimi Chirurgia, nunc iterum non mediocri studio atque diligentia à pluribus mendis purgata: cum duplici dictionum & rerum Indice* (Lugduni: apud hæredes Iacobi Iuntæ, 1559), CCPB000012773-6.

55 'Auto de bienes de difuntos: Juan de Ayllon', image 14.

Additionally, the fact that we are in the presence of books in Spanish, French and Latin, shows us that Juan de Ayllón was a learned individual, a person who, in the middle of the eighteenth century, could read books in at least three languages, and was familiar with the latest developments in medicine as well as with the classics in the subject, indicated by the fact that he owned both recent and older editions of medical texts.

Finally, this 'Inventario de Bienes de Difuntos' demonstrates one other important aspect of Ayllón: the document tells us that in addition to his activity as a surgeon he also was, at least occasionally, a trader of books. In the paragraph preceding the list of books, there is a statement made by Joseph de Arizon, captain of the ship on which Ayllón was a surgeon, that said that Ayllón had sixteen copies of a new book, in 'half-folio' format, entitled *Uso y Abuso del Agua*, that were apparently carried by the deceased to sell them to Don Gaspar Pellerel, from Cadiz.[56] This is an example of how a person who knew about a specialised subject used that knowledge to trade with it, in the form of books, establishing the existence of a close relationship between the circulation and practice of scientific knowledge.[57]

Another case that shows the active use of medical and scientific books in New Granada comes from the historical archive of Universidad del Rosario, in Bogotá (Colombia). This collection is most interesting to analyse because it contains the entire colonial library of the university, founded in 1653. In it we find several scientific books, such as the *Tesauros chirurgiae* by Ambroise Paré.[58] However, one of the more noteworthy examples of how censorship applied ton scientific books in this library is found in the copy of Newton's *Opuscula Mathematica, Philosophica et Philologica*.[59] The book was so heavily

---

56 'Manifestó el dicho Don Juan de Arizón, diez y seis libros de a medio folio, su título Orttiz Uso y abuso del agua, nuevos, expresando parece los traía el difunto de encargo para su venta de Don Gaspar de Pellerel, vezino de Cadiz'. 'Auto de bienes de difuntos: Juan de Ayllon', image 14. José Marcelino Ortiz Barroso, *Uso y abuso de el agua dulce potable, interna, y externamente practicada en estado sano, y enfermo: Dissertacion theoretico-practica que (reducida a extracto) enunció y expuso a la publica disputa en la Real Sociedad de Sevilla el jueves 21 de mayo de 1733* (En Sevilla: En la Imprenta de las Siete Revueltas, 1736), CCPB000234403-3.

57 For another good case study that confirms this, see Mariana Labarca, 'Los libros de medicina en el Chile del siglo XVIII: tipologías, propietarios y dinámicas de circulación', *Anuario Colombiano de Historia Social y de la Cultura* (2020), p. 348.

58 Ambroise Paré, *Thesaurus chirurgiae continens praestantissimorum autorum utpote Ambrosii Parei parisiensis, Ioannis Tagaultii Ambiani, Vimaci Iacobi Hollerii Stempani, Mariani Sancti Barolitani, Angeli Bolognini, Michaelis Angeli Blondi, Alphonsi Ferri Neapo* (S.l.: s.n., s.d.), Archivo Histórico de la Universidad del Rosario, E10.N68.

59 Isaac Newton, *Opuscula mathematica, philosophica et philologica* (Lausannae et Genevae: apud Marcum-Michaelem Bousquet & Socios, 1744), Archivo Histórico Universidad del Rosario, E7.N65.V3.

expurgated in some chapters, with entire pages crossed out and others even torn out, that one could be tempted to believe that scientific knowledge was harshly repressed. The censor also wrote a short essay on one of the blank pages of the book, explaining that he could not allow the commentaries of a Protestant heretic to circulate freely, and that some of his ideas were so evil that he could not expurgate them by simply crossing them out, and this was why he had to rip entire pages out of the book.[60] However, when one checks the contents of what was expurgated, it becomes obvious that all the censor's work was focused on Newton's commentaries on the Bible, specifically his *opusculas* on the Book of Daniel and the Apocalypse, leaving all the mathematical, and even the historical knowledge, without any kind of censorship.[61]

Not only were medical and scientific books allowed to circulate without any kind of censorship in the private libraries of New Granada, it was the same in the institutional libraries and libraries of government officials of the territory. Juan Gutierrez de Piñerez was one prominent government official of the early modern period, who travelled from Spain to Santafé in 1777 to take over the position of Regent of the Real Audiencia of that city, and Visitador of the New Kingdom of Granada and the provinces of Tierra Firme.[62] He also owned a rather practical collection of books to assist him in his administrative duties.[63] Most of the 118 books in his library covered subjects of law or history, such as the *Recopilación de Leyes de Indias*, but the collection also contained some scientific titles, especially dedicated to geographical knowledge.[64] Remarkably, one of the boxes in his collection was filled with forbidden books, as we can see on the following list:

> Monteschiu: Coleccion de sus obras. 6 tomos en 8° y las cartas en otro tomo suelto – 7
>
> Discursos de Fleuri, sobre las libertades de la Iglesia Galicana, con notas de un Anonimo. 1 to. en 12°. y la Apologia del mismo Anonimo en papel tambien en 12°. – 2

---

60   Alberto Campillo Pardo, *Censura, Expurgo y Control en la Biblioteca Colonial Neogranadina* (Bogotá: Editorial Universidad del Rosario, 2017), p. 64.
61   Ibid., p. 60.
62   'Expediente de información y licencia de pasajero a Indias de Juan Francisco Gutiérrez de Piñeres', Archivo General de Indias, Contratacion, 5523, N.2, R.76. Image, 1.
63   'Registro de Ida a Cartagena, 1777. Registro de la fragata nda. San Josef, alias el Coro, su Mre. Don Andres de Pazos: Memoria de equipaje y Licencia Inquisitorial Juan Gutierrez de Piñeres', Archivo General de Indias, Contratacion, 1672.
64   'Registro de Ida a Cartagena, 1777. Registro de la fragata nda. San Josef, alias el Coro, su Mre. Don Andres de Pazos: Memoria de equipaje y Licencia Inquisitorial Juan Gutierrez de Piñeres', Archivo General de Indias, Contratacion, 1672.

Pufendorf del Derecho Natural en Frances con notas de Berbeirac, 2 tomos en 4°. – 2

Grocio (Grotius Hugo) del derecho de la Guerra y de la Paz, con notas de Berbeirac. 2 tomos en 4°. – 2

El Parayso perdido de Milton 1 en 12°. – 1

Consideraciones sobre las costumbres en Frances, sin nombre de Autor, duplicado. 1 en 12° – 2

Espiritu de la Enciclopedya, o Extracto de los Articulos que se contienen en ella, libres de censura 5 en papel y 12°. – 5

Satira de Petronio en frances. 1 en 12°. – 1

Petronius, Tiberius (c.27–66), Satyricon ....

Melange de D'Alambert. 5 en 12°. – 51

Roberson. Istoria de Carlos quinto. 6 ts. en 12°. – 6

Burlamaqui. Principios del Derecho. 1 to. en 12°. – 1[65]

In this list, we find several books and authors that were listed on the Indexes of Forbidden Books. One of the emblematic examples concerned the works of Montesquieu, who was always considered a dangerous author, and his *De l'Esprit des loix*, published in 1748, was forbidden in the Inquisitorial Edict 16–1 from 1756, eighteen years before Gutierrez Piñeres traveled to America.[66] Montesquieu's works were considered subversive and their persecution persisted for the entirety of the eighteenth century. The same was true for the *Discours sur l'histoire ecclesiastique*, written by Claude Fleury, which was forbidden in the Indexes of 1747 and 1790.[67] Gutierrez Piñeres also possessed the *Melange de D'Alambert*'s *Enciclopedie*, probably one of the earliest works to try and compile all scientific knowledge in a single book. This book was originally forbidden by the inquisitorial Edict of 9 November 1759. However, the *Encyclopédie* was not forbidden because of its scientific knowledge, but due to the antimonarchical ideas of its author. If we assess the authors of forbidden books that were owned by Gutierrez Piñeres (Milton, Montesquieu, D'Alembert, Fleury, etc.), it is clear that these were considered dangerous books for their political and religious content, rather than their scientific value.

---

65 'Registro de Ida a Cartagena, 1777. Registro de la fragata nda. San Josef, alias el Coro, su Mre. Don Andres de Pazos: Memoria de equipaje y Licencia Inquisitorial Juan Gutierrez de Piñeres', Archivo General de Indias, Contratacion, 1672.

66 Jesús Martínez de Bujanda, *El Índice de libros prohibidos y expurgados de la Inquisición Española (1551–1819): evolución y contenidos* (Madrid; Biblioteca de Autores Cristianos, 2016), p. 814.

67 Ibid., p. 561.

Gutierrez Piñeres was not smuggling these books; in fact, due to his high position in the government ranks, he had an inquisitorial license to read forbidden books. We have this information thanks to the ship registers of the Indias Archive, where we can find the 'memoria' of the books, and the inquisitorial license that allowed him to possess and read them:

> Dr. D. Pedro Sánchez Manuel Beernal, *Maestre Escuela* Dignity of the Holly Cathedral Church of Cádiz, Dean Apostolic Judge, and *Real* of the Crusade's Tribunal, *Subsidio, y escusado*, Sub-collector of Confiscations, Vacancies, and *Medias Annatas*, Subdelegate of the Only Contribution of the Secular Ecclesiastic State, and Resident of that city, and its Party, and Commissioner of the Holly Office on it.
>
> Regarding the opinion of the Holy Office, I give License to Mr. Don Juan Francisco Gutierres de Piñeres, member of the King's Council, Regent of the *Real Audiencia* of Santa Fee, for him to ship four boxes of books, with the numbers listed in the margin, and other books that are in the chest containing his clothes, in the ship named *San Joseph* alias *el Coro* that is going to travel to Cartagena de Indas; because he presented a *memoria* of the books, and after revising them, we conclude that he is able to read them because he possesses a license to own and read forbidden books, given to him by the General Inquisitor in Madrid on the 17th of November of 1774, and legalised by his secretary Don Juan de Albiztegui.
> Cadiz June 25 of 1777
> Dr. Sanchez.[68]

---

68 'Registro de Ida a Cartagena, 1777. Registro de la fragata nda. San Josef, alias el Coro, su Mre. Don Andres de Pazos:Memoria de equipaje y Licencia Inquisitorial Juan Gutierrez de Piñeres', Archivo General de Indias, Contratacion, 1672. Original text: 'El Dr. D. PEDRO SANCHEZ MANUEL Bernal, Maestre Escuela Dignidad de la Sant Iglesia Cathedral de Cadiz, Juez Decano Apostolico, y Real del Tribunal de Cruzada, Subsidio, y escusado, Sub-Colector de Expolios, Vacantes, y Medias Annatas, Subdelegado de la Unica Contribucion del Estado Eclesiastico Secular, y Regular de dicha Ciudad, y su Partido, y Comisario Titular del Santo Oficio de la Inquisicion en ella &c.

Por lo que toca a dicho Santo Oficio, doy Licencia para que el Sor. Don Juan Francisco Gutierrez de Piñeres, del Consejo de S.M. su Regente de la Real Audiencia de Sta. Fee embarque quatro caxones de Libros con los numeros del margen, y otros libros en el Baul de su ropa, en la fragata nombrada San Joseph Alias el Coro que haze viaje a Cartagena de indias; atento a aver presentado nota de ellos, y reconocidos ser de los que puede leer mediante a la licencia que tiene presentada de leer y tener libros prohividos, dada por el Sor. Inquisidor General en Madrid a 17 de noviembre de 1774, refendada por su secretario Don Juan de Albiztegui. Cadiz y Junio 25 de 1777. Dr. Sanchez.'

The existence of this licence to read forbidden books given to a distinguished political figure, suggests that some of the readers of Enlightenment works in the Spanish Americas studied them in order to understand them and, if it was deemed necessary, discuss and censor them to align with the political and cultural policies of the Crown.

Our final case that illustrates the circulation of scientific books in the Viceroyalty of New Granada concerns the Jesuit library of the Peruvian mission, brought by Father Josef de Alzugaray from Cadiz to Peru through Cartagena in 1750.[69] This library, inspected by Cartagenian port officials, is one of the greatest examples of a multidisciplinary institutional library, meant to inform and educate the priests and scholars of the colonies at the 'Colegios Jesuitas' (Jesuit schools). Alzugaray, Procurator of the mission in Peru, travelled with fifty boxes that contained 1,423 books, covering every possible subject, including law, theology, history, philosophy, grammar, and, of course, science. Of this substantial library, 164 books (11.5%) were scientific in nature, with mathematics, medicine and geography making up the majority of this section. The library contained the complete oeuvre of Newton, including his *Opuscula*, his *Sistema*, and his *Natural Philosophy*, listed in the following way:

Neuton Opuscula 3–4°.
Fentamina Esperimentos Naturales 1–4°
Sisthema de Neuton 1 en 4°
Neuton Philosophia Natural 1° – 1 tom.[70]

This is evidence that the presence of Newton's works in the colonies was the result of more than the curiosity of some enlightened scholar, or the administrative need of officials: it was part of the education of the new generations of students, gradually becoming an integral part of colonial society.

The collection also had practical scientific books, such as manuals for the construction of telescopes and mathematical instruments. The percentage of scientific books in the collection might seem low, but it is interesting to note that together with these books, Alzugaray brought two boxes of scientific equipment, including telescopes, microscopes, reflective lenses and pneumatical machines,

---

69 'Registro de navío nombrado Na. Sa. del Rosario, Sn. Ignacio y S. Francisco Xavier que se despachó a Cartagena y Portovelo. Partida No. 98', Archivo General de Indias, Contratacion, 1645.

70 'Registro de navío nombrado Na. Sa. del Rosario, Sn. Ignacio y S. Francisco Xavier que se despachó a Cartagena y Portovelo. Efectos que se piden para la Mision de la Joseph de Alzugaray, cajón 38', Archivo General de Indias, Contratacion, 1645.

among other things.[71] This indicates that scientific knowledge not only circulated in print, but also in practice.

4   Conclusions: Medicine, Science and Enlightenment in the New World

In our research in the General Archive of Mexico, we found in total 123 testimonies concerning private libraries of New Spain, most of which date from the eighteenth century. These historical documents attest to the circulation of approximately 30,000 titles. We studied thirteen collections in detail, and found that that 49% of the editions in these collections were published between the sixteenth and seventeenth centuries. If we compare these statistics to the Viceroyalty of New Granada, we can see that the number of eighteenth-century books circulating there was even lower. Taking together the collections of the Universidad del Rosario, founded in 1653, and the National Library, which has the collections of several religious orders, we found that only 40% of the books in New Granadan libraries were published during the eighteenth century. This suggests that books continued to circulate through the second-hand book market for considerable periods of time. Therefore, if one wishes to study impact of intellectual fashions and trends, one has to pay attention to the practical realities of the book trade, as much as to the interests and occupations of collectors.

To study the circulation of books in New Spain in this depth, we have designed a specific database, named Kobino, to help us identify what editions were in private and institutional libraries and advertised for sale in the book market.[72] However, even these efforts only produce information on the circulation of books, not on their social interpretation or their active use. In other words, we need other elements to determine the real impact of medical and scientific books, beyond their presence in the Viceroyalty. While Doctor Peredo had one edition of Newton, we do not know what the utility of Newton's ideas were in his medical practice.[73]

---

71   'Registro de navío nombrado Nuestra Señora del Rosario, San Ignacio y San Francisco Xavier que se despachó a Cartagena y Portovelo. Efectos que se piden para la Mision de la Joseph de Alzugaray, cajón 58'. Archivo General de Indias, Contratación, 1645.
72   Available at libant.kohasxvi.mx.
73   '2 Isac Neuctoni Principia Phylosophie cum comentario perpetuo, latino 4° pasta 4 tomos Genova 1739', *Philosophiae naturalis principia mathematica, tomus primus-quartus* (Geneuae: typis Barrillot & Filii, 1739). 'Memoria de los Libros pertenecientes a los bienes de Don José Peredo (1782)', AGN, Inquisición 1268, f. 159v.

Despite this, all these historical sources can give us a good idea about the circulation and control of science in the Spanish Americas. As we have seen through this brief exposition, science was a subject that circulated freely in the eighteenth-century Spanish empire. In fact, all knowledge that was considered useful for the development of society was actively encouraged. This is evident in the ninth rule for the censors in the Index of 1747, that stated that all books of magic and heresy should be prosecuted, but:

> They are permitted [to include] the judgments and observations on nature that are written, and those that are made to help navigation, agriculture or medicine: and those regarding the knowledge of the present time and the general events of the world that come from natural causes, such as eclipses, rain, moderate or dry weather.[74]

In other words: what was understood as science was exempt from censorship.

We are left with one question: why is the idea that scientific knowledge was repressed by the Inquisition so widespread? It might be explained by as forming part of the broader Black Legend that was fostered by Spain's rivals because it suited their cultural, political and economic interests.[75] This is why it is important to go back to the sources of the period, and try to understand censorship and the Inquisition as institutions of their time. When we do so, we find that the Inquisition enjoyed much popular support, and that it played a prominent role in the circulation of useful information, including works of medicine, science and practical knowledge.

---

74 Francisco Pérez de Prado y Cuesta, *Index librorum prohibitorum ac expurgandorum novissimus pro ... Ferdinandi VI regis catholici, Hac ultima editione ... Francisci Perez de Prado ... auctus et luculenter ac vigilantissime correctus; de Consilio Supremi Senatus Inquisitionis Generalis* (Matriti: ex calcographia Emmanuelis Fernandez, 1747), p. 14.

75 Ricardo García Cárcel and Doris Moreno Martínez, 'La Inquisición y el debate sobre la tolerancia en Europa en el siglo XVIII', *Bulletin hispanique*, 104 (2002), p. 199.

CHAPTER 6

The Troubles of a Protestant Bookseller in a Catholic Market

The Nuremberg Bookseller Johann Friedrich Rüdiger (1686–1751) and the Prague Book Trade

Mona Garloff

When the Berlin publisher Friedrich Nicolai visited southern Germany in the 1780s, his verdict about the book markets of Nuremberg and Augsburg was condescending, even if he acknowledged the immense stocks and enormous financial success of the publishing houses there.[1] Similar clichés about the 'backwardness' of the south German book markets were reproduced in other eighteenth- and nineteenth-century travel accounts. The perception of a 'bibliopolar' division between north and south Germany was further enhanced by Leipzig book historians in the late nineteenth and early twentieth centuries, such as Johann Goldfriedrich in his *Geschichte des deutschen Buchhandels* (1908).[2]

---

1   Cf. on the Augsburg book trade: 'The Catholic booksellers in Augsburg are true wholesalers. The bookstores of the Brothers Veith and Mr. Joseph Wolf are among the largest and richest in Germany, and perhaps even in Europe. Their warehouses are immeasurable and in their offices they do business of such importance (in terms of the amount involved) unlike anything a single Protestant bookseller can achieve. The great important works (important in terms of prices) which they have undertaken and are still undertaking on a daily basis are sufficient to show how widespread their trade is.'['Die katholischen Buchhändler in Augsburg sind wahre Großisten. Die Buchhandlungen der Herren Gebrüder Veith und des Hrn. Joseph Wolf gehören zu den größten und reichsten in Deutschland, und vielleicht in Europa. Ihre Niederlagen sind unermeßlich, und in ihren Schreibstuben werden Geschäfte von solcher Wichtigkeit, den Summen nach, gemacht, wie sie gewiß von keinem einzigen protestantischen Buchhändler gemacht werden. Die großen wichtigen Werke (nämlich wichtig den Kosten nach) die sie unternommen haben und noch täglich unternehmen, zeigen genugsam, wie ausgebreitet ihr Handel ist.'] Friedrich Nicolai, *Beschreibung einer Reise durch Deutschland und die Schweiz, im Jahre 1781* (vol. 8, Berlin/Stettin: Nicolai, 1787), pp. 53f.; cf. Helmut Gier, 'Buchdruck und Verlagswesen in Augsburg vom Dreißigjährigen Krieg bis zum Ende der Reichsstadt', in Helmut Gier and Johannes Janota (eds.), *Augsburger Buchdruck und Verlagswesen. Von den Anfängen bis zur Gegenwart* (Wiesbaden: Harrassowitz, 1997), pp. 479–516, pp. 479–481. I am grateful to Petr Maťa (Vienna) and Jonathan Singerton (Amsterdam) for reading and commenting on this chapter.
2   Johann Goldfriedrich, *Geschichte des Deutschen Buchhandels vom Westfälischen Frieden bis zum Beginn der klassischen Litteraturperiode (1648–1740)* (Leipzig: Börsenverein der dt. Buchhändler, 1908), p. 336 et passim.

When analysing book history of the Holy Roman Empire in the eighteenth century, contemporary scholarship usually places a narrow focus on Enlightenment literature. The German-speaking world's most important trade hub from this perspective was the Leipzig fair. This is problematic, as it continues the perception of a division of the book market into a progressive Protestant section in the central and north German territories, and a 'backward', predominantly Catholic part in the Holy Roman Empire's south and south-eastern regions. Even if the commercial strength of the south German imperial cities Augsburg and Nuremberg has been acknowledged in the secondary literature, this division is upheld through a Protestant and Prussian-centred view of history until this day.[3] In this perspective, the entire German-speaking book trade is geared towards the crucial role of Leipzig and its Enlightenment publications.[4] The understanding of economic modernisation is tied too closely to normative criteria of an Enlightenment-oriented selection of books. As scholarship continues to mirror these anachronistic categorisations, this contribution proposes to investigate the activities of south German publishers, their trading agents, and markets in the Habsburg Monarchy, in order to provide a more comprehensive analysis of the book markets in the Holy Roman Empire. In-depth analysis of these important markets and long-distance trade relationships will advance our understanding of different centres of the book trade in the Holy Roman Empire, in particular with respect to distribution networks. The importance of confession in the book trade around 1700 is of particular interest, since the majority of these booksellers belonged to the Protestant faith. While they had no qualms about producing Catholic pious and devotional literature, as market players, they were subject to trade restrictions varying from territory to territory. This means, in practice, to move significantly beyond the corpus of Enlightenment literature: we will consider the book trade more comprehensively by taking the entire offer of bestselling books into account, ranging from prayer and devotional

---

3 Reinhard Wittmann, *Geschichte des deutschen Buchhandels* (3rd ed., München: Beck, 2011), p. 96, listed the centres of book production in the Holy Roman Empire with the number of relevant companies between 1701 and 1750: Augsburg (150 firms), Leipzig (145), Nuremberg (99), Frankfurt/Main (98), Cologne (93), Hamburg (76), Halle/Saale (61), Jena (58), Berlin (53), Vienna (53) und Basel (41).

4 Cf. for example Thomas Fuchs, 'Buchhandel und Verlagswesen', in Detlef Döring (ed.), *Geschichte der Stadt Leipzig* (Leipzig: Leipziger Universitätsverlag, 2016), vol 2, pp. 234–271; Monika Estermann, 'Memoria und Diskurs. Der Buchhandel in der Frühaufklärung', in Hans Erich Bödeker (ed.), *Strukturen der deutschen Frühaufklärung 1680–1720* (Göttingen: Vandenhoeck & Ruprecht, 2008), pp. 45–70; Hazel Rosenstrauch, 'Leipzig als 'Centralplatz' des deutschen Buchhandels', in Wolfgang Martens (ed.), *Leipzig. Aufklärung und Bürgerlichkeit* (Heidelberg: Schneider, 1990), pp. 103–124.

books to sermons, self-help literature, occasional works as well as almanacs and calendars.

The case study of the bookseller Johann Friedrich Rüdiger (1686–1751) will allow us to examine these general assumptions in greater detail: the Nuremberg bookseller Rüdiger established himself, over the course of for decades, as one of the most influential traders in the Prague book market. His confession deserves special attention, as do his conflicts with the authorities, which he became involved in due to his book selection, and issues related to his attempts to open a permanent bookshop in Prague.

The analysis of the long-distance book trade in the Holy Roman Empire reveals the connections between shared economic zones, that scholars usually divide along spaces and historiographies of later nation states. Investments in long-distance book trade were an influential part in the book business from the sixteenth century onwards and gained again more importance with the establishment of wholesale publishers by the end of the seventeenth century. Major publishers with sufficient capital in Augsburg and Nuremberg managed to dominate the book markets in Bavaria and the Austrian and Bohemian lands. These developments, however, apart from affecting regional trade, reduced the influence of the Leipzig book trade in these markets. It also calls into question the established division of the German-language book trade. This article expands the approach to distribution channels: the fairs of Leipzig and, to a lesser extent, Frankfurt, were significant for the book trade at the beginning of the eighteenth century, as booksellers could stock up on new publications there.[5] But we must not neglect the importance of regional markets and international publishing contacts beyond the fairs.

While most studies on German book history focus mainly on the second half of the eighteenth century, I hold that the decades after 1680 were a period of significant change for the book trade.[6] From the late seventeenth century

---

5 Cf. for an evaluation of the book fair catalogues, Carl Gustav Schwetschke, *Codex nundinarius Germaniae literatae bisecularis. Meß-Jahrbücher des deutschen Buchhandels von dem Erscheinen des ersten Meß-Kataloges im Jahre 1564 bis zur Gründung des ersten Buchhändlervereins im Jahre 1765* (Halle a.d. Saale: Schwetschke, 1850 [reprint: Nieuwkoop 1963]), Johan L. Flood, 'Omnium totius orbis emporium compendium: The Frankfurt Fair in the Early Modern Period', in Robin Myers, Michael Harris and Giles Mandelbrote (eds.), *Fairs, Markets and the Itinerant Book Trade* (New Castle/London: Oak Knoll, 2007), pp. 1–42.

6 Cf. for example Johannes Frimmel and Michael Wögerbauer (eds.), *Kommunikation und Information im 18. Jahrhundert. Das Beispiel der Habsburgermonarchie* (Wiesbaden: Harrassowitz, 2009); Giles Barber/Bernhard Fabian (eds.), *Buch und Buchhandel in Europa im achtzehnten Jahrhundert/The Book and the Book Trade in Eighteenth-Century* (Hamburg: Hauswedell, 1981); Christine Haug, Franziska Mayer and Winfried Schröder (eds.), *Geheimliteratur und Geheimbuchhandel in Europa im 18. Jahrhundert* (Wiesbaden: Harrassowitz, 2011).

onwards, the barter trade encouraged the establishment of major publishing corporations, which were based in urban centres, and offered a wide assortment of stock in addition to their own publications. Their offers, kept up to date by direct orders as well as fair purchases, were greatly sought after in all of Central Europe. Limiting the period in question to the middle of the eighteenth century is justified by the gradual transition to cash trade, which took place at that time. Booksellers in Leipzig, Berlin or Hamburg gave up the assortment trade successively. While in the central and north German territories a new system of book trade on commission was introduced, the assortment trade in the Holy Roman Empire's south and south-eastern territories proved profitable for a longer period after that. The reforming policies of Empress Maria Theresia created new economic circumstances for the booksellers in the Austrian and Bohemian lands. Starting in the 1720s, there were noticeable restrictions due to mercantilist measures, and the accompanying step-by-step standardisation of state censorship norms. By taking Johann Friedrich Rüdiger as an example, we will analyse how foreign traders adapted to changing circumstances, and protected their own businesses in most cases.

Long-distance trade requires investment in logistics and the build-up of supply chains, which influence sales practices and shape individual commercial identities. Frequently, booksellers invested in faraway markets, to stave off competition within their own city, which was growing ever more intense towards the end of the seventeenth century. Writing the history of the book trade means not only considering the successful, striving firms, but also taking into account their less fortunate competitors, sellers and publishers alike, to reconstruct a more comprehensive account of the seventeenth and early eighteenth centuries.

In research on the history of the book in the decades around 1700, bookselling publishers in the Holy Roman Empire have been almost entirely neglected so far, as have their relations within the book trade.[7] Studies on major booksellers of that era place the emphasis on local publishing, or on relationships connected to the fair trade, but rarely on book distribution and the markets in a trans-regional framework. The few individual studies on the major publishing houses of the seventeenth and early eighteenth centuries focus on the titles published, while aspects of distribution and retail are neglected. This is true for the Leipzig publishers (Fritsch, Gleditsch, Weidmann), those

---

7 Cf. Oliver Duntze, 'Verlagsbuchhandel und verbreitender Buchhandel von der Erfindung des Buchdrucks bis 1700', in Ursula Rautenberg (ed.), *Buchwissenschaft in Deutschland. Ein Handbuch.* (2 vols.; Berlin/Boston: De Gruyter, 2010), I, pp. 203–256.

in Augsburg (Veith, Wolff), and in Nuremberg (Endter, Lochner, Hoffmann).[8] The sales markets of Nuremberg and Augsburg booksellers in the Austrian and Bohemian lands, Salzburg, Bavaria or the Swiss Confederation have only been partially considered so far. The history of the book trade in Prague is limited to mere overviews for our period, and there is no systematic evaluation of long-distance book trade relationships to date.[9] The neglect of trade channels leads to research into the book trade running along the borders of present-day nation states, which prevents us from understanding the economic and cultural spheres of the early modern era as larger historic entities.[10]

By the late seventeenth century, investments in long-distance trade grew due to increased competition in the book business within a particular region or city. At this period, Nuremberg had risen to become a centre of publishing

---

[8] Cf. on Leipzig: Adalbert Brauer, 'Nachkommen des Leipziger Verlagsbuchhändlers Johann Friedrich Gleditsch. Vorfahren, Verwandtschaftskreis und soziologische Struktur', *Archiv für Geschichte des Buchwesens*, 3 (1961), pp. 77–96; Adalbert Brauer, 'Vom mittelsächsischen Obergräfenhain zum Weimarer Musenhof. Aus der Geschichte der Buchhändlerfamilie Fritsch', *Der junge Buchhandel*, 21 (1965), J149–J157; on Augsburg: Helmut Gier and Johannes Janota (eds.), *Augsburger Buchdruck und Verlagswesen. Von den Anfängen bis zur Gegenwart* (Wiesbaden: Harrassowitz, 1997); on Nuremberg: Michael Diefenbacher, Wiltrud Fischer-Pache et al. (eds.), *Das Nürnberger Buchgewerbe. Buch- und Zeitungsdrucker, Verleger und Druckhändler vom 16. bis zum 18. Jahrhundert* (Nürnberg: Stadtarchiv Nürnberg, 2003); Friedrich Oldenbourg: *Die Endter. Eine Nürnberger Buchhändlerfamilie (1590–1740)* (München/Berlin: Oldenbourg, 1911); in general David Paisey, *Deutsche Buchdrucker, Buchhändler und Verleger, 1701–1750* (Wiesbaden: Harrassowitz, 1988); Christoph Reske, *Die Buchdrucker des 16. und 17. Jahrhunderts im deutschen Sprachgebiet. Auf der Grundlage des gleichnamigen Werkes von Josef Benzing* (2nd ed., Wiesbaden: Harrassowitz, 2015).

[9] Cf. Michael Wögerbauer and Jiří Pokorný, 'Barocke Buchkultur in den Böhmischen Ländern', in Christian Gastgeber and Elisabeth Klecker (eds.), *Barock* (Graz: Akademische Druck- und Verlagsanstalt, 2015), pp. 383–426; Zdeněk Šimeček, *Geschichte des Buchhandels in Tschechien und in der Slowakei* (Wiesbaden: Harrassowitz, 2002); on Prague: Petr Voit, *Encyklopedie knihy. Starší knihtisk a obory příbuzné* (2 vol., Praha: Libri, 2008); Josef Volf, 'Zápas mědirytce Vusína s pražskými knihkupci', *Časopis Národního musea* 103 (1929), pp. 173–196; on the trade relationships with Nuremberg in general Olga Fejtová, Václav Ledvinka and Jiří Pešek (eds.), *Ztracená blízkost: Praha – Norimberk v proměnách staletí* (Praha: Scriptorium, 2010).

[10] Cf. on Germany: Wittmann, *Geschichte*; on Austria: Norbert Bachleitner, Franz M. Eybl and Ernst Fischer, *Geschichte des Buchhandels in Österreich* (Wiesbaden: Harrassowitz, 2000); Matthias Karmasin and Christian Oggolder (eds.), *Österreichische Mediengeschichte: Von den frühen Drucken zur Ausdifferenzierung des Mediensystems (1500 bis 1918)* (vol. 1, Wiesbaden: Springer VS, 2016), on Bohemia: see fn. 9; for a transnational approach: Frédéric Barbier (ed.), *Est – Ouest. Transferts et réceptions dans le monde du livre en Europe (XVIIe–XXe siècles) = L'Europe en réseaux. Contributions à l'histoire de la culture écrite 1650–1918* (vol. 2, Leipzig: Leipziger Univ. Verlag, 2005).

and sales for Catholic books. But at the beginning of the eighteenth century, Augsburg too acquired a leading role in the field of Catholic devotional literature far beyond its immediate environment. Its rise began with the arrival of the Catholic publishers Johann Caspar Bencard, originally from Dillingen, as well as Daniel Walder and Philipp Jakob Veith. The Protestant booksellers of the bi-confessional city Augsburg were represented almost in equal numbers and enjoyed an influential position as well, thanks to the wide range of their commercial relationships, and the dominant role of Protestants in copper engraving.[11] The bi-confessional status of Augsburg proved a clear advantage for the imperial city, but this inevitably caused conflicts between Catholic and Protestant publishers (about the publication of successful *catholica*, for instance).[12] The rise of Augsburg caused an economic decline of several Nurmberg firms involved in the book business. Publishers such as Felsecker sought to counteract the loss of influence by turning to newspaper publishing. Other publishers such as Johann Friedrich Rüdiger could balance their economic losses by trading with the Austrian and Bohemian lands, gradually establishing a permanent presence with storehouses and bookshops. To a significant extent, the book trade in the Habsburg Monarchy was determined by influential Nuremberg booksellers such as Johann Friedrich Rüdiger, Georg Lehmann or Peter Conrad Monath.

Looking at Prague, we will explore not only one of the most important centres of the trade in the Habsburg Monarchy, but also pursue distribution channels of long-distance trade. Companies operating in Prague could usually draw on a wide sales network for different market interests: Leipzig publishers, such as Fritsch or Gleditsch, were serious competition for Nuremberg traders in Prague. Apart from this, however, Leipzig booksellers were hardly represented in other commercial centres in the Habsburg realm, and often had to arrange commission-based deals with the Nuremberg publishers (for example in Vienna). Firms from Nuremberg and Augsburg (to a lesser extent, also those from Regensburg or Ulm) dominated the trade along the Danube, and frequented the markets of Linz and Krems. The central importance of the Danube trade for south German publishers becomes apparent through the entries in the toll registers (Aschach) and weighing and warehouse books (Krems).[13]

---

[11] A prominent example is Christoph Weigel the Elder (who moved his business to Nuremberg in 1698), cf. Étienne François, 'Buchhandel und Buchgewerbe in Augsburg im 17. und 18. Jahrhundert', in Jochen Brüning and Friedrich Niewöhner (eds.), *Augsburg in der Frühen Neuzeit. Beiträge zu einem Forschungsprogramm* (Berlin: Akademie Verlag, 1995), pp. 332–342, here pp. 339–340.

[12] Cf. Étienne François, *Die unsichtbare Grenze. Protestanten und Katholiken in Augsburg 1648–1806* (Sigmaringen: Thorbecke, 1991).

[13] Cf. the research project on Danube trade, directed by Peter Rauscher of the University of Vienna, donauhandel.univie.ac.at; for the markets of Krems: Peter Rauscher, 'Die

The legal situation of foreign traders was closely tied to conditions set by the regional authorities. Comparing Vienna to Prague, there were noticeable differences in local regulations. The Viennese wholesale trade had favoured the influential position of foreign merchants since the sixteenth century.[14] The warehouse traders ('Niederleger') could solidify their position and privileges as extraterritorial wholesalers in the face of resistance from the city-based merchants: they enjoyed freedom of religion and were exempt from taxation, except for poll taxes, and fees for customs and toll. Even if in the general scale of trade, books only played a minor role, the warehouse traders made for serious competition for the local firms. They had financially strong head offices and good connections to the fairs, to which the Viennese publishers hardly had access. Wolfgang Moritz Endter, Georg Lehmann or Peter Conrad Monath illustrate the influential position of Nuremberg booksellers in Vienna. The tightening of customs regulations and import bans from the 1720s onwards, until new legislation on wholesale trade was passed in 1774, led to foreign merchants endeavouring to set up permanent publishing branches in the Austrian territories, and to print their books in Vienna – if necessary, by purchasing a printing press there.[15]

Unlike the liberal business opportunities in Vienna, foreign merchants in Bohemia and Prague only held restricted trading rights. These regulations were directed against the dominant position of the Nuremberg trade. Decrees limited trading hours to their presence on the main markets of Prague, which

---

Kremser Märkte im 17. Jahrhundert (ca. 1620–1730). Städtischer Fernhandel und staatliche Wirtschaftspolitik im Zeitalter des beginnenden Merkantilismus', in Guillaume Garner and Sandra Richter (eds.), ‚Eigennutz' und ‚gute Ordnung'. Ökonomisierungen der Welt im 17. Jahrhundert (Wiesbaden: Harrassowitz, 2016), pp. 95–112; on the book trade in Linz: Rudolf M. Henke and Gerhard Winkler, Geschichte des Buchhandels in Linz (Linz: Archiv der Stadt Linz, 2002).

14 Cf. on the Viennese warehousers: Peter Rauscher and Andrea Serles, 'Die Wiener Niederleger um 1700. Eine kaufmännische Elite zwischen Handel, Staatsfinanzen und Gewerbe', in Oliver Kühschelm (eds.), Geld – Markt – Akteure / Money – Market – Actors (Innsbruck/Wien: StudienVerlag, 2015), pp. 154–182; Günther Chaloupek, Peter Eigner and Michael Wagner (eds.), Wien Wirtschaftsgeschichte 1740–1938: Dienstleistungen (vol. 2, Wien: Jugend und Volk, 1991), pp. 1001–1019; Helene Kuraić, Die Wiener Niederleger im 18. Jahrhundert. Diss. Univ. Wien, 1946; on the book trade: Bachleitner, Eybl and Fischer, Geschichte des Buchhandels in Österreich, pp. 69–72, 117–121; Martin Scheutz, 'Legalität und unterdrückte Religionsausübung. Niederleger, Reichshofräte, Gesandte und Legationsprediger. Protestantisches Leben in der Haupt- und Residenzstadt Wien im 17. und 18. Jahrhundert', in Rudolf Leeb, Martin Scheutz and Dietmar Weikl (eds.), Geheimprotestantismus und evangelische Kirchen in der Habsburgermonarchie und im Erzstift Salzburg (17./18. Jahrhundert) (Wien: Böhlau, 2008), pp. 209–236.

15 Cf. on the Viennese book trade in the second half of the eighteenth century: Peter R. Frank and Johannes Frimmel, Buchwesen in Wien 1750–1850. Kommentiertes Verzeichnis der Buchdrucker, Buchhändler und Verleger (Wiesbaden: Harrassowitz, 2008).

were held on the church holidays of St. Wenceslaus, St. Vitus or Candlemas.[16] Outside of these market days, wares had to be kept in sealed storehouses. Booksellers involved in the long-distance trade could offer their goods up to one third cheaper than local booksellers in Prague.[17] Because he sold books outside the regular market hours, traders such as Johann Friedrich Rüdiger repeatedly came into conflict with the authorities. In order to facilitate logistics, and to establish a permanent presence for their commercial activities, financially-savvy publishers sought to open branch stores.

For the first half of the eighteenth century, we can trace several requests from book traders to set up shops and to obtain the right of citizenship, which were, however, mostly rejected. In this context, we must also scrutinise the importance of religious confession in trade: to what extent did religion determine the integration of foreign merchants in the city? How was this used as grounds to regulate trade concessions? We will see that foreign booksellers such as Rüdiger were dependent on co-operation with local representatives in the book trade. Johann Friedrich Rüdiger's more than forty-year-long commercial operations in Prague is emblematic for the history of the book trade in that city for the first half of the eighteenth century. His establishment in the book business can be studied from four perspectives: by analysing 1) family networks in the book trade between Nuremberg and Prague; 2) Rüdiger's publishing programme; 3) his cladestine activities in the book trade and conflicts with censorship; and 4) Rüdiger's repeated attemps to acquire trade privileges to open a permanent book shop in Prague.

1   Family Networks in the Book Trade between Nuremberg and Prague

Johann Friedrich Rüdiger was born on 6 August 1686 in Heidelberg, presumably as the son of Johann Michael Rüdiger (1651–1734).[18] His father was a privileged book dealer of the Elector Palatine and the University of Heidelberg. The siege during the Palatine War of Succession (1688–1697) destroyed his father's business, so he moved to Berlin. In contrast to his older brother Johann Andreas

---

16   Cf. the decree of Emperor Leopold I of 1692 (confirming previous ordinances): *Codex Ferdinandeo – Leopoldino – Josephino – Carolinus. Pro haereditario Regno Bohemiae, ac incorporatis aliis Provinciis, utpote, Marchionatu Moraviae, et Ducatu Silesiae* (Prag: Mullem, 1720), pp. 563f.
17   Šimeček, *Geschichte des Buchhandels*, p. 31.
18   Regina Mahlke, 'Rüdiger, Michael', in *Neue Deutsche Biographie* 22 (2005), p. 215, www.deutsche-biographie.de/pnd136872115.html.

(c.1683–1751), who worked in Potsdam and Berlin as a book dealer and newspaper publisher, Johann Friedrich's biography still contains significant gaps.[19] Johann Friedrich Rüdiger completed his apprenticeship in Nuremberg and became a bookseller's assistant in the publishing house of Johann Zieger (1646–1711).[20] In 1706, Rüdiger married his employer's daughter, Clara Susanna, which granted him the rights of a citizen of Nuremberg.[21] From the 1680s onwards, Zieger regularly visited the Prague markets, so Rüdiger was able to familiarise himself with the trade in Bohemia early on. After Zieger's death in January 1712, Rüdiger took over his book stock, which was located 'in the trading shop of the house named 'Paradise' in the Old Town (Staré Město) of Prague.[22] Rüdiger traded until at least 1748 during market sessions in the Old Town of Prague. In the Nuremberg Register of Offices [Ämterbuch], he is listed as a book dealer from 1716 on. Perhaps he took over Zieger's bookstore in Prague in that year, which, in the meantime, had been run by Zieger's widow.[23] Rüdiger's appointment as a member of the Greater Council in 1720 was a further step up the social ladder in the city of Nuremberg.[24] Marriage ties further bolstered Rüdiger's trade relations: Johann Zieger had married his second daughter Elisabeth to the bookseller Georg Lehmann (1666–1735) in 1697. From this point on, Zieger and Lehmann co-operated in a joint publishing venture. From 1704 onwards, they are both listed as book dealers in the Nuremberg Register of Offices.[25]

---

19 Cf. for Johann Andreas Rüdiger: Klaus Bender, 'Vossische Zeitung, Berlin (1617–1934)', in Heinz-Dietrich Fischer (ed.), *Deutsche Zeitungen des 17. bis 20. Jahrhunderts* (Pullach bei München: Ver. Dokumentation, 1972), pp. 25–40. His brother (?) Johann Heinrich Rüdiger (died ca. 1765) was active in Berlin, Danzig and Stettin, cf. Paisey, *Deutsche Buchdrucker*, p. 217.

20 Cf. Manfred H. Grieb et al. (eds.), *Nürnberger Künstlerlexikon. Bildende Künstler, Kunsthandwerker, Gelehrte, Sammler, Kulturschaffende und Mäzene vom 12. bis zur Mitte des 20. Jahrhunderts* (4 vols.; Berlin/Boston: De Gruyter, 2007), III, pp. 1727f.; 'Johann Ziegler', in *Přispěvatelé Encyklopedie knihy*, www.encyklopedieknihy.cz/index.php?title=Johann_Zieger&oldid=15000.

21 *Nürnberger Künstlerlexikon*, vol. 3, p. 1281; Staatsarchiv Nürnberg [State Archive Nuremberg], Ratsverläße, No. 3119, fol. 115b (28 May 1706); No. 3114, fol. 40 (4 January 1706); No. 3119, fol. 110b (26 May 1706). Cf. the registers Diefenbacher, Fischer-Pache, *Das Nürnberger Buchgewerbe*, pp. 439, 476.

22 'In dem Hauß Baradeyß genandt condicirten Handels-Laaden'. Archiv hlavního města Prahy [Prague City Archives], PPL IV, 8939 (28.01.1712). The house 'im Paradies' is still to be found on the Malé náměstí (No. 1).

23 *Nürnberger Künstlerlexikon*, vol. 3, pp. 1727f.
24 *Nürnberger Künstlerlexikon*, vol. 3, p. 1281.
25 *Nürnberger Künstlerlexikon*, vol. 2, p. 902.

FIGURE 6.1 Portrait of Johann Friedrich Rüdiger
Austrian National Library (PORT_00142196_01)

The alternating sales strategy of the books they published reflects the relationship of the brothers-in-law Rüdiger and Lehmann, as does their co-ordination of the printing work. They divided the markets between themselves: Rüdiger concentrated his trade on Prague, where Lehmann initially also published books from 1702 onwards (in co-operation with Zieger). After 1706, however, Lehmann focussed his business increasingly on Brno (Brünn), where he endeavoured to obtain an official permit as a trader. His entrepreneurial activities can also be traced to Olomouc (Olmütz) and Bratislava (Preßburg). In Brno, Lehmann published a range of works, frequently reprints of his Prague editions. In 1717, his repeated request to establish a bookstore in the Brno 'Landhaus' was finally rejected, most likely because Lehmann was a Protestant. As a consequence, his stock of books in Brno was confiscated. Lehmann kept his main store in Nuremberg, and managed to set himself up, from 1710 onwards, as a warehouse trader in Vienna.[26] Rüdiger's relations with his brother-in-law Lehmann enabled him to use the direct channels of trade to Brno and Vienna. Rüdiger also benefited from Lehman's publishing focus on catholic sermons and devotional literature for his own book assortment.

2   Rüdiger's Publishing Programme

Johann Friedrich Rüdiger was continuously present at the fairs in Frankfurt and Leipzig for three decades. Between 1710 and 1743, he presented, on average, six of his books at the fairs, and was absent for only five years during this period.[27] It is remarkable, however, that – according to the sources – Rüdiger never applied for imperial printing privileges. In the files of the imperial book commission in Frankfurt am Main, he is listed only with non-privileged books. This is worth mentioning, because a large number of book traders who operated in the long-distance trade of the Habsburg Monarchy applied for such privileges.[28] The books he printed in Prague were intended for the Bohemian

---

26   Cf. Zdeněk Šimeček, *Knižní obchod v Brně od sklonku 15. do konce 18. Století* (Brno: Archiv města Brna, 2011), passim; Bachleitner, Eybl and Fischer, *Geschichte des Buchhandels*, pp. 71f.; *Nürnberger Künstlerlexikon*, vol. 2, p. 902; Karel Chyba, *Slovník knihtiskařů v Československu od nejstarších dob do roku 1860*. 1966[–1976] [Příloha Sborníku PNP Strahovská knihovna 1966[–1976], pp. 171f.

27   According to the information in Schwetschke, *Codex nundinarius*, pp. 188–221.

28   Cf. Hans-Joachim Koppitz (ed.): *Die kaiserlichen Druckprivilegien im Haus-, Hof- und Staatsarchiv. Verzeichnis der Akten vom Anfang des 16. Jahrhunderts bis zum Ende des Deutschen Reichs (1806)*, (Wiesbaden: Harrassowitz, 2008); Hans-Joachim Koppitz: 'Die Privilegia impressoria im Haus-, Hof- und Staatsarchiv in Wien', *Gutenberg-Jahrbuch*, 69 (1994), pp. 188–207.

market, where official approval by the archbishop was more useful than imperial printing privileges.[29]

Rüdiger's continuous presence at the Frankfurt and Leipzig fairs, as well as his book list prove that he was a successful assortment retail trader. Secondly, this shows that the books he published were meant to be sold over a wide geographic area, and that his German-language *Bohemica* were directed at readers in the entire Holy Roman Empire.[30] Today, in the library catalogues of the Czech Republic, Austria and Germany, we can identify 96 books which were published by Rüdiger in one or several print runs between 1710 and 1751. Around 45 of these were published in Prague, or with the double impressum 'Nuremberg – Vienna'.

Rüdiger's publishing profile indicates several points of thematic focus. Aside from dictionaries and grammar books in French, Spanish and Latin, as well as medical and alchemistic treatises, a special emphasis was placed on legal works.[31] A number of these books, such as *Extractus iuris provincialis* (1710) or *Manuductio ad praxim juridicam* (1729, 1751) were printed in Prague. Early on, Rüdiger specialised in the publication of *Bohemica* in German. Under the false impressum 'Amstelædami, Apud Joh. Frider. Rüdigerum 1713', he published Pavel Stránský's *Respublica bohemiae* (first edition: Leiden, 1634).[32] The *Bohemica* also included specialist studies of Bohemian Law, such as the *Alphabetische[n] Auszug der gesammten alt und neuen Böhmischen Gesetze*

---

29 From 1708 onwards imperial printing privileges no longer included the territories of Bohemia, Moravia and Silesia. For these markets booksellers would have had to apply for territorial printing privileges (approved by the Bohemian Court Chancellery) or to request an extension of the imperial privileges at the Imperial Aulic Council.

30 Antonín Měšťan, 'Die Produktion von Büchern in tschechischer Sprache im 18. Jahrhundert', in Herbert Göpfert, Gerard Kozielek and Reinhard Wittmann (eds.), *Buch- und Verlagswesen im 18. und 19. Jahrhundert. Beiträge zur Geschichte der Kommunikation in Mittel- und Osteuropa* (Berlin: Camen, 1977), pp. 130–137; Mirjam Bohatcová, 'Die Anfänge der typographischen Zusammenarbeit zwischen Nürnberg und. Böhmen', in *Gutenberg-Jahrbuch*, 1976, pp. 147–155; Elisabeth Beare, *Fremdsprachiger Buchdruck in Nürnberg (15.–20. Jh.)* (Ausstellungskatalog, Nürnberg: Stadtbibliothek Nürnberg 1984).

31 A selection of first editions: Antoine Perger, *Parfaite Grammaire Françoise* (Nürnberg: Rüdiger, 1713); *Teutsch-Lateinisches WörterBüchlein. Zum Nutz und Ergötzung der Schul-Jugend zusammen getragen* (Nürnberg: Rüdiger, 1722); Johann Helferich Jüngken, *Wohlunterrichtetender Sorgfältiger Medicus. Welcher nach denen Grund-Reguln so aus der heutigen Anatomie und Chymie hergenommen* (Nürnberg: Rüdiger, 1725); *Die gantz neue eröffnete Pforte zu dem Chymischen Kleinod. Oder einige vornehmste Chymische Arcana* (Nürnberg: Rüdiger, 1728).

32 Pavel Stránský, *De Republica Bojema. Opus utilisimum, quod propter excellentiam suam Typo novo donatum, addita Præfatione Frider. Roth-Scholtzii* (Amstelaedami [Nürnberg: Rüdiger], 1713).

(1741) by Johann Georg Miller von Muehlensdorf.[33] Books describing countries and cities proved successful too: *Das Sehens-würdige Prag* von Carl Adolph Redel saw several reprints.[34] In another case, Rüdiger cleverly adapted an earlier edition: the *Historisch- und Geographische Beschreibung des Königreichs Böhmens* (Nuremberg – Prague, 1742) almost resembled *Das Jetzt-lebende Königreich Böhmen* by Moritz Johann Vogt, with only minor variations. Rüdiger had probably published the latter work already in 1712, under the name of his meanwhile deceased father-in-law Zieger. Rüdiger also used the copper engravings of the earlier version.

At the beginning of the book, there is a highly detailed description of the estates of Franz Anton Graf von Sporck, and of the towns of Kuks (Kukus) and Lysá nad Labem (Lissa at the Elbe river).[35] The copper engravings bear Zieger's dedication to Sporck. Thus, we may assume that Sporck financed the printing of this volume, and if not entirely, at least those chapters describing his estates as well as the illustrations. Rüdiger evidently benefited from the publication network and relations that Zieger had already established earlier in Bohemia.

The publication history of the *Biblia Sacra*, a work which was in the hands of the Nuremberg printing houses, illustrates again the inter-generational process of creating a publishing identity, and reveals at the same time business pragmatism by keeping successful titles in the publishing catalogue. In 1701, Johann Zieger and Georg Lehmann reprinted Caspar Ulenberg's German translation of the Bible, which had first appeared in 1630.[36] Since there was a

---

33 See Wenceslas X. Neumann von Puchholtz, *Tractatus Juridico-Practici de Abusibus Quibusdam Praxeos Boemiae et de Specialitatibus Juris Boemici* (Nürnberg: Rüdiger, 1731 (Nürnberg 1733, Prag 1729)); [Johann Georg Müller von Müllendorf], *Alphabetischer Auszug der gesammten Alt und Neuen Böhmischen Gesetze* (Prag: Rüdiger, 1741).

34 *Das Sehens-würdige Prag. Worinnen Alle sehens- merck- und Wunderwürdige Begebenheiten, Denckmahle und Antiquitäten ... kürtzlich vorgestellet werden* (Nürnberg/Prag: Rüdiger, s.d. [1728], second edition 1730).

35 Cf. Heinrich Benedikt, *Franz Anton Graf von Sporck (1662–1738). Zur Kultur der Barockzeit in Böhmen*. (Wien: Manz, 1923); Pavel Preiss, *František Antonín Špork a barokní kultura v Čechách*. (2nd ed., Praha: Paseka, 2003); Joachim Bahlcke, 'Bücherschmuggel. Die Versorgung ostmitteleuropäischer Protestanten mit Bibeln, Gesangbüchern und lutherischen Erbauungsschriften in der Zeit der Gegenreformation', in Joachim Bahlcke, Beate Störtkuhl and Matthias Weber (eds.), *Der Luthereffekt im östlichen Europa. Geschichte – Kultur – Erinnerung* (Berlin/Boston: De Gruyter, 2017), pp. 161–176.

36 Cf. Uwe Köster, Studien zu den katholischen deutschen Bibelübersetzungen im 16., 17. und 18. Jahrhundert (Münster: Aschendorff, 1995), p. 226; Arnd Müller, 'Zensurpolitik der Reichsstadt Nürnberg. Von der Einführung der Buchdruckerkunst bis zum Ende der Reichsstadt', *Mitteilungen des Vereins für Geschichte der Stadt Nüremberg*, 59 (1959), pp. 66–169.

ban on printing Catholic books in Nuremberg itself, they moved to Bamberg, using the printing press in Fürth.[37] Here, the translation saw five print runs. After Zieger's death, Rüdiger published again two print runs in Bamberg (1713 and 1718). In 1730, Rüdiger prepared a further edition for the Bohemian book market, which was printed in Prague by Matthias Adam Höger.[38] The publication was approved by the Prague archbishop, which was gratefully acknowledged at the first pages of the *Biblia Sacra*. With this official permission, which included the right to produce future editions (Prague 1731), it became possible for the Protestant publisher Rüdiger to print a Catholic work in Prague. Further approbations, granted by Adolf Franziskus Steckel, the president curator [Praeses curatus] of the *Deutsches Haus* [German House] in Nuremberg, and by the Bamberg theologian and dean Johann Ernestus Schubert in 1703 for a previous print of this work to Zieger, were also reproduced in the Prague edition. Perhaps Rüdiger and Lehmann had agreed on a common strategy for this new edition. While Rüdiger's version was intended for sale on the book markets of Prague, Lehmann was planning a new edition of the *Biblia Sacra* for Vienna. For this and subsequent editions, Lehmann applied for an imperial printing privilege, which was granted to him on 27 June 1731 for six years.[39] Lehmann's edition of the *Biblia Sacra*, which was published in Vienna between 1732 and 1734, mentioned Zieger's version from 1701 in the preface, but completely ignores Rüdiger's prints, in order to safeguard the printing privilege.[40]

Rüdiger continued to publish religious works, such as Catholic devotional books and sermons. This included reprints of titles from the fifteenth and sixteenth centuries, including the *Nachfolge Christi* of Thomas à Kempis and *Das Leben des Geistes, oder geistliche Leben* of Antonio de Rojas. Rüdiger published the German translation of *Das Christliche Jahr, oder Die Messen auf die*

---

37 *Sacra Biblia Das ist: Die gantze Heilige Schrifft, Alten und Neuen Testaments. Nach der letzten Römischen Sixtiner Edition* (Bamberg: Zieger/Lehmann, 1701).

38 *Sacra Biblia, Das ist die gantze Heil. Schrifft Alten nd Neuen Testaments, Nach der letzten Römischen Sixtiner Edition* (Prag: Rüdiger 1730). The title page indicates that this edition was the sixth print run ('In diesem sechsten Druck aufs neue mit Fleiß übersehen'). It was printed for the first time at Cologne and Bamberg; the Prague edition of 1730 was printed by Matthias Adam Höger, printer of the Prague archdiocese, and published by Johann Friedrich Rüdiger ('Erstlich gedruckt zu Cölln und Bamberg, anjetzo aber zu Prag in Königs-Hoff bey Matthias Adam Höger, Hochfürstlich-Ertz-Bischöflichen Buchdruckern, An. 1730. Verlegts, Johann Friedrich Rüdiger').

39 Österreichisches Staatsarchiv, Wien [Austrian State Archives, Vienna], Haus-, Hof- und Staatsarchiv, Reichshofratsakten, Impressorien 41, Nr. 7, Bl. 26–30.

40 *Sacra Biblia, Das ist Die gantze Heilige Schrifft Alten und Neuen Testaments* (Wien: Lehmann, 1732–1734: three parts in one volume: *Das Alte Testament* (1734), *Die Propheten* (1733), *Das Neue Testament* (1732)).

Sonn- Gemeine- Ferial- und Fest-Täge des gantzen Jahrs of the Jansenist Nicolas Le Tourneux, an interpretation of the epistles and the gospels for the liturgical year. This work, commissioned by Franz Anton Graf von Sporck, was banned for print in Bohemia. Due to the interdiction of printing Catholic books in Nuremberg, Rüdiger had this work (according to the impressum) printed in Würzburg.[41] Nevertheless, the final luxury edition voluminous edition of the *Christliches Jahr*, illustrated with elaborate copper engravings by the Nuremberg artists Michael Heinrich Rentz and Johann Daniel de Montalegre, was printed in Prague in 1733–34.[42] This commission by Sporck arose from the connections that Rüdiger's father-in-law had already established, and which were strengthened by his assistant Friedrich Roth-Scholtz.

We have evidence that Roth-Scholtz accompanied Zieger and, later, Rüdiger on business trips to Prague in the years between 1709 and 1714.[43] It is likely that the two book traders encountered Franz Anton Graf von Sporck in Prague. Sporck's autobiography, *Leben Eines Herrlichen Bildes Wahrer und rechtschaffener Frömmigkeit*, which also contains a substantial collection of his trial records, was probably smuggled out of the country by Rüdiger and Roth-Scholtz. Both remained in touch with the count over the following years, who was getting into increasing difficulties because of a number of trials for heresy. As the correspondence between Sporck and Roth-Scholtz proves, the publisher took several years to prepare the release of the count's autobiography. The first edition mentions the author's pseudonym Ferdinand van der Roxas, and gives the false impressum 'Amsterdam: Rudolph van der Leewen 1715'.[44] As we have seen in the case of Pavel Stránský's *Respublica bohemiae*, Rüdiger used

---

41 [Nicolas Le Tourneux], *Das Christliche Jahr, Oder Die Messen auf die Sonn- Gemeine- Ferial- und Fest-Täge des gantzen Jahrs, in teutscher Sprach* (11 parts in 2 vols.; Würtzburg [Nürnberg]: Rüdiger, 1716–1718).

42 [Nicolas Le Tourneux], *Das Christliche Jahr, Oder, Die Episteln und Evangelien, : auf die Kirchen-Fest-Täge und Gelübd-Messen durch des gantze Jahr* (2 vols.; Prag: Labaunische Erben, 1733–1734).

43 For more on the contacts and academic networks created by Roth-Scholtz in Leipzig and Prague see the first of two *Alba amicorum* which belonged to Friedrich Roth-Scholtz (entries 1710–1716). It is held in the British Library, Egerton Ms. 1391. Cf. Antonín Kostlán, 'Bohemikálni alba amicorum ve fondech British Library', *Folia Historica Bohemica*, 23 (2008), pp. 91–214; see Mona Garloff, 'Friedrich Roth-Scholtz (1687–1736). Eine gelehrte Verlegerbiographie zwischen Schlesien und Nürnberg', in Marek Hałub (ed.), *Śląska Republika Uczonych – Schlesische Gelehrtenrepublik – Slezská vědecká obec* (vol. 9, Wroclaw/Dresden: Oficyna Wydawnicza ATUT, 2020), pp. 46–66.

44 [Ferdinand van der Roxas], *Leben Eines Herrlichen Bildes Wahrer und rechtschaffener Frömmigkeit, Welches Gott in dem Königreich Böhmen, in der Hohen Person Sr. Hoch-Gräfl. Excellenz, Herrn Herrn Frantz Antoni, Des Heil. Röm. Reichs Grafen von Sporck* (Amsterdam, 1715 [1717]).

the false imprint Amsterdam for titles destined for unofficial distribution at the Bohemian book market. Amsterdam was often used as a false impressum in these decades: Rüdiger had no specific business relations to Amsterdam, the choice of this city has to be seen as a general identification of the Dutch city as a place of religious toleration and refuge for religious exiles (like Johann Amos Comenius).

In fact, Sporck's juridical defence and autobiography was not printed until 1717, presumably in a Frankfurt printing shop. The pseudonym includes the initials of Roth-Scholtz. Only 200 copies of the autobiography were published for this first print run. In 1720, a marginally extended version followed under the nom de plume Gottwald Caesar von Stillenau, of which 3,000 copies were published in an unknown printing shop.[45] As the correspondence with Sporck after 1717 is lost, we cannot prove that Rüdiger and Roth-Scholtz were involved in the publication of the second edition. In two letters to Rüdiger (1720 and 1724), Sporck tried to renew the business relationship with his publisher. But Rüdiger did not publish any more of Sporck's work. Similarly, the commercial dealings with Georg Lehmann, Peter Conrad Monath and the engraver Michael Heinrich Rentz, help us to grasp the central role of Nuremberg as an alternative place for publishing Sporck's books outside the Bohemian territories.[46]

Apart from the surviving titles of his publishing programme, two comprehensive booksellers' catalogues, dated 1716 and 1748, give us clues as to Rüdiger's trading activities in Prague. The catalogue from 1716 consists of three bound individual volumes, divided according to academic disciplines: *Catalogus Librorum Catholicorum* (Prague, 1716), *Catalogus Librorum Judicorum* (Nuremberg, 1716) and *Catalogus Librorum Medicorum* (Prague, 1716).[47] The catalogue was generous to the reader, printed in a spacious quarto format. Some copies were interleaved. In addition, the wide margins next to the titles offered plenty of space for notes, as the handwritten comments in the Strahov copy indicate. The catalogues of the theological and medical works had been compiled especially for the Prague book markets ('qui prostant Pragae apud Jo. Fridr. Rudiger'). The legal books were offered in Nuremberg ('qui prostant Norimbergae apud Jo. Fridr.

---

45 [Gottwald Caesar von Stillenau], *Leben Eines Herrlichen Bildes wahrer und rechtschaffener Frömmigkeit* ([s.l.] 1720). Cf. Benedikt, *Graf von Sporck*, pp. 421–424.

46 For more detail, see: Mona Garloff, 'Nürnberger Buchhandelsnetzwerke und die Verbreitung jansenistischen Schrifttums in Böhmen im frühen 18. Jahrhundert', in Christoph Schmitt-Maaß (ed.), *Der Jansenismus im deutschsprachigen Raum, 1670–1789, Bücher, Bilder, Bibliotheken* (Berlin: De Gruyter, 2023), pp. 103–127.

47 *Catalogus Librorum ... qui prostant* (Nürnberg/Prag: Rüdiger, 1716), Strahovská knihovna, Praha [Strahov Library], AY III 50.

Rudiger'), but also in the Prague markets. The titles are listed in alphabetical order, sometimes arranged in sub-categories by discipline, and the entries provide substantial bibliographical information: first and last name of the author, a short title, the format, number of volumes, as well as the place and year of publication are all listed. In some cases, the abbreviated title deviates slightly from the original title. In all three catalogues, German and Latin books are listed separately. Works in Czech hardly feature at all. Together with author and title, the places of publication are of great importance for the following analysis.

In the Nuremberg catalogue of legal works, Leipzig, Stuttgart, Gotha, Nuremberg, Jena and Halle are the most prominent places of publication, directed as it was to a Protestant readership. It contains works by Matthias Bernegger, Christoph Besold, Benedict Carpzov, Ahasverus Fritsch, Hugo Grotius and Samuel Pufendorf. The catalogue of medical works, which also includes works of chemistry and the natural sciences, lists many Protestant writers of the sixteenth century through to the eighteenth century. In general, books from these categories, which did not directly involve theological issues, could be traded freely on the Prague markets. Individual cases, such as the confiscation of a book by the Flemish-Dutch mathematician and engineer Simon Stevin (see further below), show, however, that even works of the natural sciences could be banned from trade on censorship grounds.

Most revealing for the functioning of the south German assortment trade is the *Catalogus Librorum Catholicorum*. This 97-page catalogue is divided into different sections. Apart from Latin and 'German-theological-Catholic books' [Teutsch-theologisch-Catholische Bücher] it contains 'monastic texts' [libri ord. monast.], 'sermon books' [Predigt-Bücher] and 'prayer books' [Gebeth-Bücher], underlining the popularity of these genres. Traditional Catholic places of publication predominate, such as Antwerp, Paris, Cologne and Augsburg. But the efficiency of the Protestant book production in south Germany is equally apparent. We see this in the works of Abraham a Sancta Clara (1644–1709): with 16 titles, this Augustinian preacher has a larger number of books to his name than other authors in Rüdiger's programme. Only four of these titles were printed by Catholic publishers: the *Grammatica religiosa* (Salzburg, 1699), *Reim Dich oder ich ließ Dich* (Cologne, 1684), *Gack Gack Gack* (Cologne, 1689) und *Geistliche Tugend-Schul* (Cologne, 1699). Other works were published in Nuremberg (10 titles), Ulm (1), Amsterdam (1) and Brno (1). Only in individual cases were these first editions or works which were not (posthumous) compilations. The sermon against the Turks, *Auff, auff Ihr Christen* was first printed in 1683 by Melchior Haan in Salzburg, and reprinted in the same year by Matthäus Wagner in Ulm. The treatise on the plague, *Mercks Wien*, was initially published by Peter Paul Vivian in Vienna in 1680, and in the same year by Johann Hoffmann in Nuremberg. Rüdiger had a later version from 1689 in stock.[48]

The publication of Abrahams *Sterben und Erben* (Amsterdam 1702 and Brno 1708) reveals a complex story of adaptions and false imprints: as for the Amsterdam edition of 1702, we are dealing with a translation by Abraham of De Chertablon's *La manière de se bien préparer à la mort*. In its French version this *ars moriendi* work was printed by the Huguenot George Gallet in Amsterdam in 1700 with the false imprint 'Anvers'. Rüdigers brother-in-law Georg Lehmann had first published the German version in 1702 in Prague (by using the impressum Amsterdam: Gallet), copying the original copper engravings of the Dance-of-Death motif.[49] Rüdiger also advertised Lehmann's print of 1708, which was published in Brno. In his catalogues, Rüdiger included the entire publishing programme of his brother-in-law, who was more strongly specialised in Catholic preaching and devotional literature. The close family ties thus also contributed to the mutual expansion of the Lehmann's and Rüdiger's respective book assortments.

Aside from stock and publisher's catalogues, book dealers used newspapers to advertise their wares. In journals such as the *Wienerisches Diarium* or the *Prager Post-Zeitungen*, we find the first advertisements from booksellers starting in the 1720s. The very first adverts in the *Prager Post-Zeitungen* were placed by Johann Friedrich Rüdiger. Rüdiger used this form of advertising at least until 1747.[50] In this paper, he mainly listed his own publications, but also titles from his stock. In addition to the title, Rüdiger mentioned format and price. He usually advertised cheap books. As an example, he promoted the legal textbook, which he published in several editions, *Manuductio ad praxim iuridicam tam apud superiores quam inferiores instantias in regno Bohemiae*, for sale for

---

48   Cf. Franz M. Eybl, *Abraham a Sancta Clara. Vom Prediger zum Schriftsteller* (Tübingen: Niemeyer, 1992); Gertien Deneke, 'Johann Hoffmann. Ein Beitrag zur Geschichte des Buch- und Kunsthandels in Nürnberg', *Archiv für Geschichte des Buchwesens*, 1 (1958), pp. 337–364.

49   De Chertablon is a pseudonym. This work is a revision and extension of David de la Vigne's *Miroir de la bonne mort*. David de la Vigne's work was first printed in Paris 1646 and in Amsterdam in 1673 with the copper engravings of the Dance-of-Death motif by Romeyn de Hooghe. Cf. Christian Coppens, *Een Ars moriendi met etsen van Romeyn de Hooghe: Verhaal van een boekillustratie* (Brussels: AWLSK, 1995), pp. 281–283; 'Georg Lehmann', in *Příspěvatelé Encyklopedie knihy*, www.encyklopedieknihy.cz/index.php?title=Georg_Lehmann&oldid=14054.

50   For the period in question, the following years of the *Prager-Post-Zeitungen* have been preserved and digitised: 1725, 1744, 1745, 1746 and 1748 (Czech National Library).

12 Kreutzer.[51] As for his book selection, Rüdiger would announce new publications on current affairs. In 1745, for instance, he printed several anonymous commentaries on the election of Franz I Stephan as Holy Roman Emperor, stating his sympathy for Maria Theresia.[52] As for the political writings on offer, Rüdiger was careful to present himself as being on the side of the imperial government, so as not to risk his already limited privileges as a foreign trader in Bohemia. In contrast, he was prepared to take issue with the municipal and territorial authorities as well as the Archdiocese of Prague in religious matters.

3 The Clandestine Book Trade and Rüdiger's Encounters with Censorship

In his catalogues, Rüdiger presented his official selection as entirely conforming censorship regulations. However, we can find records of numerous legal proceedings against Rüdiger for trading in banned religious books. The multitude of procedures taken against foreign booksellers shows us the difficulties that authorities had to control the wholesale book trade in these decades. Censorship measures in the first half of the eighteenth century in Bohemia included ecclesiastical bans, based on the Roman *Index librorum probibitorum* or the Index *Clavis haeresim* (1729) by the Jesuit Antonín Koniáš, and imperial edicts prohibiting literature critical of the government or political pamphlets.[53]

The procedures against Rüdiger demonstrate the efforts to establish a censorship commission, which unified state censorship measures and was intended to bring about a clearer distinction between secular and ecclesiastical competences in censorship matters. However, the difficulty in distinguishing between

---

51 *Prager-Post-Zeitungen*, 28 September 1745: *Manuductio ad praxim iuridicam tam apud superiores quam inferiores instantias in regno Bohemiae* (Prag: Rüdiger, 1729, 2nd ed. 1751) [1 Gulden = 60 Kreutzer].

52 *Prager-Post-Zeitungen*, 28 September 1745: *Die Untersuchung der Frage: Warum die Königin in Ungarn so ausserordentlich geliebet werde?* (s.l. 1745); *Germania Triumphans Sub Aquila Austriæ oder Pragmatischer- und vornemlich ex Ratione Status hergeleiteter Beweißthum* (s.l. 1745); *Prager-Post-Zeitungen*, 10 July 1745; *Prager-Post-Zeitungen*, 2 October 1745: *Christoph Gottlieb Richter: Lebens- und Staats-Geschichte der Allerdurchlauchtigsten, Grosmächtigsten Fürstin und Frauen, Frauen Maria Theresia, Königin in Ungarn und Böheim, Erzherzogin zu Oesterreich* (Nürnberg: Albrecht, 1744).

53 Antonín Koniáš: *Clavis haeresim in claudens et aperiens* (Hradec Králové: Tibelli, 1729, 2nd ed. 1749); Jiří Pokorný, 'P. Antonín Koniáš s. j. jako teoretik české knižní kultury', *Documenta Pragensia*, 10 (1990), pp. 327–334; cf. the imperial edict (18 July 1715) by Charles VI, Adolph Wiesner: *Denkwürdigkeiten der Oesterreichischen Zensur vom Zeitalter der Reformation bis auf die Gegenwart* (Stuttgart: Krabbe, 1847), pp. 82–85.

secular and ecclesiastical censorship matters is repeatedly demonstrated in specific cases: in 1733, a censorship commission was formed, chaired by the supreme burgrave of Prague, who was also the president of the Lieutenancy Council ['Statthalterei']. In reality, cases of confiscation reveal that the University of Prague, headed by Jesuits, could bring considerable influence to bear on these decisions. The commission was not in continuous session, but it was re-established as a permanent institution in 1749, in the course of the establishment of a central office (the *Directorium in Publicis et Cameralibus*) for the Habsburg lands by Maria Theresia. In the decades before this, the case-by-case starting point of confiscations became clear time and again.[54] Confiscations were based on ecclesiastical censorship or imperial edicts without clear lines of procedure. The frequency with which foreign booksellers were subjected to those measures demonstrates that censorship was used to regulate their dominant position in the Bohemian book markets. I will analyse three lawsuits against Rüdiger that were driven by different interest groups. All three cases took place in the mid-1730s, which signals the efforts of the authorities to unify and centralise the censorship practise in Bohemia around this time.

In the first case, in February 1734, an order was given to confiscate books from Rüdiger's stock. Previously, the Procurator of the Bohemian Province of the Jesuits, Pater Ferdinand Hoffmann SJ, had brought serious pressure to bear on the captain and magistrate of the Prague Old Town, where Rüdiger's warehouses were located, and where he offered his products at the Candlemas-of-Mary and the St.-Wenceslaus markets. The object of the complaint was a book denigrating Pater Jean-Baptiste Girard SJ. The priest in question, who had been involved in a number of scandals, had died only shortly before, in July 1733, in Dole.[55] The latest volume in the series *Der Genealogische Archivarius* from 1733, published by Johann Samuel Heinsius in Leipzig, was also confiscated. Rüdiger had also worked in commission for Heinsius (see below), which points to a closer business co-operation between the two publishers. This backs the

---

54　On censorship in Bohemia cf. Marie-Elizabeth Ducreux and Martin Svatoš (eds.), *Libri prohibiti. La censure dans l'espace habsbourgeois 1650–1850* (Leipzig: Leipziger Univ. Verlag, 2005); on later periods Petr Píša and Michael Wögerbauer, 'Das Königreich Böhmen (1750–1848)', in Norbert Bachleitner et al., *Die literarische Zensur in Österreich von 1751 bis 1848* (Wien: Böhlau, 2017), pp. 193–215, pp. 193f.; M. Wögerbauer, Petr Píša and Petr Šámal et al., *V obecném zájmu. Cenzura a sociální regulace literatury v moderní české kultuře, 1749–2014* (2 vols.; Praha: Academia, 2015); Grete Klingenstein, *Staatsverwaltung und kirchliche Autorität im 18. Jahrhundert* (Wien: Böhlau, 1970); Jean-Paul Lavandier, *Le livre au temps de Marie-Thérèse. Code des lois de censure du livre pour les pays austro-bohémiens (1749–1780)* (Bern: Lang, 1993).

55　Národní archiv, Praha [National Archive], Staré české místodržitelství (SČM), 1734/II/d/22, 1734/II/d/38 (no pag.).

earlier observation that Leipzig traders were often not present at the book markets of the Habsburg Monarchy in person, but had intermediaries working for them on a commission basis. The controversial aspect of *Der Genealogische Archivarius* was a detailed description of Pater Girard's sexual abuse scandal. This outrage, which ended with Girard's acquittal by a court in Aix-en-Provence, later inspired Voltaire to his novel *Thérèse philosophe* (1748).[56] Pater Hoffmann insisted on withdrawing the latest *Archivarius* from the market, as it sullied the honour of the deceased French priest. The captain of the Prague Old Town ordered a hearing and a confiscation of the copies in Rüdiger's warehouse. The stores of other foreign booksellers such as Paul Lochner were ordered to be searched as well.

In the second case, Rüdiger became involved in a business conflict with Jews in Prague in the New Town (Nové Město). The head of the Jewish community, Isaac Simon Lowotitz, accused him of selling an anonymous anti-Jewish pamphlet ('a book most disadvantageous to the Jewish community, having neither an author nor a printing license') at the annual market of the New Town.[57] Rüdiger confessed to having sold ten copies of this no longer identifiable book to various Jews in Prague. The Jewish community's council of the elders denied that these were bought by their own community. As the market season was drawing to a close, the captain of the New Town urged the inspection of Rüdiger's stocks, since at the end of the market period, the warehouses were sealed, and foreign merchants such as Rüdiger left Prague. The limitation of the trading and residency permit of foreign traders to market sessions impeded the authorities' control of their books on offer, and favoured loopholes for the semi-clandestine trade and distribution.

In the third case of confiscation, two books were seized directly in Teynhof by the Ungelt-Amt (Office for Import and Export Customs) and handed over to the Censorship Commission for examination.[58] The first theologically controversial title was *Neu Catholisch Handbüchlein. Darinnen Das gantze Papsthum und dessen vornemeste Irrthümb* by the court preacher of Lübz, Georg Rost (Rostock, 1629), the anti-Catholic position of which is very clear. The second title was Simon Stevin's *Kurzer doch gründlicher Bericht von Calculation der*

---

56 *Der genealogische Archivarius, welcher alles, was sich unter den ietztlebenden hohen Personen in der Welt an Geburten, Vermählungen, Avancements und Todes-Fällen veränderliches zuträgt, mit Eindrückung vieler Lebens-Beschreibungen sorgfältig anmercket* (8 vols.; Leipzig: Heinsius, 1731–1738), III, pp. 234–244.
57 'Der Judenschaft sehr nachtheiliges weder Authorem noch licientiam imprimendi habendes Büchlein'. Národní archiv, Praha, Staré české místodržitelství (sčm), 1734/VII/d/6, no pag.
58 Národní archiv, Praha, Staré české místodržitelství (sčm), 1736/X/d/12, no pag.

Tabularum Sinuum, Tangentium und Secantium, which Daniel Schwenter had translated into German, and which had first been printed in 1628 in Nuremberg. Stevin (1548–1620), a Flemish-Dutch mathematician and engineer, was a Calvinist and subscribed to Copernican heliocentrism. In principle, scientific works could be advertised and sold in early eighteenth-century Prague irrespective of the confessional allegiance of the author. Both of these books were published in the 1620s in Protestant cities. This case shows the efforts to institutionalise a mechanism of (state) censorship that still functioned without a fixed catalogue of prohibited books.[59] The ban upon these titles was placed in the phase of 're-Catholicising' Bohemia after the Battle of White Mountain, but the interdiction of those publication was still used as an argument for confiscations in the 1730s.

The confiscation of censored works aside, there were no long-term restrictions on Rüdiger's bookselling activities in Prague in consequence of the three cases presented here. Taking other conflicts with censorships into account we see in the majority of the cases, that foreign booksellers did not face any grave sanctions in consequence. Due to their comprehensive book selection, foreign traders such as Rüdiger had no serious competition to fear from local traders.

4   Rüdiger's Rise as a Privileged 'Imperial-Royal' Bookseller

In Prague, Rüdiger had no fixed bookshop until 1748, as the advertisements of the *Prager-Post-Zeitungen* indicate. Rather, he offered his wares in different shops during the market periods. In the newspaper advertisements up to 1747, the store 'In Paradise' in the town centre is mentioned as a venue for his sales during the markets of Candlemas and St. Wenceslaus. We may assume that foreign booksellers shared these stores, for, as of 1743, Conrad Georg Walther used the same house in the centre of Prague for commercial purposes. For the markets of Mid-Lent and St. Margaret, Rüdiger rented a shop in the Lesser Town (Malá Strana) district, 'At Three Rings'. On 22 April 1747, Rüdiger gave a shop at the Rossmarkt (Václavské náměstí today) in his adverts for the New Town's market. In 1747, Rüdiger traded at five markets in Prague, instead of the usual two to four annual visits.

Rüdiger's increased market presence was certainly also due to competition from other foreign traders from beyond Prague. Rüdiger placed four advertisements in the *Prager-Post-Zeitungen* in 1725, the only other foreign trader at this time in the newspaper was Paul Lochner, with one advertisement. Johann

---

59   Cf. *Catalogus librorum rejectorum per Consessum censuræ* (Viennæ, 1754).

THE TROUBLES OF A PROTESTANT BOOKSELLER IN A CATHOLIC MARKET

Conrad Mullem was the sole local bookseller advertising his offers. By 1747, the number of adverts had increased noticeably: Prague printers could promote their wares outside of the market times, as well. We can find advertisements from Ulrich Gröbel, Joseph Heck and the widow Sophia Johann Rosenmüller.[60] Aside from Rüdiger, three other foreign traders were making publicity for their trade in Prague: the firm of Lochner (Lochner Erben & Johann Caspar Mayer) from Nuremberg, Conrad Georg Walther from Dresden as well as Johann Samuel Heinsius from Leipzig.[61] The Heinsius company rarely visited the Prague markets, but let Rüdiger act on commission for them. For instance, the *Allgemeines Juristisches Oraculum* or the translation of La Martinière's *Le Grand Dictionnaire* were sold by Rüdiger.[62] This commercial agreement extended to Rüdiger's range of customers, and also to return services from his colleagues in Leipzig. From the early 1740s on, the companies of Paul Lochner and Johann Caspar Mayer, Gregor Mangoldt and Conrad Georg Walther were in competition with considerable influence in the Prague market.[63] They

---

60 In spite of statements to the contrary, the bookseller Ulrich Gröbl must have been active in Prague already in the 1740s., cf. Chyba, *Slovník knihtiskařů*, p. 101, Claire Madl, Petr Píša and Michael Wögerbauer, *Buchwesen in Böhmen 1749–1848. Kommentiertes Verzeichnis der Drucker, Buchhändler, Buchbinder, Kupfer- und Steindrucker* (Wiesbaden: Harrassowitz, 2019), p. 64. 'Oldřich Gröbeľ, in *Přispěvatelé Encyklopedie knihy*, www.encyklopedieknihy.cz/index.php?title=Oldřich_Gröbel&oldid=14770; Chyba, *Slovník knihtiskařů*, p. 112; Madl, Píša and Wögerbauer, *Buchwesen in Böhmen*, pp. 75, 175f.; Claire Madl, Michael Wögerbauer and Petr Píša, *Na cestě k výborně zřízenému knihkupectví. Protagonisté, podniky a sítě knižního trhu v Čechách (1749–1848)* (Praha: Academia 2019); Chyba, *Slovník knihtiskařů*, pp. 224f.

61 'Heinsius, Johann Samuel', in *Deutsche Biographie*, www.deutsche-biographie.de/pnd1359 04838.html.

62 *Prager-Post-Zeitungen*, 28 September 1745.

63 The firm Lochner & Mayer merits a more exact analysis, as the secondary literature proves contradictory. Paul Lochner of Nuremberg (1689–1733/4) ran a bookstore in Prague at least since 1716. His widow married the bookseller Johann Caspar Mayer (died 1788/90) from Würzburg. This bookstore was registered in the Nuremberg List of Offices as the successor to the heirs of Lochner and Mayer until 1790. We may assume that Mayer continued the bookstore in Prague with one of Lochner's sons (Paul), cf. *Nürnberger Künstlerlexikon*, p. 937; Chyba, *Slovník knihtiskařů*, p. 175; Madl, Píša and Wögerbauer, *Buchwesen in Böhmen*, p. 131; Koppitz, *Die kaiserlichen Druckprivilegien*, pp. 322–324; Šimeček, *Knižní obchod*, pp. 98–100, 115, 124–126; 'Joachim Lochner', in *Přispěvatelé Encyklopedie knihy*, www.encyklopedieknihy.cz/index.php?title=Joachim _Lochner&oldid=13653; Gregor and his son Felician Mangoldt, from Oberammergau, both received full citizens' rights during the war of Austrian Succession (1742/3). This procedure was scrutinised in 1744, when the Archduchy of Austria was at war with Bavaria. The argument of their Catholic confession was instrumental in allowing Georg and Felician Mangoldt to remain citizens and traders in the city of Prague. Cf. Mona Garloff, *Foreign Booksellers in Vienna and Prague: Markets, Actors, Politics,*

exemplified a new generation of booksellers, whose firms existed until the 1780s or even later. Under changing circumstances, they managed to integrate into the Prague trade successfully.[64]

Security in the face of this heightened competition may have been the reason why Rüdiger applied once more, in 1748, for a permanent bookshop in Prague. In addition, the ongoing travel between Nuremberg and Prague for the market sessions must have become increasingly wearing, since Rüdiger was now over sixty years of age. He reduced his publishing activities, evidenced by the fact that there are no new publications of his listed at the fairs of Frankfurt or Leipzig after 1743. The level of his debt is yet to be determined from primary sources. But is seems likely that the economic losses of his bookstore were the key factor which prompted him to move his business to Prague completely. Rüdiger is listed as a book trader and member of the Great Council of the city of Nuremberg only until 1745.[65] He probably did not give up his citizen's rights in this year, however. Only in December 1746 did he apply for privileges in Prague, the procedure of which stretched on until April 1748.

Already in 1724, Rüdiger had filed his application with the Bohemian Commercial College, requesting to set up an 'open bookstore' in Prague.[66] Rüdiger listed the great usefulness of a 'permanent bookshop' ['beständige Officin'] for an 'improved import and spread of commercial goods' ['besserer Einfuhr und emporbringung des Comercii']. He argued that there were only two local booksellers, who 'trade little' ['wenig treiben'], making a 'completely and well-stocked bookstore' ['vollkommen wohl versehener Buchladen'] vital. If he had one, Rüdiger stated, he could provide 'many more practical and high-quality books' ['allerhand nützlicher und guter Bücher'] than there was

---

1680–1750 (in preparation). The information on Gregor Mangoldt's biography is sparse, cf. Madl, Píša and Wögerbauer, *Buchwesen in Böhmen*, p. 135; Chyba, *Slovník knihtiskařů*, pp. 178f; For Conrad Georg Walther (1710–1778) and Walther's court bookshop, cf. Madl, Píša and Wögerbauer, *Buchwesen in Böhmen*, pp. 224–226.

64 Cf. Madl, Wögerbauer and Píša, *Na cestě*.

65 Cf. *Nürnberger Künstlerlexikon*, p. 1281. Diefenbacher and Fischer-Pache, *Das Nürnberger Buchgewerbe*, p. 679. Due to the total closure of archives and libraries in March and April 2020, I was not able to complete the primary research in the City and State Archive of Nuremberg.

66 Národní Archiv, České gubernium – Commerciale, D1, K. 12 (1716–1730), 1724, no pag. For more on the Bohemian Commercial College, cf. Alfred Francis Přibram, *Das böhmische Commerzkollegium und seine Thätigkeit* (Prag: Verlag des Vereins, 1898); Grete Klingenstein and Eva Faber, 'Kommerzbehörden und Staatswirtschaftsdeputation', in Michael Hochedlinger, Petr Maťa and Thomas Winkelbauer (eds.), *Verwaltungsgeschichte der Habsburgermonarchie in der Frühen Neuzeit* (2 vols.; Wien: Böhlau, 2019), II, pp. 985–990.

available now, when his trade was restricted to the 'prescribed, few market hours' ['aufgesetzten wenigen Marcktzeiten']. Rüdiger drew on another argument popular with foreign traders: his bookstore would boost the weak local printing industry as well as paper production.[67] So far, he only imported books. With the new privilege, he could move his publishing business to Prague. It may be because of the institutional developments of 1724 that Rüdiger filed his application in August of that year. In May 1724, an imperial edict had granted wider powers to the Commercial College (founded in 1714/15).[68] As similar cases show, the booksellers of Prague could exert considerable influence on the decisions of the College by means of expert reports. The reports on Rüdiger's application have not survived. But we can assume that the strong resistance of the local booksellers was the main reason why his application was turned down in 1724.

Along with other traders, Rüdiger was able to benefit, however, from the mercantilist measures instigated from the early 1720/30s onwards and intensified by the government of Maria Theresia. This particular economic policy was geared towards encouraging national production and trade, but it could also provide foreign traders, who had already established themselves as influential market players over a longer period of time, with local advantages: the concession of permanent bookshops was also used as an argument to stimulate the regional industry (the production of paper, printing and book binding). The question of confession was still an important criterium, though, when it came to granting trade concessions and citizens' rights.

The second petition for trading privileges, a lengthy procedure dating from late 1746, illustrates this. It is rare that application processes of this nature are so well documented in the files of the Bohemian Court Chancellery, now part of the Czech National Archives.[69] Rüdiger (referring to himself as a 'bookseller in Nuremberg') did not appeal to the Bohemian Commercial College for his second case, but directly to the territorial sovereign, Maria Theresia. In his application, dated 19 December 1746, Rüdiger draws on mercantilist

---

67   Between 1622 and beginning of the eighteenth century there existed twenty printing shops in total in Prague, and in the year of 1740 there were seven printing shops and six bookshops in Prague. Cf. Bohatcová, *Česká kniha v proměnách staletí*, pp. 289–290; Michael Wögerbauer and Jiří Pokorný: 'Barocke Buchkultur in den Böhmischen Ländern', p. 388; Šimeček, *Geschichte des Buchhandels*, p. 33; Chyba, *Slovník knihtiskařů v Československu*.
68   Přibram: *Das böhmische Commerzkollegium*, p. 32.
69   It is rare that application processes of this nature are so well documented, cf. the files of the Bohemian Court Chancellery (Národní archiv, Česká dvorská kancelář (ČDK), IV, D7 (Rüdiger box 675, conv. 46, no pag.). These privileges of the book trade constitute a central corpus of primary sources for my research project: Foreign Booksellers in Vienna and Prague: Markets, Actors, Politics, 1680–1750.

arguments: his trading permit, making him a regular bookseller in the towns of Prague, would boost the local industry with the increased demand for paper production and book printing of his publishing house. Furthermore, his trade connections and visits to the Frankfurt and Leipzig fairs would ensure that a wide selection of foreign-language books and their translations would be available in Prague permanently. Rüdiger requested merely a temporary trading privilege, as he would not pass it on to his heirs. He was a widower, and both of his daughters were already married.[70]

Over the course of 1747, the Commercial College commissioned expert reports, drawn up by the university and the magistrates of the three Prague districts, Old Town, New Town and Lesser Town. In April and October of the same year, the Commercial College prepared two statements of its own. The reports reveal the different market interests of the individual players: the Commercial College considered the number of established booksellers in Prague sufficient for existing demand. The magistrates of the three districts listened to the views of their respective booksellers on a possible trading privilege for Rüdiger. The mayors and councils of both New Town and Lesser Town mentioned that there were no permanent bookstores in their areas, and welcomed Rüdiger's request.[71] The established book trade was located in the Altstadt, and the magistrate there was of a different opinion. His argument drew on the statements of the four booksellers Kaspar Zacharias Wussin, Joseph Heck, Gregor Mangoldt and Ulrich Gröbl, who spoke for their trade in the city centre. They feared even more serious economic losses than those already caused by the visiting foreign traders with their much larger selection of books. The booksellers from Nuremberg, personified by Johann Friedrich Rüdiger, were considered the strongest competition. These booksellers caused the 'pauperisation of our lands with many thousands of guilders being taken out of our country' ['zur Depauperierung des Landes viele Taußendt Gulden außer Landes'], the Prague traders stated, while the local book trade could hardly raise its own tax requirements.[72] Rüdiger's assortment was not a unique selling point, for every

---

70   Petition for privilege by Rüdiger (s.d., praes. 19 December 1946); Johann Friedrich Rüdiger's wife Clara Susanna (née Zieger) had died already in 1741, cf. *Nürnberger Künstlerlexikon*, p. 1281.

71   ČDK, IV, D7, box 675, conv. 46, statements of the magistrate of the Lesser Town (24 March 1747); statement of the magistrate of the New Town (10 April 1747).

72   'The prague markets dominated by Nurmberg booksellers causing us to cease trading since we are not able to turn over any more of our book stock for the rest of the year; we are not able to live by our trade, while meanwhile the Nuremberg traders cause the pauperization of the land with many thousands of guilders being taken out of our country.' ['Gestallten nur die ausgesetzte JahrMärckte hindurch von denen hereinkommenden Nürnbergern, haubtsächl. aber von ihm Rüdiger, uns solcher Abbruch beschieht, daß wir

Prague bookseller, they continued, was in a position to obtain 'the required stock of books in sufficient quantitiy'.⁷³

The principal argument which the traders brought forward to prevent Rüdiger being granted a trading privilege, however, was his confession. As in other reports, they referred to article twenty-three of the *Verneuerte Landesordnung*, decreed in 1627 by Ferdinand II, stating that the Roman Catholic faith constituted the only acceptable religion.⁷⁴ It was not the fact that Rüdiger's Lutheran belief alone that was the issue of contention. The book dealers of Prague fortified their argument, claiming that Rüdiger's confession would facilitate the import of heretical books to Bohemia. The Prague booksellers pointed to previous cases of confiscation, in which Rüdiger had been responsible for dealing with banned publications. This proved, they claimed, that Rüdiger's real motivation was to spread heretical beliefs in Bohemia. Finally, the magistrate added an example from history, mentioning that since the Battle of White Mountain in 1620, religion had been considered 'such a formidable obstacle' ['derley obstaculum'], 'because of which many thousand people born and settled in Bohemia had been required to emigrate' ['daß wegen derselben ebenmahlen viele tausende Ingebohren und wohl ansässige Leuthe emigrieren und das Landt haben räumen müssen']. Because of this, the magistrate saw no reason to grant Rüdiger, a Protestant, citizens' rights in the Old Town of Prague.⁷⁵

The vice chancellor and academic council of the University of Prague employed similar arguments, with the main point focussed on Rüdiger's confession. According to the academic council, Rüdiger did not want to 'adopt the catholic religion or the rights of a citizen' ['sich weder zur Catholischen Religion noch zum Bürgerrecht bequemen']. Its members continued that there was also no economic necessity to grant Rüdiger a trading permit. He claimed that there was a deficiency in the book stock available in Prague, which did not exist in reality, they stated, but instead only served the 'self-interest' ['Eigennutz']

---

hinnach die übrigen Jahrs-Zeit von unserer Bucherey-Waare schier nichts mehr auszuwerfen, folgsamb von unserem Handel nicht zu leben vermögen, wo inzwischen [...] von denen Nürnbergern zu Depauperierung des Landes viele Taußendt Gulden außer Land geführet werden.'] ČDK, IV, D7, box 675, conv. 46, statements of the booksellers of the Prague Altstadt (s.d., praes. 16 March 1747).

73 'Den benöthigten Bücher-Vorrath genüglich zu verschaffen'. ČDK, IV, D7, box 675, conv. 46, statements of the booksellers of the Prague Old Town (s.d., praes. 16 March 1747).

74 'Von der Religion' (A. XXIII). Hermenegild Jireček (ed.), *Codex Juris Bohemici. Tomi v. Pars 2: Constitutiones Regni Bohemiae anno 1627 reformatae* (Prag: Tempsky, 1888), pp. 33–35.

75 ČDK, IV, D7, box 675, conv. 46, statements of the magistrate of Prague Old City (23 March 1747).

of the 'applicant' ['Supplicanten'].[76] It would be perfectly sufficient, the council points out, to purchase Rüdiger's books during the two-week-long market sessions, or to read them in libraries.[77] The university further reflected that no report on Rüdiger had been requested from the Archiepiscopal Consistory, which was responsible for censorship.

In their assessment of 13 November 1747, the Bohemian Court Chancellery passed all of these documents on to the Lieutenancy Council in Prague, adding its own contrasting opinion: the Lieutenancy Council inverted the arguments of the Commercial College, mentioning that further competition by foreign sellers would provide an economic incentive. This meant that book production in Bohemia would benefit along the lines of major literary centres such as Nuremberg, Leipzig, Frankfurt, Cologne, Augsburg and Hamburg. There was a high demand for 'foreign academic books' ['auswärtige gelehrte Bücher'].[78] On condition of the payment of public charges, the Lieutenancy Council recommended that a trading permit be granted to Rüdiger. In its report, it still pointed to the issue of confession, however, and leaves the final decision to the sovereign. With the commercial privilege Maria Theresia awarded Rüdiger on 1 April 1748, he was granted the right 'to trade freely books in Prague' ['auf den freien Bücher-Handel zu Prag']. Thus, after thirty-eight years of trading at the markets of Prague, Rüdiger finally received formal commercial rights. But this document still limited his rights as a privileged bookseller: it limited Rüdiger's trading rights to three years. Rüdiger was allowed to keep a permanent store, but was still subject to the special legal terms for non-Catholic merchants, which barred him from obtaining citizens' rights in one of the three Prague districts. Outside of market times, a Catholic assistant ['factor'] had to run the shop. Nonetheless, Rüdiger had to pay the 'praestationes publicas', the full public charges, like every (Catholic) merchant in the city.[79]

Even if trading rights had been conceded only in part, Rüdiger was still one of the very few Protestant merchants granted a commercial privilege in Bohemia in these decades: in 1753, for instance, the publisher and bookseller Conrad Georg Walther from Dresden applied to the Commercial College to

---

76   ČDK, IV, D7, box 675, conv. 46, report of the university (s.d., praes. 8 August 1747).
77   'In vorhandenen Bibliothecen gelesen werden können'. ČDK, IV, D7, box 675, conv. 46, report of the university (s.d., praes. 8 August 1747). Libraries in plural were a reference to the former individual libraries of each collegium of the Charles University, together with the library of the Jesuit order. All those holdings were transferred to the new Klementinum building in 1727, today the building of the Czech National Library.
78   ČDK, IV, D7, box 675, conv. 46, report of the Lieutenancy Council (13 November 1747).
79   ČDK, IV, D7, box 675, conv. 46, (1 April 1748), cf. also the copies for the Lieutenancy Council and the Commercial College (13 April 1748), Staré české místodržitelství (SČM), B 56,3.

run a bookstore. Walther's confession was used as an argument against him, and it was not until 1771 that he was permitted to open a branch in Prague.[80] Rüdiger's case illustrates that confessional reasons could still be employed to regulate trade, but that they were no longer an exclusive criterium for commercial policy in Austria and its territories.[81] Rüdiger used his official establishment on the Prague book market for a large-scale publicity offensive: already in his petition, he had pointed out his planned comprehensive catalogue, in which he wanted to offer his books at fixed prices – a sales tactic unavailable to him before his trading concession.

In his subsequent catalogue of 1748, Rüdiger presents himself as 'imperial-royal privileged bookseller' ['kayserl. königl. Privilgierter Buchhändler']. His catalogue would be appearing on a monthly basis: 'This serves as a friendly announcement that every month a sheet from my Universal Catalogue will be distributed, in accordance with the regulations and God willing, beginning in June' ['Es dient zur freundlichen Nachricht, daß von diesem meinen Universal-Catalogo, nach der Ordnung alle Monat ein Bogen, mithin im Junio, geliebts Gott, die erste Continuation, und so fort, wird zu haben seyn']. These catalogue extracts were printed in octavo booklets of 16 pages. The first one was decorated with an elaborate seal ('collegio flores'), hinting at the printing shop of the widow Sophia Johanna Rosenmüller in Prague.[82] The two different versions of Rüdiger's catalogue of 1748, preserved in the library of the Strahov Monastery and the National Museum (both in Prague),[83] permit us to draw several conclusions: with his alphabetically ordered catalogue, Rüdiger did not provide a complete list of all the titles in his stock. While the catalogue in Strahov Monastery only runs until the letter K and until volume number XXIII, the

---

80   Národní Archiv, České gubernium – Commerciale (CG Com), H9, box 75; Šimeček, *Geschichte des Buchhandels*, p. 32; Madl, Píša and Wögerbauer, *Buchwesen in Böhmen*, pp. 224–226.
81   Cf. Mona Garloff, 'Confessio et commercium. Konfessionelle Selbst- und Fremdwahrnehmung protestantischer Buchhändler in der Habsburgermonarchie (1680–1750)', in Mona Garloff and Christian V. Witt (eds.), *Confessio im Konflikt. Religiöse Selbst- und Fremdwahrnehmung in der Frühen Neuzeit. Ein Studienbuch* (Göttingen: Vandenhoeck & Ruprecht, 2019), pp. 202–205.
82   Cf. Madl, Píša and Wögerbauer, *Buchwesen in Böhmen*, p. 175f.; esp. on the seal: 'Karel Frantisek Rosenmüllter st.', in *Příspěvatelé Encyklopedie knihy*, www.encyklopedieknihy .cz/index.php?title=Karel_Franti%C5%A1ek_Rosenm%C3%BCller_st.&oldid=16710.
83   *Catalogus oder Verzeichnuß aller Büchern, Welche in Prag in dem Buchladen im Paradeyß um billigen Preis zu haben seyn bey Johann Friedrich Rüdiger, Kayserl. Königl. Privilegirten Buchhändlern* (s.l. 1748) [Strahovská knihovna, ET XV 36; Národní muzeum Praha [National Museum Prague], 57 F 8.].

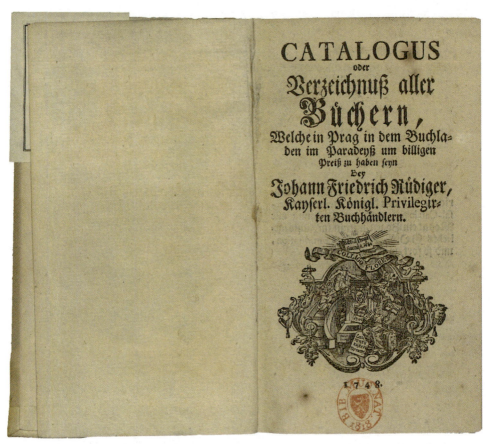

FIGURE 6.2   Title-page of Johann Friedrich Rüdiger's *Catalogus oder Verzeichnuß aller Büchern* (1748). Národní muzeum Praha [National Museum], 57 F 8.

catalogue in the National Museum runs until the letter P.[84] This practice of the individual catalogue volumes appearing every month was continued until the middle of 1750. After this, Rüdiger discontinued cataloguing his stock, as we can see by the list of titles (in the National Museum edition) continued by hand after the letter P. Furthermore, the manual crossing out in the Strahov catalogue impressum indicates that as a privileged bookseller, Rüdiger gave up his book warehouse 'in Paradise' in the town centre after 1748, and moved to a shop in the Lesser Town instead.[85]

---

84   This catalogue carries the ex libris, 'Ex Bibliotheca Clauseriana', from the library of Johann Josef Clauser, who had been married with Sophia Johanna Rosenmüller since 1761.

85   For the transfer of the bookshop to the Lesser Town district, see Šimeček, *Geschichte des Buchhandels*, p. 32.

The comparison between the catalogues of 1716 and 1748 cast a spotlight on Rüdiger's establishment as a wholesale publisher. We may also deduce general developments in the practices of book advertising and catalogue design: in the book market of the early eighteenth century, there were several prevalent catalogue formats, each fulfilling different functions (fair catalogues, catalogues for new releases, stock catalogues, etc.). Generally speaking, we can trace the tendency from specific catalogues, ordered by genre, to more comprehensive retail catalogues, so-called 'universal catalogues', in which the major booksellers listed all the titles from their stock, and which could be used, irrespective of location, also in long-distance trade.[86] If the desired title was not to be found in a local branch, it could be delivered by the trader on their next visit to the market. Rüdiger's 'Universal-Catalogo' from 1748 lists 7,700 books from his warehouses on 532 pages.[87] It is likely that Rüdiger, who was no longer young and without direct heirs in Prague, intended to sell his entire stock with the help of this catalogue. Listing the titles with fixed prices is evidence for this. In his petition for trading privileges, Rüdiger had already mentioned that 'respecting the current ordinary sales prices' ['Respectu des jetzigen ordinari verkaufspreyßes'], he wanted to get rid of his books 'for a full half cheaper' ['umb die halfte wohlfeiller loßschlagen'].[88] Fixed prices began appearing around the 1730s in the German-speaking book trade, but they were far from being common practice, especially in the long-distance trade, where different currencies made for difficult conversion rates, and catalogues with fixed prices could not be used as a means of advertising over longer periods. Prices were mostly set as fixed when traders wanted to sell their whole book stock in large portions at a time. Since we have no verified, quantifiable statements on book prices in the early eighteenth century, and none for Prague, it is worth examining Rüdiger's pricing practice more closely.

Publishing titles in alphabetical order on a monthly basis enabled Rüdiger to bring out his catalogue regularly, and to establish long-term ties with customers. In contrast to other retail or stock catalogues, the alphabetical list contained several sub-categories with rough divisions by genre ('History',

---

86   Cf. Ernst Weber, 'Sortimentskataloge des 18. Jahrhunderts als literatur- und buchhandelsgeschichtliche Quelle', in Reinhard Wittmann (ed.), *Bücherkataloge als buchgeschichtliche Quellen in der frühen Neuzeit* (Wiesbaden: Harrasowitz, 1984), pp. 209–257; Goldfriedrich, *Geschichte des deutschen Buchhandels*, pp. 296–325; Marie-Kristin Hauke, *'In allen guten Buchhandlungen ist zu habe'. Buchwerbung in Deutschland im 17. und 18. Jahrhundert* (Diss., Univ. Erlangen, 1999), urn:nbn:de:bvb:29-opus-1301 [08.04.2020].

87   Pravoslav Kneidl, 'Pražský knihkupec Johann Friedrich Rüdiger a jeho nabídka knih v roce 1748', *Knihy a dějiny*, 2 (1995), pp. 1–8, p. 1.

88   ČDK, IV, D7, box 675, conv. 46, no pag., petition for privileges by Rüdiger (s.d., praes. 19 December 1746).

'Chemical-Philosophical Books', 'Biographies', 'All Kinds of Dictionaries', etc. ['Geschichte', 'Chymisch-Philosophische Bücher', 'Lebens-Beschreibungen', 'Lexica allerhand']). In the sections on Medicine and Law Rüdiger sold exclusively Protestant authors, yet in the section on theological works exclusively Catholic authors. One exception to this rule was Johann Amos Comenius, whose works belonged to the bestselling *Bohemica* of the period. Rüdiger offered new releases and some antiquarian books. The early printed books included the rare *Conciliator differentiarum* by Pietro d'Abano (Venice, 1496, 3 guilders), more recent second-hand books like the *Nürnbergische Hesperides* (Nuremberg, 1708) with 'beautiful engravings' for 10 guilders, the sermon *Auff, auff Ihr Christen* by Abraham a Sancta Clara (Vienna, 1683) for 12 kreutzer or Gottfried Wilhelm Leibniz' *Ars combinatoria* (Erfurt, 1690) for 10 kreutzer.[89]

According to the survey of Rüdiger's catalogue by Pravoslav Kneidl, German-language titles predominate, but Latin and French titles also constitute a regular feature. It is worth noting that books in Czech are a rarity, which is also true for other foreign booksellers' catalogues of that time. The titles Rüdiger collected under the German heading 'Bohemian' ['böhmisch'] were in their majority German-language and Latin *Bohemica* (148 titles).[90] In this catalogue, Rüdiger presents his books as conforming to censorship standards. With stocks of this considerable scale, it was easy to sell books on the side which were not to be found in the catalogue. In the last years of Rüdiger's life, which we do not know much about, it was probable that his trading activities were restricted by disease or old age. One indication of this is that his catalogue was not continued after 1750. The last biographical evidence is a publication from 1751. This is the reprint of a legal work, *Manuductio ad praxim iuridicam tam apud superiores quam inferiores instantias in regno Bohemiae*, which Rüdiger had first published in Prague in 1729. It seems likely that Rüdiger died in 1751, when, coincidentally, his three-year trading privilege ended. As there is no company archive, we do not know how Rüdiger's book stock was sold after his death, or if his bookstore was bought up in its entirety. Like for many publisher's biographies, we can reconstruct Rüdiger's role in the book trade of the early eighteenth century only through limited aspects.

---

89 *Catalogus od. Verzeichnuß aller Büchernn, welche in Prag* (Prag: Rüdiger, 1748), pp. 3, 5, 385, 478.
90 Kneidl, 'Pražský knihkupec', pp. 1f.

5   Conclusion

Johann Friedrich Rüdiger's biography illustrates the establishment of a foreign Protestant bookseller at a central book market of the Habsburg Monarchy in the first half of the eighteenth century. His case reveals the uncertainties of publishing which characterise the history of book production in the early modern era. In spite of this, long-distance trade proved profitable from the perspective of booksellers, because retail publishers from major book centres such as Nuremberg could participate in fairs, and outclass local book dealers with their large selection.

For a retail publisher such as Rüdiger, who virtually worked as a one-man business, long-distance trade brought with it considerable logistical challenges and entrepreneurial insecurities. Apart from his publishing activities and his political function (as a member of the Greater Council) in Nuremberg, Rüdiger was compelled to near-permanent travel: he visited the Prague markets at an average three times a year and participated in two fair sessions in Frankfurt am Main, usually also in Leipzig. These three destinations (all 250–300 kilometers from Nuremberg) required long travels over land for at least ten days. The investment in long-distance trade could not halt the decline of his main business in Nuremberg, however. An increasing level of debt for his Nuremburg publishing house and bookshop led to Rüdiger's commercial reorientation in 1745. As his move to Prague shows, it was often difficult for smaller firms to sustain both a main and branch business in the long-distance trade over the long term. Rüdiger was only able to benefit from his privilege as an imperial-royal bookseller, and the running of a bookstore connected with that, for a few years. Even though restrictions on Rüdiger's commercial activities were still in force despite his trade permit, the award of this privilege should be regarded as a tremendous achievement. For the economic history of Bohemia in the first half of the eighteenth century, it is an exception that a Protestant such as Rüdiger was granted a trading concession as a bookseller in Prague. This case underlines that confession could still be used to regulate trade, but it was no longer a criterium for exclusion according to the commercial policy of the Habsburg Monarchy. The argument of religious faith could be used by the authorities and competitors alike to restrict market access for foreign traders. On the merchants' side, issues of confession were usually subordinated to those of business. The instances of censorship make clear that in contrast to itinerant peddlers, established foreign traders did not have to fear serious sanctions when trading in banned literature.

Johann Friedrich Rüdiger's catalogues from 1716 and 1748 show not only his comprehensive assortment of books, but also his wide-ranging commercial ties, thanks to which he managed to secure an influential capacity for himself in the book markets of Prague. Only a few local booksellers, such as Kaspar Zacharias Wussin, were in a position to participate in fairs and thus compete with Rüdiger. Rüdiger's retail trade faced rising competition from the market presence of other foreign wholesale traders, such as Lochner and Mayer, Mangoldt, or Walther, from the 1740s onwards. By placing advertisements in the *Prager-Post-Zeitungen*, and by publishing monthly catalogue extracts with fixed prices, Rüdiger drew upon the contemporary book advertising practices of his day. Rüdiger's case offers the rare opportunity to study long-distance trade relationships between Nuremberg and Prague for nearly four decades. The fact that Rüdiger's trade activity can only be partially reconstructed today reveals how problematic the records are for the history of the book trade in the first half of the eighteenth century. But Rüdiger's biography makes clear that this phase of the book trade in central Europe is much more than simply a transition period to the Enlightenment, allegedly pointing onwards into the modern era. Instead, it deserves detailed research and scholarly attention for its intrinsic historical value. The in-depth analysis of these important markets and long-distance trade relationships will advance our understanding of different centres of the book trade in the Holy Roman Empire and the Habsburg Monarchy, in particular with respect to distribution networks. The example of Johann Friedrich Rüdiger's trade relations between Nuremberg and Bohemia emphasise that book history in the early modern era can only be understood by taking spatial perspectives of book production fully into account.

CHAPTER 7

Disclosing False Imprints: a New Look at Eighteenth-Century French Printed Production

Dominique Varry

The purpose of this article is to demonstrate that our supposed knowledge of eighteenth-century French printed production is imprecise and false, despite the numerous and serious investigations undertaken since the middle of the twentieth century. We do not know, and we will probably never know what was really printed in France during the last century of the *Ancien Régime*. Such is my conviction after more than twenty-five years spent researching the people involved in Lyon's book trade in the eighteenth century. This research began as a prosopographical inquiry which allowed me to collect biographical information on more than five hundred individuals who were in some way involved in the book trade in Lyon between 1700 and 1800: printers-cum-booksellers, but also companions, apprentices, pedlars, binders and people who participated in the production and trade of prohibited books. In a second phase of research, I have employed the techniques of material bibliography to reveal a small portion of the hidden production of my Lyonnais printers. The analysis of paper, watermarks, type, ornaments, page layout, and typographical practices (signatures, catchwords, etc.) led to interesting and surprising discoveries. In all these investigations, it is the conjunction of elements, which taken alone do not mean anything, that can prove an attribution to a hidden printer. Furthermore, the evidence revealed by material bibliography must be compared and collated with information available in archival records. The few bibliographical cases I have solved are only the tip of the iceberg, and they point to our ignorance of the real printed production of the time.

1 The Limitations of Early Quantitative Approaches to Book History

If you try to find when a work by Montesquieu was first printed in Lyon by examining, as I did twenty years ago, the printed volumes of the Bibliothèque nationale de France's *Catalogue des imprimés*, you will find the first edition under the name of the Bruyset brothers and the date of 1792.[1] For such a prolific and popular author of the eighteenth century, this is really quite astonishing. Is there nothing before 1792? In fact, as I have since proven, numerous editions of Montesquieu's writing appeared in Lyon before this date, but all bore false foreign imprints and cannot be identified as Lyonnais without close examination using the methods of analytical bibliography. This example is a good illustration of the false impression of reality that official records, library catalogues, and historical scholarship can give.

In France, it is this official record that has been at the forefront of book history since the Annales School adopted a more scientific approach to history in the 1930s. Under the patronage of Marc Bloch and Lucien Febvre, this school of historians abandoned diplomatic and political history, factual events, and instead concentrated on economic and social approaches, using statistics and series of documents over the long term. One of the first such publications in the history of the book was Robert Estivals' *thèse d'état* (a thesis requiring at least twenty years of work): *La Statistique bibliographique de la France sous la monarchie au XVIIIe siècle*, published in 1965.[2] It is a very serious and imposing book full of figures, curves, and diagrams, all of which rely on the official sources that are the records of the *Ancien Régime*'s *Direction de la Librairie*, especially its registers of publishing privileges and permits. Today however, we know the historical narrative presented by this book to be partial, no matter how thoroughly researched it was, since it is limited to only one part of the story: the official one.

In the same period, a group of scholars led by François Furet launched a great inquiry which culminated in the publication of the two volumes of *Livre et société dans la France du XVIIIe siècle*.[3] For the first time, computers were used to organise the information recorded in the manuscript registers of privileges of the *Direction de la Librairie*. One of the well-known members of the Annales School was Emmanuel Le Roy Ladurie, who was very keen on the quantitative approach which he used in his research on the history of climate, of the peasants of Languedoc, of military conscripts, and on books, even though he was not a specialist in this domain. In an article published by the weekly *Nouvel*

---

1 Dominique Varry, 'Les imprimeurs-libraires lyonnais et Montesquieu', in Michel Porret and Catherine Volpilhac-Auger (eds.), *Le Temps de Montesquieu, actes du colloque international de Genève 28–31 octobre 1998* (Geneva: Droz, 2002), pp. 43–63.
2 Robert Estivals, *La Statistique bibliographique de la France sous la monarchie au XVIIIe siècle* (Paris and The Hague: Mouton, 1965).
3 François Furet (ed.), *Livre et société dans la France du XVIIIe siècle* (2 vols.; Paris and The Hague: Mouton, 1965 and 1970).

Observateur in 1968, he defended the use of computing by historians, and wrote: 'Tomorrow's historian will be a programmer or will disappear'.[4]

Later, after serving as General Administrator of the Bibliothèque nationale de France (BnF) between 1987 and 1994, Le Roy Ladurie published, in association with collaborators, several articles about book history with all the visual trappings of a quantitative approach.[5] The last two use data issued from the retro-conversion of the general catalogue of the BnF. However the material collected on this occasion can be deceiving for an uninformed user. For instance, I personally heard Le Roy Ladurie insisting on the importance of Cologne as a printing place. Evidently he was unaware that the imprint 'à Cologne chez Pierre Marteau' (in Cologne by Pierre Marteau) was in fact false. As was pointed out by Janmart de Brouillant at the end of the nineteenth century, Pierre Marteau, Pierre du Marteau, Peter Marteau or Peter Hammer never existed, though he ostensibly published dozens of books in Cologne, alone or in association with his son-in-law Adrien L'enclume (= the Anvil), from 1660 until the nineteenth century.[6] Pierre Marteau was used as a figurehead by numerous printers from the Low Countries, France, Germany, Switzerland and elsewhere. The importance of Cologne as printing place must therefore be considered cautiously, especially when including French-language books.

Printed bibliographies and library catalogues are hardly more reliable than this literature. Pierre Conlon's six volumes of the *Prélude au siècle des Lumières* and thirty-four volumes of *Le Siècle des Lumières*, for example, only list, year after year, first editions legally published under their given imprints, and ignore all the re-impressions.[7] For its part, the *Répertoire bibliographique des*

---

4   Emmanuel Le Roy Ladurie, 'La fin des érudits: l'historien de demain sera programmeur ou ne sera pas', *Le Nouvel Observateur*, 8 May 1968, pp. 38–39; reprinted in Emmanuel Le Roy Ladurie, *Le Territoire de l'historien* (Paris: Gallimard, 1973), pp. 11–14.
5   See for example: Emmanuel Le Roy Ladurie, 'Une histoire sérielle du livre 1452–1970', *Histoire, économie et société*, 1 (1995), pp. 3–24; Emmanuel Le Roy Ladurie, Yann Fauchois, Annette Smedley-Weill and André Zysberg, 'L'édition francophone (1470–1780) Paris – Province – 'Étranger' par tranches diachroniques', *Histoire, économie et société*, 4 (1996), pp. 507–523; Emmanuel Le Roy Ladurie, Annette Smidley-Weill and André Zysberg, 'French Book Production From 1454: A Quantitative Analysis', *Library History*, 15 (1999), pp. 83–98; Emmanuel Le Roy Ladurie, 'Histoire quantitative de l'édition en langue française d'après les collections de la Bibliothèque nationale de France (1460–1969)', *Revue de la Bibliothèque nationale de France*, 9 (2001), pp. 20–27.
6   Léonce Janmart de Brouillant, *La Liberté de la presse en France aux XVIIe et XVIIIe siècles, histoire de Pierre Du Marteau, imprimeur à Cologne (XVIIe–XVIIIe siècles)* (Paris: Quantin, 1888; reprinted Geneva: Slatkine, 1971).
7   Pierre-Marie Conlon, *Prélude au siècle des Lumières en France, répertoire chronologique de 1680 à 1715* (6 vols.; Geneva: Droz, 1970–1975); Pierre-Marie Conlon, *Le siècle des Lumières. Bibliographie chronologique* (34 vols.; Geneva: Droz, 1983–2009).

livres imprimés en France au XVIIIème siècle lists books by place of publication but only includes those officially produced under the real names and imprints of their printers.[8] As a result, there too, the image is incomplete and blurred.

The problem shared by all of these studies, catalogues and bibliographies is that they rely exclusively on official sources. First and foremost among these are the archives of the *Direction de la Librairie*, nowadays held in the manuscript department of the BnF, and especially the registers of printing permissions (*privilèges du roi* and *permissions tacites*). The next most used source are the collections themselves of the BnF and of provincial public libraries. It is evident that pirated books or prohibited ones would not have entered the king's library through the legal deposit established by François I in 1537. The unauthorised books that are now on the shelves of the national library arrived mostly with the private libraries confiscated during the Revolution. These are found more easily at the Bibliothèque de l'Arsenal than in the main collections at the Tolbiac site, since in the eighteenth century, the Arsenal was a private library belonging to a great book collector, the marquis de Paulmy. Similarly, provincial public libraries were constituted by private libraries bequeathed to different institutions (such as cities or convents) under the condition that they would be opened to the public. As a result, and in contrast to the King's library, these could include pirated editions previously owned by the donors.

Further complicating the identification of false imprints is the fact that the librarians who created the catalogues of the BnF and of other Parisian and provincial libraries only copied the imprints that were placed on the title-pages of the books they described. They had no possibility of identifying the real printers of books parading as having been published in Amsterdam or in London. The catalogue of the BnF is moreover one of three main parts that make up the *Catalogue collectif de France* (CCFr), along with the collective catalogue of French university libraries, and the *base patrimoine* (heritage database).[9] The latter brings together records prepared in different periods, according to variable rules, for the nineteenth-century printed catalogues or twentieth-century card catalogues of a certain number of provincial city libraries. All this explains why the *Catalogue collectif de France* is useful for locating extant copies of books, but bibliographically unreliable and full of doubles, errors and ghosts.

On the other hand, there is an important source traditionally ignored by librarians and book historians: the catalogues of newly issued titles published in the eighteenth century by booksellers, and auction sales catalogues

---

8 *Répertoire bibliographique des livres imprimés en France au XVIIIe siècle* (17 vols.; Baden-Baden: Valentin Koerner, 1988–2001).
9 *Catalogue collectif de France* ccfr.bnf.fr/portailccfr/.

of that time.[10] In the description of the books they list, after the name of the city as it is printed on the title-page, they often give the name of the real place of printing and sometimes the name of the printer. The constitution of a database gathering this kind of information would be very useful, and could allow for another vision of the printed production of this period. The booksellers who disclosed these imprints in their catalogues knew very well from whom they had purchased and from where they had received them.

Despite many constraints, scholars have not been unaware of the widespread use of false imprints on piracies and prohibited books. In the second half of the nineteenth century, Emil Weller published an important study disclosing false imprints.[11] Still used today, Weller's work must be used with caution; it is not always reliable as it attributes to Paris numerous impressions printed elsewhere, and notably in the French provinces. The doctoral thesis of Jean-Paul Belin, a descendant of the Parisian printers, published on the eve of the First World War, gave a first overview of the trade of prohibited books, opened new trails for further investigations and is still useful.[12] Later in the twentieth century, François Moureau published a stimulating article demonstrating that false imprints serve not only to protect the printer's real identity, but also as a marketing tool to attract the customer's attention and trigger the purchase of books.[13]

2   Strict Regulations and General Surveillance

From the very beginning of the sixteenth century, and until the fall of the monarchy, French royal authorities took numerous measures to control authors, printers and booksellers, and their production: they introduced censorship, limited the number of print shops, and created a complex system of necessary and compulsory authorisations to publish a book. These measures had the effect of strengthening the position of Parisian printers who, by their proximity to the royal administration, received most of the privileges for new books, and condemned their provincial colleagues to choose between publishing only

---

10   The latter have been the object of attention by book historians since the studies of Françoise Bléchet and conferences held in Paris and Lyon. Françoise Bléchet, *Les ventes publiques de livres en France 1630–1750. Répertoire des catalogues conservés à la Bibliothèque nationale* (Oxford: The Voltaire Foundation, 1991); Annie Charon and Elisabeth Parinet (eds.), *Les ventes de livres et leurs catalogues XVIIe–XXe siècle* (Paris: École des chartes, 2000).

11   Emil Ottokar Weller, *Die Falschen und fingirten Druckorte. Repertorium der seit Erfindung der Buchdruckerkunst unter falscher Firma erschienen deutschen, lateinischen und französischen Schriften* (2 vols.; Leipzig: W. Engelmann, 1864; reprinted New York: G. Olms, 1970).

12   Jean-Paul Belin, *Le commerce des livres prohibés à Paris de 1750 à 1789* (Paris: Belin, 1913).

13   François Moureau, 'Le libraire imaginaire ou les fausses adresses', *Corps écrit*, 33 (1991), pp. 45–56.

old titles fallen into the public domain, and secretly printing counterfeits and pirated editions to survive. This is how Lyon and Rouen, respectively the second and third most productive centres of print in France, were the first and second centres in terms of the production of piracies and prohibited books in the early modern period.

On 20 October 1521, François I forbade booksellers and printers from selling or publishing anything without the authorisation of the university of Paris and its Faculty of Theology. This date is considered the birth of French royal censorship. Soon, the faculty was overwhelmed with manuscripts and asked the king for help. In January 1629, Louis XIII authorised the keeper of the seals to appoint royal censors, in spite of the protests of the Faculty of Theology. From that point on, royal censorship became a lay administration organised by the *Direction de la Librairie*.[14]

On 28 December 1537, by the *Ordonnance de Montpellier* (Ordinance of Montpellier), François I established the legal deposit of all books printed in the kingdom. If the official aim of such a decision was the transmission of these works to posterity, this measure also made it possible to keep an eye on all authors, printers and booksellers.

Additional control was exercised in limiting the number of printers. In 1704, the government decided to limit the number of printers to 250, working in 110 cities of the kingdom. In fact, this goal was only reached on the eve of the Revolution. The number of print shops in Lyon and Rouen was originally fixed at 18, and was later reduced to 12 in 1739. The number of printers in Paris had already been reduced to 36 in 1686.

On top of all this, the system of publication permissions was very complex. We must distinguish the *permission du sceau* (permission of the seal), given in the name of the king by his chancellor and sealed with the royal seal, from other local permits. The most ancient *permission du sceau* is the *privilège du roi* (royal privilege), which appeared at the beginning of the sixteenth century, and gave its owner the monopoly of publication of a title for a stated number of years in the whole kingdom. In 1563, Charles IX reserved for himself the possibility of granting such *privilèges*. Three years later, he decreed that no book could be printed in France without a royal privilege. From 1653 onwards, to be valid, a royal privilege had to be recorded in the registers of Paris' printers *Chambre syndicale*, and the title submitted for legal deposit.[15]

---

14 The functioning of the *Direction de la Librairie* in eighteenth-century France has been studied by different scholars, notably Nicole Hermann-Mascard and more recently Raymond Birn. See Nicole Hermann-Mascard, *La censure des livres à Paris à la fin de l'Ancien Régime, 1750–1789* (Paris: Presses universitaires de France, 1968); Raymond Birn, *La censure royale des livres dans la France des Lumières* (Paris: Odile Jacob, 2007).

15 The *Chambre syndicale* was more or less equivalent to the London Worshipful Company of Stationers.

In 1709 a sort of lesser privilege was created: the *permission tacite* (tacit permit). This kind of authorisation was used on a large scale after 1750 to publish books, such as novels, which were not considered serious enough to warrant a royal privilege, especially in the period when Chrétien Guillaume de Lamoignon de Malesherbes (1721–1794) was *Directeur de la Librairie* from 1750 until 1763. The tacit permit was based on a fiction: a French bookseller was allowed to import and sell in France a book supposedly printed abroad. In actual fact, the French bookseller was the printer but was obliged to use a foreign imprint to give the illusion of the work having been imported. Often in these cases the title-page indicates two locations: a foreign locale printed in bold type, and, in smaller type, a French place name. For instance: '*A Amsterdam et se trouve à Paris chez ...*' (printed in Amsterdam, and found in Paris at the address of ...). In such cases the tacit permit is easily recognisable. However we know of numerous cases in which the title-page bears only a foreign imprint so that the tacit permit cannot be recognised at a glance, nor distinguished from either a true foreign book or from an illicit publication. Like royal privileges, tacit permits theoretically had to be registered in the records of the *Chambre syndicale* in Paris, and to comply with legal deposit. But we have proof that this was not always the case, especially when the tacit permit was given by the *intendant* (official representative of the king) in Lyon. It is a little-known fact that provincial *intendants* could deliver such publishing authorisations themselves. These permits may have been recorded in local archives, but we do not have any evidence of this. Unsurprisingly then, the system of tacit permits remains poorly understood by historians and bibliographers, though some new investigations have been launched.[16]

The records of royal privileges and tacit permits constitute an important part of the *Archives de la Librairie*, nowadays held in the manuscript department of the national library as the Anisson-Duperron collection.[17] These archives were the main source used by Estivals, Furet and others. This documentation ignores a part of the tacit permits given in the provinces by local *intendants* and the other existing permits given and recorded locally. These were of two kinds: *Permission locale* (local permit) granted in the provinces for books in small formats and with a maximum of 48 pages; and a *Permission simple* (simple permit), created in 1701, and widely used after 1777. These allowed for the publication of books having fallen into the public domain, for a duration of three years before 1777 and thereafter for five years, though without any protection from

---

16   Jean-Dominique Mellot, 'Pour une 'cote' des fausses adresses au XVIIIe siècle: le témoignage des éditions sous permission tacite en France', *Revue française d'histoire du livre*, 100–101 (1998), pp. 323–348.

17   Ernest Coyecque, *Inventaire de la collection Anisson sur l'histoire de l'imprimerie et de la librairie, principalement à Paris* (2 vols.; Paris: Leroux, 1900). This material has been digitised and is available on the digital collections platform of the BnF: *Gallica* <gallica.bnf.fr>.

competition.[18] There was a third kind of permit, by which the royal administration shut its eyes to books it could not officially allow, but whose production was tolerated for economic purposes, as it was considered preferable to have these books printed in French workshops rather than abroad only to be smuggled in. This last kind of permit, the *permission orale* (oral permit), did not leave any traces in the archives.

Several royal edicts of the summer of 1777 tried to stop general piracy, by pardoning existing counterfeits, but announcing the fierce repression of new counterfeiters.[19] To be legalised, each pirated copy had to be brought to a designated commissioner of the local 'chambre syndicale' who signed and stamped it with a special seal. The stamping began in 1778 and lasted until 1780. This new legislation appears to have been effective as the number of counterfeits fell after 1777, and it also gave new impulse to the use of simple permits.

Beginning in the reign of Louis XIV, French police forces were increasingly organised, and progressively became more efficient. In the eighteenth century, they benefitted from the help of numerous police spies, nicknamed *'mouches'* (flies), active at all levels of society. One of the most efficient sleuths of the time was police inspector d'Hémery, whose papers are still a great source for the historian today.

Joseph d'Hémery was born on 22 February 1722 in Stenay. He was an upper middle-class illegitimate child. He began a military career in 1739 at the Clermont cavalry Regiment and joined the Paris police in 1741. Gradually, from 1754, he became specialised in policing the book trade. The Paris bookseller Hardy wrote in his diary that he was a trustworthy man for all secret police cases, even abroad. We can add that he practised material bibliography before it was invented, being able to identify prohibited impressions by their type, ornament or layout. He gave himself the unofficial title of *Inspecteur général de la librairie* (General inspector of the book trade). He left his duties progressively after 1773 and died on 5 October 1806 in Belleville (now a district of Paris). His archives and papers, bound in 143 manuscript registers, were bought in 1792 by the director of the *Imprimerie nationale*, Étienne-Alexandre Anisson-Dupéron. They form the main part of the above-mentioned Anisson-Dupéron collection, now held at the BnF. D'Hémery created three important tools for the police of

---

18 Such permits given after 1777 have been studied and listed by Robert Dawson in *The French book trade and the 'permission simple' of 1777: copyright and public domain with an edition of the permit registers* (Oxford: The Voltaire Foundation, 1992).

19 Anne Boës and Robert L. Dawson, 'The legitimation of contrefaçons and the police stamp of 1777', in *Studies on Voltaire and the 18th Century* (Oxford: The Voltaire Foundation, 1985), vol. 230, pp. 461–484. See also Jeanne Veyrin-Forrer, 'Livres arrêtés, livres estampillés traces parisiennes de la contrefaction', in François Moureau (ed.), *Les Presses grises. La contrefaçon du livre XVIe–XIXe siècles* (Paris: Aux Amateurs de livres, 1988), pp. 101–112.

the time, and for today's historians and bibliographers.[20] The first is his diary, written every Thursday between 1750 and 1769, which he called the *'Journal de la librairie'*. Each week he listed publications that had appeared in the kingdom of France, indicating if they were authorised or not, and identifying, if possible, their printers.[21] The second tool created by d'Hémery, written between 1748 and 1753, was a file on 500 authors entitled *'Historique des auteurs'*, in which he gave information on the identity, age, country, description, residence and the history of each author.[22] Robert Darnton has presented and used this material in several publications.[23] The third, compiled between 1749 and 1752, is entitled *'Historique des libraires'* and was published recently.[24] It gives biographical information on 261 Paris printers-cum-booksellers, eleven in the provinces, and one foreigner, Marc-Michel Rey of Amsterdam.

3 Identifying Illicit Imprints

Detecting counterfeits is not always easy. Some signs can warn the historian, for instance the use of armillary spheres on title-pages, or the presence above the imprint of phrases in tiny type such as *'jouxte la copie imprimée'*, *'sur la copie'*, *'sur l'imprimé'*. Such expressions can be understood to mean 'I am copying the genuine edition printed at …' For instance, a book entitled *La Charge des gouverneurs des places* by Antoine de Ville appeared in Paris in 1639, which was printed under a royal privilege by Mathieu Guillemot. The book was a small folio and bore an engraved frontispiece preceding the title-page. A year later a

---

20   Jean-Pierre Vittu, 'L'inspecteur d'Hémery organise ses fiches: les instruments de la police du livre à Paris dans la seconde moitié du XVIIIe siècle', in Gaël Rideau and Pierre Serna (eds.), *Ordonner et partager la ville XVIIe–XIXe siècle* (Rennes: Presses universitaires de Rennes, 2011), pp. 75–87.

21   Kept in the Anisson collection of the Bibliothèque nationale, this diary is available online on *Gallica*. The annual distribution of the *Journal de la Librairie* is as follows: ms. fr. 22156: 1750–1751; ms. fr. 22157: 1752; ms. fr. 22158: 1753; ms. fr. 22159: 1754–1755; ms. fr. 22160: 1756–1758; ms. fr. 22161: 1759–1760; ms. fr. 22162: 1761; ms. fr. 22038: 1762; ms. fr. 22163: 1763–1765; ms. fr. 22164: 1766–1767; ms. fr. 22165: 1768–1769.

22   BnF: ms. NAF. 10781–10783.

23   Robert Darnton, 'A police inspector sorts his files: the anatomy of the Republic of Letters', in idem, *The Great Cat Massacre and Other Episodes in French Cultural History* (New York: Basic Books, 1984), pp. 145–190; 'Les encyclopédistes et la police', *Recherches sur Diderot*, I (1986), pp. 94–109 and 'Policing Writers in Paris circa 1750', *Representations*, 5 (Spring 1984), pp. 1–31.

24   BnF: ms. fr. 22106–22107. Jean-Dominique Mellot, Marie-Claude Felton, Élisabeth Queval (eds.), *La police des métiers du livre à Paris, au siècle des lumières: Historique des libraires et imprimeurs de Paris existans en 1752, de l'inspecteur Joseph d'Hémery* (Paris: Bibliothèque nationale de France, 2017).

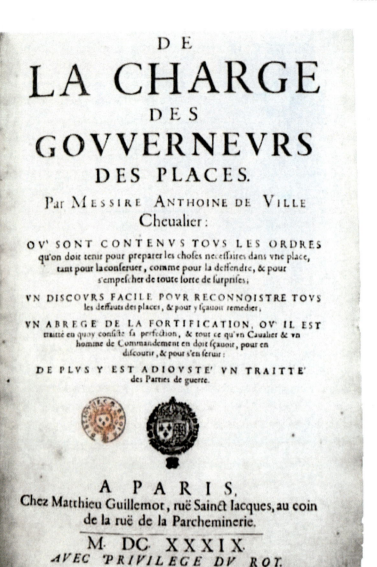

FIGURE 7.1   Title-page of the original 1639 edition of *La Charge des gouverneurs des places*

counterfeit duodecimo was published, without any illustrations. Its title-page bore an armillary sphere and the imprint '*Iouxte la copie imprimée A Paris*'.[25]

As a general rule, counterfeits were printed in a smaller format than the original, on paper of poor quality, with worn types and ornaments. The *Soirées hélvétiennes, alsaciennes et fran-comtoises*, written by the marquis de Pezay,

---

25   See USTC 6040501 and 6040277.

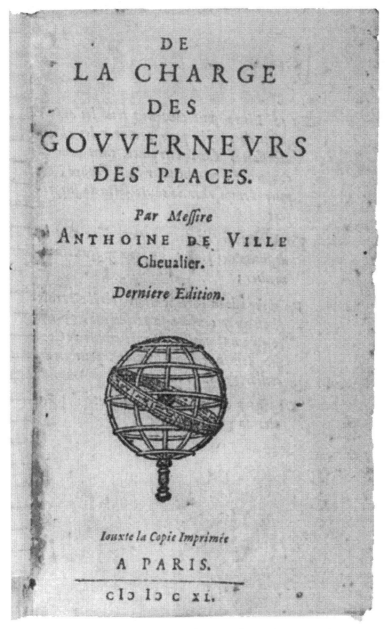

FIGURE 7.2　Title-page of the counterfeit 1640 edition of *La Charge des gouverneurs des places*

received a tacit permit on 29 November 1770 from the royal censor Jean-Henri Marchand. The book was published as an octavo under the imprint '*A Amsterdam, et se trouve à Paris chez Delalain ... 1771*'. A few months later a counterfeit appeared in two little duodecimo volumes bearing the imprint '*A Londres, 1772*'. It was printed on paper bearing watermarks of grapes and 'M CuvellieR' which corresponds to the paper mill of Moïse Cuvellier from Esquernes, near Lille. This mill is known to have been active from at least 1764 to 1783. The pirated edition was probably printed by a member of the Boubers family, either Jean-Louis de Boubers (1731–1804), who tried to open a print shop at Lille in 1760–1762 before running away to Liège and then Brussels, or Charles-Louis (1740–1811), a bookseller in Dunkirk, then printer in Lille.[26]

Counterfeiters do not often reveal themselves easily, but we have an exceptional confession of Lyon printer Jean-Marie Barret in a letter he wrote on 10 April 1772 to the Société typographique de Neuchâtel, evoking his piracy in progress of Jean Jacques Rousseau's *Oeuvres* under the Amsterdam imprint of Marc-Michel Rey:

> My edition of Rousseau will be finished in August. It will contain the eleven volumes of the Dutch edition I am imitating, and with which it will go entirely hand in hand [...] The edition of the works of J.J. Rousseau is a piece of work which will cost me a lot because of the expenses and the care I take: I am using paper that costs 12 pounds per ream, I am having the engravings, tailpieces and music made in Paris, so that they are of better quality.[27]

Examination of a copy of the pirated edition held in the Besançon municipal library reveals paper used in Lyon bearing watermarks from Montgolfier of Annonay or Corchon and Richard from Ambert, engravings signed by the

---

26 Dominique Varry, 'Le Marquis de Pezay témoin de son temps. *Les Soirées helvétiennes, alsaciennes et fran-comtoises* (1771)', in François Lassus, Paul Delsalle, Corinne Marchal and François Vion-Delphin (eds.), *Mélanges offerts au professeur Maurice Gresset: des institutions et des hommes* (Besançon: Presses de l'université de Franche-Comté, 2007), pp. 509–519.

27 Bibliothèque publique et universitaire de Neuchâtel: Société typographique de Neuchâtel: ms. 1117, ff. 229–293, 41 letters from Jean-Marie Barret (1 April 1772–23 September 1784). 'Mon édition de Rousseau sera fini [*sic*] au mois d'août. Elle contiendra les onze volumes de l'édition de Hollande que j'imite et avec laquelle ira de pair en tout [...] L'édition des oeuvres de J.J. Rousseau est un ouvrage qui me reviendra très cher par la dépense et les soins que j'y prends; j'y employe du papier de 12 livres la rame, je fais faire à Paris les figures, culs de lampe et musique, pour qu'elles soient mieux exécutées'.

FIGURE 7.3   Title-page of the original 1770 edition of *Soirées hélvétiennes, alsaciennes et fran-comtoises*

French engraver Martinet, and Barret's tailpieces recorded in the Lausanne database *Fleuron* and Montpellier database *Maguelone*.[28]

Paris printers often complained about Lyon counterfeiters. In turn, Lyon printers complained about Avignon counterfeiters. Most printers did not know how

---

28   Fleuron database (db-prod-bcul.unil.ch/ornements/scripts/Info.html) tailpieces: bar007, bar019, and Maguelone database (maguelone.enssib.fr) m0148, all identified as Jean-Marie Barret's ornaments.

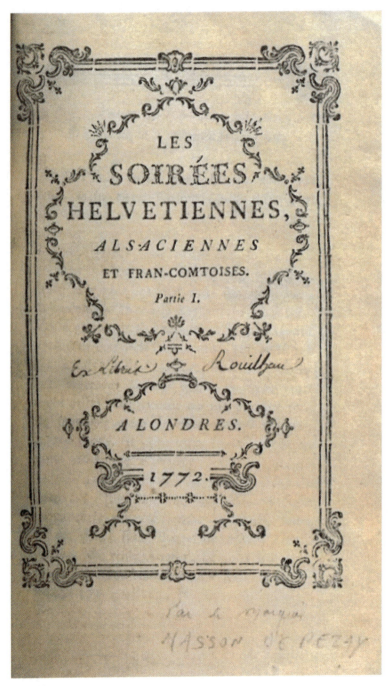

FIGURE 7.4   Title-page of the counterfeit 1772 edition of *Soirées hélvétiennes, alsaciennes et fran-comtoises*

to protect themselves against this plague. In 1716, the author Nicolas Barreme signed each copy of his *L'Arithmétique du Sr Barreme* published in Paris, and promised in a notice printed in the book, his part of the fine punishing counterfeiters to their whistle-blower. At the end of the century, the widow Desaint, from Paris, printed a warning against counterfeiters on the verso of the half-title, and similarly hand-signed the verso of the title-page of each copy of the eight volumes published between 1783 and 1789 of her *Collection de décisions nouvelles et de notions relatives à la jurisprudence, donnée par Me Denisart*.

Some false imprints refer to improbable locations: '*Ici A Présent*' (here and now), '*à Constantinople l'année présente*' (in Constantinople in the present year), '*aux enfers, de l'imprimerie de Belzébuth*' (in Hell, from Belzebuth's print shop).[29] Others evoke exotic places: '*à Constantinople chez le Grand Turc*' (in Constatinople by the Sultan), '*à Pékin chez le Grand Moghol*' (in Beijing by the Great Mogul), '*à Gibraltar chez Pierre Chinois*' (in Gibraltar by Peter Chinese).[30] Pornography was often supposedly printed in Rome: '*à Rome de l'imprimerie du Vatican*' (in Rome from the Vatican print shop), '*à Rome sous les yeux du Saint-Père*' (in Rome under the Holy Father's eyes), '*à Rome de l'imprimerie du général des jésuites*' (in Rome from the print shop of the Jesuits general).[31] Masonic books often bore the name of cities such as Philadelphia or Edinburgh.

Other false imprints refer to various European cities and often under the last name, but not necessarily the first name, of an existing professional. When a printer used a colleague's name, was it with the latter's approval? Most often, the borrower would change the Christian name or used the name of a printer who had recently passed away. Take for instance, the edition of Caraccioli's *La Jouissance de soi-même* which appeared in 1762 under the imprint '*à Lyon, chez Dominique Reguillat*'. To the common customer of the time, and later to the non-specialist, the imprint seems genuine. But not to a specialist of Lyon printing history. Cursory analysis of the paper and of the ornamental material reveals that this edition was in fact printed by Louis Chambeau in Avignon,

---

29 See for example: Paul Baret, *Le Grelot, ou les &c., &c., &c. Ouvrage dédié à moi* (Ici: A present [1754]); Pierre-François Godard de Beauchamps, *Histoire du prince Apprius, &c. Extraite des Fastes du Monde, depuis sa Création. Manuscrit Persan trouvé dans la Bibliothèque de Schah-Hussain, Roi de Perse, détrôné par Mamouth en 1722. Traduction françoise. Par Messire Esprit, gentilhomme Provençal, servant dans les troupes de Perse* (Imprimé à Constantinople, l'année présente [1728]); Claude-Marie Giraud, *Épître du diable à Monsieur de Voltaire, avec des notes historiques. Aux Délices, près Genève* (Aux Enfers: de l'imprimerie de Béelzébuth, 1760). Available on *Gallica*.

30 For example: Jean-Louis-Claude Taupin d'Orval, *Épitre à Mlle de C ... Par M. D ... Qui n'est d'aucune Académie* (A Gibraltar: De l'imprimerie de Pierre Chinois [1761]).

31 For example: Honoré-Gabriel Riquetti comte de Mirabeau, *Erotika Biblion* (A Rome: De l'imprimerie du Vatican, 1783). Available on *Gallica*.

which was then a foreign enclave in the heart of the French kingdom. There was no printer named Dominique Reguillat active in Lyon in 1762. Reguilliat was however, the name of a local family of printers-cum-booksellers. At that time, Jean-Baptiste Réguilliat, who signed and printed his name with an 'i', was an active printer in Lyon and known for producing forbidden books.[32] The Avignon printer only played with the fame of his Lyon colleague, borrowing his surname and composing it with a mistake.

We know of at least one case, however, in which the foreign printers whose names were borrowed by a French colleague had consented to their use. In 1762, the Lyon printer Jean-Marie Bruyset produced a shared edition of a book entitled *Esprit des Loix de la tactique* with three editions under the imprints of Pierre Gosse junior in The Hague, George Weidmann in Leipzig and Henri-Louis Broenner in Frankfurt.[33] In this case we have the proof that foreign printers occasionally lent their name in exchange for receiving a certain number of copies, since Broenner (Brönner) published an advertisement for the book bearing his name in the *Gazette de Cologne* as soon as the book was published. D'Hémery's diary informs us that the book had been granted a tacit permit, which obliged Bruyset to use a foreign imprint.[34] The majority of the print run bears the name of Pierre Gosse active in The Hague, and it is likely that he too agreed to lend his name since the book is listed in his own catalogue of 1766.

4 The Use of the False Imprint *Londres* in the Eighteenth Century

Among the false imprints used in the eighteenth century, '*Londres*' (as opposed to 'London') is, with '*Cologne*', one of the most frequently recurring. The reputation of the United Kingdom as a country of liberty explains this, as it does one of the most famous false imprints of the time: that of the *Gazetier cuirassé ou Anecdotes scandaleuses de la cour de France* by Charles Théveneau de Morande: '*Imprimé à cent lieues de la Bastille, à l'enseigne de la liberté*'

---

[32] In August 1762, Réguilliat was arrested in the act of re-printing a forbidden edition of Rousseau's *Contrat social*, and jailed. Five years later, he was dismissed by royal authorities for having published prohibited books, paying dearly for his illicit printing of Rousseau. See Dominique Varry, 'Un lyonnais pris en flagrant délit d'impression du *Contrat social* (1762)', *Histoire et civilisation du livre: revue internationale*, 13 (2017), pp. 123–141.

[33] Dominique Varry, 'Quatre villes pour une adresse typographique: enquête autour de l'impression de l'Esprit des loix de la tacticquz (1762)', *Livre – Revue historique*, 2018, hal.science/hal-01900690.

[34] BnF: ms. fr. 22038, fol. 45v (17 June 1762).

(*printed at a hundred leagues from the Bastille at the sign of liberty*). This surprising imprint insinuated that London was the supposed printing place of the book, whose author, if identified, could have been sent to the Bastille. Some lampoons of members of the French court, printed in French, for a French public, really were printed in London and were hunted there by the French police. An example is the case of the *Vie privée ou Apologie de tres-sérénissime prince Monseigneur le duc de Chartres*, also with the imprint 'A cent lieus [sic] de la Bastille' in 1784.[35] Though in this case one can read in English on its last printed page that this book was available alongside similar titles in bookshops in London and Edinburgh.

The imprint '*Londres*' was used by numerous French and European printers for a production they could not avow. In an article published in 1988, James Mitchell documented 322 editions bearing a false London imprint produced between 1787 and 1800.[36] Among them, 292 were French, and of these most were printed in Paris. For his part, Robert Darnton listed 720 forbidden titles for the years 1769–1789 in his *Corpus of Clandestine Literature in France*, 141 of them (19.6%) bearing the false imprint '*Londres*'.[37] I have analysed the most reliable source, the *English Short Title Catalogue* (ESTC), and found 5,514 titles in French published under a '*Londres*' imprint between 1701 and 1800. This corpus includes books truly printed in London in French, and foreign impressions under false imprints. Parisian and French printers were not the only ones to use this false address, as the ESTC identifies books with this imprint as having been printed in the cities of Amsterdam, Rotterdam, Basel, Frankfurt, Geneva, Lausanne, and Neuchâtel, among others. These include scandalous titles as well as piracies such as the *Soirées Helvétiennes, alsaciennes et fran comtoises*.

---

35   ESTC T114476.
36   James Mitchell was one of the first researchers to work on 'Londres' as a false imprint. He presented his first results at a conference held at the Bibliothèque nationale in May 1987, the proceedings of which were published (James Mitchell, 'La fausse rubrique 'Londres' durant la Révolution française', *Livre et Révolution, Mélanges de la Bibliothèque de la Sorbonne*, n° 9, 1988, pp. 157–164). He published this work in English in 1992 in the *Australian Journal of French Studies* (James Mitchell, 'The Use of the False Imprint 'Londres' during the French Revolution, 1787–1800', *Australian Journal of French Studies*, n° 29, 1992, pp. 185–219.) Simon Burrows later studied French impressions made in London in his doctoral dissertation (published as *Blackmail, scandal, and revolution. London's French libellistes, 1758–92*, Manchester: Manchester University Press, 2006.) We must also mention the book of Robert Darnton, *The Devil in the Holy Water. The Art of Slander from Louis XIV to Napoleon* (Philadelphia: University of Pennsylvania Press, 2009).
37   Robert Darnton, *The Corpus of Clandestine Literature in France 1769–1789* (New York and London: W.W. Norton & Company, 1995).

But the *'Londres'* imprint also appears on numerous title-pages of books published with tacit permission. Introduced in 1709, tacit permits were used on a large scale after 1750. Of the 5,514 titles listed by the ESTC, I have found 748 (13.5%) published before 1789 with tacit permits, recognisable by their double imprint '*A Londres*' in large type, and '*et se trouve à Paris chez …*' in a smaller typeface.

The books published under tacit permits with the *'Londres'* imprint were mostly printed in Paris. Of the 5,514 titles listed by the ESTC, 14% were printed in France under tacit permits, a further 36% (1,972 titles) can be reliably attributed to a French printer, but 50% (2,794 titles) cannot.

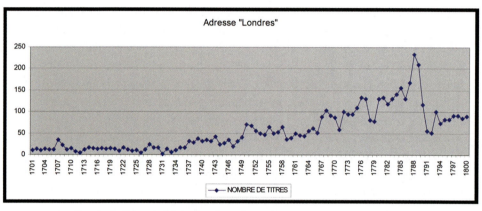

FIGURE 7.5 *'Londres'* editions published in the eighteenth century

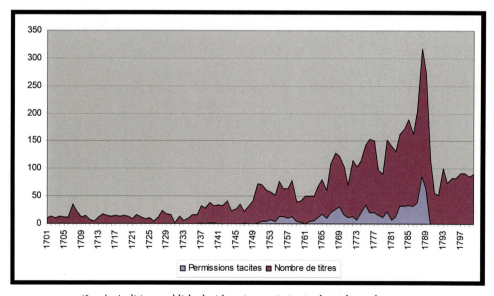

FIGURE 7.6 *'Londres'* editions published with tacit permission in the eighteenth century

5 An Unknown Pirate Printer

Who knows Geoffroy Regnault? Nobody. He is not even mentioned in Joseph d'Hémery's *Historique des libraires*, though, in my opinion, he deserved to be. Born in Lyon in 1710, he began to work as a bookseller in 1743, became a printer in 1757 and was active until at least 1791. He opened one of the first reading rooms in Lyon in 1759, had three printing presses running in 1763, and left his bookshop to his son Gabriel in 1773. He was a deputy officer of Lyon's 'Chambre syndicale' in 1784, and is known for having collaborated with Joseph Duplain, Panckoucke and the *Société typographique de Neuchâtel* on the quarto edition of the *Encyclopédie*. Robert Darnton considers him Panckoucke's agent and spy in Lyon. According to the catalogue of the Bibliothèque nationale de France, he printed a scant six titles under his own name between 1758 and 1773. To the authorities, he was a very suspect printer. In his report to Sartine, the *Directeur de la Librairie* (Director of the book trade) in 1763, before leaving his functions of 'inspector of the book trade in Lyon', Claude Bourgelat wrote:

> I shall cite Réguillat and Renaud [Regnault], without fearing that you ask me for proof of what I say. Their print shop is the workshop where a quantity of bad books of all manner are constantly made, which sometimes flood the capital and provinces, and secret warehouses harbour all of these books from the shadows.[38]

Geoffroy Regnault was a Lyon printer-cum-bookseller who, until now, has gone unnoticed. Recent inquiries in material bibliography have demonstrated that he may have been one of the city's most important printers in the eighteenth century, that he produced, either alone or in collaboration with his colleagues Claude-André Vialon and Claude-André Faucheux, numerous best-sellers of the Enlightenment, though always under false foreign imprints.

In his *Bibliography of the writings of Helvetius*, David Smith identified several editions made in Lyon by Claude-André Faucheux and pointed out others probably printed by Regnault, without being able to attribute them to him

---

[38] BnF: ms. fr. 22128, ff. 291–302. Léon Moulé, 'Rapport de Cl. Bourgelat sur le commerce de la librairie et de l'imprimerie à Lyon en 1763', *Revue d'histoire de Lyon*, 13 (1914), pp. 51–65. '[...] je citeray Réguillat et Renaud [*i.e.* Regnault], sans craindre que vous ayez à me demander des preuves de ce que j'avance. Leur imprimerie est l'atelier où se fabrique sans cesse une quantité de mauvais livres en tous genres, dont la Capitale et les provinces se trouvent quelquefois inondées, et des magazins cachés recèlent tous ces ouvrages des ténèbres.'

with certainty.[39] Due to the development of the Maguelone and Fleuron databases of ornaments, this is now possible, and we can affirm that Regnault was the printer of the second edition of *Le Bonheur* (Smith B2), and of *De l'Homme* (Smith H4) published under the false imprint 'A Londres' respectively in 1772 and 1773, in both of which his ornamental material is now easily recognisable.[40] For her part, Claudette Fortuny demonstrated that Regnault, alone or in collaboration with Vialon and Faucheux, printed seven of the twelve editions of Raynal's *Histoire des deux Indes* which appeared in Lyon between 1772 and 1782 under false foreign imprints of Amsterdam, The Hague or Geneva.[41]

I have also shown that Regnault was the printer of one of the two framed editions of Voltaire's works to appear in 1775 in 40 volumes. Regnault's impression is known as W75X, and should now be called W75L. Long considered a piracy probably printed in Lyon, I have demonstrated that this edition made by Regnault was in fact a collaboration with the Geneva printers of the genuine edition W75G, in order to provide a slightly amended edition which could be accepted by French royal censorship.[42] We know that Panckoucke obtained the authorisation to introduce a certain number of copies under the condition that he insert cancels. On 16 February 1776, Bachaumont wrote in his *Mémoires secrets* that 'the framed edition spreads furtively'.

More recently, we have proven that Regnault was the printer of the *Collection complette des œuvres de M. de Voltaire* published *sine loco* in 10 octavo volumes in 1772, copying the Geneva edition of 1770 and known as Trapnell 72X.[43] In all, some 108 volumes printed by Geoffroy Regnault are currently listed in the ornament database *Maguelone*: 17 bear his name, 91 have false imprints. This is how physical bibliography can reveal the true importance and activities of an unknown provincial printer, considered in his time, and until now, to be a

---

39 David Smith, *Bibliography of the writings of Helvetius* (Ferney-Voltaire: Centre international d'étude du 18ème siècle, 2001).

40 See maguelone.enssib.fr; db-prod-bcul.unil.ch/ornements/scripts/Info.html.

41 Claudette Fortuny, 'Les éditions lyonnaises de l'*Histoire des deux Indes* de l'abbé Raynal', in Dominique Varry (ed.), *Lyon et les livres, Histoire et civilisation du livre: revue internationale*, 2 (2006), pp. 169–188.

42 Dominique Varry, 'L'édition encadrée des œuvres de Voltaire: une collaboration entre imprimeurs-libraires genevois et lyonnais ?', in François Bessire and Françoise Tilkin (eds.), *Voltaire et le livre* (Ferney-Voltaire: Centre international d'étude du 18ème siècle, 2009), pp. 107–116. For the previous evaluation, see Jeroom Vercruysse, *Les éditions encadrées des Œuvres de Voltaire de 1775* (Oxford: The Voltaire Foundation, 1977).

43 See Dominique Varry, 'Faire tomber le masque: Geoffroy Regnault imprimeur lyonnais de Voltaire', paper presented at the conference (*Ré*)-*éditer Voltaire. Geste éditorial et réception*, Bern University, March 1–2 2018. William H. Trapnell, 'Survey and analysis of Voltaire's collective editions, 1728–1789', in *Studies on Voltaire and the eighteenth century*, volume 77 (Oxford: The Voltaire Foundation, 1970), pp. 103–199.

second-rate professional, but who was probably one of the principal printers of the Enlightenment in Lyon, acting always under false imprints, never using his real name.

6   The French Authorities' Double Game

Archival material cannot necessarily prove it, but we must consider that a significant proportion of the books printed in France under false foreign imprints such as 'Londres', especially in the second half of the eighteenth century, were published with the backing of the authorities, for economic reasons. Numerous books were printed without official approval but were tolerated by the authorities to prevent unemployment in French printing shops, and the smuggling of foreign impressions into the kingdom. We know that oral permissions could sometimes be given to French printers, especially in Paris, by the *Directeur de la Librairie*, on condition of using a false foreign imprint, and of avoiding public scandal. In case scandal did ensue, the authorities could deny having given any authorization, and sue the author and the printer, if they could be identified, or at least have the publication condemned to be publicly burnt by the executioner. I would like to cite two examples of these practices.

Two clandestine editions of the *Œuvres du philosophe de Sans-Souci* appeared in January 1760. One, printed in Lyon, was issued on January 15. It was printed without any authorisation by Jean-Marie Bruyset, but as he always denied it, the police could not prove it. Another edition was offered at the end of the month in Paris by the printer Saillant who, in the summer of 1759 had discretely requested a permission from Malesherbes, the *Directeur de la Librairie*. These two editions were published while France was at war with Prussia. Malesherbes did not impeach the publication of the Saillant edition to begin with, but when in February the archbishop of Paris objected to the publication, Malesherbes forbade the book. At the same time, Choiseul, the minister of Foreign Affairs, took the opportunity to discredit the 'heinous' Frederick II of Prussia and to order the arrest in Lyon of the Prussian officer who had brought Frederic's manuscript, whom he suspected of being a spy. In his diary of the book trade, inspector d'Hémery wrote:

> Thursday January 17 1760: *Œuvres du philosophe Sans souci*. 299 pages in 12. Printed without any permission. These are the works of the King of Prussia who had only six copies printed [of the original edition].[44]

---

44   BnF, ms fr. 22161, f° 70 (available on *Gallica*): D'Hémery: *Journal de la librairie*, 1759–1760: 'Du jeudy 17 janvier 1760: Œuvres du philosophe Sans souci. 299 pages in 12 imp.

Thursday January 31 1760: *Œuvres du philosophe Sans souci*. 2 volumes in 8° printed by Saillant and Durand, with a sort of tolerance. **Nevertheless, since it has appeared M. de Malesherbes has given the most precise orders to stop it.** This edition is far more extensive than the one previously published in the provinces.[45]

The second example concerns Voltaire's *Dialogues chrétiens ou Préservatif contre l'Encyclopédie*, published in the same year, 1760.[46] François Rigollet, a Lyon bookseller sold this little pamphlet without its author's permission. When Voltaire heard about the publication in the first days of September 1760, he undertook to find a copy and to get information about Rigollet. In fact, Rigollet had had the pamphlet printed in Geneva and brought into France. In his *Journal de la Librairie*, d'Hémery wrote: 'Thursday September 11, 1760: Dialogues chretiens ou preservatif contre l'Encyclopedie by M. Vxx Geneva. 16 pages in 8° printed with a sort of tolerance'.[47] This means that though printed abroad, the sale of the pamphlet was tolerated in France. In numerous letters to different correspondents, Voltaire denied being the author of this text, and declared himself to be scandalised that someone had dared to put his name on its title-page. With the help of his friend Charles Borde in Lyon, he first attempted, though unsuccessfully, to get the manuscript back from Rigollet. Then, on 10th of September, he wrote to the minister Choiseul, to Malesherbes and to the Royal Prosecutor in Lyon to complain about Rigollet, whose home and bookshop were searched as a result. Only 22 sheets of the *Epître du diable à M. de Voltaire* were found. Satisfied, Voltaire gave up the prosecution on 16 September. On 13 September, he wrote to Tronchin: 'I only want to beat Rigollet, or at least prevent him from disturbing our rest in Geneva; a literary war is only worthwhile in Paris'.

---

sans p[ermissi]on. Ce sont les œuvres du roy de Prusse qui n'en a fait imprimer que six exemplaires'.

45 BnF, ms fr. 22161, fol. 72 (available on *Gallica*): D'Hémery: *Journal de la librairie*, 1759–1760: 'Du jeudy 31 janvier 1760: Œuvres du philosophe sans souci. 2 vol. in 8° imp. par de Saillant et Durand, avec une espece de tolerance. **cependant depuis qu'elle a paru M. de Malesherbes a donné les ordres les plus precis pour l'empecher.** Cette edition est beaucoup plus ample que celle qui a paru precedt et qui a été imp. en province' [underlined in the original].

46 Dominique Varry, 'Voltaire et les imprimeurs-libraires lyonnais', in Ulla Kölving and Christiane Mervaud (eds.), *Voltaire et ses combats. Actes du colloque international Oxford Paris 1994* (2 vols.; Oxford: The Voltaire Foundation, 1997), I, pp. 483–507.

47 BnF, ms fr. 22161, fol. 114v (available on *Gallica*): D'Hémery: *Journal de la librairie*, 1759–1760: 'Du jeudy 11 7bre 1760: Dialogues chretiens ou preservatif contre l'Encyclopedie par M. Vxx Geneve. 16 pages in 8° imp. avec une espece de tolerance'.

The royal authorities were not fooled. Lyon's Governor wrote to Malesherbes: 'I do not doubt that M. de Voltaire is the author, and the procedures he made to get the manuscript are the proof of it. [...] Furthermore, these Dialogues do not seem to me to contain anything which could not be printed in France'. For his part, Malesherbes replied 'I would confess, for the honour of such a great man, that I would like him to be more temperate in what he feels against his enemies, or less passionate in the tracking of those who write against him'. The only victim of the case was the bookseller François Rigollet. Scared by the police searches, all of his creditors asked for their money at the same time, and Rigollet went bankrupt. In 1763, the Lyon book-trade inspector Bourgelat wrote that he was 'reduced to begging'.[48]

In both of the above cases, d'Hémery used the same phrase: *'avec une espèce de tolérance'*. I would be very grateful indeed to whomever could explain what *'une espèce de tolérance'* (a kind of tolerance) really meant, but it seems that this expression referred to an oral permit.

7 The Sovereignty of Dombes

Until the mid-eighteenth century, the sovereignty of Dombes was a small foreign principality, near the little city of Trévoux, then on the French border, today situated in the department of Ain. It belonged to the house of Bourbon. During the seventeenth century, princes of Dombes made several attempts, mostly unfruitful, attracting Lyon printers to develop a print shop at Trévoux.[49] Things changed under the reign of the Duke of Maine. Louis Auguste de Bourbon (1670–1736), Duke of Maine, was the legitimate and favourite son of Louis XIV and Madame de Maintenon. In 1692 he had married Anne Louise Bénédicte de Bourbon (1676–1753), Mademoiselle de Charolais, daughter of the prince de Condé and Palatine princess Anne of Bavaria, granddaughter of the 'Grand Condé'. She is well-known for having created the Order of the Honey Fly ('Mouche à miel') at her court at Sceaux castle.

On 25 June 1699, the Duke of Maine gave the privilege of the Trévoux print shop to the Parisian printer-cum-bookseller Jean Boudot. The duke invested money in the print shop, erected a special building to house it, and bought

---

48   'Réduit à la mendicité'. BnF: ms. fr. 22128, ff. 291–302. Léon Moulé, 'Rapport de Cl. Bourgelat sur le commerce de la librairie et de l'imprimerie à Lyon en 1763', *Revue d'histoire de Lyon*, 13 (1914), pp. 51–65, see p. 54.
49   Dominique Varry, 'Le livre prohibé à Lyon au XVIIIe siècle et l'imprimerie de Trévoux', in Isabelle Turcan (ed.), *Quand le Dictionnaire de Trévoux rayonne sur l'Europe des Lumières* (Paris: L'Harmattan, 2009), pp. 57–67.

printing material. When Jean Boudot died in 1706, his assistant Etienne Ganeau succeeded him, and in 1707 was the only printer of the Sovereignty of Dombes.[50] When Ganeau returned to Paris in 1710, his younger brother Louis, who died in 1716, succeeded him at Trévoux. After him, the print shop was run by the foreman, François Boulay. This print shop is well known for having published the first two editions (1704 and 1721) of the *Dictionnaire de Trévoux*, and until the middle of the 1730s the *Journal de Trévoux*, thereafter printed first in Lyon and then Paris. In fact, Trévoux was, for French authorities, a useful comic-opera principality. It was outside of the kingdom, close by, but not subject to French law, yet still ruled by a French prince. It allowed for a triple manipulation.

The *Journal des savants*, launched in 1695 in Paris, obtained in 1701 a royal privilege which gave it a monopoly in the kingdom. The same year, the French Jesuits wanted to create their own publication, but came up against the privilege of the *Journal des savants*. The sovereign principality of Dombes soon appeared useful to bypass the privilege, and the Jesuits could publish the *Mémoires pour l'histoire des sciences et des beaux arts*, better known as *Journal de Trévoux*. Furthermore, Trévoux was used to discreetly counterbalance the foreign-printed French-language production made in the Dutch Republic and smuggled into France by publishing books bearing false imprints.

Finally, printers from Lyon and Paris used the sovereignty of Dombes and its print shop as an alternative to secretly produce pirate editions of works protected in France by a royal privilege, or to print prohibited books. However in 1762, Trévoux ceased to be a place of interest, when the Jesuit order was suppressed and the Sovereignty was annexed to France. The print shop disappeared soon thereafter. For more than sixty years it had published books under the imprint of Trévoux and the coat of arms of the prince, and, all the while, also had an illicit production under false foreign imprints. Aimé Delaroche, who was the most important printer in Lyon during the better part of the century, as well as one of the last owners of the print shop in Trévoux, summarised the situation when he wrote, around 1770:

> The print shop based at Trévoux was, under the government of the princes of Dombes, an object of speculation for several Paris booksellers, who were quick to take advantage of the ease of printing books in the heart of France, in a foreign city, the impression of which would not have been tolerated in Paris under the eyes of the government. This is the reason for

---

50   Jean Delay, 'Libraires à Saint Séverin', in *Avant Mémoire II. D'une minute à l'autre (Paris 1555–1736)* (Paris: Gallimard, 1980), pp. 204–261.

the fame of the Trévoux print shop. The company of booksellers at Paris which ran the print shop there was necessarily in the sovereign's service because there was no other print shop [to do this work]. It is superfluous to point out that this service alone could not have formed the basis of a commercial enterprise.[51]

8 Conclusion

As the material presented here demonstrates, the picture of French eighteenth-century print production given by traditional historiography is blurred, imperfect, partial and, simply put, false. The official records on which this vision is based only report a part of historical reality, and this is the part that has remained visible. Using the metaphor of an iceberg, we must remember that the visible part, official production bearing genuine imprints, is relatively small, and that the greater portion remains hidden. We will likely never know the true extent of this printed production. We have no means to unravel the mystery. False imprints were widely used, and not only by French printers. These false addresses hide counterfeits and prohibited books of course, but also authorised books printed with tacit permission, and, though few people are aware of this, books which were not forbidden, but whose production was tolerated for economic reasons and to avoid unemployment. In my opinion, it is more than probable that the majority of books printed in France under false imprints belonged to the two latter categories. Contrary to common belief, a false imprint is not by definition synonymous with illegality.

---

51 Rhône Department Archives: 1 C 221 file Aimé Delaroche [c.1770]. 'L'Imprimerie établie à Trévoux a été, sous le Gouvernement des Princes de Dombes, un objet de spéculation de quelques libraires de Paris empressés de profiter de la facilité d'imprimer au cœur de la France, dans une ville étrangère, des ouvrages dont l'impression n'eût pas été tolérée à Paris sous les yeux du Gouvernement. C'est à cette raison qu'a été düe la célébrité de l'Imprimerie de Trévoux. La Compagnie des Libraires de Paris qui a élevé l'Imprimerie qui y existoit devoit nécessairement être chargée du service du Souverain puisqu'il n'y avoit pas d'autre Imprimerie. Il est superflu d'observer que ce service, envisagé seul, ne pouvoit former un objet de commerce'.

PART 3

Auctions, Collectors and Catalogues

∴

CHAPTER 8

Early Modern English Parish Libraries: Collecting and Collections in the Francis Trigge Chained Library and the Gorton Chest Parish Library

Jessica G. Purdy

The early modern English parish library is difficult to conceptualise. Despite approximately 165 parish libraries being established between 1558 and 1709, the differences in their size, scope and character make generalisations problematic. Surviving early modern English parish libraries range in size from collections of around twenty books, to several hundred volumes, to up to three thousand texts. The importance of these libraries in the sixteenth and seventeenth centuries derived from their role as repositories of both spiritual edification and secular education for the clergy and laity alike. This chapter will examine the collecting practices and collections of the Francis Trigge Chained Library in Lincolnshire (1598) and the Gorton Chest parish library in Lancashire (1653) to demonstrate that, despite these libraries being established over fifty years apart and the differences in the size and scope of their collections, their educational incentives and objectives remained the same. Both collections were compiled with the religiously divided people of their respective counties in mind, and both collections included books that were intended to provide their readers with a religious education and moral instruction.

Books have been housed in England's parish churches since at least the thirteenth century. In the late thirteenth century, Robert Winchelsey, Archbishop of Canterbury (1293–1313), decreed that parishioners must supply eight service books to their parish churches. This decree became so widely circulated that by the mid-fourteenth century it was treated as an official decree of the archdiocese of Canterbury.[1] Between 1350 and 1536, 192 parish churches had at least one religious reference book, with many churches owning small collections of liturgical works, clerical manuals and other works of religious instruction

---

1 John Shinners, 'Parish Libraries in Medieval England', in Jacqueline Brown and William P. Stoneman (eds.), *A Distinct Voice: Medieval Studies in Honor of Leonard E. Boyle* (Notre Dame, Ind.: University of Notre Dame Press, 1997), p. 208.

and edification.[2] However, the vast majority of books that were in churches at the start of the Reformation were lost in that very process, and it would take time to rebuild their collections.[3] The time taken for parish churches to rebuild their book collections in the wake of this religious upheaval has led historians such as Sarah Gray and Chris Baggs to suggest that 'for some fifty years after the Reformation ... nothing that could be described as a library is known to have existed in a parish church'.[4] That is not necessarily the case, as the first post-Reformation parish library was recorded as established in Steeple Ashton in Wiltshire in 1568.[5] Furthermore, the years during which collections of books were re-established in parish churches do not necessarily equate to fundamental change. Arnold Hunt has demonstrated that there were important elements of continuity between the pre-Reformation collections of service books, liturgical texts and other religious works, and post-Reformation parish libraries. He suggested that rather than pre-Reformation texts having been lost or destroyed during the processes of religious change in the mid-sixteenth century, they were actually saved by conservative members of the clergy and may eventually have found their way into the hands of post-Reformation clergymen and parish libraries through testamentary bequests.[6]

Books came to be housed in parish churches in numerous ways before and after the Reformation: as well as testamentary bequests, books also came to be in churches through donations or through the gift of money to purchase books. Clergymen often donated their books to the church of the parish in which they had been born or employed, usually for use by other clerics or local parishioners. In 1383, for example, Thomas de Lexham, canon of Hereford, bequeathed one of his books to Feltwell St Mary church in Norfolk 'with the condition that it should remain forever in the church for the common use of all the ministers of that church and of other churches'.[7] In 1457, John Edlyngton, rector of Kirkby Ravensworth, gave a bible, a history text, a devotional work, and the rest of his books that were not otherwise sold or given away, to Boston

---

2 Stacey Gee, 'Parochial Libraries in Pre-Reformation England' in Sarah Rees Jones (ed.), *Learning and Literacy in Medieval England and Abroad* (Turnhout: Brepols, 2003), pp. 199–200.
3 C.B.L. Barr, 'Parish Libraries in a Region: the Case of Yorkshire', in *Proceedings of the Library Association Study School and National Conference, Nottingham, 1979* (London: The Association, 1980), p. 33; Sarah Gray and Chris Baggs, 'The English Parish Library: A Celebration of Diversity', *Libraries and Culture*, 35 (2000), p. 417.
4 Gray and Baggs, 'The English Parish Library: A Celebration of Diversity', p. 417.
5 Michael Perkin, *A Directory of the Parochial Libraries of the Church of England and the Church in Wales* (London: Bibliographical Society, 2004), pp. 59, 357–358.
6 Arnold Hunt, 'Clerical and Parish Libraries', in Elisabeth Leedham-Green and Teresa Webber (eds.), *The Cambridge History of Libraries in Britain and Ireland, Volume 1: To 1640* (Cambridge: Cambridge University Press, 2013), pp. 405–407, 412.
7 Gee, 'Parochial Libraries in Pre-Reformation England', p. 201.

church in Lincolnshire.[8] This practice continued after the Reformation and into the seventeenth and eighteenth centuries. George Dunscomb, vicar of Wootton Wawen in Warwickshire, for example, left his books to the church for the use of his parishioners after his death in 1652. Bradley Hayhurst, former minister of Macclesfield, bequeathed his books to the parish church of Ribchester in Lancashire, his hometown, in his will of 1684. Similarly, Richard Newte, rector of Tiverton in Devon, bequeathed his library to his son and successor as rector, John Newte, in 1678. John, in turn, left the books to Tiverton church to form a parish library in the early eighteenth century.[9]

Donations of books to parish churches also came from the laity across the medieval and early modern period. Prior to the Reformation, these books were often donated in the hope of some sort of spiritual benefit for the donor. In 1435, for example, the York merchant Richard Russel left six service books, amongst other objects, to his parish church, on condition that the minister 'forever would especially pray in the church pulpit' for the souls of Russel and his wife, and others.[10] After the Reformation, and with the decline of belief in purgatory and the efficacy of good works, spiritual benefit became less of an incentive for lay donations of books. It was replaced by a desire to educate. In 1616, Lady Anne Harington gave 'two hundred Latin and Greek Folio's, consisting chiefly of Fathers, Councils, School-men, and Divines' to the parish church of Oakham in Rutland 'for the use of the vicar of that Church, and ... the Neighbouring Clergy'.[11] Similarly, in 1631, Sir John Kedermister of Langley Park bequeathed to St Mary the Virgin church in Langley Marish in Buckinghamshire, 'for the benefit as well of ministers of the said towne [Langley Marish] and such other in the Countie of Bucks ... those books which I have already prepared ... together with soe many more as shall amount to the summe of Twenty pounds'.[12] Even towards the end of the seventeenth century, the desire to educate motivated men to establish parish libraries. In 1680, Sir Richard More established a library in More, Shropshire, 'for the use and benefit of the inhabitants of the village and for the encouragement of a preaching minister'.[13] Conal Condren has argued that 'when Richard More gave the library ... the

---

8   Ibid., p. 202.
9   Perkin, *A Directory of Parochial Libraries*, pp. 329–330, 371–372, 400.
10 Shinners, 'Parish Libraries in Medieval England', pp. 210–211.
11 James Wright, *The History and Antiquities of the County of Rutland* (London: Printed for Bennet Griffin, 1684), p. 52. This edition not listed on the USTC.
12 The National Archives, Kew, (PROB 11/159/567), Will of Sir John Kidderminster of Langley Marish, Buckinghamshire, 7 May 1631.
13 Conal Condren, 'More Parish Library, Salop', *Library History*, 7:5 (1987), pp. 141–144; Shropshire Archives, Shropshire, (P193/S/1/1), More Church Library Trust Deeds with Rules.

evidence from the books themselves indicates that he was trying to maintain a literate local community'.[14]

Books could also be purchased by parish churches using money bequeathed or gifted to them specifically for that purpose. This practice seems to have been more common after the Reformation than before it. Two of the most prominent examples of post-Reformation parish libraries that were established by this process are the Francis Trigge Chained Library in Grantham, Lincolnshire, which was established in 1598, and the Gorton Chest parish library in Manchester, Lancashire, established in 1653, which will form the basis of this chapter. The Francis Trigge Chained Library was established by the gift of £100 from Francis Trigge for the purchase of 'books of divinitie and other learninge'.[15] The Gorton Chest was founded by Humphrey Chetham's testamentary bequest of £200 to establish five parish libraries in and around Manchester. Just £30 was allocated to purchasing books for the Gorton Chest.[16] The practice of donating or bequeathing money to parish churches for the purchasing of books continued into the first half of the eighteenth century, as demonstrated by the will of Nathaniel Symonds. Symonds was vicar of Ormesby in Norfolk and in his 1727 will he bequeathed to the minister of Great Yarmouth 'three pounds p[er] anno ... [to be] laid out in buying of Books of practicall divinity of one or more sort or sorts such as he shall think most proper to be ... distributed ... amongst the poorer and best deserving sort of people'.[17]

The ways in which books were acquired by parish churches had a significant impact on the nature of the library collection itself. Before the Reformation, when books were donated in the hope of spiritual benefit, the books donated to parish churches tended to be aimed at the clergy, from whom the laity received their religious and devotional instruction. 'Manuals to help the clergy with their liturgical, sacramental and pastoral duties' were, Stacey Gee has argued, 'the most ubiquitous volumes found in parish churches' before the Reformation.[18] Gee has also demonstrated William of Pagula's *Oculus Sacerdotis* to be the most popular pastoral manual of the fourteenth century, before it was replaced by John

---

14   Condren, 'More Parish Library, Salop', p. 150.
15   Lincolnshire Archives, Lincolnshire, (Grantham St Wulfram Par/23/1), Documents relating to the Trigge Library: Agreement.
16   Chetham's Library, Manchester, (Uncatalogued), Last Will and Testament of Humphrey Chetham; Chetham's Library, Manchester, (Chet/1/2/1), Minute Book, 6 Dec 1653–16 Apr 1752.
17   The National Archives, Kew, (PROB 11/617/416), Will of Nathaniel Symonds, Clerk of Ormesby Saint Margaret, Norfolk, 12 October 1727.
18   Gee, 'Parochial Libraries in Pre-Reformation England', p. 213.

de Burgh's *Pupilla Oculi* in the fifteenth century.[19] The subject of theology continued to dominate the collections of post-Reformation parish libraries, even as their intended readership expanded to include the laity as well as the clergy. W.M. Jacob has therefore argued that the subject was not solely the purview of the clergy, and that 'the laity of the better sort were usually theologically literate, and often theologically well educated'.[20] As the seventeenth century progressed, secular literature became a more noticeable presence in many parish library collections, particularly when they were established by a layman. The parish library in More, for example, was established using a portion of its founder, Sir Richard More's own library collection, and as such demonstrated the kinds of books More was interested in and believed to be most useful to his intended readers. Theological books were present, but so were works of poetry, history and geography.[21]

The nature of the collections in the Francis Trigge Chained Library and the Gorton Chest parish library demonstrate the successful realisation of their founders' educational motivations. Francis Trigge established his library for the 'better encreasinge of learninge and knowledge', and the collection includes numerous works in Latin on topics as diverse as religious history, secular and natural histories, cosmography, and medical works, in addition to numerous Biblical commentaries and works of doctrine and theology by both Catholic and Protestant authors. Humphrey Chetham founded his five parish libraries, including the Gorton Chest, specifically 'for the edificac[i]on of the common people' and they were to be filled with 'godly English Bookes, such as Calvins, Prestons, and Perkins works, comments of annotac[i]ons uppon the bible or some parts thereof, or such other bookes' as his trustees thought most appropriate.[22] The Gorton Chest parish library thus contains works written almost exclusively by Protestant authors of different confessions; only one book in the collection was written by a Catholic, and that work expresses strong anti-papal sentiments. This chapter will argue that the collections of these two parish libraries were in keeping with the educational intentions of their founders, and that there was method in the selection practices employed when compiling their collections.

---

19 *Ibid.*, pp. 213–214.
20 W.M. Jacob, 'Parochial Libraries and their Users', *Library and Information History*, 27 (2011), p. 212.
21 Condren, 'More Parish Library, Salop', p. 146.
22 Chetham's Library, Manchester, (Uncatalogued), Last Will and Testament of Humphrey Chetham.

1 The Founders: Francis Trigge and Humphrey Chetham

Francis Trigge was born in Lincolnshire in around 1547. Very few details have survived about Trigge's early life until 1564, when he matriculated to University College, Oxford at approximately seventeen years of age. Trigge pursued 'degrees in arts' and proceeded BA in 1568 and MA in 1572. Thereafter he 'entered into the sacred function' and took orders in 1582, before being appointed rector of Welbourne in Lincolnshire in 1583.[23] Trigge held this post for over twenty years, until his death in 1606.[24] His marriage to an unnamed daughter of Elizabeth Hussey of Honington seemingly did not produce any surviving children, as none are mentioned as beneficiaries in Trigge's will.[25]

Trigge was a Calvinist whose belief in the importance of preaching and of Scripture as the primary source of religious authority suggests moderate Puritan sympathies. He was an active preacher and author throughout his career, and eight of his published works in either English or Latin survive. Trigge revealed his Calvinism in his earliest surviving work, *An apologie, or defence of our dayes, against the vaine murmurings & complaints of manie....* Published in 1589, in this politico-religious commentary on social and religious conditions in Lincolnshire, Trigge described the Reformed religion as a light that 'was spread farre and wyde ... it encreaseth every daye, and is more brighter and clearer'.[26] His *A Godly and Fruitfull Sermon Preached at Grantham 1592*, which was first published in 1594, demonstrates Trigge's desire for ministers to keep 'the gospel of Jesus Christ in their heartes' and live an exemplary life in order to 'be able to say [to their parishioners] ... do those things which you have both seene & heard of me'.[27] In preaching and publishing this sermon, Trigge stated his wish to 'pul some out of the fire of sinne and wickednes', suggesting an attempt to convert through his words some of Lincolnshire's remaining Catholics to Protestantism.[28] The publication of this sermon also reveals

---

23 Joseph Foster (ed.), *Alumni Oxonienses, Volume IV – Early Series* (Oxford: James Parker & Co., 1891), p. 1510; A. Wood and P. Bliss (ed.), *Athenae Oxonienses, Volume I* (London: T. Bensley, 1813), p. 759.
24 E.I. Carlyle and A. McRae, 'Trigge, Francis (1547?–1606)', *Oxford Dictionary of National Biography* (online: 2004).
25 Lincolnshire Archives, Lincolnshire, (LCC Wills/1606), Wills proved in the Lincoln Consistory Court, number 252.
26 Francis Trigge, *An apologie, or defence of our dayes, against the vaine murmurings & complaints of manie wherein is plainly proved, that our dayes are more happie & blessed than the dayes of our forefathers* (London: John Wolfe, 1589), p. 4. USTC 511333.
27 Francis Trigge, *A Godly and Fruitfull Sermon Preached at Grantham 1592* (Oxford: Joseph Barnes, 1594), sig. C6v–C7r. USTC 512686.
28 *Ibid.*, sig. A4v.

a connection to Grantham that may explain Trigge's choice of St Wulfram's church as the location for his library – the market town was less than twelve miles from the town of Welbourn, where Trigge was rector.[29]

Humphrey Chetham was born in Manchester in 1580 and was educated at Manchester Grammar School until the age of 17, when he was apprenticed to the draper Samuel Tipping on 2 October 1597. Chetham completed his apprenticeship some time before 1605, when he went into business with his elder brother, George. The two men were active as wool and cloth merchants for several years and formed an extremely successful partnership until George's death in 1627.[30] Chetham purchased the Clayton Hall estate in Manchester with his brother in 1620 and Turton Tower in 1627, after George's death. His purchase of several small farming properties and minor estates in and around Manchester meant that Chetham quickly became one of the largest landowners in the area.[31] Chetham's primary source of income came from his money-lending business, which he charged at a rate of eight percent, the highest rate of interest allowed by law.[32] Throughout his lifetime, Chetham held a range of influential administrative positions, including High Sheriff of Lancashire in 1634 and 1648 and Treasurer of the county in 1643, which strengthened his standing in society.

By the time of his death in 1653, Chetham had amassed a vast fortune. His will provided for three important philanthropic endeavours. The first was a school for poor boys from the Manchester area; the second was the provision of a public library for scholars and the educated elite; and the third was the bequest of £200 to be used in purchasing 'godly English bookes' to establish five parish libraries.[33] These libraries were to be placed in churches that had a personal significance to Humphrey Chetham. The first was Manchester Collegiate Church, with which the Chetham family had a longstanding personal and business relationship and where Humphrey Chetham had purchased a family pew

---

29 Thomas Cox, *Magna Britannia, Volume II* (London: printed for and sold by Caesar Ward and Richard Chandler Booksellers, 1738), p. 1417; John Speed, 'Lincolnshire', *Britain's Tudor Maps: County by County* (London: Pavilion Books Limited, 1995), pp. 118–119.

30 Francis Robert Raines and Charles W. Sutton, *Life of Humphrey Chetham, founder of the Chetham Hospital and Library, Manchester, Volume I*, printed for the Chetham Society (Manchester: James Stewart, 1903), pp. 9–12.

31 Alan G. Crosby, 'Chetham, Humphrey (*bap.* 1580, *d.* 1653)', *Oxford Dictionary of National Biography*, (online: 2008).

32 Raines and Sutton, *Life of Humphrey Chetham, Volume I*, p. 113.

33 Chetham's Library, Manchester, (Uncatalogued), Last Will and Testament of Humphrey Chetham.

in the early 1620s.[34] The second church that Chetham identified in his will was in Bolton, where Chetham had professional connections, and the third was Gorton chapel, which was close to Chetham's primary residence at Clayton Hall.[35] The final two churches named by Chetham in his will were the chapels of Turton and Walmsley, both of which were situated in reasonably close proximity to Turton Tower, Chetham's second residence.

2   Collecting Practices for the Francis Trigge Chained Library

In the nineteenth century, historians believed that the library's collection was comprised of a portion of Francis Trigge's personal library.[36] Documents relating to the establishment of the Francis Trigge library were unearthed in the Lincolnshire Borough Archives in 1957 that demonstrate that this was not, in fact, the case. Evidence for the compilation processes for the original collection of the Francis Trigge library, however, remains at best circumstantial. The suggestions made by John Glenn in the 1980s as to how the collection was assembled arose from the substantial piecing together of small items of information.[37]

Detail about the original provision of the library comes from the foundation indenture from October 1598. The indenture noted that Francis Trigge 'at his own charges and expenses endevored to have a library erected in the said towne of Grantham' and that he 'hath provided or intendeth to provide at his like costs for the furnishinge thereof books of divinitie and other learninge to the value of one hundreth pounds or thereaboutes'.[38] The agreement also makes reference to a list of named books with which the library was to be stocked, which, if it was ever drawn up, no longer survives.[39] The wording of this document led Glenn to argue that Francis Trigge did not draw the books for the library in St Wulfram's church from his own collection. Instead, Glenn posited that phrases such as 'hath provided or intendeth to provide' were merely

---

34   Raines and Sutton, *Life of Humphrey Chetham, Volume 1*, p. 35; S.J. Guscott, *Humphrey Chetham, 1580–1653: Fortune, Politics and Mercantile Culture in Seventeenth-century England* (Manchester: The Chetham Society, 2003), pp. 53, 70, 170, 188.

35   Guscott, *Humphrey Chetham, 1580–1653*, p. 183.

36   John Glenn, 'A Sixteenth-Century Library: the Francis Trigge Chained Library of St Wulfram's Church, Grantham', in Daniel Williams (ed.), *Early Tudor England: Proceedings of the 1987 Harlaxton Symposium* (Woodbridge: The Boydell Press, 1989), p. 63.

37   *Ibid.*, pp. 61–71.

38   Lincolnshire Archives, Lincolnshire, (Grantham St Wulfram Par/23/1), Documents relating to the Trigge Library: Agreement.

39   Angela Roberts, 'The Chained Library, Grantham', *Library History*, 2 (1971), p. 76.

legal terminology and that the lack of any named books in the agreement itself demonstrates that the books were sourced from elsewhere.[40] Trigge's promise to provide 'books to the value of one hundreth poundes or thereaboutes' is also suggestive of his intention to purchase books rather than to donate his own.

The books for the Francis Trigge Chained Library were bought in Cambridge and London, though there is no record of Francis Trigge himself ever having visited the university town. In the 1980s, work was carried out on the bindings of a large quantity of books in the library that enabled the identification of several binders. The first known binder was Garrett Godfrey, a Dutchman living in Cambridge who was appointed one of three university stationers in 1534. The second, Thomas Thomas, was a Cambridge scholar who was appointed printer to the University in 1583. Thomas was known for printing works of a Puritan nature, and was linked with continental Reformers.[41] Books bound by several other binders who are known only by their initials, as well as other, anonymous binders known to have been active in either London or Cambridge have also been identified in the collection.[42] Glenn suggested that an agent presumably purchased the books, *en masse* and indiscriminately, in one six-day roundtrip from Grantham to Cambridge and back.[43] He asserted that the books in the Francis Trigge collection were broadly theological in their nature but arbitrary in their religious ideology. Analysing the mixture of Protestant and Catholic works in the collection, which includes Calvinist sermons and Lutheran propaganda, the works of the Catholic theologians who refuted Protestant doctrines, books of Catholic canon law, and numerous Biblical commentaries, Glenn stated that 'one does not see an attempt to bring together a library as useful and comprehensive as possible'.[44]

This chapter argues rather the contrary: the Francis Trigge Chained Library is not as eclectic and indiscriminate as Glenn suggested and actually seems to bear numerous similarities to the libraries of some of the most prominent bishops of the early seventeenth century. The English clergy in the sixteenth and seventeenth centuries knew that in order to defend the Anglican Church from attacks by Roman Catholics and other confessions, they had to have a profound understanding of a range of subjects. David Pearson has demonstrated that the need to

---

40   Glenn, 'A Sixteenth-Century Library', p. 64.
41   Ibid., p. 64; R.B. McKerrow (ed.), *A Dictionary of Printers and Booksellers in England, Scotland and Ireland, and of Foreign Printers of English Books 1557–1640* (London: Blades, East & Blades, 1910), pp. 264–265; E. Gordon Duff, *A Century of the English Book Trade* (London: Blades, East & Blades, 1905), pp. 56–57.
42   Glenn, 'A Sixteenth-Century Library', p. 64.
43   Ibid., p. 66.
44   Ibid., p. 65.

understand different religious beliefs was the impetus behind the collecting practices of many bishops, whose collections included both Protestant and Catholic works.[45] Many of the lower ranking clergy employed similar principles in compiling their collections and it is through this lens that the Francis Trigge collection should be seen. At the end of the sixteenth century, Trigge and his colleagues were consciously trying to provide a comprehensive repository of religious materials to educate their readers and provide clerics with assistance in their ministerial and pastoral duties. In this context, the variety of books does demonstrate an attempt to bring together a library as useful and comprehensive as possible. The inclusion of works by the noted Jesuit Robert Bellarmine and the Catholic Hector Pintus, texts by the Church Fathers, including Saint Augustine, Saint Cyril and Saint John Chrysostom, alongside works by various prominent Reformers including John Calvin, Theodore Beza, Heinrich Bullinger and Martin Bucer, evidence the fulfilment of Trigge's desire to provide 'books of divinitie' from a range of confessional standpoints to the users of his library. Similarly, the small number of secular volumes in this collection demonstrate that Trigge's provision of books on the 'liberall sciences' was acted upon, with natural and secular histories, medical textbooks, and works of geography that discussed the territories of the New World appearing in the corpus.[46] Far from being indiscriminate and undiscerning in collecting the books for the Francis Trigge Chained Library, the person responsible for purchasing these books acquired a collection the nature of which would be replicated throughout the seventeenth century and beyond.[47]

Collecting continued in the Francis Trigge Chained Library into the mid-eighteenth century. Donations began with the testamentary bequest of the library's founder, upon his death in 1606. Trigge left several books, many of which bear Trigge's ownership inscription, to the library in his will, including

> My Theatru[m] vitae humanae, and Scotus his works, and all Antoninus, and my great Pagnen his lexicon, Concordantiae grecae Phillippus de dies his postill with that p[ar]te wh[ich] Mr Pontell of Carleton hath of it, Vigeas upon the Revelation, Fox upon the Revelation and Catholicon ..., and Hugo Cardinalis wh[ich] Mr Mills of Stamford hath.[48]

---

45 David Pearson, 'The Libraries of English Bishops, 1600–40', *The Library*, 14 (1992), *passim*.
46 For example: Simon Grynaeus, *Novus Orbis regionum ac insularum veteribus Incognitarum una cum tabula cosmographica* ... (Basel: Johann Hervagium, 1555), USTC 678745.
47 David Pearson, 'Patterns of Book Ownership in Late Seventeenth-Century England', *The Library*, 11 (2010), p. 139.
48 Lincolnshire Archives, Lincolnshire, (LCC Wills/1606), Wills proved in the Lincoln Consistory Court, number 252; Theodor Zwinger, *Theatrum humanae vitae* in four volumes

These titles are in keeping with Trigge's vision for the library as a repository of education in religion and the liberal sciences and most of them are still in the collection. Exceptions include the copy of Hugo Cardinalis' work that was in the possession of Mr Mills of Stamford at the time of Trigge's death and seems never to have been returned, and the lexicon of 'Pagnen' (the Italian Dominican Friar, Sante Pagnini) which has since been lost.[49] In the mid-seventeenth century, the library received another notable donation, this time from Henry More, the Grantham-born theologian and writer. More donated many of his own works to the Library, three of which bear the Latin inscription '*ex dono auctoris* [a gift of the author]' on the first leaves of the book in an unknown hand.[50] Like Trigge's testamentary bequest, More's gift was in keeping with the rest of the collection and consisted of books on theology and philosophy. Similar volumes were donated by John Newcome to the Francis Trigge Chained Library in 1765. Newcome, another Grantham-born theologian and cleric, bequeathed books on morality, Christian divinity, commentaries on the Bible, sermons, and some secular texts, to the Trigge library.[51] These books were never merged with the Trigge collection, for reasons unknown, and were instead kept in the South chancel of the church until 1806, the vestry until 1878 and then were moved to the bottom of the belfry stairs.[52] Nevertheless, they represent a recognition of the aims and intentions of the Trigge library and demonstrate a desire to further that mission, over one hundred and fifty years after the library was established.

(Basel: ex officina Episcopiorum, 1586–1587), USTC 606525; Duns Scotus, *Scriptum primum Oxoniense doctoris subtilis Ioannis Duns Scoti Ordinis minorum super primo Sententiarum pristine integritati restitutum. Cui tabula generalis miro artificio elaborata superadditur universam doctoris subtilis peritiam octo sectionibus compraehendens ab excellentissimo doctore Antonio de Fantis Taruisino primario eius inventore ac Scotice discipline illustrator* (Venice: Pietro Quarengi for Gregorio de Gregori, 1515), USTC 827877; Antoninus Forciglione, *Historia Venerabilis Antonini, Volumes I–III*, (Basel: Nicolaus Kasler, 1502), USTC 686502; Philippe Diez, *Concionum quadruplicium libri* (Lyon: Peter Landry, 1589), USTC 138040; Blaslo Viegas, *Commentaria exergetici in Apocalypsim Joannis apostoli* (Lyon: Horatio Cardon, 1602), USTC 690139; Johannes Balbus, *Summa que Catholicon appellatur* (Lyon: Nicolaus Wolff, 1503), USTC 142905.

49 B. Roussel and R.E. Shillenn (trans.), 'Pagnini, Sante (1470–1536)', *The Oxford Encyclopedia of the Reformation*, (online: 2005).

50 Henry More, *An explanation of the grand mystery of godliness* (London: J. Flesher, 1660), USTC 3077286; Henry More, *Enchiridion ethicum praecipua moralis philosophiae rudimenta complectens* (London: J. Flesher, 1669), USTC 3087169; Henry More, *Enchiridion metaphysicum. Pars prima* (London: E. Flesher, 1671), USTC 3089625.

51 National Archives, Kew, (PROB 11/907/118), Will of Reverend John Newcome, Doctor of Divinity, Master of Saint John's College University of Cambridge, proved 12 March 1765.

52 *Grantham Journal*, Saturday 26 October 1878, p. 3.

3   Collecting Practices for the Gorton Chest Parish Library

The instructions left by Humphrey Chetham in his will pertaining to the establishment of five parish libraries is a clear demonstration of his desire to provide the 'common people' with a strongly Protestant religious education. He stipulated that the collections were to comprise only religious texts written in English, such as Biblical commentaries and any other, similar works deemed appropriate by his three trustees. Chetham reinforced this aspiration through his choice of those three trustees – Richard Johnson, a Calvinist non-conformist, and Richard Hollinworth and John Tildsley, both committed Presbyterians – all of whom were known to Chetham personally. Johnson, Hollinworth and Tildsley oversaw the selection of books for these repositories and evidently employed collecting practices in line with the vision Chetham prescribed for the libraries. Hollinworth took responsibility for choosing the books for Gorton chapel and Manchester Collegiate Church; Tildsley for Bolton church, Turton chapel and Walmsley chapel. Johnson, because he resided in London at the time, was responsible for purchasing the books his fellow executors requested.[53]

At a meeting of the trustees in October 1654, the £200 left by Chetham for the parish libraries was divided: 'For Manchester, seaventie pounds, for Gorton thirtie pounds, for Boulton Fifty pounds, for Turton thirtie pounds, for Walmesley twentie pounds'.[54] Considering the number of books required to stock these parish libraries, Johnson, Hollinworth and Tildsley turned to London's second-hand book market and to two prominent London-based booksellers, Robert Littlebury and John Rothwell, to supply them. Littlebury had a shop at the sign of the Unicorn and then at the King's Arms in Little Britain that was well-stocked with both new and second-hand volumes, as well as many that had been imported from the continent.[55] Rothwell had a print shop first in St Paul's Churchyard, before moving to Goldsmith's Row, Cheapside; both he and his father, also a bookseller, dealt mainly in theological texts.[56] The exact circumstances under which the trustees came into

---

[53]   Richard Copley Christie, *The Old Church and School Libraries of Lancashire*, printed for the Chetham Society (Manchester: Charles E. Simms, 1885), pp. 21–22.

[54]   Chetham's Library, Manchester, (Chet/1/2/1), Minute Book, 6 December 1653–16 April 1752.

[55]   Matthew Yeo, *The Acquisition of Books by Chetham's Library, 1655–1700* (Leiden: Brill, 2011), pp. 85, 87.

[56]   Henry R. Plomer, *A Dictionary of the Booksellers and Printers who were at work in England, Scotland and Ireland from 1641 to 1667* (London: Blades, East and Blades for the Bibliographical Society, 1907), pp. 157–158.

contact with Littlebury and Rothwell are unknown. However, both Rothwell's and Littlebury's shops were located within a mile of the Temple Church where Richard Johnson was Master from 1647 to 1658, and Johnson had already procured books from Littlebury, either asking him to supply Bibles to the Temple Church or as a customer at his shop. As specialists in theological works, Johnson would undoubtedly have visited the Rothwells as well. It is therefore likely that the choice of Littlebury and Rothwell as suppliers of books to the parish libraries was a result of Johnson knowing them personally.[57]

In compiling a collection that achieved Chetham's vision of providing educational opportunities to the laity, Johnson, Hollinworth and Tildsley simultaneously promoted Puritan and Presbyterian religious ideas and actively omitted any works that challenged or opposed those ideas. The writings of John Calvin, the leading theologian of the Reformed tradition, John Preston, the Puritan priest and author, and William Perkins, the theologian and celebrated Elizabethan author of Puritan texts of practical divinity, mentioned in Chetham's will, provided the trustees with the foundation they needed to build up the rest of the collection. When selecting books for the public library that Chetham endowed in his will, Johnson, Hollinworth and Tildsley probably worked from lists of titles drawn from their own collections and their experiences of other religious libraries that they had had cause to visit, bibliographies and booksellers' catalogues, and through advice and recommendations from colleagues and booksellers.[58] Matthew Yeo has suggested that these selection practices can also reasonably be applied to the parish libraries. It is worth noting, however, that no catalogues or bibliographies remain in the collections of the public or parish libraries.[59]

Once the books had been selected by the trustees, with the help of Littlebury and Rothwell, they needed to be transported from London to Manchester. Deliveries of the selected religious books began in August 1655. Parcels of English books were delivered to the trustees on 2 August and 20 September 1655, 7 May and 28 July 1657, 30 June 1659, and 1 October 1666.[60] The invoice of 'books delivered to Gorton Chappell' is undated (Figure 8.1), but it must have occurred at some point between October 1654, when the meeting to allocate funds took place, and the end of 1655, the date inscribed on the Gorton Chest itself.[61]

---

57 Yeo, *The Acquisition of Books*, p. 86; Joseph Foster (ed.), *Alumni Oxonienses, Volume II – Early Series* (Oxford: James Parker & Co., 1891), p. 815.
58 *Ibid.*, p. 47.
59 *Ibid.*, pp. 47–56.
60 Chetham's Library, Manchester, (Chet/4/5/2), Invoices of Books, 1655–1685, f. 6r, f. 8r, f. 17r, f. 19r, f. 58r, f. 58v.
61 *Ibid.*, f. 59r.

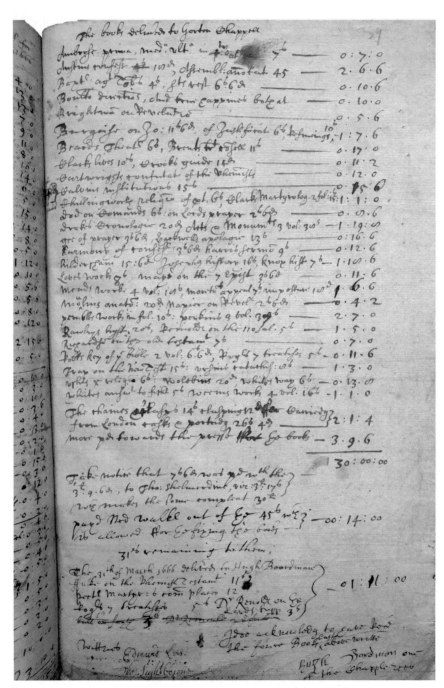

FIGURE. 8.1 The list of books sent to Gorton Chapel for the Parish Library
© CHETHAM'S LIBRARY, MANCHESTER (CHET/4/5/2) INVOICES OF BOOKS, 1655–1685, F. 59R. REPRODUCED WITH THE KIND PERMISSION OF CHETHAM'S LIBRARY, MANCHESTER

Some of these parcels were sent individually, whilst others were sent together with a delivery of books intended for the public library. The invoice dated 2 August 1655, for example, states that 'these [English books] came with the first parcell' of books for the public library, and the invoice of 7 May 1657 asserts that these 'English books [were] sent with 5th parcell' of books for the public library.[62] As well as including details on the size and cost of the books, the number of copies of each title and, occasionally, binding information, these invoices also sometimes included packing and transportation costs. The invoice for books delivered to Gorton, for example, notes a cost of 14s. for chains for the books, and 26s. 4d. for 'Carriedg from London casks & portridg'.[63]

4   The Collections of the Francis Trigge and the Gorton Chest Libraries

Francis Trigge envisioned a religious library that emulated and, in many ways, pre-empted those owned by late sixteenth and early seventeenth century English bishops. Humphrey Chetham intended for his parish libraries to be repositories of Protestant education for the laity. Both were comprehensive religious libraries, but in different ways.

The Francis Trigge Chained Library included works by Catholics, such as Hector Pintus and the committed Jesuits Robert Bellarmine and Francisco Ribera, and Protestants, including the English Puritan clergyman John Rainolds, the German Lutheran Martin Chemnitz, and the French Calvinist Wolfgang Musculus, as well as John Calvin himself and his theological successor, Theodore Beza. The Trigge library collection also has a significant number of Early Christian authors, alongside numerous volumes by the Church Fathers and Doctors of the Church. The balance between Catholic and Protestant authors in the collection is relatively equal: Catholic authors represent thirty-seven percent and Protestant authors wrote thirty-eight percent of the total collection, which consists of 263 surviving volumes. However, the same equality does not apply to the number of titles, which are instead weighted heavily in favour of Protestant authors, as might be expected. Protestant books account for fifty-two percent of the total collection, whilst the works of post-Reformation Catholic authors account for the more modest figure of ten percent of the collection. This dominance of Protestant texts reflects not only Francis Trigge's own religion, but also the religion that he was

---

62   *Ibid.*, f. 6r, f. 17r.
63   *Ibid.*, f. 59r.

trying to promote in the religiously divided county of Lincolnshire at the end of the Elizabethan era.

Commentaries on the Bible, both Catholic and Protestant, are overwhelmingly predominant in the Trigge library's collection, with ninety-one volumes. Christians had been writing Biblical commentaries since the end of the apostolic era and so they were nothing new by the sixteenth and seventeenth centuries, but they remained overwhelmingly popular with wide ranging audiences.[64] Of the eighteen non-Protestant commentaries on the Bible included in this collection, thirteen were republished versions of patristic and medieval Biblical commentaries that were widely available in the late sixteenth and seventeenth centuries.[65] Post-Reformation Catholic authors, including Hector Pintus and Georg Eder, were responsible for writing the remaining five non-Protestant commentaries in the collection. Protestant Biblical commentaries were more common than Catholic ones after the English Reformation. Within this collection, there were nine Biblical commentaries by Calvin, nine by Wolfgang Musculus, four by Martin Bucer and six by Peter Martyr Vermigli, amongst numerous others. Both Protestant and Catholic commentators focused on presenting to their readers the literal meaning of Scripture, and attempting to simplify complex Scriptural messages for a more general audience.[66]

Within the theological texts in the Francis Trigge collection, the preponderance of Calvinist theology is particularly noticeable. Calvinist authors wrote eighteen of the thirty-eight theological texts in the collection, though only one was by Calvin himself. The theological texts in the Trigge library include Theodore Beza's *Tractatus theologicarum*, a compilation of theological treatises on Calvinist theology, as well as works on more specific aspects of that theology, such as Hieronymus Zanchius's various works on predestination, *Miscellaneorum libri tres. Tertium nunc editi. De praedestinatione sanctorum*. Catholic theology was also represented, most likely to enable the clergymen of the Church of England to properly refute it. Texts such as Diego de Payva de Andrada's *Defensio Tridentinae fidei catholicae et inegerrimae quinque libris*

---

64 Ulrich G. Leinsle, 'Sources, Methods, and Forms of Early Modern Theology', in U.L. Lehner, R.A. Muller and A.G. Roeber (eds.) *The Oxford Handbook of Early Modern Theology, 1600–1800* (Oxford: Oxford University Press, 2016), p. 32; Ian Green, *Print and Protestantism in Early Modern England* (Oxford: Oxford University Press, 2000), pp. 113–119.

65 Carl R. Trueman, 'Scripture and Exegesis in Early Modern Reformed Theology', in U.L. Lehner, R.A. Muller and A.G. Roeber (eds.) *The Oxford Handbook of Early Modern Theology, 1600–1800* (Oxford: Oxford University Press, 2016), p. 188.

66 Marius Reiser, 'The History of Catholic Exegesis, 1600–1800', in U.L. Lehner, R.A. Muller and A.G. Roeber (eds.) *The Oxford Handbook of Early Modern Theology, 1600–1800* (Oxford: Oxford University Press, 2016), p. 77.

comprehensa that defended Catholic doctrine as outlined at the Council of Trent in 1563 and reprints of medieval works of theology such as the *Summa theologica* of Saint Antonio Forciglione and Peter Lombard's *Sacratissima sententiarum totius theologie quadripartita volumina* were included in the collection.[67]

In addition to Protestant and Catholic works, this library includes works by all four Fathers of the Western Church, as well as the four Fathers of the Eastern Church. These books were staples of clerical libraries throughout the seventeenth century and are also to be found in numerous parish libraries from the sixteenth and seventeenth centuries, most notably at Wimborne Minster in Dorset, which holds over eighty patristic volumes. There were also those books that tended towards the 'liberall sciences' referred to in the foundation indenture for the Francis Trigge Chained Library. These works, which included natural and secular histories, medical texts and works of morality, reflected Trigge's desire to enhance learning and knowledge of as wide a range of topics as possible amongst the people of Grantham and its surrounding areas.

The Gorton Chest, on the other hand, was comprised almost exclusively of Protestant texts from authors of various confessional identities, with the Catholic Paolo Sarpi's *History of the Council of Trent* being the only exception. Each of the books chosen for the Gorton Chest library served to reinforce the message the trustees wanted to promote through the libraries, of religious unity within Protestantism and the encouragement of the laity to live godly lives in preparation for death and salvation. Whilst Sarpi's inclusion may initially seem at odds with this vision and intent – his confessional identity represents a stark juxtaposition to the religious positions of the other authors – he was a vocal opponent of the papacy and his works were, in fact, in alignment with the anti-papist stance of Chetham's trustees.[68] Many of the authors whose works were included in the collection had confessional identities that were shared by Johnson, Hollinworth and Tildsley. They included Calvinist and Puritan stalwarts such as William Perkins, Richard Rogers, John Dod and John Calvin himself, all of whom shared a similar religious outlook to Richard

---

67   Theodore Beza, *Tractatus Theologicarum*, 2nd edition ([Geneva]: Eustathius Vignon, 1582), USTC 450918; Hieronymus Zanchius, *Miscellaneorum libri tres. Tertium nunc editi. De praedestinatione sanctorum* (Neapoli Palatinorum: Matthaeus Harnisius, 1592), USTC 662676; Diego de Payva de Andrada, *Defensio Tridentinae fidei catholicae et inegerrimae quinque libris comprehensa* (Ingolstadt: David Sartorius, 1580), USTC 632166; Antonio Forciglione, *Summa theologica* (Lyon: Johannes Cleyn, 1516); Peter Lombard, *Sacratissima sententiarum totius theologie quadripartita volumina* (Venice: Gregorio De Gregori, 1514), USTC 847956.

68   K. Brinkmann Brown, 'Sarpi, Paolo (1552–1623)', *The Oxford Encyclopedia of the Reformation*, (online: 2005).

Johnson. There were also a number of influential Presbyterians' works in the collection, including John Knox, Thomas Brightman, Anthony Burgess and Thomas Cartwright, whose views reflected those of Richard Hollinworth and John Tildsley. The trustees' commitment to spreading the broader messages of Protestantism is evidenced by their inclusion of works by the Arminian Francis White and the Anglican John Mayer, and their conscious omission of works by Catholics and Independents, whom Tildsley singled out for exclusion from the parish library collections in a letter to Hollinworth dated April 1655.[69] Unlike Trigge and those responsible for selecting books for that collection, Chetham and his trustees seem to have had no desire to create a comprehensive library of both Catholic and Protestant religious and secular knowledge.

The Gorton Chest library corpus encompassed a variety of texts that can be divided into eight categories: catechisms, Christian apologetics, church histories, Christian life (or practical divinity), Biblical commentaries, theological works, doctrinal texts, and sermons. Printed sermons, which were popular and widely available in the mid-seventeenth century, are plentiful within the collection, accounting for thirty-four percent of the corpus.[70] Many of the sermons in the Gorton Chest library focussed on the importance of living a good life 'to show the fruits of one's faith'. They urged people to eschew sin in favour of following the teachings of Christ and endeavouring to emulate His life by expounding particular passages of Scripture that stressed the importance of obedience, morality and faith. Reading them in conjunction with the Puritan practical divinity texts also in the Gorton Chest would have presented a particularly persuasive argument in favour of godly living.[71] Theological and doctrinal works each account for fifteen percent of the corpus in its entirety. The theological texts notably covered eschatology, the Final Judgement and the soul's eternal destiny. Such subjects are discussed in John Napier's *A Plain Discovery of the Whole Revelation of St. John*, which argued that the Final Judgement would take place between 1688 and 1700, and Richard Baxter's *The Saints' Everlasting Rest*, framed as a dying man's legacy to his readers.[72] Other theological books served

---

69   Chetham's Library, Manchester, (CPP/2/141), Letter from John Tildsley to Rev. Hollinworth at Manchester.

70   James Rigney, 'Sermons into Print', in Peter McCullough, Hugh Adlington and Emma Rhatigan (eds.), *The Oxford Handbook of the Early Modern Sermon* (Oxford: Oxford University Press, 2011), pp. 204–205.

71   Ian Green, 'Preaching in the Parishes', in Peter McCullough, Hugh Adlington and Emma Rhatigan (eds.) *The Oxford Handbook of the Early Modern Sermon* (Oxford: Oxford University Press, 2011), pp. 151–152.

72   John Napier, *A Plain Discovery of the Whole Revelation of St. John*, 5th edition (Edinburgh: Andrew Wilson, 1645), USTC 3059920; Richard Baxter, *The Saints' Everlasting Rest* (London: printed for Thomas Underhill and Francis Tyton, 1656).

to set out the paradigms of the Reformed religion, as seen in John Calvin's *The Institution of Christian Religion*. This text divided systematic theology into four sections that were designed to enable readers to better recognise God.[73]

The eight Biblical commentaries in the collection, designed to increase accessibility to the Bible for the less educated, include Francis Roberts's *Clavis Bibliorum, The Key of the Bible*, John Mayer's *Ecclesiastica Interpretatio*, and Thomas Cartwright's *A Confutation of the Rhemists Translation, Glosses and Annotations on the New Testament*.[74] John Napier's *A Plain Discovery of the Whole Revelation of St. John* can also be included in this category and, with Thomas Brightman's *Works* on the Book of Revelation, can perhaps be seen as a reflection of a wider preoccupation with the apocalypse in the mid-seventeenth century.[75] By providing the Gorton Chest parish library with such a rich plethora of expository and instructive works, Chetham's trustees gave people who were unaware or unsure of the fundamental principles of Protestantism a way in which to edify and educate themselves on matters of religion. It may also suggest that, in such a Catholic county as Lancashire remained in the mid-seventeenth century, Chetham and his trustees were hoping to encourage the conversion of any Catholics who may read these volumes.

The people responsible for collecting books for both the Francis Trigge Chained Library and the Gorton Chest parish library made extensive use of the second-hand book market. As Ian Mitchell has argued, 'old texts were and are a vital part of the canon' as 'new books remained expensive' throughout the sixteenth and seventeenth centuries.[76] Considering the consistently high costs of newly published books and the relatively limited funds provided for the establishment of these libraries, the preponderance of older titles in both collections is perhaps unsurprising. It is also demonstrative of the continued popularity of certain older titles and their ease of availability. The Francis Trigge Chained Library was established in 1598, but the publication dates of books

---

73   John Calvin, *The Institution of Christian Religion* (London: Eliot's Court Press, 1611), USTC 3004572.
74   Francis Roberts, *Clavis Bibliorum. The Key of the Bible*, 2nd edition (London: Thomas Ratcliffe and Edward Mottershed, 1649), USTC 3052315; John Mayer, *Ecclesiastica Interpretatio* (London: John Haviland, 1627), USTC 3013294; Thomas Cartwright, *A confutation of the Rhemists translation, glosses and annotations on the New Testament* ([Leiden: William Brewster], 1618), USTC 3008255 and 1436816.
75   Thomas Brightman, *The workes of that famous, reverend, and learned divine, Mr. Tho: Brightman* (London: John Field for Samuel Cartwright, 1644), USTC 3046550.
76   Ian Mitchell, '"Old Books – New Bound"? Selling Second-Hand Books in England, c. 1680–1850', in Jon Stobart and Ilja Van Damme (eds.), *Modernity and the second-hand trade: European consumption cultures and practices, 1700–1900* (Basingstoke: Palgrave Macmillan, 2010), p. 140.

in its collection demonstrate that only around a quarter of the books were new when they were purchased for the library. The collection includes 193 volumes published in the 1580s or earlier, meaning that seventy-four percent of the collection was printed over a decade prior to the library's foundation. Even taking into consideration the length of time books could sit in booksellers' warehouses or back rooms, these books were unlikely to have been new when they were bought for the library. In the Gorton Chest parish library, the situation is similar: just thirty-one percent of the titles in this collection were published in the 1650s, the decade in which the library was established. As such, it is unlikely that the remaining sixty-nine percent of the corpus was new when these books were placed into the library. They were published over a seventy-year period between the 1580s and the 1640s and had probably had at least one, if not multiple, prior owners. The Gorton library was allocated just £30 for books by the trustees, which may have been both a reason for the predominance of second-hand books in the collection and another factor in their choice of Robert Littlebury as their bookseller, as he was proficient in the second-hand book trade and was one of its principal practitioners in England.[77]

5 Conclusion

Francis Trigge and Humphrey Chetham were by no means unique in the post-Reformation period in their desire to promote and provide for the education of the parish clergy and laity: over 165 parish libraries were established in England between 1558 and 1709. Throughout the sixteenth and seventeenth centuries, the men (and, occasionally, women) who founded these collections were consistently focussed on providing a religious education to their intended readers. Both the Francis Trigge Chained Library collection and that of the Gorton Chest parish library were methodically compiled in order to reflect the religious situation of their respective counties. Lincolnshire at the end of the sixteenth century was a religiously divided county that still contained a considerable number of Catholics, despite largely having accepted Protestantism. As a result, the collection included a combination of Catholic and Protestant works that were designed to allow the local clergy to increase their knowledge of the religious opposition in order to be better able to refute their arguments. The range of genres in the collection also reflected the combined clerical and lay readership, with Biblical commentaries, expository texts

---

77   Yeo, *The Acquisition of Books*, p. 87.

and works of liberal science appealing to both kinds of readers. In contrast, the Gorton Chest parish library retained its educational nature, but was comprised almost exclusively of Protestant works written by predominantly Calvinist, Puritan and Presbyterian authors. Being situated in what was one of England's most Catholic counties in the mid-seventeenth century and intended solely for use by the ordinary laity, this was a deliberate choice on the part of Chetham and his trustees and was perhaps the result of a wish to avoid confusing relatively uneducated readers. The genres of texts focussed on sermons, Biblical commentaries and theological texts intended to explain complex passages of Scripture to the 'common people' of Chetham's intended audience, thus both increasing their religious knowledge and, through numerous texts on Christian life, providing them with moral instruction. Taken together, these two parish library collections demonstrate that the Protestant focus on religious and moral instruction remained the same in the mid-seventeenth century, after the Civil War and Interregnum, as it was at the end of the Elizabethan era, over fifty years earlier.

CHAPTER 9

'Libri Anglici': English Books in Danish and Dutch Library Collections, c.1650–1720

Hanna de Lange

When Joachim Gersdorff died in 1661, he bequeathed his entire library of around 8,000 books to King Frederick III of Denmark. Gersdorff's book collection, together with those of Laurids Ulfeldt and Peder Lauridsen Scavenius, formed the foundation of the Royal Danish Library in Copenhagen as it still survives today.[1] Unlike Scavenius, Joachim Gersdorff did not write his name on the title-pages of his books to mark them as his property. Without these provenance marks it would normally be impossible to identify the former owner of these books. To complicate matters further, once transferred to the royal collection, many of Gersdorff's books were uniformly bound with the owner's mark of King Frederick III on the spine. But thanks to the king's first librarian, we do know which books had belonged to Gersdorff. Marcus Meibom compiled a five-volume handwritten catalogue of the collection, the *Catalogi Bibliothecæ Gerstorffianæ*.[2]

In the third volume of this catalogue separate sections were dedicated to books from Spain, the Low Countries, Italy, France, Sweden and England, the 'Libri Anglici'. Despite the fact that the catalogue was in Latin, the 373 books described in this part were in English. Meibom scrupulously recorded the author, the title, the format, the year and finally the place of publication of each book. Among these books in English, some were printed in The Hague, Amsterdam, or even Middelburg. These, however, were exceptions: most of them were printed in London. In the other volumes, little tabs on the fore-edge mark the different sections of 'theologici', 'juridici', 'philosophici', 'medici', and so forth. Under these classifications works of more English authors can be found, but the books listed are in other languages like Latin, Greek or French.[3] The amount of books printed on the British Isles that found their way to the

---

1   Joachim Gersdorff (1611–1661), Steward of the Danish Realm, bequeathed his library to King Frederick III. The book collections of both Laurids Ulfeldt (1605–1659), land commissioner, and Peder Lauridsen Scavenius (1623–1685), Attorney General, were bought by the King.
2   Marcus Meibom and Joachim Gersdorff, KB's arkiv (indtil 1943) E2 Bd3: *Catalogi Bibliothecæ Gerstoffianæ*, Det Kongelige Bibliotek (The Royal Library), Copenhagen, Denmark.
3   Marcus Meibom, *Catalogi Bibliothecæ Gerstoffianæ*, vols. 1–5.

'LIBRI ANGLICI'

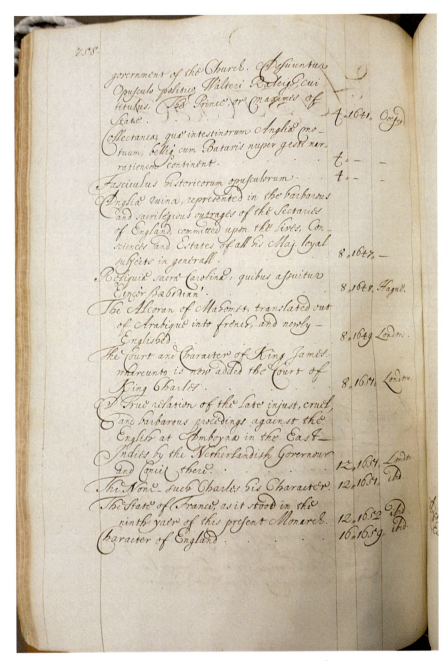

FIGURE 9.1   Page 758 of the *Catalogi Bibliothecæ Gerstorffianæ*, volume 3
COURTESY OF THE ROYAL DANISH LIBRARY IN COPENHAGEN, DENMARK.
SHELFMARK: KBS ARKIV (INDTIL 1943) E 2

Danish Royal collection in the early 1660s comes as a surprise. From the total of 2,570 books that Ulfeldt sold to the king, 224 were printed in England, and of Scavenius' library nearly 4% of the books were printed on the British Isles (236 out of a total of 5,895 books).[4]

The purpose of this article is to explore the presence of books printed on the British Isles in personal libraries in Denmark and the Dutch Republic. In the first centuries of print, the printing industry in England and Ireland was a peripheral business. The London trade was curtailed by the monopoly of the corporate Stationers Company. This was not the only hindrance for the development of a successful international export trade. Very little paper was made in Britain, and therefore most of it had to be imported. At first local printers were not able to meet the demand of the domestic market and better-financed printers on the continent produced books of better quality and at lower prices. The importation of books from abroad was the so-called 'Latin Trade'. This was largely a successful trading relationship, one that allowed English collectors to build up substantial libraries, while English booksellers could make a handsome profit as intermediaries. As a result, no more than half the books in the collection of the philosopher John Locke, assembled largely at the end of the seventeenth century, were printed in England. The playwright and poet William Congreve also relied heavily on imported books for his collection; these took up 40 % of the titles he owned.[5] In the seventeenth century, English printers began to increase their production, both in the vernacular and in Latin. First, they focused mainly on the domestic market, but gradually the dissemination of British books on the European continent began to take off. London retained its status as the capital of British printing, with Oxford and Cambridge coming a distant second and third. Rarer still on the European continent were books printed in Dublin, Edinburgh, Glasgow or Aberdeen.[6]

---

4   *Catalogus Librorum selectissimorum bibliothecae rarae et quoad librorum compactionem nitidissimae Generosi ac Strenui Dni. Laurentii Ulfeldii, Nobilis Dani Quorum auctio constituta est Hafniae ad diem 15. Junij: Anno 1662. Hafniae, Typis Christiani Weringii Acad. Typog.* (Copenhagen: Christian Wering, 1662) and *Designatio librorum in qvalibet facultate, materia & lingva rariorum, summa cura, tum quoad librorum, editionum ve perfectionem, tum quoad eorundem compactionem varijs in locis, in amorem patriæ, & supplementum instructissimæ Bibliothecæ Regiæ, conqvisitorum. [à P. L. Scavenio.] Nullus Amicus magis liber, quam Liber. Hafniæ, Typis Christiani Weringii Acad. Typogr. Anno 1665.* (Copenhagen: Christian Wering, 1665).

5   John Barnard, 'Introduction', in *The Cambridge History of the Book in Britain, Vol. IV, 1557–1695* (Cambridge: Cambridge University Press, 2002), p. 6; and David Pearson, 'The English Private Library in the Seventeenth Century', *The Library: The Transactions of the Bibliographical Society*, 13:4 (2012), pp. 379–399, here p. 383.

6   Wherever books printed in England or on the British Isles are mentioned in this chapter, all books printed in England, Scotland and Ireland are included. But here, for reasons of readability I will refer to 'England' and 'English'.

Traditionally, scholarship of the English book was undertaken from a national perspective. This resulted in invaluable inventories of what was published on the British Isles, and an unrivalled national bibliography in the form of the English Short Title Catalogue.[7] Recent scholarship has shifted this focus and explored which authors and works published in England found international resonance. Paul Hoftijzer researched English books on the continent from different angles. He explored the dissemination of English books by looking at trade lists of continental booksellers and the Frankfurt book fairs. He also examined the production of exiled English booksellers in seventeenth-century Amsterdam.[8] Hans Bots wrote about the role of periodicals in the dissemination of books, including English books, whereas Katherine Swift has conducted research on Dutch booksellers penetrating the London book market in the eighteenth century.[9] While focussing largely on books in the English language in sixteenth- and early seventeenth-century book fair catalogues, in his latest work Ian Maclean investigated how publishers of learned English works of medicine and natural philosophy sold their scholarly works on the northern European market at the end of the seventeenth century.[10] A consensus among these authors is that the English presence in the continental book trade was very small and only started to blossom in the eighteenth century. This does appear to be the case when focussing on the retail and fair trade. However, this article claims that book ownership of private library owners tells a different story. By looking at the contents of book auction catalogues a more nuanced

---

[7] On English books see the English Short Title Catalogue: estc.bl.uk and the Cambridge series on the book in Britain: Lotte Hellinga and J.B. Trapp (eds.), *The Cambridge History of the Book in Britain, Vol. III, 1400–1557* (Cambridge: Cambridge University Press, 1999); John Barnard and D.F. McKenzie (eds.), *The Cambridge History of the Book in Britain, Vol. IV, 1557–1695* (Cambridge: Cambridge University Press, 2002); Michael Suarez and Michael L. Turner (eds.), *The Cambridge History of the Book in Britain, Vol. V, 1695–1830* (Cambridge: Cambridge University Press, 2010).

[8] Paul G. Hoftijzer, 'British books abroad: the Continent', in John Barnard and D.F. McKenzie (eds.), *The Cambridge History of the Book in Britain, Vol. IV, 1557–1695* (Cambridge: Cambridge University Press, 2002), pp. 735–743; Paul G. Hoftijzer, *Engelse boekverkopers bij de Beurs. De geschiedenis van de Amsterdamse boekhandels Bruyning en Swart, 1637–1724* (Amsterdam: APA-Holland Universiteits Pers, 1987).

[9] Hans Bots, 'Le rôle des périodiques Néerlandais pour la diffusion du livre (1684–1747)', in C. Berkvens-Stevelinck, et al. (eds.), *Le Magasin de L'Univers. The Dutch Republic as the Centre of the European Book Trade* (Leiden: Brill, 1992), pp. 49–70; Katherine Swift, 'Dutch penetration of the London market for books, c. 1690–1730', in Berkvens-Stevelinck, *Le Magasin de L'Univers*, pp. 265–280.

[10] Ian Maclean, 'English Books on the Continent, 1570–1630', in his *Learning and the Market Place. Essays in the History of the Early Modern Book* (Leiden: Brill, 2009), pp. 339–370; Ian Maclean, *Episodes in the Life of the Early Modern Learned Book* (Leiden: Brill, 2020), pp. 212–213.

picture emerges: one of book collectors who gathered English books carefully and purposefully.

The present choice in focussing on Denmark and the Dutch Republic can be justified by a number of reasons. First of all, like England, these were Protestant countries. Even though there were differences, these countries took a particular interest in the confessional publications, disputes and developments in other Protestant states. There were also long-standing trading networks between these countries. Their merchants and sailors became familiar with each other's languages long before scholars or polyglots did.[11] This brings us to another important aspect: what Denmark and the Dutch Republic had in common with England was the limited linguistic impact of their vernacular language. Both the Danes and the Dutch were obliged to master languages other than their own as soon as they crossed the borders of their homeland or met foreigners. This could explain why they did not shy away from buying books in languages other than those in the diplomatic and scholarly standards of Latin and French.[12] Finally, the Danes and Dutch were prolific adopters of book auctions, and book auction catalogues from Denmark and the Dutch Republic are digitally available. This makes the information they contain easily accessible.

This chapter begins by looking at what could have sparked an interest in English books among (future) book collectors. Then it will examine the main sources used here: the book auction catalogues, their limitations and uses. To further illustrate their contents, a closer look will be taken at four library owners and the auction of their collections in Denmark and the Dutch Republic. Finally, this chapter investigates where collectors turned to for information about the availability of English books on the market in the period around 1650–1720.

1   The English Connection

In 1645, Johan and Cornelis de Witt, then 20 and 22 years old, undertook a Grand Tour, a voyage typically undertaken by privileged young men and – to a smaller degree – women. A Grand Tour was part of their education: the brothers visited places that symbolised the cultural heritage of Antiquity and the Renaissance. Johan de Witt kept track of their adventures by taking notes and keeping a little account book. Their tour took almost two years, most of which

---

11 According to Maclean, even polyglots around 1600 rarely spoke the English language. See: Maclean, 'English Books on the Continent', pp. 339–370.
12 Peter Burke, *Languages and Communities in Early Modern Europe* (Cambridge: Cambridge University Press, 2004).

time they spent in France. Here, at the University of Angers, they graduated with a law degree. The final six weeks of their tour in 1647 were dedicated to a visit to England. The brothers had been away from home for nearly twenty months when they took a boat from Calais to Dover. Travelling around in a horse drawn carriage was time-consuming, so they did not get to see a great deal of the country. Nevertheless, they did visit some major attractions that modern tourists still favour today. In London they went to see the Tower, the Houses of Parliament and Westminster Abbey with its royal tombs. To the west their destinations included Stonehenge, Salisbury, Bristol and Bath. And, last but not least, they visited the university town of Oxford, where they went to see the Bodleian Library.[13]

Unfortunately we have no list of the books the brothers De Witt owned which could enable us to see which English books they came to possess before they met their untimely and violent death in 1672.[14] Still it is important to bring up the trip they made, because excursions like this one were a popular pastime and an indispensable part of the upbringing of young members of privileged families. This was not just the case in the Dutch Republic. In Denmark too it was common for young noblemen to study abroad for a period of time. Students with less wealthy parents could apply for one of the four annual travel grants introduced by King Frederick II in 1569. Vello Helk has mapped the Danish-Norwegian study trips in detail, and popular destinations in England were London, Oxford and Cambridge.[15] Along the way, just like their Danish counterparts, the De Witt brothers broadened their horizons. They were the book collectors of the future and visiting England must have sparked their interest in English culture and encouraged them to purchase English books.

---

13   Janneke Groen, 'De Grand Tour', in Ineke Huysman and Roosje Peeters (eds.), *Johan de Witt en Engeland* (Soest: Catullus, 2019), pp. 32–41. See for different editions of the *Catalogi Bodleiana*, USTC 3002175, 3009219, 3002177 and 3002176.

14   The books of Johan and Cornelis de Witt were not auctioned after they were murdered in 1672. When Johan de Witt's son, Johan jr. died in 1701 his collection was auctioned and a catalogue was printed: *Catalogus Bibliothecae luculentissimae, & exquisitissimis ac rarissimis in omni disciplinarum & linguarum genere libris, magno studio, dilectu & Sumptu quaesitis, instructissimae, a Joanne de Witt, Joannis Hollandiae Consiliarii & Syndici, magnique Sigilli Custodis, Filio. Illius Auctio habebitur Dordraci, in aedibus defuncti, 20 Octobris 1701. Dordraci, Apud Theodorum Goris, & Joannem van Braam, Bibliopolas* (Dordrecht: Theodorus Goris and Johannes van Braam, 1701). This library probably still contained books previously owned or collected by his father.

15   Vello Helk, *Dansk-norske studierejser: 1661–1813* (Odense: Universitetsforlag, 1991) and Ejvind Slottved and Ditlev Tamm, *The University of Copenhagen. A Danish centre of learning since 1479* (Copenhagen: The University of Copenhagen, 2009), p. 26.

The question remains which language they preferred to read in, and if they would choose books in Latin over books printed in English, if both were available. Could they indeed read the books in the English language that came into their possession? Did the De Witt brothers speak and read the English language or did they manage in Latin or French during their trip to England? Johan de Witt did not master the English language very well. We may wonder whether that was necessary. From some of his later diplomatic correspondence, from 1653 onwards, when Johan de Witt became the Grand Pensionary of the Dutch Republic, this does not seem to be the case. The letters show us that even Englishmen corresponded with him in languages other than English. Walter Strickland wrote to Johan de Witt in French (March 1654), Oliver Cromwell sent him a letter in Latin (October 1654), Charles II wrote in French (Sept 1660), just as Elizabeth Stuart (June 1661) and William Temple did (in October 1668). Actually, few people wrote to him in English, except for George Monck (in June 1655) and George Downing (March 1662).

English correspondents appear to have been well aware of the exotic status of the English language abroad. To the original letter of Edward Hyde to Johan de Witt dated 3 March 1663 and undersigned 'Clarendon' in English, a translation in Dutch was attached.[16] When William Temple added a letter of the Lord Keeper in English to one of his own, he appended a postscript in which he stated that in case De Witt did not understand the English of The Lord Keeper, he could rely on the messenger bringing him the letter to translate it for him into French.[17] These examples show the low status of the English language at the time and the unfamiliarity with the language among foreigners. It would still be long before English would become the international language it is today.

2 Book Auction Catalogues

To learn more about collecting practices of book owners we need to look beyond trade lists and fair catalogues. These stock lists – often structured in alphabetical order sorted by author – tell us what was available on the book market,

---

[16] The politician, historian and chancellor of Oxford University Edward Hyde, was the first earl of Clarendon. See for the Clarendon letter EMLO: tinyurl.com/y536dqhr. Both the original and the translation are written in 'secretary hand'. Clarendon clearly signed the original in his own hand.

[17] For the correspondence of Johan de Witt see the ING Huygens project and EMLO (Early Modern Letters Online, emlo.bodleian.ox.ac.uk); Ineke Huysman, 'Alleen voor uw ogen', in Ineke Huysman and Roosje Peeters (eds.), *Johan de Witt en Engeland. Een bloemlezing uit zijn correspondentie* (Soest: Catullus, 2019) pp. 148–152.

but we need to keep in mind that they were commercial tools. Booksellers listed what they thought would sell best. These catalogues do not inform us of the works that eventually found their way into private libraries. For this we must turn to other sources, like estate inventories and book auction catalogues. An example of such an inventory list is that of the library of Albertine Agnes (1634–1696), the wife of the Frisian stadtholder Willem Frederik of Nassau-Dietz, composed in 1681. The books are mainly in French, some are in Dutch and fewer still in German. At first glance there are no English titles, but a curiosity about the English language may be detected. There are 'the French Englis[h] dictionary', a 'Grammaire Angloise' and a 'Dictionaire English Duyts'. A further interest in English affairs is displayed by the mention of an 'Histoire d'Elisabeth d'Angleterre' and 'Theologisch[e] werken van Goodwin' (*Theological works by Goodwin*).[18] Although the entries in this inventory are interesting, unfortunately, they are imprecise. Without additional information about author, year and place of publication, this inventory, and others like it, lack the information that help us identify particular editions of books and allow us to reconstruct private book ownership with any certainty.

The major sources used for the present investigation are book auction catalogues that documented private libraries. The first printed auction catalogue known to us appeared in the Dutch Republic in 1599.[19] Although with considerable delay, Denmark was among the first European countries to take up this phenomenon. It was not before 1661 when the first printed Danish book auction catalogue emerged. The auction catalogues of the Dutch Republic are available digitally through Brill's database *Book Sales Catalogues Online*, and their Danish counterparts are available via the online catalogue of *Det Kongelige Bibliotek*, the Royal Library in Copenhagen.[20] When collectors passed away, the heirs usually sold their books at auction. A catalogue listing all the items in the collection was then compiled, printed and distributed in advance of such auctions. A careful analysis of the contents of book auction catalogues of library owners give us a good indication of the resonance that English authors and works found on the European continent. The catalogues reveal which books printed in England reached buyers and collectors on the European book market, and show that these works were by no means

---

18   Tresoar, Leeuwarden, Archive no. 323–3707, 'Inventaris van de roerende goederen van prinses Albertine Agnes te Leeuwarden', in: 'Familie Van Eysinga-Vegelin van Claerbergen'.
19   Bert van Selm, *"Een menighte treffelijcke Boecken". Nederlandse boekhandelscatalogi in het begin van de zeventiende eeuw* (Utrecht: HES, 1987).
20   For the Dutch catalogues, see Brill's Book Sales Catalogues Online (BSCO). For the Danish catalogues, see *Cataloger over bogauctioner*, Royal Danish Library.

restricted to one single topic. On the contrary, a wide variety of subjects, fields of study and years of publication are reflected in the titles.

Title-pages of book auction catalogues contain valuable information.[21] In addition to the date and place of the auction, the title-page indicates the provenance of the books contained therein. Sometimes the former owner of the books remained anonymous, but in the cases examined here the names of the late owners were mentioned. Among them were statesmen, ministers, bishops, university professors, jurists and medical doctors. To be able to trace the book back to a single edition with any certainty, some basic information is required. This includes the name of the author, the title of the book, the year of publication, the place of publication and the format of the book. The language that the work was written in can generally be derived from the title and the separate sections it was composed of. The name of the printer or publisher may confirm the specific edition of a book. A catalogue can contain further information that may not be strictly necessary for the identification of specific editions, but does provide us with a better understanding of the machinations of the trade. Lot numbers, for instance, structured the proceedings during the auction itself. Occasionally, the price paid for each book and the name of its buyer were added by hand in the margin. These pieces of information reveal the value contemporaries attached to certain works and the people involved at the auctions.

The catalogues came in different shapes and sizes. A common ordering principle of book auction catalogues is by subject category and format. These divisions added some structure to the lists of books. The biggest books in folio and quarto were often well described. But the description of octavo, duodecimo, 16mo and even smaller formats tended to be shorter, often limited to title and author: enough for the auctioneer to sell a book, but insufficient to identify the exact edition of the work for this research. Sometimes, frustratingly, 'a variety of packages' or similar phrases were mentioned towards the end of the catalogue. The auction catalogue of the Danish statesman Henrik Matthesius concluded with vague descriptions like 'bundles of disputations', *forordninger* (regulations) and 'various'. Similarly, we will never know which books were hidden in the packages of the Dutch bookseller Pieter van den Berge, but they may have contained smaller format books, pamphlets or broadsheets.[22]

---

21   On general trends in European book catalogues, see Arthur der Weduwen, Andrew Pettegree and Graeme Kemp (eds.), *Book Trade Catalogues in Early Modern Europe* (Leiden: Brill, 2021).

22   *Designatio Librorum, Viri Nobiliss. & Amplissimi Beatæ memoriæ Henrici Mathesii Sereniss. Reg. Majest. Quondam Consiliarii &c. Quorum auctio in instituenda est* [August] *d: [1] Hor. VIII. In ædibus Viduæ Ernstianæ in foro vulgo Amager-Torff* (Copenhagen: Christian

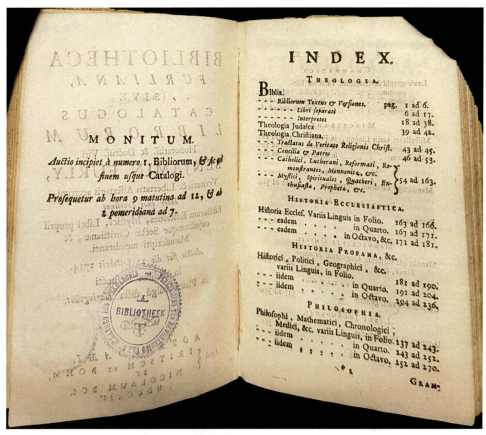

FIGURE 9.2   Page from the index of the *Bibliotheca Furliana*
COURTESY OF ALLARD PIERSON, UNIVERSITY OF AMSTERDAM. SHELFMARK: KVB NV 76A

Whoever compiled the catalogue thought these items in themselves were not valuable enough to deserve separate listings.

Book auction catalogues can reveal as much as they hide. Consider, for example, the so-called 'lost books' of which no copy has survived, and so which are not described in retrospective bibliographies. Scholars have recently drawn our attention to books used intensively like school books and prayer books, or printed material that was produced for temporary use, like almanacs, pamphlets and newspapers. Such works could have easily been discarded

Wering, 1687) and *Catalogus, Variorum Insignium ac Rarissimorum (in omni Facultate & Lingua) Librorum Compactorum, Officinae Petri Van Den Berge. Quorum Auctio habebitur in AEdibus ejusdem, in de Berg-straat, by Jan-Roden-poorts Thoorn, in de Berg Parnas.* (Amsterdam: Pieter van den Berge, 1670), USTC 1846623.

not long after they had been produced. Other works did not survive because of natural disasters, destruction and war.[23] Consequently, the only trace of their existence may be their inclusion in catalogues.

Before taking a closer look at some cases of private book ownership a general overview of the presence of English books in Dutch and Danish collections seems appropriate. The book auction catalogues analysed for this article – 60 Danish and 107 Dutch auction catalogues – were inspected for the presence of books printed on the British Isles, resulting in 5,816 English books in the Danish catalogues and 9,092 English books in the Dutch catalogues. The proportion of books printed in England varied as much as the size of the collections in which they were housed. The smallest collection at auction in Copenhagen contained no more than a total of 288 works and its Dutch counterpart was even smaller with 189 books.[24] At the other side of the spectrum we find collections with over 15,000 works.[25] These numbers represent high averages that do not give us a reliable picture of what was common. Figure 9.3, however, shows that collections between 1,000 and 3,000 books occurred most frequently.

No matter what their size was, the books printed in England were not evenly distributed among the different collections. The catalogue of the Danish statesman Cornelius Pedersen Lerche contained a total of 3,095 publications, of which only twenty-one (0.6%) were produced in England. The collection of Johan Adolph Bornemann, on the other hand, was modest with 986 works, but included 180 books printed in England (18%). (See Table 9.1).[26]

---

23 Van Selm, *"Een menighte treffelijcke Boecken"*, pp. 315–316; Flavia Bruni and Andrew Pettegree (eds.), *Lost books: reconstructing the print world of pre-industrial Europe* (Leiden: Brill, 2016); Andrew Pettegree and Arthur der Weduwen, *The Bookshop of the World. Making and Trading Books in the Dutch Golden Age* (New Haven: Yale University Press, 2019), pp. 13–17 and Robert Ovenden, *Burning the Books. A History of Knowledge Under Attack* (London: John Murray, 2020).

24 Minister Petrus Norman from Denmark and minister Thomas Laurentius from the Dutch Republic respectively.

25 The catalogue of Danish councillor Janus Rosencrantz contained 15,828 books and the catalogue of the late Dutch Grand Pensionary Adriaen Pauw contained 15,646 publications.

26 *Catalogus Selectissimorum Librorum Omnium Facultatum & Linguarum, Nobilißimi & Illustrißimi Dni.b.m. Cornelii Lerke, Quondam Regis Daniæ ad Hispanos Legati nunc demum in Collegio Status Consiliarii & Laalandiæ Præfecti, &c. Quorum Auctio instituenda est Hafniæ in ædibus Nobilißimi Domini Petri Lerke, s.r.m. à Justitiis & Commerciis Consiliarii, &c. bey den Wage. Ad diem [] Septembris Anno 1682. Hafniæ, Literis Conradi H[artwigi Neuhofii]* (Copenhagen, 1682) and *Catalogus Librorum maxime Theologicorum B.M. Mag. Joannis Adolphi Bornemanni, Quondam In Diaecesi Saelandia, & nominatim in Nomarchia Socchelundensi, Præpositi primi, adq; Templum Divae Virginis Hafniense Pastoris Primarii,*

'LIBRI ANGLICI'   221

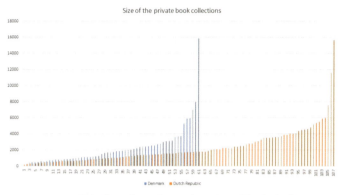

FIGURE 9.3   This chart shows the total number of books in the
            Danish and Dutch catalogues surveyed for this chapter

TABLE 9.1   Percentage of English imprints found in the collections surveyed

	Number of catalogues	Total number of books	English books	Percentage
Denmark	60	137,693	5,816	4.2%
Dutch Republic	107	244,876	9,092	3.7%

Which authors and works did these collectors buy for their libraries? A number of collectors turned to the catalogues of the Bodleian Library in Oxford for inspiration. It was for good reason that Oxford became a Grand Tour destination. The treasures its university library held were famous throughout Europe and catalogues of its holdings were widely disseminated, whether it was the 1620 edition compiled by Thomas James or the 1674 Hyde version. Even though scholars did not yet possess or purchase books from England in large quantities, these *Catalogi Bodleiana* set an example of the works a good library should contain.[27]

An extraordinary work of scholarship and printing was the *Biblia Sacra Polyglotta*, edited by Brian Walton and printed in London. We could, anachronistically, use the term 'collector's item' for this multi-volume work in nine

---

    Quorum auctio habebitur die 12. Septembris in habitatione Pastorali. (Copenhagen: widow
    Joh. Phil. Bockenhoffer, 1698).
27 See for different editions of the *Bibliotheca Bodleiana*, USTC 3002175 (1605), 3009219
    (1620), and 3092045 (1674).

different languages. Numerous ministers and statesmen, professors and doctors from Denmark and the Dutch Republic owned the work. The Bible consisted of six volumes and a separate introduction to the Oriental languages used therein. Customers could subscribe to obtain the entire work, after which they patiently had to wait until all the volumes were published. The project took two years to complete, between 1655 and 1657. The editor, Brian Walton, cooperated with a number of well-known and learned scholars to accomplish this work, which was modelled after the famous Parisian and Plantin polyglot Bibles.[28]

Certain English authors were particularly popular among Dutch and Danish collectors. Their names appear again and again in various catalogues. One of these is Francis Bacon. Some of his works in the catalogues were printed during his life, like the *Instauratio magna* (London, 1620). Others were published posthumously, like his *History of the Reigne of King Henry the Seuenth* (London, 1628).[29] For Scottish history collectors turned to George Buchanan. His name appears less frequently in the catalogues, but when mentioned it is mostly thanks to his *Historia rerum scoticarum*, printed in Edinburgh in the early 1580s.[30] James Ussher's name adorns the catalogues in different spellings. He was called Usser, Usserii, Usher or Ussher, sometimes confusingly several variants would be used in one catalogue. Nearly all his works were published in Latin and some in Dublin instead of in London. Not surprisingly for this Irish Anglican Bishop, his publications revolved around theological subjects and continued to be printed after his death, like the *Chronologia Sacra* (Oxford, 1660).[31] Another author not to be missed was John Selden. His publication about maritime law, *Mare Clausum* (London, 1635), often found its way bound in a volume together with works from other authors on the same subject, resulting in lively debates. In this case supporters and opponents of the closed seas envisaged by Selden and his royal patrons could be found in the same binding.[32] Collectors on the European continent also took an interest in the defence John Milton wrote against accusations made by Claudius Salmasius. Salmasius had claimed that Cromwell's Parliament had unjustly executed

---

28   See Nicolas Barker, 'The Polyglot Bible', in John Barnard and D.F. Mckenzie, *The Cambridge History of the Book in Britain* IV, pp. 648–651. USTC 3071814, 6040442 and 401394.
29   USTC 3009366 and 3013821.
30   USTC 509496.
31   USTC 3074642.
32   USTC 3018258. The Royal Danish Library holds a Sammelband in which works by William Welwood, Theodoor Graswinkel, an anonymous writer and John Selden all engage in a debate about the dominion of the sea. They were all printed in 1653 in The Hague and London respectively. Shelfmark 45.255.00771.

'LIBRI ANGLICI'   223

King Charles I. Milton disputed this in *Pro populo Anglicano defensio* (London [or Utrecht], 1650 [or 1651]). On the European continent this work sold far better than his *Paradise Lost* (London, 1667). Innumerable editions and reprints of Milton's work were published, both in England and abroad. In the book auction catalogues it is not always clear to which edition of *Pro populo* was referred.[33] A last author in this far from extensive list is Robert Boyle. His works could be found in both Latin, *Chymista scepticus* (London, 1662), and English, *The Origine of formes and Qualities* (Oxford, 1667).[34]

To illustrate these findings further, four examples of private book collectors and their book auction catalogues will be analysed in more detail. Two were auctioned in the Dutch Republic and two in Denmark. The auctions took place between 1650 and 1714 in Leiden, Copenhagen and Rotterdam. In many ways these were different: the year of auction, the profession of the owners, the size of the collections and the number of English books they contained. These case studies give us an idea of the various collecting practices and different motives that collectors had for collecting English books. Ministers looked for works by English authors because of their shared Protestant background. Danish collectors in particular had often travelled to or studied in England. Others found English men and women in their (trade) networks. Even those who had never set foot ashore the British Isles were curious about the learned works published there. During the seventeenth century England became a European power to be reckoned with. This, in addition to the growth of London as a centre of the print industry, added to the appeal for collectors on the European mainland.[35]

3   Johannes de Laet

The books of Johannes de Laet (1581–1649) were sold at auction in Leiden in 1650, one year after his death. De Laet was a merchant and one of the founders and directors of the Dutch West India Company, but he was also a renowned geographer, writer and polyglot. His parents had left Antwerp in 1585, when Johannes was four years old, and moved to Leiden. There Johannes studied philosophy and theology, notably under Josephus Scaliger. After his studies, from 1603–1607, De Laet lived in London where he married Jacomijntje van Loor, or Jacquemine Vanlore, as she was called in England, the daughter of

---

33   USTC 3062370 is an example of a false London imprint, whereas the work was actually printed in Utrecht. This edition is just one of many examples of *Paradise Lost*, USTC 3085931.
34   USTC 3081867 and 3081097.
35   Barnard, 'Introduction', in *The Cambridge History of the Book* IV, pp. 1–2.

a merchant from the Dutch Republic. Through this marriage he became relatives with members of the administrative and intellectual elite of London. Upon his return to the Dutch Republic he continued to help select ministers for the Reformed Church in London. In 1619, De Laet was sent to the Synod of Dordrecht, held by the Dutch Reformed Church, as a deputy in his capacity as elder of the church of Leiden. At the Synod of Dort, he must have met the English delegates from the Church of England and of Scotland. Among them were John Davenant, Joseph Hall and George Carleton. Books written by Carleton were in De Laet's book collection: *Jursidiction Regall, Episcopale, Papale* (London, 1610) and *A thankfull remembrance of Gods Mercy* (London, 1624).[36] Besides his English connections, as director of the West India Company, De Laet also travelled to the New World. This may explain the presence of titles such as *The generall Historie of Virginia, New England; A key into the language of America,* or, *A discovery of New-found-land* (London, 1620).[37]

De Laet's library collection contained 1,816 books of which 212 (11.6 per cent) were printed in England. Inevitably, the overwhelming majority of these books had a London imprint. Striking is that of his books printed in England, 127 were written in English, compared to 68 in Latin. Further proof that De Laet had a good command of the English language is reflected in four lot numbers in the catalogue with 'severale English Pamphlets bound together'. It is also noteworthy that De Laet's choice of English books was rather selective. Some 30 per cent of his English books were in folio format, and around half were in quarto. Compared to the rest of his collection, this indicates that, in general, his English books were larger and more expensive.[38]

It was common for seventeenth-century libraries to contain many theological works and Bibles, often constituting up to a third of the collection. This was no different with De Laet's books, but alongside theology his collecting

---

36 *Biografisch lexicon voor de geschiedenis van het Nederlands protestantisme*, part 5, 2001, pp. 324–326, resources.huygens.knaw.nl/retroboeken/blnp/#source=5&page=324. Leneth Witte, *The English Book in the Dutch Golden Age. Three Well-Read Men and their Libraries in the Seventeenth Century'* (MA-Thesis, Leiden University, 2017), pp. 35–37. USTC 3004436 and 3011425.

37 John Smith, *The generall Historie of Virginia, New England* (London, 1632), USTC 3016371; Roger Williams, *A key into the language of America* (London, 1643), USTC 3046162; Richard Whitbourne, *A discourse and discovery of New-found-land* (London, 1620), USTC 3009422.

38 *Catalogvs Bibliothecae Amplissimi & Clarissimi Viri D. Joannis De Laet, Antwerpiani, dum viveret Societas Indiae Occidentalis praefecti, In qua varii ac rarissimi in qualibet scientia ac lingua Libri continentur, Quorum auctio habebitur in aedibus Francisci Hackii, Bibliopolae in de Choorsteech, 27 Aprilis, Anno 1650. Die Mercurii, stylo novo. Lvgdvni Batavorvm. Ex Officina Francisci Hackii. MDCL* (Leiden: Franciscus Hackius, 1650), USTC 1121740. The lot numbers 31, 32, 38 and 45 in quarto format contain various bound English pamphlets.

habits betrayed other interests. Thirty-eight of his English works were historical books. The work of Buchanan on Scotland could also be found in his collection, just like John Selden's *Mare Clausum*. This should not strike us as odd for a man directing one of the largest early modern seafaring companies in the world. The geopolitical ambition of England as an upcoming global power was something to be reckoned with.

De Laet was a well-read man, an author, and an intrepid traveller. His own work featured in his catalogue on several occasions, both in bound and unbound copies. His knowledge of geography in general and of the British Isles in particular must have given the Elzevier publishing firm the notion that he was the best man to write for their *Respublicas* series with descriptions of countries. De Laet contributed to no less than eleven out of forty-one volumes, notably one on Ireland and Scotland (1627).[39] And although this last work does not feature in his book collection, it does reflect his fascinations as a polyglot and geographer.

4 Rasmus Hansen Brochmand

During his lifetime Rasmus Hansen Brochmand (1626–1664) collected nearly 2,000 books. These were auctioned on 17 April 1665 in Copenhagen. Brochmand worked at the University of Copenhagen as a professor in history and theology. Just like the De Witt brothers, Brochmand had travelled through Europe and studied, among other places, in Leiden, and from 1650–1652 in London and Oxford. He was responsible for several works of philosophy, printed in Denmark as well as in Leiden.[40]

The books printed in England in his collection tallied up to a considerable 373 works (18 per cent of the total). The majority of Rasmus Hansen Brochmand's books from England, two-thirds, was comprised of books in quarto format, whereas forty-one books were large folios. He owned the multi-volume polyglot

---

39   Johannes de Laet, *Respublica, sive Status regni Scotiæ et Hiberniæ* (Leiden: ex officina Elzeviriana, 1627), USTC 1514958.

40   *Catalogus Librorum Viri Plur. Reverendi & Excellentissimi b.m. M. Erasmi Joh. Brochmand s.s. Theolog. Professoris Publ. in Regia Hauniensi Academia, Quorum auction in œdibus Viduæ habebitur a.d. 17 April. St.v. 1665* (Copenhagen: Matthiæ Godicchenii, 1665). Note that the date is in 'Stylo veteri', or 'old style', according to the Julian Calendar. Bjørn Kornerup, 'Rasmus Brochmand, f. 1626', in *Dansk biografisk leksikon*, 3rd ed., Gyldendal 1979–84. Retrieved from biografiskleksikon.lex.dk/Rasmus_Brochmand,_f._1626; Erasmi Joh. Brochmand, *Ethices historicæ specimen* (Leiden: Adriani Wyngaerden, 1653), USTC 1808757.

Bible edited by Brain Walton, a Bible in English as well as some Bible parts in English and in Latin. He also possessed two library catalogues of the Bodleian library plus an appendix and the library catalogue of Sion College London. It is not hard to imagine that he purchased these catalogues while he was studying in England, afterwards bringing them back with him to Denmark. Other works that clearly link back to the time Brochmand spent in England are John Taylor's *Catalogue of Tavernes in ten Shires about London* and *Astrologicall predictions for the Year 1652* written by William Lilly.[41]

Brochmand's interest in history manifests itself in the works he owned about the history of theology and the political history of England, Kings, Queens and Parliament. He owned no less than seven works written by John Selden. To name just two of these, alongside *Mare Clausum*, Brochmand owned *Titles of Honor* (London, 1631) and *Uxor Hebraica* (London, 1646).[42] Closely related to his profession, this Copenhagen professor owned many university dissertations, listed in an appendix. As we would assume, most of these theses were published in Copenhagen, but others originated in the Dutch Republic and England. A title that stands out among his works is the curious *Newes from the Dead, or a True and exact narration of the miracolaus deliverance of Anne Greene, who being executed at Oxford afterwards revived* (Oxford: Leonard Lichfield, 1651). This work was, according to the title-page, written by a scholar from Oxford, named Richard Watkins.[43] The story was concerned with the miraculous recovery of Anne Green, falsely accused of infanticide, sentenced to death and hanged. But Anne miraculously survived and her story was captured in a poem; contemporaries judged that God had saved an innocent woman. Considering its dissemination abroad, this was a popular work and Brochmand was not the only collector on the continent who owned a copy. Today we can still find copies in the university libraries of Ghent and Leiden, amongst others. The collection of Brochmand not only reflects his interest in England and the time he spent there, but also the interest in works of history and theology that came with his profession.

---

41 Lot number 312 in the auction catalogue: John Taylor, *A catalogue of tavernes in ten shires about London* (London, 1636). This octavo work was printed twice in 1636 by different London printers: Augustine Matthews and Henry Gosson, see USTC 3018460 and 3018478. But since the printer name is not mentioned in the catalogue it remains unclear to which edition is referred. The Royal Library of Denmark owns a copy of each. Lot number 279, also in 8° is: William Lilly, *Merlini Anglici ephemeris: astrological predictions for the year 1652* (London: printed for the Company of Stationers, and H. Blunden, 1652).

42 USTC 3015374 and 3043528.

43 Anne Green's fate has not ceased to intrigue scholars until today. Be it from a historical or a medical point of view. See: Caoimhghin S. Breathnach and John B. Moynihan, 'Intensive care 1650: the revival of Anne Greene (c. 1628–59)', *Journal of Medical Biography*, 17 (2009), pp. 35–38. USTC 3066816.

5   Petrus Holm

The auction of the library of the Swede Petrus Holm (1634–1688) took place in Copenhagen. This is noteworthy because Holm lived and worked at the Universities of Lund and Uppsala for most of his career. Until 1658, Lund, located in the Skåne region, had been a part of Eastern Denmark. After the Peace of Roskilde, Lund became part of Sweden. It took eleven years after Holm's death before the auction finally took place in Copenhagen on 7 August 1699. Could the political and military struggles between Sweden and Denmark have been the reason his books were not sold sooner? This question lays bare one of the risks of using book auction catalogues as a historical source, because we do not know what happened to the collection in the intervening years. May we assume the collection was still intact after all these years? We cannot rule out the possibility that alterations were made. Therefore, we need to take extra precaution in analysing the collection. What we do know with certainty is that these books came on the Danish market and that the compiler felt the need to put the name of Petrus Holm on the title-page.[44]

The catalogue listed 3,190 books, of which a mere 61 were printed in England. The most recent English book in Holm's collection was a theological work published in 1684. Petrus Holm was a theology professor and orientalist. He studied both in Greifswald and in Uppsala before touring Europe, but there is no evidence that he ever visited England. In Jena he wrote *Theologiae Muhammedanae brevis*, a work on Islam.[45] Next to his academic work he was a vicar of the parishes of Hobys and Håstads, situated north of Lund. Naturally, as a theologian, he owned many Bibles. Again we find the complete run of the *Biblia Sacra Polyglotta*, edited by Walton, in his collection. Information that the catalogue did not reveal was whether Holm purchased the series on subscription, if he had bought these works unbound and brought them to a bookbinder in Lund or if the volumes were bound for him in England before being shipped.[46]

Holm also owned historical chronicles and five volumes of Matthew Poole's *Synopsis Criticorum*, a synopsis of Bible interpretations, printed in London.[47]

---

44   *Catalogus Librorum Variorum B.M. Mag. Petri Holmii Quondam Assessoris in Collegio Consistoriali, & Lectoris Christianiensis Quorum auctio habebitur Hafniae d. 7. Aug: in Platea Snaregeden, in aedibus Dni. Mauritii Mandix* (Copenhagen: Justini Hòg, 1699).
45   Petrus Holm, *Theologiae Muhammedanae brevis Consideratio* (Jena: Joh. Jacobi Bauhofer, 1670), USTC 2594050.
46   See Nicolas Barker, 'The Polyglot Bible', *The Cambridge History of the Book in Britain IV*, pp. 648–651 and USTC 3071813, 3071814 and 3071815.
47   Matthew Poole, *Synopsis Criticorum aliorumque S. Scripturae interpretum* (London: J. Flesher & T. Roycroft, 1669), UST 3087632.

The presence of a Syriac grammar (London, 1658) and an Arab-English dictionary (Oxford, 1661) demonstrated his linguistic interests. *Mare Clausum* by John Selden (London, 1636), in a duodecimo edition, was also present.[48] Maritime laws and the debates about these between seafaring countries like England, Denmark and Sweden must have been a lasting and urgent theme for someone living near the Sound. At the end of the catalogue, in the appendix, various volumes of dissertations from Germany and Denmark were listed.

We could question whether Holm mastered the English language, because he owned just two books printed in that language: one on algebra and the other on 'the art of preaching'.[49] Assessing his career and his interests in the Orient it may not strike us as odd that his library consisted of very few works from England. The majority, forty-seven books were in Latin and two in Arab. This closer look at the catalogue leaves a strong impression that, even after the years that passed before its sale, this was still Holm's collection. The works certainly did not match that of a bookseller's stock. The works listed were the ones desired by a specialist, someone with specific linguistic interests and skills.

6   Benjamin Furly

The auction of the library of Benjamin Furly (1636–1714), a merchant and Quaker leader, was a remarkable event. No less than 4,500 titles were brought under the hammer, along with furniture and objects from Furly's estate. They were listed in the catalogue as 'Curiositates', with items ranging from a magic lantern and a barometer, to a watch and a spinning wheel.[50] To compile the 362-page catalogue itself must have been an immense undertaking, just as its dissemination was. Copies of the catalogue found their way to places far beyond the Dutch Republic. Today, surviving copies can still be found in Budapest, Cambridge, Göttingen, Copenhagen, London, Oxford, Paris and St. Petersburg. This gives us a sense of the scale of the circulation of these catalogues. The auction took place on six consecutive days, from 22–27 October 1714, some

---

48 This work was actually printed in the Dutch Republic. See my chapter about its printing history: Hanna de Lange, 'Print and Piracy: The Publication History of John Selden's *Mare clausum*', in Esther van Raamsdonk, Sjoerd Levelt, Michael D. Rose (eds.), *Anglo-Dutch Connections in the Early Modern World* (London: Routledge, 2023), pp. 159–170.

49 Richard Balam, *Algebra* (London: J.G., 1653), USTC 3068311 and *Ecclesiastes, or, A discourse concerning the gift of preaching* (London: Samuel Gellibrand, 1659), USTC 3074855.

50 See Hanna de Lange, '"Bibliotheca Furliana, 1714". The Public Sale of a Private Book Collection', in Ineke Huysman and Michaël Green (eds.), *Perspectives on privacy in the early modern Netherlands* (Turnhout, BE: Brepols, 2023), pp. 225–246.

six months after Furly died. The place of the auction was Rotterdam, at the house of the deceased. All of this was announced in the *Gazette de Rotterdam* and in the Haarlem newspaper, the *Oprechte Haerlemse Courant*.[51]

We need not search long for the reason Benjamin Furly chose to collect books printed in England, as he was born to and grew up in a Colchester family of linen drapers. He sought refuge in the Dutch Republic after being persecuted for his beliefs in England. He first went to Amsterdam around 1658, but later settled in Rotterdam where he became a leader of the Quaker community. Furly had British friends who visited him on a regular basis and helped him collect books for his collection. Among them were the 3rd Earl of Shaftesbury, Anthony Ashley Cooper, the politician Algernon Sidney and the philosopher John Locke. Benjamin Furly's collection included 1,467 books printed on the British Isles (a third of the total). This number may be even higher, since 234 English-language books are listed in the catalogue without mention of a place of publication.[52]

The size of the catalogue is noteworthy, as is the presence of printer's names for many items. There is one surviving catalogue, now in the possession of the British Library, that reveals even more exciting information. This was the copy owned by Benjamin's son, Benjohan Furly. During the auction, he added the price paid for each lot and the buyer that purchased the book on inserted sheets. Among the buyers were members of the Quaker community that were attracted by the many works on their denomination. Another group of buyers that were present in force were professionals of the book trade. Various booksellers bought works at this auction. Even the printers of the catalogue, Caspar Fritsch and Michel Böhm, were noted by Benjamin's son as buyers. They bought 105 lots for 253 guilders and 17 stuivers, no doubt with the aim of selling them on once again. These second-hand English titles thus found their ways into other private collections.[53]

First and foremost, Furly collected theological works. These books were not just related to the Quaker creed, but also works that Furly contested in his

---

51   *Bibliotheca Furliana, Sive Catalogus Librorum Honoratiss. & Doctiss. Viri Benjamin Furly, Inter quos excellunt Bibliorum Editiones, Mystici, Libri proprii cujuscumque Sectae Christianae, & Manuscripti membranei. Auctio fiet die 22 Octobris 1714. in AEdibus Defuncti in Platea vulgô dicta Haringvliet* (Rotterdam: Fritsch & Böhm, 1714). *Gazette de Rotterdam* (Rotterdam, 8, 11 and 15 October 1714) and *Oprechte Haerlemse Courant* (Haarlem, 20 October 1714).

52   William I. Hull, *Benjamin Furly and Quakerism in Rotterdam* (Swarthmore, PA: Swarthmore College, 1941), pp. 3–11.; Frank van Lamoen, 'Bibliotheca Furliana (1714). Over het innerlijke licht in "De Lantaarn"', *Jaarboek Nederlands Genootschap van Bibliofielen*, (2014), pp. 1–23.

53   The copy of Furly's son was digitised and made available by Brill through BSCO. Some of the surviving catalogues have a different title-page on which 'Nicolaum Bosch' is mentioned as a third printer next to Fritsch & Böhm. And this Nicolaas Bos deserved an extra mention in Benjohan Furly's notes: he bought books up to a total value of 201 guilders and 17 stuivers.

sermons for the Quaker congregation in the Dutch Republic. Bibles, of course, could not be absent. Furly owned eleven Bibles printed in England, of which nine were in the vernacular. Like Brochmand and Holm in Denmark, he possessed Walton's multilingual *Biblia Sacra Polyglotta*. In addition, Furly had also bought the accompanying *Lexicon Heptaglotton*.[54]

Furthermore, he owned thirty-five Old or New Testaments. Twenty-five of these were printed in English. Remarkable are the hundred English titles with 'history' or 'historical' in their title. Again, these works often touched on religion, like the lives of the Apostles or Quaker history. But Furly's interest went beyond religion as well. Some books carried sweeping titles like these: *History of the World* by Walter Raleigh (London, 1617), *Naturall History in ten Centuries* by Francis Bacon (London, 1628), or *Metallographia, or an History of Metals*

FIGURE 9.4   Pages 99 and 98 of *Introductio ad lectionem linguarum orientalium* by Brian Walton (London: Tho. Roycroft, 1655)
COURTESY OF THE UNIVERSITY OF ST ANDREWS LIBRARIES AND MUSEUMS.
SHELFMARK: R17 PJ70.W2

54   Edmund Castell, *Lexicon Heptaglotton* (London, 1669), USTC 3087290.

by John Webster (London, 1681).[55] The sheer number of works about the lives of Kings and Queens of England bear witness to his persistent links to his native country. As in the other collections, John Selden could not be missed. Like Holm, Furly owned several works by this author, including *History of Tithes* (London, 1618) and an English translation of *Mare Clausum*, entitled *Right and Dominion of the Sea* (London, 1663). Last but not least, William Harvey featured twice in this Rotterdam library with his work on embryology. The first was in Latin printed in Amsterdam in 1651 and the other an English translation that was printed in London two years later.[56]

7 Gathering English Books

The four book collectors discussed above all had their own motives to purchase English books. Johannes de Laet had lived in England, married the daughter of a successful immigrant and became acquainted with some famous contemporary Englishmen. He wanted to keep up with devotional developments in England, but also showed a keen interest in the geopolitical ambitions and in the history of the country. Rasmus Hansen Brochmand had similar interests. As a scholar of theology and history he collected many books from all over Europe on these subjects. Some English titles indicate a feeling of nostalgia he may have felt for his former host country. The knowledge gathered in Oxford and Cambridge on Oriental languages appealed strongly to the Swedish philologist Petrus Holm as the Syriac grammar showed. Lastly, Benjamin Furly, as an exile, purchased books in his native tongue from England, the land to which he could not return. Instead, he found a considerable English community in the Dutch Republic, with whom he shared his interest in English culture and the desire for English books.

The question remains how representative these catalogues were for the wider community of collectors in Denmark and the Dutch Republic. The number of books owned by both De Laet and Brochmand fell within the average size of the catalogues studied here. A different picture arises when it came to language. Taking into account that nine of the book collections from Denmark and forty-two from the Dutch Republic did not contain any work in the English language, the collection of Petrus Holm was most representative of the collecting habits found. However, private owners who mastered the English language apparently preferred English to Latin works.

---

55 USTC 3007753, 3013928 and 3089671. This work was printed in 1671 and not in 1681. Could this have been a misinterpretation of the Roman numerals of the year?
56 USTC 3007954 and 3065782.

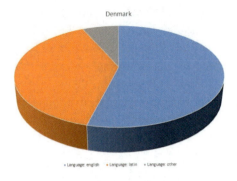

FIGURE 9.5
Subdivision by language. Of the 5,816 books from England in the Danish collections, 3,146 were in English, 2,284 in Latin and 386 in other languages

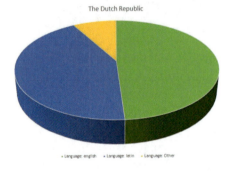

FIGURE 9.6
Subdivision by language. Of the 9,092 books from England in the Dutch collections, 4,445 were in English, 3,906 in Latin and 741 in other languages

Another important aspect concerns the age of the collected books. Sixteenth-century works are underrepresented in the catalogues. Brochmand collected more books from around the time he spent in England, as did De Laet. Furly, with his vast collection, owned books from an entire range starting in the sixteenth century up until the year of his death. With the extraordinary number of English imprints in general and works in English in particular, his collection did not represent a common collecting style. But it did accelerate the spread of English print on the European mainland.

A final question that needs to be addressed is how books from England ended up in the collections of book collectors on the continent. How and where did these people purchase them? Personal connections, networks and friendships were important. Collectors would buy the books themselves while travelling, commission friends living in or travelling to England to buy books for them or they received them as gifts.

Dutch customers could learn about new publications booksellers offered for sale in newspapers. From the 1620s onwards, advertisements started to appear in Dutch newspapers, at the bottom of the back page, right after the news reports, below a horizontal line. In this section of the newspaper Dutch authorities made announcements, relatives looked for missing loved-ones, stolen

TABLE 9.2 This table shows the composition of the four collections. The decades indicate the year of publication of the books in the collections. The year below the owner's name indicates the year in which the auction took place

Year of publication	De Laet (1650)	Brochmand (1665)	Holm (1699)	Furly (1714)
1551–1560	1			2
1561–1570	5	1		3
1571–1580	6	3		4
1581–1590	11	3		6
1591–1600	22	10		12
1601–1610	46	14		26
1611–1620	39	35	2	43
1621–1630	25	31	2	53
1631–1640	36	89	4	83
1641–1650	21	116	8	140
1651–1660		68	34	264
1661–1670		3	8	106
1671–1680			2	162
1681–1690			1	208
1691–1700				106
1701–1710				189
1711–1720				60

goods were reported and booksellers tried to sell their newly published books.[57] Usually they advertised for books they printed and published themselves. But on occasion the advertisements referred to books with a 'Londini impt' they had in stock, such as a Latin title for sale with Joannes Boeckholt in Amsterdam. Or for tracts by William Temple 'int Engels beschreven' ('written in English'), for sale in the shop of Anthony Schouten in Utrecht.[58] In this section of the newspaper, upcoming book auctions, which were another important avenue by which collectors could purchase English books, were also announced. On Monday 17/27 June 1689 several bound books, on various subjects and in

---

57   See: Arthur der Weduwen and Andrew Pettegree, *The Dutch Republic and the Birth of Modern Advertising* (Leiden: Brill, 2020), and Arthur der Weduwen and Andrew Pettegree, *News, Business and Public Information. Advertisements and Announcements in Dutch and Flemish Newspapers, 1620–1675* (Leiden: Brill, 2020).

58   *Oprechte Haerlemse Courant* (Haarlem, 7 March 1684 and 11 October 1692).

different languages, among which were English books, were to be auctioned in the university town of Harderwijk. Even an auction in London could not escape the attention of Dutch newspaper readers. In the *Oprechte Haerlemse Courant* of 22 January 1688 the upcoming sale of the stock of 'Robbert Scott, Konincklijcke Boeckverkoper te London, in Ave-Mary-Lane, by Ludgate-street' (Robert Scott, Royal Bookseller in London), was announced.[59]

In Denmark, as of 1693, it was ordained that all auctions had to be announced via printed or written placards. These were distributed throughout Copenhagen. Still, this did not mean that before then Danish customers received no information about new books. English printers gave notice of forthcoming works in the books they printed. They promoted works by the same author, or they recommended other books they produced. A book that contained such an advertisement was *De ipsa natura* by Robert Boyle (London, 1687).[60] This book was printed in Latin, but the advertisement at the back of the book read in English:

> Advertisement.
>
> The Declamations of *Quintillian*, being an Exercitation of Praxis upon his twelve Books, concerning the Institution of an Orator. Translated (from the *Oxford* Theatre Edition) into *English*, by a Learned and Ingenious hand; with the approbation of several Eminent Schoolmasters of the City of *London*: Very useful for Scholars and Students in the Law.
>
> *Bazilica Chymica, & Praxis Chymiatricæ*, or Royal and Practical Chymistry, in three Treatises; being a Translation of *Oswald Crollius* his Royal Chymistry: Inlarged by *John Hartman*. To be sold by *John Taylor*, at the *Globe* in St. *Paul*'s Chuch-yard.[61]

Advertisements like these were aimed at the domestic market, but they also gave collectors abroad an idea of what was being published in England. To purchase books they relied on bookshops closer to home. Booksellers

---

59 *Amsterdamse Courant* (Amsterdam, 14 June 1689) and *Oprechte Haerlemsche Courant* (Haarlem, 22 January 1688).
60 USTC 3108799.
61 Robert Boyle, *De ipsa natura* (London: H. Clark, 1687), Det Kongelige Bibliotek, shelfmark KB 132, 9.

published trade or stock catalogues regularly, listing the titles they could provide. Judging by these catalogues, books from England were not very high on their list. In 1662 the stock of jurisprudential books of the late bookseller Johannes Verhoeve was auctioned; of 250 listed editions, only two were printed in London. And in the 1690 catalogue of the Danish bookseller Christian Cassube no more than eleven books out of the total 3,340 were from England. Three of these were in English.[62] Could this mean that collectors had little choice in acquiring English imprints? Or was it a matter of simple demand, as the Hamburg bookseller Gottfried Schultze lead us to believe? In his sales catalogue of 1668 he urged his customers to ask for 'foreign language' books. Besides books in Italian, Dutch and Spanish, he could also lay his hands on English ones.[63]

Still, fluency in the English language was not something to be taken for granted and it was not yet fashionable to speak English on the continent. For collectors who were not fluent in English, but still interested in works by British authors, there were several options to choose from. First of all, they could take lessons to learn the language themselves. Considering the number of dictionaries the book auction catalogues contained this was a popular option. There was the plain 'English dictionary', but Latin-English, Dutch-English, French-English, Italian-English and dictionaries featuring more than two languages could be found in many continental libraries. If learning English was too complicated or time-consuming, there were faster solutions. Printers solved the problem by translating works from English into Latin or Dutch. Again, we see this reflected in advertisements in Dutch newspapers, where schoolteachers promoted English lessons and booksellers advertised their

---

62 *Catalogus Librorum, Eller Fortegnelse paa een deel Boger som i Christian Cassubes huus tilfommendis 19. May 1690. ssal Auctioneis. Der ester stal iligemaade hans Mobilier og huus, ved G. Nicolai Kircke-Taarn paa Hjornet af lille Kircke-Stroede, til den Meest-bijdende selgis. Kiøbenhafn, Prentet af Christian Wering Universit. Bogt* (Copenhagen, 1690) and *Catalogus Variorum Insignium ac rarissimorum in omni Facultate ac Lingua Librorum, praecipe Iuridicorum, Quorum Auctio habebitur Hagae-Comitis in officina Johannis Verhoeve, Bibliopolae Op de groote Zael van 't Hof. Die Lunae 13 Martii 1662.& sequent. Hora nona matutina* (Den Haag: Johannis Verhoeve, 1662), USTC 1846380.

63 *Catalogus Variorum & insignium undiq, compactorum Librorum. Qui nunc temporis honesto ac civili pretio venales reperiuntur. Hamburgi. In platea vulgo dicta Die Bohnenstrasse. In Bibliopolio noviter instructo. à Godofredo Schultzen. Bibliopola. Impressus. 1668* (Hamburg: Godfried Schultzen, 1668), USTC 2674295.

translated books.[64] Danish newspapers, however, did not contain any advertisements, and in Denmark there were fewer efforts to translate English works into Danish.[65] This may also explain why, on average, more English-language books could be found in Danish collections than in Dutch libraries of the seventeenth century.

Books printed on the British Isles found their way to the continent thanks to Dutch intermediaries and booksellers, or via Hamburg. Dutch publishers and booksellers saw opportunities in the Baltic as well as in their local market. One of the strategies they used was producing reprints of popular works by English authors. This could be very profitable, since the books printed in England were of lesser quality and more expensive than the Dutch ones. One example of a work in the auction catalogues that was printed both in England and abroad is *Mare Clausum* by John Selden that we have already encountered. It was first printed in London in 1635, but quickly followed by three editions printed in the Dutch Republic in 1636.[66] If English authorities or printers complained about this pirating, printers could go underground and produce the book under a misleading or even a false imprint.[67]

For contemporary readers it must not always have been obvious where a book was produced. The Dutch printer Elzevier reprinted an edition of Buchanan's *Rerum Scoticarum Historia*. Back in 1582 this work was first published by the Edinburgh printer Alexander Arbuthnot. In 1643, Elzevier republished it twice, the first time bearing Edinburgh in the imprint and the second time with Amsterdam as place of publication. Looking at the 'Edinburgh' edition more closely, the imprint states 'ad Exemplar Alexandri Arbuthneti editum' printed in black ink, right above 'Edimburgi', printed in red ink.[68] The printer's device left no question: this was an Elzevier production. Moreover, the year was noted in Roman numerals with reversed c's, another characteristic mark of this

---

64 *Amsterdamse Courant* (Amsterdam, 11 December 1687); *Oprechte Haerlemsche Courant* (Haarlem, 28 December 1669).

65 *Den Danske Mercurius* (1666–1683) and *Mercurius* (1683–1691), two seventeenth-century newspapers in which the news reports were written in rhyme. They did not contain any advertisements. See: www2.statsbiblioteket.dk/mediestream/avis.

66 Pettegree and Der Weduwen, *The Bookshop of the World*, pp. 281–284. John Selden, *Mare Clausum* (London 1635 and Leiden/Amsterdam[?], 1636). USTC 3018258, 3018464 and 3018465.

67 George Buchanan, *Rerum Scoticarum Historia* (Edinburgh, 1582; 'Edinburgh', 1642 and Amsterdam, 1643). USTC 509496, 3042160 and 1013723.

68 On this practice more broadly, see chapter 7 in this volume.

publishing company. For some buyers it may have been crystal clear that this book was produced in Amsterdam 'after an example of Arbuthnot', and not in Edinburgh. It could have fooled others, though.

Book auction catalogues of private library owners are a valuable source of information for the presence of English books in European continental collections. This article has shown that the number of books printed in England circulating on the European book market in the seventeenth century was clearly on the rise. This development kept pace with the emergence of England as a global power. People on the continent were increasingly interested in English books, the English language, English authors and their ideas. After Paris and Rome, destinations like London and Oxford gained a permanent place in the traditional itinerary of educational trips. Moreover, study trips brought young scholars to the British Isles for longer periods of time, which further encouraged scholarly exchange. These developments explain a growing curiosity about and knowledge of the English language. Danish collectors showed a preference for English imprints in English rather than in Latin, demonstrating a growing acceptance of the language on the continent. Even though many books by English authors were in fact not printed in England at all, but on the continent, that did not reduce their impact. On the contrary, these reprints only added to the growing presence of English works and their international influence. It was the start of a shift in favour of English book production.

CHAPTER 10

The Government at Auction: Urban Policy and the Market for Books in Eighteenth-Century Lübeck

Philippe Bernhard Schmid

On his visit to Lübeck in February 1710, Zacharias Conrad von Uffenbach (1683–1734) went to see Georg Heinrich Götze (1667–1728), the orthodox superintendent of the Lutheran Church. He was dissatisfied that Götze could not be won for a learned discourse. Even though he was supposed to have a prodigious memory, Götze was confused, preferring to gossip about ministers of the town. August Hermann Francke (1663–1727) and Johann Wilhelm Petersen (1649–1727) were particularly preoccupying his imagination. Francke was born and raised in Lübeck, until his family moved to Gotha. Later, he went on to become a Pietist leader, the religious movement so much despised by Götze. Petersen, another child of Lübeck, had received a stipend from the church to study theology, but Götze thought that he had misused it, not strengthening the Lutheran community in Lübeck but, as an ally of Francke, damaging it, and eventually leaving the town. To Uffenbach's further dismay, Götze seemed unwilling to show him his private library, which he thought not worth the effort. Instead, he recommended visiting the larger collection of books owned by Christoph Gensch von Breitenau (1638–1732), whose brother was a bookseller in Halberstadt, and who would understand the book trade well.[1]

Uffenbach's visit to Götze reveals the small world to which the book trade of Lübeck was confined at the outset of the eighteenth century. What Wolf-Dieter Hauschild called the 'confessional absolutism' of the Lutheran orthodox elite forced bright young people to leave the town, like Francke and Petersen, and led to difficulties in attracting new intellectual talent.[2] Yet the account also hints at the presence of a small community of learned people interested in buying, collecting and exchanging books, embodied by Christoph Gensch von Breitenau, who possessed one of the most substantial private libraries in

---

1 Zacharias Conrad von Uffenbach, *Herrn Zacharias Conrad von Uffenbach Merkwürdige Reisen durch Niedersachsen Holland und Engelland* (Ulm: Johann Friedrich Gaum, 1753), vol. 2, pp. 31–32.
2 Wolf-Dieter Hauschild, *Kirchengeschichte Lübecks. Christentum und Bürgertum in neun Jahrhunderten* (Lübeck: Schmidt-Römhild, 1981), pp. 311–342. See also Wolf-Dieter Hauschild, *"Suchet der Stadt Bestes": Neun Jahrhunderte Staat und Kirche in der Hansestadt Lübeck*, ed. Antjekathrin Graßmann and Andreas Kurschat (Lübeck: Schmidt-Römhild, 2011).

eighteenth-century Lübeck. With the introduction of book auctions in the last decades of the seventeenth century, new opportunities arose for collectors, with printed catalogues announcing what would be sold publicly. However, this foreign form of selling books meant that the city elite had to find new ways of controlling the circulation of texts. What role did the learned community, hinted at in Uffenbach's account, play in the regulation of the market for books? And how did it interact with the city officials and the Lutheran Church? This article studies the regulation of the auction trade in Lübeck from the late seventeenth to the middle of the eighteenth century. It focuses on urban policy and its enforcement, following the groups and institutions that the city council was dependent on for an effective governance.

Recovering from the Thirty Years' War, the decades after 1680 saw an increase in legislative output in the German territories. General ordinances, which sought to impose social discipline on the private life of their subjects, were often replaced by more specific mandates.[3] However, a higher rate of legislation does not imply more effective governance. Enforcement of law was selective, and norms were often developed in response to local demand. Corporative states such as guilds and the nobility retained an important position in local communes, and governments were dependent on their cooperation in order to enforce new legislation.[4] The effectiveness of governance is based on the support of local communities and corporate bodies, and it seems doubtful whether social disciplining can be seen as 'an expression of the modernizing forces of the state and the market'.[5]

Book auctions were introduced to the Holy Roman Empire during the late 1650s, with the first event supposedly taking place at the University of Helmstedt in 1657.[6] From the 1680s on, the first official ordinances on book auctioning were printed in Leipzig, Jena, Dresden, Wittenberg and Halle, bringing to an end the first phase of auctioning in the German territories.[7] The regulation of these auctions should be seen as a part of the wider trend of increased legislative action. Ordinances were often developed as a response to local complaints against abuses ('Mißbräuche') and disarray ('Unordnungen')

---

3 Joachim Whaley, *Germany and the Holy Roman Empire, Volume 2: The Peace of Westphalia to the Dissolution of the Reich, 1648–1806* (Oxford: Oxford University Press, 2012), pp. 257–259.
4 See Sheilagh Ogilvie, "'So that Every Subject Knows How to Behave": Social Disciplining in Early Modern Bohemia', *Comparative Studies in Society and History*, 48/1 (2006), pp. 38–78.
5 Ibid., p. 74.
6 Hans Dieter Gebauer, *Bücherauktionen in Deutschland im 17. Jahrhundert* (Bonn: Bouvier, 1981), pp. 20–34. For a more detailed account of book auctioning in Lübeck, see Philippe Bernhard Schmid, *A Culture of Reuse: Libraries, Learning and Memory in Early Modern Germany* (Dissertation: University of St Andrews, 2022), pp. 114–142.
7 Ibid., pp. 34–39. In contrast, Denmark had already issued an official ordinance on book auctioning in 1661.

at the public sales.[8] Nonetheless, the book trade is something of a special case. Regulations of the market for books can be studied as economic policy. But since they entail a programme of public censorship by enforcing the publication and posting of official catalogues, they can be analysed as forms of social discipline as well. Political, religious and economic considerations in effect all played their role for policy makers and the groups that supported new legislation.

Since Lübeck never issued a printed ordinance on book auctioning, it was passed over by Hans Dieter Gebauer in the only comprehensive account of German book auctions to date.[9] A focus on printed sources, such as ordinances or book catalogues, can also exclude certain institutions of importance to the history of book auctioning, since their activities are not directly reflected in legislation. The defensive character of Lutheran orthodoxy, with its theological emphasis on the verbal inspiration of the Bible, added to a negative image as well as a neglect of the eighteenth century in the historiography of Lübeck.[10] But the guilds, the Lutheran Church and the learned community played an important role in the book trade. This study will address these groups, using the council minutes of the city council of the Hanseatic City of Lübeck.[11] It finds that besides the traditional corporative states of the guild and the church, the scholarly community had a decisive influence on the regulation of the market for books.

Both as buyers of books and as the community of learned families interested in selling the libraries of their deceased, this group of citizens shared a common interest. It clearly matches the definition of what Laurence Brockliss called a mini-Republic of Letters, which is a local community of scholars.[12] Yet this group is more than a web of intellectuals belonging to the universal Republic of Letters, since it has political influence and can play a specific role

---

[8] See the printed ordinance for Leipzig, 'Des Raths zu Leipzig Verordnung/wie es mit Ver=auctionirung derer Bücher oder Bibliotheken zu halten. Leipzig/den 13. Junii/Anno 1680', reprinted in *Der Stadt Leipzig Ordnungen wie auch Privilegia und Statuta* (Leipzig: Fritsch, 1701), pp. 237–241.

[9] See Gebauer, *Bücherauktionen*, p. 35, where he briefly mentions the case of Lübeck, but without discussing its history.

[10] In addition to Hauschild's important monograph, see especially Antjekathrin Graßmann (ed.), *Lübeckische Geschichte* (Lübeck: Schmidt-Römhild, 2008); with an essay on eighteenth-century Lübeck by Franklin Kopitzsch, 'Das 18. Jahrhundert. Vielseitigkeit und Leben', in Graßmann (ed.), *Lübeckische Geschichte*, pp. 501–538; for the seventeenth century, see Antjekathrin Graßmann, 'Lübeck im 17. Jahrhundert: Wahrung des Erreichten', in Graßmann (ed.), *Lübeckische Geschichte*, pp. 445–500.

[11] For a comparable study on auctioning in the city of Mechelen, see Stefanie Beghein and Goran Proot, 'Book auctions in Mechelen, 1773–1800', *De Gulden Passer*, 89/2 (2011), pp. 97–183. I am grateful to Ian Maclean for pointing out this article to me.

[12] Laurence Brockliss, *Calvet's Web: Enlightenment and the Republic of Letters in Eighteenth-Century France* (Oxford: Oxford University Press, 2002), pp. 79–96.

in urban history, even when not connected to a corporate group, such as a university. As a micro-study of the auction trade in the Hanseatic City of Lübeck, this essay then presents a study of the role that the Republic of Letters could play in the enforcement of legislation. It argues that the small world which the community of the learned made up in Lübeck represents the main financial interest behind the auction trade, and that the official regulation of the market was less pervasive and 'absolutist' than the general picture painted by older scholarship of the Lutheran town of eighteenth-century Lübeck. Furthermore, it reveals that the community supporting auctions was part of a learned memory culture, and that the auction culture of early modern Germany was essentially a culture of commemoration.

1   A Fanatical Auctioneer

Compared to the early printing history of Lübeck, with its production of incunabula for the foreign markets of Scandinavia, the eighteenth-century book trade was focused on domestic demand.[13] The guilds were in general a protectionist influence on the local economy, with the guilds of the printers and the booksellers and bookbinders defending privileges and limiting foreign competition. On his visit to Lübeck, Uffenbach mentions the shops of booksellers outside St Mary's Church, the stalls of booksellers inside the church and the bookbinders selling their calendars in a large chapel known as the 'Briefkapelle' or Chapel of Indulgences.[14]

The 'confessional absolutism' of the Lutheran Church did not go unchallenged, however. The 1660s saw some spiritualist groups appear in Lübeck, many of whose leaders were expelled, such as Thomas Tanto and Jakob Taube.[15] Petersen visited Lübeck from 1675 to 1676, introducing news of the newly published book *Pia desideria*, and its Pietist ideals, by Philipp Jakob Spener (1635–1705). Forced to leave in 1676, Petersen and his wife Johanna Eleonora maintained close contact with the Pietist circles in Lübeck from their home

---

13   See Manfred Eickhölter, 'Lübeck', in W. Adam and S. Westphal (eds.), *Handbuch kultureller Zentren der Frühen Neuzeit. Städte und Residenzen im alten deutschen Sprachraum* (Berlin and Boston: De Gruyter, 2012), pp. 1299–1348, here p. 1337; Graßmann, 'Lübeck im 17. Jahrhundert', pp. 482–483. On the history of printing in Lübeck, see A. Bruns and D. Lohmeier (eds.): *Die Lübecker Buchdrucker im 15. und 16. Jahrhundert* (Heide, Holstein: Boyens, 1994); and Wolfgang Undorf, *From Gutenberg to Luther: Transnational Print Cultures in Scandinavia, 1450–1525* (Leiden: Brill, 2014).

14   Uffenbach, *Merkwürdige Reisen*, pp. 19–23.

15   See Markus Matthias, *Johann Wilhelm und Johanna Eleonora Petersen: Eine Biographie bis zur Amtsenthebung Petersens im Jahre 1692* (Göttingen: Vandenhoeck, 1993), pp. 272–278.

in Eutin, which was some 35 kilometres from Lübeck.[16] During the 1680s, official action against these groups began to increase. In 1687, Peter Günther was killed by the sword for blasphemy, and Adelheid Sibylla Schwartz (1656–1703) was expelled as a would-be prophetess. The city council issued a mandate in 1692 *Wider die Schwermer und Neuen Propheten* (*Against Enthusiasts and New Prophets*) and superintendent August Pfeiffer (1640–1698) wrote a theological response to spiritualism and Pietism in 1691, aptly titled *Anti-Chiliamus*.[17] After a few decades of peace, under the more moderate leadership of superintendent Götze, who was host to Uffenbach in 1710, the late 1730s witnessed the new direction of Johann Gottlob Carpzov (1679–1767), who showed an incomparable zeal for fighting the Moravian Church.

The introduction of book auctions to Lübeck was perceived both as a part of the heterodox challenge to Lutheran orthodoxy and as a threat to guild authority. Furthermore, the 'Bürgerrezeß' of 1669, a legislative record induced by the citizens, brought a new distribution of power between the council and the citizenry, with a loss of influence of the 'Zirkelgesellschaft', the society of patricians. The patricians were known for their display of wealth, especially leading up to the events of 1669.[18] Lübeck was facing a crisis between 1665 and 1669, comparable to what John Pocock famously called a 'Machiavellian Moment', with a defensive reaction by the citizenry.[19] The general fear of luxury, dissent and heterodoxy can to some extent explain the negative reception of auctioning in Lübeck.

The first auctions were held by Jasper Köneken (1629–1715), who had studied theology in Copenhagen. He would be banned from the Danish capital for his heterodox views, which were inspired by the radical mysticism and theosophy of Valentin Weigel (1533–1588).[20] After longer visits to Schonen and Amsterdam, he tried to return to Copenhagen, but had to leave again because of

---

16 Hauschild, *Kirchengeschichte Lübecks*, pp. 318–320.
17 Ibid., pp. 320–324.
18 On the 'Bürgerrezeß', see Graßmann, 'Lübeck im 17. Jahrhundert', pp. 468–471; Eickhölter, 'Lübeck', pp. 1308–1309.
19 J.G.A. Pocock, *The Machiavellian Moment: Florentine Political Thought and the Atlantic Republican Tradition* (Princeton, NJ: Princeton University Press, 1975), p. viii, defines the 'Machiavellian Moment', beyond its concrete Florentine context: 'It is a name for the moment in conceptualized time in which the republic was seen as confronting its own temporal finitude, as attempting to remain morally and politically stable in a stream of irrational events conceived as essentially destructive of all systems of secular stability.' For a critical discussion of the term, see Mary Lindemann, *The Merchant Republics: Amsterdam, Antwerp, and Hamburg, 1648–1790* (Cambridge: Cambridge University Press, 2015), pp. 9–11.
20 See Alken Bruns, 'Köneken, Jasper', in *Biographisches Lexikon für Schleswig-Holstein und Lübeck: Band 13* (Neumünster: Wachholtz, 2011), pp. 270–272.

THE GOVERNMENT AT AUCTION 243

his arguments with orthodox Lutheran ministers. Finally, he arrived in Lübeck in late 1677 or early 1678, and began to make a living by auctioning books. He also became a part of the Pietist circle at the *Hundestraße*, which gathered around Adelheid Sibylla Schwartz.[21] Book auctioning was still unknown in Lübeck, but Köneken would have witnessed book auctions in Copenhagen or Amsterdam.

After approximately one and a half years of pursuing his new profession, Köneken was found out by the guild of booksellers and bookbinders, which must have seen his enterprise as a threat to their own business. The guild was strongly opposed to these auctions, banned Köneken's sales and issued a fine. Köneken recalled the incident in a petition to the city council in 1679 (see Figure 10.1):

> No citizen or inhabitant of this city who is not a bookseller or bookbinder or has a special permit or privilege from the council or the police shall sell books or calendars, or else the books will be confiscated. And so the senior of the police issued a fine of 10 *Reichsthaler* and banned me from selling books in the future.[22]

Köneken appealed to the city council to allow him to continue auctioning books by issuing an official decree. It is significant that the council only debated the case, without – in contrast to other cities – ever issuing a printed ordinance. The protocol of the council's session on 5 April 1679 shows that Köneken was allowed to auction books, with some restrictions. He had also asked for the right to sell some of his own stock at auction, which was denied.[23]

Both the guild and the council believed that Köneken had, in addition to his auctions, sold new titles, infringing the rights of the guild.[24] This is the reason why the council decided that he 'has to stop the selling [of books], but he may auction books'.[25] In the petition, Köneken gives an accurate description of what the guild might have found problematic about his sales: he produced a printed catalogue for each auction, which included some of his own stock;

---

21 Matthias, *Johann Wilhelm und Johanna Eleonora Petersen*, pp. 273–274. On conventicles in Radical Pietism, see Douglas H. Shantz, *An Introduction to German Pietism: Protestant Renewal at the Dawn of Modern Europe* (Baltimore: Johns Hopkins University Press, 2013), pp. 147–178; and Hans Schneider, 'Der radikale Pietismus im 17. Jahrhundert', in Martin Brecht (ed.), *Geschichte des Pietismus. Band 1: Der Pietismus vom siebzehnten bis zum frühen achtzehnten Jahrhundert* (Göttingen: Vandenhoeck, 1993), pp. 391–437.
22 Lübeck, AHL: ASA Interna, Nr. 02263, petition of Jasper Köneken, 1679, fol. 1r–fol. 1v, here fol. 1r.
23 See ibid., fol. 1v: 'daß in denen auctionen, wie vorhin, einige alte Bücher selbst mit Verkauffen möge'.
24 See ibid., fol. 1r: 'haben so fort der hiesigen Buchbinder etzliche solches vor einen Eingriff ihrer rolle achten'.
25 Lübeck, AHL: ASA Interna, Nr. 02263, 'Extractus Protocolli', 1679, fol. 1r: 'Er muß das Verkauffen bleiben laßen, sonst mag er, die auctiones der Bücher treiben und verrichten …'

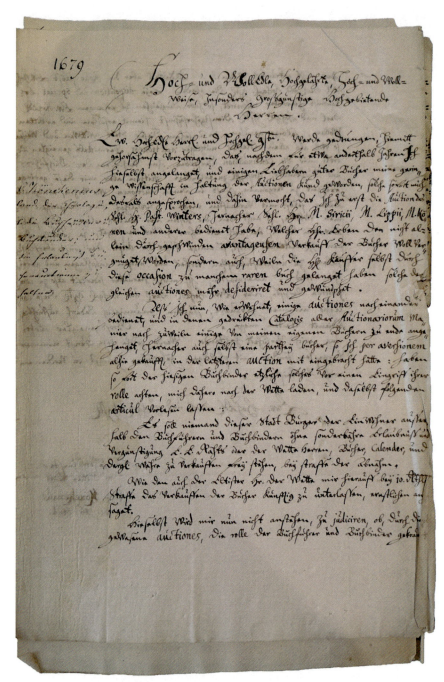

FIGURE 10.1   Petition of Jasper Köneken (1629–1715) to the city council in 1679; Lübeck, AHL: ASA Interna, Nr. 02263, fol. 1r
WITH KIND PERMISSION, ARCHIV DER HANSESTADT LÜBECK

and he resold books at his own auctions which he acquired himself at earlier sales.[26] However, these would be common practices for auctioneers at the time, Köneken stated. So what was the issue? And why did the guild wait for almost two years before taking action against him?

What the guild and the council were implying was that Köneken used his auctions as a front to spread dissent. The ecclesiastical historian Carpar Heinrich Starck (1681–1750) wrote a polemical article against Köneken in 1746, titled *Kurtze Nachricht von dem fanatischen Auctionario zu Lübeck Iaspar Könekenio*.[27] According to Starck's account, during his first two years in Lübeck from 1677 to 1679, Köneken chose to receive the communion with the archdeacon Thomas Carstens (1631–1679) at St Gile's Church, not being allowed to do so by Thomas Honsted (1642–1704) at the Maria-Magdalenen-Kirche, who was his assigned confessor. However, after Carstens passed away in 1679, Köneken refused to accept the communion. This might then have alarmed the Lutheran ministry, the representative body of all ministers, urging the guild of booksellers and bookbinders to denounce Köneken to the city council to ban his book auctions in 1679.

Starck also claimed that Köneken spread spiritualist propaganda at his auctions, decorating the walls with quotations from the Bible, and sneaking heterodox pamphlets into the catalogue past official censorship. A rare extant copy of a catalogue which was arranged by Köneken indeed shows how he auctioned off unbound pamphlets. One lot comprises different treatises that concerned the dispute between Abraham Hinckelmann (1652–1695), a Pietist who lived in Lübeck from 1675 to 1685, and the orthodox theologians Johann Winckler (1642–1705) and Johann Friedrich Mayer (1650–1712) in Hamburg.[28] The pamphlets are advertised without mention of any bibliographical details. Only two auction catalogues by Köneken survive, limiting the available evidence.[29] However, it seems as if Köneken tried to hide his clandestine titles

---

26   See ibid., fol. 1r: 'aller Auctionariorum Manier nach zuweiln einige von meinen eigenen Büchern zu andr angehanget'; and ibid., fol. 1r: 'so ich per aversionem alhir gekaufft'.

27   Carpar Heinrich Starck, 'Kurtze Nachricht von dem fanatischen Auctionario zu Lübeck Iaspar Könekenio', *Dänische Bibliothec: oder Sammlung von alten und neuen Gelehrten Sachen aus Dännemark*, 8 (1746), pp. 663–674.

28   Jasper Köneken, *Catalogus Librorum paucor. quidem iterum & Miscellaneorum; Sed tamen & non minimam partem non contemnendorum: una cum Append. nonn. Auctionando vendendorum; Benedicente Dei Gratia Lubecae, d. 31. Octobr. & sq. Anno 1698 In Auditorio Cathariniano per J. Könekenium* (Lübeck: Schmalhertz, 1698), Erlangen-Nürnberg, UB: H61/TREW.Nx 49/55, pp. 28–29.

29   Stephen Rose, 'A Lübeck music auction, 1695', *Schütz-Jahrbuch*, 30 (2008), pp. 171–190, discusses a catalogue issued by Köneken in 1695: Jasper Köneken, *Catalogus Librorum egregiae cujusdam Bibliothecae, Medicorum Imprimis, & Philologis Naturae Curiosis*

at the very end of his catalogues. This had the obvious benefit of postponing their sale to the last day of the auction, when public interest was minimal. It also meant that they were harder to spot by censors, since they were conglomerated in one large lot without any typographical distinction, such as line breaks or indentations. And finally, catalogues were required to be posted publicly as official announcements for the sales, and the typographical camouflaging would again draw limited public attention from the uninitiated.

However, Starck's polemical perspective should not dictate the narrative of events. The most pressing question is not why Köneken was denounced by the guild, but why he was allowed to continue auctioning books by the city council. It must be stressed that the catalogue containing heterodox literature was issued in 1698, some ten years after the decision of the council. Obviously, Köneken did not comply with the restrictions of the council, and continued to sell his own books at auction. The campaign against Köneken by the combined efforts of the guild and the ministry was unsuccessful, and the order of the council relatively ineffective. Since Köneken retained his position as auctioneer until his death in 1715, the council showed a remarkable tolerance, even though he repeatedly got into quarrels with the ministry between 1679 and 1691.[30] With Köneken introducing his heterodox titles into the auction catalogues, official censorship by Lutheran authorities was hardly as absolute as older histories of Lübeck in the eighteenth century indicate.[31]

2 The Widows and Orphans of This City

Who then had supported the book auctions of Jasper Köneken? Manfred Eickhölter has shown that there was a considerable group of citizens who owned books in seventeenth-century Lübeck.[32] Books were listed in almost

---

miscellaneorum, Ex recentiorib. sui ante bien. temporis aeque ac veterib. exquisitissime selectorum; Una cum rarioribus quibusdam Manuscr. & lib. Musicis: Quorum Auctio Benedicente Dei Gratia Lubecae habenda d. 26. Aug & sq. 1695. In Auditorio Cathariniano per J. Könekenium Lubecae Typis Mauritii Schmalhertzii (Lübeck: Schmalhertz, 1695), London, BL: s.c.65. Gebauer, *Bücherauktionen*, pp. 139–169, lists two surviving auction catalogues by Köneken in A 71 and A 75.

30 Bruns, 'Köneken, Jasper', pp. 270–272.

31 See Alken Bruns, quoted in Kopitzsch, 'Das 18. Jahrhundert. Vielseitigkeit und Leben', p. 520: 'Nie hat Lübeck in seiner geistigen und literarischen Geschichte auf einem tieferen Punkt gestanden als zu Beginn des 18. Jahrhunderts. Das gesamte wissenschaftliche und literarische Leben wurde von einer verknöcherten lutherischen Orthodoxie beherrscht, jede freiere Regung schon im Keim erstickt.'

32 Manfred Eickhölter, 'Buchpreise und Bücherwert in Lübeck im 17. Jahrhundert', *Zeitschrift für Lübeckische Geschichte und Altertumskunde*, 76 (1996), pp. 131–155.

every second inventory drawn up after a death. Religious works were most commonly found among the books which were inventoried.[33] The petition of Köneken gives further evidence of this group of book owners. He mentioned a few citizens whom he could serve by selling their libraries at auction: the minister Gerhard Winter (1589–1661), the minister Gerhard Siricius (–1677), a member of the Lippius family, possibly the minister Jacob Lippius (1638–1674), and a magistrate by the name Könen.[34] Apparently, the sales went well, since he later recalled that his customers demanded that more auctions be held in the future. The reason for this is not only that these bibliophiles or 'Liebhaber' would be able to find some rare books otherwise not available with booksellers in Lübeck; his customers were also interested in selling their own books at auction quickly and profitably.[35]

33 Eickhölter, 'Lübeck', p. 1321: 'Im Bestand zeigen sich klare Befunde. In vielen, wenn nicht sogar in jedem zweiten Verzeichnis finden sich Bücher. Es liegen Verzeichnisse vor aus den Haushalten von Mitgliedern der Zirkelkompanie, von Kaufleuten, Juristen, Krämern, Brauern, Handwerkern, aber auch Ausrufverzeichnisse von Bewohnern in Wohnstiften und Armengängen. In jedem Buchbestand gibt es einen „harten Kern" von religiösen Titeln (Bibel, Gesangbuch, Erbauungsschrift). Daran änderte sich bis in die Zeit um 1800 nichts, dann löste das Konversationslexikon die Hausväterliteratur allmählich ab. Der Umfang der verzeichneten Sammlungen reicht von summarisch erwähnten „etlichen Bücheren", einigen wenigen namhaft genannten Titeln bis hin zu einer Bibliothek von mehr als 1.000 Bänden.'

34 Lübeck, AHL: ASA Interna, Nr. 02263, petition of Jasper Köneken, 1679, fol. 1r. The identification of these names is somewhat tentative. The auction of Siricius is confirmed by the last will of Joachim Wulff; see Eduard Hach, 'Joachim Wulffs Testament und Nachlaß', *Mittheilungen des Vereins für Lübeckische Geschichte und Altertumskunde*, 9 (1900), pp. 145–197, here pp. 153–154. Jacob Lippius (1638–1674) was the son of Daniel Lippius (1635–1690), who taught at the Katharineum until 1682, and the brother of Daniel Lippius (1640–), who was deputy head at the gymnasium in Wismar until *c.* 1677. Jacob was educated at Jena and Rostock and became a minister in Lübeck in 1667. See the articles on Daniel and Jacob Lippius in Johann Heinrich Zedler's *Grosses vollständiges Universal-Lexicon aller Wissenschafften und Künste* (Halle and Leipzig: Zedler, 1731–1754), vol. 17, p. 800, cols. 1561–1562; and the entry for Daniel Lippius in Ernst Deecke, *Das Catharineum zu Lübeck vor 1800. Eine Jubelschrift im Namen jener Anstalt verfasst* (Lübeck: Rohden, 1843), p. 55. The passage is worth quoting in full: '... nachdem für etwa anderthalb Jahren Jch hinselbst angelanget, und einigen Liebhabern guter Bücher meine geringe Wissenschaft in Haltung der Auctionen kund geworden, solche sofort mich deshalb angesprochen, und dahin vermocht, das Jch zu erst die Auction des Sehl. Herrn Past. Winters, Jernacher Sehl. Hrn. M. Siricii, M. Lippii, M. Könen und anderen bedienet habe, welcher Hrn. Leben den nicht allein durch geschwinden avantageusen Verkauff der Bücher woll vergnüget worden, sondern auch, weiln die Hrn. Käuffer selbst durch diese occasion zu manchem raren Buch gelangt, haben solche dergleichen auctiones mehr desideriret und gewünschet.'

35 Uffenbach, *Merkwürdige Reisen*, p. 24, complained about the high prices of books in the bookshop of Wiedemeyer: '... als wir aber lange vergebens gewartet, giengen wir in den Wiedemeyrischen Buchladen, allein dieser Mann war so theuer, daß wir nichts kaufen konnten. Es scheinet, daß Herr Wiedemeyer zu seiner grossen Aufführung viel verdienen

The widows of learned men, for example, sometimes had an urgent need to sell the libraries of their deceased husbands in order to pay debts or raise cash.[36] Köneken states in his petition, that his auctions would be 'beneficial to the widows and orphans of this city as well as to all the literati'.[37] Scholars might also wish to auction off their duplicates, or dispose of their library, if they had financial troubles. What becomes clear is that the local scholarly community did not have an abstract intellectual interest in the book market. Their support for the auction trade, which is implied by the petition, was motivated by financial incentives. The social discipline attempted by the Lutheran ministry, partly successful by prohibiting the sale of new books and the censorship of printed catalogues, was set against the monetary interests of bibliophiles and learned families to sell or buy books.

The competition between the guild, the church, the council and the learned community was not restricted to the case of the 'fanatical auctioneer' Jasper Köneken.[38] The same issues arose around the activity of Johann Wessel between 1709 and 1715. Wessel was active as an auctioneer from the 1690s until the 1750s, the first extant catalogue being dated to 1698.[39] He was a bookbinder by trade,

---

muß, wie er uns dann auf ein Glas Rheinischen Wein, so gut wir ihn in unserm Lande tränken, sogleich zu sich bate; allein ich mochte es ihm vorher an den Büchern nicht erst bezahlen; wir giengen also auch nicht zu ihm.'

36 See Lübeck, AHL: ASA Interna, Nr. 02263, petition of Jasper Köneken, 1679, fol. 1v: 'Welches den denjenigen armen Witwen, so nicht eben die Kosten der auction erlegen, solche selbst abwarten laßen, oder auch fort bahres geldes benötiget, ja zuweilen denen H. Literatis selbst, so einige Bücher in duplo oder sonst überflüssig haben, zu unzweiffelhafften Vortheil und nutzen auspflagen und gereichen wird ...'

37 See ibid., fol. 1v: 'in Ansehen dieser Stadt Wittwen und Waisen so woll als allen Literatis nützlicher auctionen'.

38 See Starck, 'Kurtze Nachricht', pp. 663–674. Starck described Köneken as the 'fanatical auctioneer in Lübeck'.

39 Four auction catalogues by Johann Wessel are listed in VD17 and VD18 between 1698 and 1743: Johann Wessel, *Catalogus Librorum Theologicorum, Cum Appendice Medicorum, Quorum Auctio Benedicente Dei Gratia habebitur Lubecae Anno 1698 d. 10. Octobr. & sq. In Auditorio Cathariniano per Johannem Wesselium* (Lübeck: Schmalhertz, 1698), Erlangen-Nürnberg, UB: H61/TREW.Nx 49/55; ibid., *Catalogus Librorum Theologicorum, Quorum Auctio Benedicente Dei Gratia Lubecae, d. 28. Nov. Ann. 1698 In Auditorio Cathariniano per Johannem Wesselium* (Lübeck: Schmalhertz, 1698), Erlangen-Nürnberg, UB: H61/TREW.Nx 49/55; ibid., *Catalogus Bibliothecae Medicae admodum selectae: externoque pariter vultu splendentis, Quae Una cum Antlia Pneumatica Boyleana instructissima, ac Museo curioso, publico Auctionis ritu Lubecae, In Auditorio Cathariniano, die 31. Octobr. & seqq. A. 1701, distrahetur per Johannem Wessell* (Lübeck: Schmalhertz, 1701), Erlangen-Nürnberg, UB: H61/TREW.Nx 49/55; ibid., *Catalogus Librorum Theologicorum Aliorumque etc. Die XVIII. Februarii An. MDCCXLIII Lubecae In Autitorio Cathariniano Auctionis Lege Distrahendorum Per Jo. Wessel* (Lübeck: Willer, 1743), Göttingen, SUB: DD2001 A 420. Gebauer, *Bücherauktionen*, pp. 169–184, lists seven confirmed book auctions for Wessel

but became Köneken's business partner during the 1690s. The accusations that were directed at him repeated the main arguments used against Köneken. The first was that he would acquire books at auctions which he was supposed to supervise, selling these books at later auctions for a profit. Secondly, it was claimed that he would arrange terms with some of his customers, keeping prices down and thereby diminishing the profit earned by the heirs of the library's owner. And thirdly, Wessel was accused of presenting commissioned bids without mentioning the names of the customers, in effect purchasing books for his own stock.[40]

The repetition of the same criticisms made about Köneken in 1679 reveals that the measures introduced by the city council had been far from adequate. Most of the allegations were part of a larger moral discourse on what could go wrong at book auctions. Georg Paul Hönn (1662–1747) discussed many of the possible pitfalls facing auctioneers and customers in his *Betrugs-Lexicon*, published in 1721.[41] Auctions should, Hönn concluded, only be supervised by officially licensed auctioneers, and there should also be a general mandate regulating how the auctions should take place. That these fears were fairly widespread can be seen by the fact that Johann Heinrich Zedler (1706–1751) took up Hönn's considerations in the article on auctions in his popular lexicon.[42] Auctioneers selling their own stock as part of an auction were indeed, as Hönn contended, still fairly common during the early eighteenth century.[43]

None of the recommendations made by Hönn were implemented in Lübeck. Köneken received only a concession for auctioning from the council in 1679, not an official license. There was also no decree or ordinance regulating proceedings at the sales, and the *Statuta, Stadt-Recht und Ordnungen*, reprinted in 1728, did not contain any mandates on the auction trade.[44] The legal vacuum was filled in 1709, when St Catherine's Church issued a privilege for Wessel to

---

for the seventeenth century in 1693, 1694, 1696, 1698 (2), 1699 and 1700; with two printed catalogues not listed in VD17, published in 1699 and 1700 respectively.

40 Lübeck, AHL: ASA Interna, Nr. 02254, 'Die in denen Auctionen eingeschlichenen Un=Ordnungen', 1711, fol. 1r.

41 Georg Paul Hönn, *Betrugs-Lexicon: worinnen d. meiste Betrügereyen in allen Ständen nebst denen darwider guten Theils dienenden Mitteln entdecket* (Coburg: Pfotenhauer, 1721), pp. 25–26.

42 See the article 'Auction' in Zedler, *Universal-Lexicon*, Suppl. S2, p. 364, cols. 717–718.

43 See Michael F. Suarez, S. J., 'English Book Sale Catalogues as Bibliographical Evidence: Methodological Considerations Illustrated by a Case Study in the Provenance and Distribution of Dodsley's Collection of Poems, 1750–1795', *The Library*, vol. s6–21/4 (1999), pp. 321–360, especially pp. 324–332.

44 See *Der Kayserlichen Freyen und des Heiligen Reichs-Stadt Lübeck Statuta und Stadt Recht. Samt der Ehrbaren Hanse-Städte Schiffs-Ordnung und See-Recht* (Lübeck: Green, 1727–1728).

become Köneken's successor, since book auctions used to take place in the 'Auditorium of St Catherine's'.[45] The privilege was nullified by the city council that same year, and an investigation was launched.[46] However, it never seems to have been carried out, so the uncertainty regarding who was licensed as an official auctioneer remained. Even though no steps were taken towards an ordinance by the city council, St Catherine's Church was not to have jurisdiction over book auctions taking place on their premises. In spite of promises made as part of a decree on 12 March 1711, no regulation was drafted by the council, and Johann Wessel continued to auction books, together with Köneken, until Wessel was replaced in 1751.

Booksellers were, not surprisingly, the most influential group in the auction trade. If their financial interest was at stake, issues could be resolved rather quickly. When Burchard Stöter, a bookseller from Hamburg, began to auction books in Lübeck in 1736, local booksellers and auctioneers closed ranks and submitted a petition to the council, led by Peter Böckmann (1703–1774), the principal publisher in town.[47] Stöter was allowed to go through with an already planned event, but he was prohibited from staging any further auctions within the jurisdiction of Lübeck.[48]

Interestingly, the petition against Stöter used arguments similar to those that Köneken had made more than fifty years earlier. Foreign competition would harm the interests of local widows and orphans who needed to sell the libraries of deceased family members; the importation of scholarly collections from outside would not just be a detriment to their own trade as booksellers, but also to the learned citizens of Lübeck.[49] Again, scholars, their wives and

---

45 Lübeck, AHL: ASA Interna, Nr. 02254, privilege by St. Catherine's Church, April 1709, fol. 1r–fol. 1v, here fol. 1r. St Catherine's Church grants a privilege to Wessel, 'daß er nach dem Abgang Jasp. Köneken die Bücher Auctiones allein haben und behalten'. One of the conditions for the privilege is that Wessel should sell 'alle Bücher in den Auditorio zu St. Catharinen ..., damit weder Jetzo noch Künfftig ein ander Orth sein solle', effectively restricting auctions to the auditorium of St Catherine's, which was probably located in the lecture hall of the Katharineum.

46 Ibid., decree of the city council against St Catherine's Church, 22 April 1711, fol. 1r.

47 Burchard Stöter is listed as a bookseller in Hamburg in Ute Schneider, 'Ein Erfolgsroman im gelehrten Programm. Samuel Richardsons *Clarissa* (1748–1753) bei Abraham Vandenhoeck', in M. Estermann, E. Fischer and U. Schneider (eds.), *Buchkulturen. Beiträge zur Geschichte der Literaturvermittlung* (Wiesbaden: Harrassowitz, 2005), pp. 211–232, here p. 231.

48 Lübeck, AHL: ASA Interna, Nr. 02276, decree of the city council against Burchard Stöter, 7 March 1736.

49 Ibid., petition of auctioneers against Burchard Stöter from Hamburg, 1736, fol. 1r–fol. 3r, here fol. 1v: 'Wenn aber durch solche Bücher Schacherey und hereinführung frembder auch verstorbener Gelehrter Bibliothequen zur öffentlichen auction nicht allein unsrer

THE GOVERNMENT AT AUCTION 251

their families are presented as the main instigators of auctions, obscuring the booksellers' own interests. Since nobody could argue with economic protectionism, and since the booksellers could be sure of the support of the guild and the learned community, the decree by the council proved relatively effective.

As the various petitions and decrees make clear, the church, the booksellers, the council and the learned community were often competing for dominance in the auction trade. The enforcement of decrees by the authorities remained selective, depending on the degree of support by these communities. The same allegations were repeatedly raised against different auctioneers during the seventeenth and eighteenth centuries. Auctioning without a privilege, issuing a privilege without the necessary jurisdiction, the selling of booksellers' stock at auction, the acquisition of books by auctioneers at their own sales – all of these practices were prohibited by printed regulations such as the ordinance issued in Leipzig in 1680.[50] It ruled that each auction had to be officially registered with the city council. The auctioneer was to be selected by the authorities. A catalogue of the books to be sold had to be submitted in advance for censorship. The books should also be laid out before the auction for inspection. Speculating on customers and manipulating prices was illegal, and books were only allowed to be sold at auction if they were part of a library that was rightfully inherited.

Nonetheless, only a few cases of forbidden practices which were brought to the attention of the authorities in Lübeck were actually resolved effectively, in each case depending on the political context. Three groups played a central role for the auction trade: firstly, the booksellers and the auctioneers themselves, who had the largest stake in the trade; secondly, the collectors of books who could afford to buy books at auction; and thirdly, the families, widows and children of deceased scholars who had to sell their books in order to survive. Together, they made up the local Republic of Letters – a miniature Republic indeed, but one which had a larger influence on politics, culture and the market for books in Lübeck than has previously been acknowledged.

    Handlung ein großer abbruch geschiehet sondern auch Wittwen und Weysen hiesieger und im dieser Stadt Jurisdiction verstorbener Gelehrter die Jhre Bücher verkauffen müßen ein großer Schade zu wächset ...'
50   'Des Raths zu Leipzig Verordnung', pp. 237–241. See also Gebauer, *Bücherauktionen*, pp. 34–39.

FIGURE 10.2 Front of St Catherine's Church in Lübeck (Katharinenkirche Lübeck). Book auctions took place in the auditorium on the premises of the old St Catherine's Monastery (Katharinenkloster)
WITH KIND PERMISSION, MUSEUMSQUARTIER ST. ANNEN

3 The Republic of Letters in Lübeck

Since Lübeck was not a university town, scholars may not have played a large role in city life.[51] Only some 120 academics were among the 2,000 citizens living within the city walls in 1789.[52] However, these ministers, lawyers, physicians and teachers made up a close-knit network of buyers and sellers of books. The scholar-collectors, academics, booksellers and auctioneers attending book sales made up a community of bibliophiles with a shared financial interest. They also built a memory community, writing eulogies for funerals and assisting in the sale of inherited books.[53]

This small community was centred around the Katharineum, the old gymnasium of the town. It was founded in 1531 as a part of the social reforms of Johannes Bugenhagen (1485–1558). The school is adjacent to St Catherine's Church and the city library, the institutions which were part of the old structure of St Catherine's Monastery, and which made use of its former building fabric (see Figure 10.2). Uffenbach visited both the church and the city library during his stay in Lübeck.[54] The students of the school took part in funeral processions, where the status and order of appearance of participants was strictly regulated. Most of Köneken's customers were associated with the Katharineum in some way. Winter, Siricius and Lippius, for instance, had been students of the gymnasium. The directorship of the city library came with the post of the third professorship at the gymnasium. It had originally been a rector of the gymnasium, Johann Kirchmann (1575–1643), who initiated the establishment of the city library between 1616 and 1622.[55] Uffenbach was impressed not just

---

51 See Eickhölter, 'Lübeck', pp. 1326: 'Lübeck war wie die anderen großen reichsfreien Städte Frankfurt am Main und Nürnberg keine Universitätsstadt, Gelehrte spielten im gesellschaftlichen Leben eine untergeordnete Rolle.'

52 Kopitzsch, 'Das 18. Jahrhundert. Vielseitigkeit und Leben', p. 502. The estimate of Kopitzsch includes ministers, lawyers, physicians and teachers at higher schools, such as the Katharineum.

53 For a study of collecting as a memorial practice, see Philippe Schmid, 'Catalogues in Catalogues: Imitation and Competition in Early Modern Book Collecting', in Arthur der Weduwen, Andrew Pettegree and Graeme Kemp (eds.), *Book Trade Catalogues in Early Modern Europe* (Leiden: Brill, 2021), pp. 399–424.

54 Uffenbach, *Merkwürdige Reisen*, pp. 23–24 and pp. 32–34.

55 See Gerhard Meyer, 'Bibliothek der Hansestadt Lübeck (Stadtbibliothek)', in Bernhard Fabian (ed.), *Handbuch der historischen Buchbestände in Deutschland. Digitalisiert von Günter Kükenshöner* (Hildesheim: Olms Neue Medien, 2003), art. 1.2 (https://fabian.sub.uni-goettingen.de/fabian?Stadtbibliothek(Luebeck).

by some 8,000 books, but also by the gallery of portraits which paid homage to the most celebrated citizens of the town.[56]

The city library and the Katharineum had close ties to the auction trade. Book auctions took place in the auditorium on the premises of the old St Catherine's Monastery.[57] Auctioneers also had to deliver a book which was worth at least 6 *Groschen* to the city library for every auction which exceeded 50 *Reichsthaler* in profit as of 1679, which was later changed to a regular fee of 2% of the profits to be paid.[58] The history of the gymnasium further reveals that it could not have been such a hostile world to Köneken. From 1675 to 1685, Abraham Hinckelmann was rector of the Katharineum, who entertained his own 'Kollegio biblico' in Lübeck, a small Bible study group.[59] From 1676 until 1692, the deeply learned Martin Lipenius (1630–1692) was deputy head

---

56 Uffenbach, *Merkwürdige Reisen*, p. 47: 'Ganz oben über den Büchern stunden sehr viele Burgermeister in Lebens-Grösse abgemalt, gegen über aber einige Superintendenten und Prediger von hier.'

57 A reference given by Jacob von Melle, *Ausführliche Nachricht von dem Leben und Charakter des Doctor Samuel Pomarius, eines in der letzten Hälfte des vorigen Jahrhunderts berühmt gewordenen Gottesgelehrten*, vol. 2 (Lübeck: Christian Gottfried Donatius, 1787), pp. 242–247, in a chapter titled 'Pomarius hält Vorlesungen im Auditorio zu St. Catharinen und disputirt' strongly suggests that the 'Auditorio Cathariniano' is identical with the lecture hall ('Aula') of the gymnasium (Katharineum). Melle writes about the lectures of the superintendent Samuel Pomarius (1624–1683), here pp. 243–244: 'Er [= Johannes Bugenhagen (1485–1558), who initiated the first church ordinance in Lübeck in 1531] fand es in Betracht der damaligen Zeiten … für höchst nützlich, daß der Lübeckische Superintendent [= Pomarius] über die Theologischen Wissenschaften vorzüglich über die Bücher der heiligen Schrift in dem öffentlichen Hörsaal unsers Gymnasii zu St. Catharinen Vorlesungen in lateinischer Sprache hielte und zugleich öftere Uebungen im Disputiren mit fähigen Köpfen unter den Mitgliedern des Gymnasiums und mit seinen Candidaten des Ministeriums, auch zu Zeiten mit den Ministerialen selbst anstellete.' This is confirmed by Starck, 'Kurtze Nachricht', pp. 670, who refers to the 'Auditorio zu S. Catharinen' as the 'ordentlichen dazu gewidmeten Orte', mentioning students of the gymnasium who were present in the room. Neither *Die Bau- und Kunstdenkmäler der Freien und Hansestadt Lübeck*, vol. 4 (Lübeck: Nöhring, 1928) nor Lübeck, AHL: 6.1–7 St. Katharinen, Nr. 281, renovation of the auditorium, 1655, give any evidence of an auditorium on the premises of St Catherine's Church. Many sources misleadingly refer to the 'Auditorio Cathariniano', but the auditorium was actually located within the gymnasium and not inside of the church. Cf. Heike Trost, *Die Katharinenkirche in Lübeck* (Kevelaer: Butzon & Bercker, 2004). I am grateful to Dominik Kuhn and Birgit Börngen for the latter references, and for kindly offering to scan the documents for evidence of the auditorium.

58 Lübeck, AHL: ASA Interna, Nr. 02263, 'Extractus Protocolli', 1679, fol. 1r; see Meyer, 'Bibliothek der Hansestadt Lübeck (Stadtbibliothek)', art. 1.5.

59 Abraham Hinckelmann to Philipp Jacob Spener (14 September, 1677); reprinted in Theodor Wotschke (ed.), 'Fünf Briefe von Seelens an Löscher', *Mitteilungen des Vereins für Lübeckische Geschichte und Altertumskunde*, 15 (1929), pp. 1–18, here p. 2.

of the gymnasium, and from 1693 until 1708, his son Sixt Christian Lipenius (1664–1708) was the second deputy head of the school and director of the city library. Finally, beginning in 1728, Carl Heinrich Lange (1703–1753) took up different positions at the gymnasium, introducing Enlightenment thought to Lübeck, corresponding with Johann Christoph Gottsched (1700–1766) in Leipzig and bequeathing his entire collection of books to the city library after his death.[60]

No one had more influence on the Katharineum than Johann Heinrich von Seelen (1687–1762). He became its rector in 1717, and tried to balance Lutheran orthodoxy with the scholarly erudition of the Republic of Letters. He corresponded with the orthodox theologian Valentin Ernst Löscher (1673–1749), but he also maintained contact with institutions of the early Enlightenment, such as the journal *Der Patriot* in Hamburg.[61] Seelen represents a new generation of young scholars and theologians in Lübeck after 1700, who were focused more on erudition than on dogma, and his letters to Löscher show a certain reservation towards the hard-line theologian Carpzov, who became superintendent in Lübeck in 1730 instead of Löscher, who declined.[62] Yet Seelen was not only a prolific writer in the fields of theology and history. From 1725 onwards, he was also at the centre of a small circle that edited the learned journal *Bibliotheca Lubecensis*, which appeared until 1732; from 1753 to 1757, again under Seelen's editorship, the journal was published as *Nova Bibliotheca Lubecensis*. The circle of the *Bibliotheca* was one of the earliest forms of citizen association in Lübeck, promoting the local exchange of ideas and the scholarly study of the history of learning, which was known at the time as the academic field of *historia litteraria*.[63] The learned community of Lübeck then had two epicentres, the

---

60   Kopitzsch, 'Das 18. Jahrhundert. Vielseitigkeit und Leben', pp. 520–521. For a list of the faculty of the Katharineum, see Deecke, *Catharineum zu Lübeck*, pp. 49–56.
61   Erdmann Neumeister to Valentin Ernst Löscher (15 February, 1726); reprinted in Wotschke, 'Fünf Briefe von Seelens an Löscher', pp. 1–18, here pp. 8–9. In his letter to Löscher, Erdmann Neumeister (1671–1756) characterised Seelen as a moderate who would be acceptable to both Pietist and orthodox ministers: 'Die Widersacher können nicht sagen, daß er ein harter Eiferer ist, und die Orthodoxen können aus seiner Disputation, die er jüngst bei der Promotion zum Licentiaten zu Rostock gehalten, auch sicher hoffen, daß er der Wahrheit nichts vergeben wird, und an seiner Erudition wird niemand etwas auszusetzen haben.' See Kopitzsch, 'Das 18. Jahrhundert. Vielseitigkeit und Leben', p. 520.
62   Johann Heinrich von Seelen to Johann Christian Wolf (19 November, 1730); reprinted in Wotschke, 'Fünf Briefe von Seelens an Löscher', pp. 1–18, here p. 16. Seelen had supported Löscher and was disappointed, when Johann Gottlob Carpzov became superintendent instead of Löscher. See Hauschild, *Kirchengeschichte Lübecks*, pp. 343–344.
63   Eickhölter, 'Lübeck', pp. 1338–1339. On *historia litteraria*, see Ann M. Blair, *Too Much to Know: Managing Scholarly Information Before the Modern Age* (New Haven: Yale University Press, 2010); Paul Nelles, 'Historia litteraria at Helmstedt: Books, professors and students

Katharineum and the *Bibliotheca*. Both were supported by a new generation of young university-educated humanists, and both were connected to Seelen and his network.

Seelen was also a supporter and historiographer of the local book culture. In 1740 he wrote a history of printing for the anniversary of the invention of the printing press by Gutenberg, entitled *Nachricht von dem Ursprung und Fortgang der Buchdruckerey*.[64] It was initiated by Johann Nicolaus Green (ca. 1721–1766), who was the official 'Rathsbuchdrucker' or printer of the council, as Seelen reveals in the preface.[65] His account mentions a selection of books which were printed in Lübeck, together with their producers, and is peppered with learned anecdotes about cultural life in the town. Since Seelen's history of printing commemorates the jubilee, its depiction of printers took part in local memory culture. His correspondence with his patron Valentin Ernst Löscher further reveals a first-hand knowledge of the local bookshops and their wares. When Seelen was classified as an 'indifferentist' in regards to the disputes between Lutheran orthodoxy and Pietism in 1732, he asked Löscher for help.[66] The theological journal *Fortgesetzte Sammlung von alten und neuen theologischen Sachen*, which was edited by Löscher, mistakenly listed Seelen as author of a heterodox work published in 1729, titled *Religio Bibliopolae: Oder die Religion eines Buch-Händlers*.[67] Seelen defended himself by assuring Löscher that he

---

in the early Enlightenment university', in Helmut Zedelmaier and Martin Mulsow (eds.), *Die Praktiken der Gelehrsamkeit in der Frühen Neuzeit* (Tübingen: Niemeyer, 2001), pp. 147–176; Paul Nelles, 'Historia litteraria and Morhof: Private Teaching and Professorial Libraries at the University of Kiel', in Françoise Waquet (ed.), *Mapping the World of Learning: The Polyhistor of Daniel Georg Morhof* (Wiesbaden: Harrassowitz, 2000), pp. 31–56; Frank Grunert and Friedrich Vollhardt (eds.), *Historia literaria. Neuordnungen des Wissens im 17. und 18. Jahrhundert* (Berlin: De Gruyter, 2007).

64   Johann Heinrich von Seelen, *Nachricht von dem Ursprung und Fortgang der Buchdruckerey in der kays. freyen und des H. Röm. Reichs Stadt Lübeck: worinnen die Lübeckischen Buchdrucker u. allerley von Ihnen gedruckte merckwürdige Bücher u. Schriften angeführt u. beschrieben werden* (Lübeck: Schmidt, 1740), Berlin, SBB-PK: RLS Fc 9029.

65   See the preface of Seelen, *Nachricht von dem Ursprung und Fortgang der Buchdruckerey*, f. 2r.

66   Johann Heinrich von Seelen to Valentin Ernst Löscher (15 November 1732); reprinted in Wotschke, 'Fünf Briefe von Seelens an Löscher', pp. 1–18, here pp. 11–15.

67   John Dunton, *Religio Bibliopolae: Oder die Religion Eines Buch-Händlers: Auch Leuten von andern Ständen und Profeßionen sehr angenehm und nützlich zu lesen. Wegen Seldenheit der darinnen enthaltenen Sitten-Lehren Aus dem Englischen ins Teutsche übersetzet* (Hof (Saale): Martinus, 1729). The book seems to have been rather popular, since a new edition of the work was published in 1737: John Dunton, *Religio Bibliopolae: Oder Die Religion Eines Buch-Händlers: Auch Leuten von andern Ständen und Profeßionen sehr angenehm und nützlich zu lesen; Wegen Seltenheit der darinnen enthaltenen Sitten-Lehren Aus dem Englischen ins Teutsche übersetzet* (Frankfurt am Main and Leipzig: Martinus, 1737).

had never even seen the book, since it was not available with local booksellers in Lübeck, and it would have been too troublesome to order it from abroad. Likewise, Seelen was aware of the new work by Carl Heinrich Lange, his colleague at the gymnasium, whose *Kurtze Anleitung zu der rechten und eigentlichen Art einen deutlichen und geschickten Periodum zu schreiben* was printed by Christian Heinrich Willers (c. 1727–1748) in Lübeck. Seelen was critical of some of its theological contents and knew that the author had bypassed official censorship by the authorities in Lübeck.[68]

The history of printing which Seelen wrote for the Gutenberg jubilee shows that the learned network which supported the book trade also formed a memory community. In the early modern period, auctions were part of a larger academic memorial culture, which included scholars, families, widows and their children. They cared for deceased scholars in different ritualised ways. Selling the libraries of deceased academics was no small task, and it included the careful study and cataloguing of the collection with its books and manuscripts, the publication and public posting of a printed catalogue, the advertising of the sale in local newspapers or journals, cooperation with auctioneers and booksellers and the shipping of the books that were bought by foreign customers on commission during the sale, not to mention the organisation of the sale itself.[69]

Printed catalogues often became public memorials for the dead. When Christoph Gensch von Breitenau passed away in 1732, Seelen prepared a massive catalogue, which was issued in three parts in 1747. Uffenbach had visited Breitenau in February 1710 and recalled some 3,000 volumes of high quality,

---

Indeed, the register of *Fortgesetzte Sammlung von alten und neuen theologischen Sachen, Büchern, Uhrkunden, Controversien, Anmerckungen und Vorschlägen: Anhang* (Leipzig: Braun, 1731), lists 'a Seelen, Io. Henr. verfält in einen gemäßigten Indifferentismum' as author of the *Religio Bibliopolae*, which is referenced on p. 1061: 'Es ist p. 640. sq. die Religion eines Buchhändlers recensiret worden. Hierbey ist folgendes noch zu mercken. Der Verfasser giebt viel gute Erinnerungen von der Mäßigkeit in Religions-Sachen auf beyden Theilen, u.s.f. fält aber selbst in einen gemässigten Indifferentismum, u. versündiget sich selbst an der Religion, obwohl mäßig. Er behält sonst die Calvinischen Irrthümer, bleibt aber im Mittel zwischen den Episcopalen und Presbyterianern. Sonst hat er seine moralische Reflexiones.'

68 M. Carl Heinrich Lange, *Kurtze Anleitung zu der rechten und eigentlichen Art einen deutlichen und geschickten Periodum zu schreiben: zum besondern Gebrauch seiner Privatisten aufgesetzet* (Lübeck: Willers, 1730). See Johann Heinrich von Seelen to Valentin Ernst Löscher (19 September 1730); reprinted in Wotschke, 'Fünf Briefe von Seelens an Löscher', pp. 1–18, here pp. 9–11.

69 My dissertation research focused on the rituals of caring for the libraries of deceased scholars in early modern Germany. For a general introduction to memory culture in the early modern period, see Judith Pollmann, *Memory in Early Modern Europe, 1500–1800* (Oxford: Oxford University Press, 2017).

mostly printed in folio format and with a focus on ecclesiastical history. Breitenau, who was a successful lawyer and diplomat, had originally collected his library as a donation to the gymnasium in Plön, to which he had already bequeathed 8,000 Reichsthaler.[70] Since the books were stored in a small room, it is questionable whether Uffenbach saw the whole collection. Parts of the library were sold following the publication of the catalogue of the library in 1747. The sale of some books to Carl Joseph Freiherr von Palm (1698–1770) between 1750 and 1751, using his book agent as an intermediary, is well documented.[71] The catalogue which Seelen edited was printed by Green, the printer of the city council, and became a posthumous eulogy for both Breitenau and his collection years after his death. It lists some 13,000 volumes and begins with a preface by Seelen, followed by a *Memoria Breitenaviana*, an extensive biography of Breitenau.[72] In the preface, Seelen discloses his model for the catalogue, which is based on the elaborate classification of subjects of the library of Jacques Auguste de Thou (1553–1617). The catalogue of de Thou's library had just been reissued in 1704 by booksellers in Hamburg and remained a widely imitated model for scholar-collectors.[73]

70 Uffenbach, *Merkwürdige Reisen*, pp. 66–67: 'Er hat sich in Ruhe leben hieher begeben, und hat zur Aufnahme des Gymnasii in Ploen, und Bestellung mehrerer Schul-Präceptoren acht tausend Thaler verehrt, er soll auch seine kostbare Bibliotheck zu dem Ende zu sammeln angefangen haben, um sie dahin zu vermachen. Nachdem er mit uns von allerhand geredet, und von alten Bekannten in Frankfurt Nachfrage gethan, bate ich uns das Glück aus, seine Bibliotheck, die uns so sehr gerühmt worden wäre, zu sehen; welcher er aber sehr weit warfe, endlich aber sein Alter und Unvermögenheit im Steigen entschuldigte, und einen Menschen, der vermuthlich sein Secretarius, mit uns hinauf gehen hiesse. Dieser führte uns dann in ein nicht gar grosses Zimmer, allwo bey drey tausend Bände, aber meist lauter Folianten waren, darunter viele kostbare Werke, sonderlich zur Kirchen-Historie gehörig, vorkamen, welche das vornehmste und meiste von diesen Büchern ausmachten.'
71 Lübeck, AHL: ASA Externa, Nr. 4651, acquisition of books from the Breitenau library by Carl Joseph Freiherr von Palm, 1750–1751, using Johann Georg Barth from Regensburg as book agent.
72 Johann Heinrich von Seelen (ed.), *Bibliotheca Breitenaviana, Sive Operum, Librorum, Scriptorum, Ad Omne Literarum Genus Spectantium, Editorum Et Ineditorum: Quae Vir Perillustris, Generosissimus Atque Excellentissimus, Christophorus Gensch A Breitanau, Eques Auratus Ordinis Dannebrogici, Haerediatrius In Grunenhoff, Augustissimi Daniae Et Norvegiae Regis Consiliarius Intimus, Magno Comparavit Digessitque Studio Catalogus, In Tomos III. Et Partes VIII. Divisus Ac Selectis Quibusdam Annotationibus Instructus; Praemissa Est Memoria Breitenaviana; Accessit Conspectus Bibliothecae Breitenavianae Et Auctorum Index / Scriptore Io. Henr. A Seelen, SS. Theol. Lic. Et Gymn. Lubec. Rect* (Lübeck: Green, 1747), sig. ar–a3r for the preface and pp. 1–82 for the eulogy of Breitenau.
73 Joseph Quesnel (ed.), *Catalogus Bibliothecae Thuanae: a Clarissimis Viris Petro & Jacobo Puteanis ordine Alphabetico primum distributus; Tum a Clarissimo Viro Ismaele Bullialdo Secundum Scientias & artes digestus; Denique editus a Josepho Quesnell, Parisino, &*

As one of the leading scholars in Lübeck, Seelen was involved in the auction trade. His catalogue and biography for the commemoration of the library of Breitenau was a monumental contribution to bibliography and learned memory culture. Seelen also wrote eulogies for deceased colleagues and friends for most of his adult life, starting with his post as rector of the Katharineum in 1717, and continuing until the late 1750s. He wrote dozens of funeral orations for the ministers and academics of Lübeck, some of whom are rather obscure, such as Georg Heinrich Götze (1728), Heinrich Engenhagen (1728), Zacharias Stampeel (1731), Adolf Christian Beisner (1735), Heinrich Sivers (1736), Hermann Adolph Le Fèvre (1745), Carl Friedrich Mensching (1746), Johann Heinrich Scholvin (1748), Johann Fleegen (1750), Hermann Anton Rhon (1750), Carl Heinrich Lange (1753) and Johann Hermann Becker (1759).[74] Most of these funeral orations were

Bibliothecario; Cum Indice Alphabetico Auctorum M. DC. LXXIX. (Hamburg and Lauenburg: Liebezeit, 1704). See Schmid, 'Catalogues in Catalogues', pp. 416–419.

[74] Johann Heinrich von Seelen, *Memoria Viri Summe Reverendi Atque Excellentissimi Domini Georgii Henrici Goetzii, ... Ecclesiarum Lubecensium Superintendentis Meritissimi Literis Consignata / A Jo. Henr. A Seelen* (Lübeck: Green, 1728); ibid., *Memoria Viri Nobilissimi Consultissimique Domini Henrici Engenhagen, Reip. Lubecensis Actuarii Optime Meriti, Literis Consignata A Jo. Henr. A Seelen, SS. Theol. Lic. Et Gymn. Lub. Rect.* (Lübeck: Green, 1728); ibid., *Memoria Viri Praecellentissimi, Clarissimi Doctissimique Domini Zachariae Stampeelii, Subrectoris Lubecensis Meritissimi, Literis Consignata A Jo. Henr. A Seelen, SS. Th. Lic. Et Gymn. Lub. Rect.* (Lübeck: Green, 1731); ibid., *Memoria Viri Admodum Reverendi Et Praeclarissimi, Domini M. Adolphi Christiani Beisneri, Ecclesiastae Laurentiani Optime Meriti: ... d. XXIX. Mart. A. MDCCXXXV. / Literis Consignata A Jo. Henr. A* (Lübeck: Green, 1735); ibid., *Ehren-Gedächtnis, Dem weiland Wol-Edlen, ... Herrn Henrich Sivers, ... Cantori in Lübeck, am Tage seiner Beerdigung den 14. Novemb. 1736. / aufgerichtet Von Jo. Henr. von Seelen, Theol. Licent. und des Lübeckischen Gymnasii Rectore* (Lübeck: Willers, 1736); ibid., *Memoria Viri Nobilissimi, Consultissimi Et Amplissimi, Domini Hermanni Adolphi Le Fevre, I.V.L. Secretarii De Republica Lubecensi Praeclarissime Meriti: ... d. XXIII. Iul. A. MDCCXLV. / Literis Consignata A Jo. Henr. A Seelen, Ss. Theol. Lic. Et Gymn. Lubec. Rect.* (Lübeck: Green, 1745); ibid., *Memoria Viri Nobilissimi, Consultissimi Et Amplissimi, Domini Caroli Friderici Mensching: Juris Utriusque Doctoris Et Causarum Patroni Excellentissimi Celeberrimique / Literis Consignata A Jo. Henr. A Seelen, SS. Theol. Lic. Et Gymn. Lubec. Rect. D. VI. April. A. MDCCXLVI* (Lübeck: Green, 1746); ibid., *Memoria Viri Admodum Reverendi Et Praeclarissimi, Domini Johannis Henrici Scholvin, Symmystae Mariani Meritissimi: ... d. VII. Mart. A. MDCCXLVIII. / Literis Consignata A Jo. Henr. A Seelen, SS. Theol. Lic. Et Gymn. Lub. Rect.* (Lübeck: Green, 1748); ibid., *Memoria Viri Admodum Reverendi Et Praeclarissimi, Domini Johannis Fleegen, Pastoris Kalckhorstensis Pereximie Meriti, Literis Consignata A Jo. Henr. A Seelen, SS. Theol. Lic. Et Gymn. Lubec. Rect.* (Lübeck: Green, 1750); ibid., *Memoria Viri Admodum Reverendi Et Praeclarissimi Domini M. Hermanni Antonii Rhon, Archi-Diaconi Mariani Pèreximie Meriti, Literis Consignata A Jo. Henr. A Seelen, SS. Theol. Lic. Et Gymn. Lubec. Rect.* (Lübeck: Green, 1750); ibid., *Memoria Viri Praecellentissimi, Clarissimi, Doctissimiqve, Domini M. Caroli Henrici Langii, Conrectoris Lubecensis Meritissimi, Societatum Teutonicarum, Lipsiensis, Ienensis Ac Goettingensis; Latinae Ienensis, Membri Honorarii, Literis Consignata: P. P. Lubecae. d. XXVII. Febr. A. M DCC LIII. / A Io. Henr. A*

printed by Green, the official printer of the council, and were issued as broadsheets. His service to the recently deceased intelligentsia of the town should be read in context of his larger work, *Athenae Lubecenses*, which was published in four volumes between 1719 and 1722, at the very beginning of Seelen's career at the Katharineum. It is a collection of biographies and epitaphs of the most distinguished citizens from the past, and forms a part of the early historiography of Lübeck and *historia litteraria* more generally during the eighteenth century.[75]

When Seelen passed away in 1762, his library was brought to auction, and a catalogue of his collection was printed by Green in 1763 (see Figure 10.3).[76] It was edited by Peter Böckmann, a leading local publisher of schoolbooks and hymnals who, in 1758, had also became official auctioneer of Lübeck. In that year the city council introduced a formal oath for auctioneers, with a list of the auctioneers and their signatures.[77] The introduction of an official municipal privilege finally put an end to the competition between the booksellers, the church, the guild and the academics for an auction privilege. Breaking into the corporative guild structure in 1679, book auctions had by 1758 become a regular part of city life, with customers, booksellers and auctioneers forming a close-knit community of shared interest. With the new privilege and oath, the city at last established a minimal set of normative practices for licensed auctioneers.[78]

Seelen, ss. Theol. Lic. Et Gymn. Lubec. Rect. (Lübeck: Green, 1753); ibid., *Memoria Viri Maxime Reverendi, Amplissimi Et Praeclarissimi, Domini Iohannis Hermanni Becker, ss. Theologiae Doctoris Celeberrimi Et Pastoris Mariani Meritissimi, Literis Consignata A Io. Henr. A Seelen, ss. Theol. Lic. Et Gymn. Lubec. Rect.* (Lübeck: Fuchs, 1759).

75   Johann Heinrich von Seelen, *Athenae Lubecenses, sive de Athenaei Lubecensis Insignibus Meritis, per institutionem optimorum virorum acquisitis, in Rempublicam sacram, civilem & litterariam Commentarius, praeter gloriosas Memorias quorundam Consulum Lubecensium, ... multas praestantissimorum Theologorum, Ictorum, Medicorum, Philologorum Et Philosophorum Vitas ... complectens ... / Auctore Ioan. Henr. Von Seelen Rect. Lubec.* (Lübeck and Lauenburg: Böckmann and Pfeiffer, 1719–1722).

76   Peter Böckmann (ed.), *Catalogus Bibliothecae Seelenianae: Libros selectissimos In Theologia, Historia Civili, Ecclesiastica Et Literaria, Philologia, Philosophia, Antiquitatibus &c. Complectens, quos magno olim studio & sumtu comparavit sibi Io. Henr. A Seelen s.s. Theol. Lic. & Gymnas. Lubec. Rector; nunc vero a. d. XXVII. Iun. An. MDCCLXIII. Lubecae In Auditorio Catharinian publicae Licitationi exponet Petrus Boeckmann* (Lübeck: Green, 1763).

77   Lübeck, AHL: ASA Interna, Nr. 02255, 'Der Bücher-Auctionarii Eyd', 1758–1790, fol. 1r. The office was later taken up by his son in 1776.

78   Ibid., fol. 1r: 'Ich gelobe und schwere, daß ich dem Dienst eines Bücher-Auctionarii nach meinem besten Vermögen getuldig und unpartheyisch fürstehen, mithin dabey nichts zum Schaden des Verkaufes, ohne Vortheil des Käufers vornehmen, auch selbst für mich, und zu meinem Vortheil nicht bieten, noch durch andere bieten laßen, nicht weniger kein Buch, worauf nur etwas geboten worden, unverkauft wegsetzen, auch insonderheit,

FIGURE 10.3   Interior of St Catherine's Church in Lübeck (Katharinenkirche Lübeck) with Epitaph of Johann Heinrich von Seelen (1687–1762)
WITH KIND PERMISSION, MUSEUMSQUARTIER ST. ANNEN

4   Epitaphs of Another Kind

The introduction and the regulation of the auction trade in eighteenth-century Lübeck cannot be summed up in a simple narrative of enlightened modernisation. Governance was often far from effective and in each case dependent on the support of the church, the guild, the booksellers or the academic customers, confirming the trends of legislation on social discipline at the time. The traditional corporative structures of the guild and the church retained an important influence on the regulation of the trade until the introduction of the oath of the auctioneers in 1758. Control of the trade by authorities was limited, resulting in a certain tolerance towards heterodoxy. One of the most influential groups supporting the auction trade was the learned community. As a mini-Republic within the larger universe of erudition, its members had a financial interest in the book trade. In many cases, their financial incentives were dominated by the family, and not by an individual, forming a memory community. Debts had to be paid or cash raised in order to support the family when a husband or father passed away. Since the library was often of little use after such a loss, it had to be sold to generate liquid assets.

When Uffenbach visited St Mary's Church during his stay in Lübeck in February 1710, he was impressed by the elaborate epitaphs of the Flemish artist Thomas Quellinus (1661–1709).[79] They were made of marble and alabaster and showed the councillors and mayors of the city of Lübeck. This was the small world that the auction trade of eighteenth-century Lübeck was a part of: it was a baroque memory culture of epitaphs and eulogies, public sales and memorial catalogues. As much as books in the early modern period were bought by the living, they were sold by the dead.[80]

---

wenn ich auswärtige Commissiones bekommen, und selbige an andere übertragen solte, wir überhaupt nicht ehender, als nach dreymahligem vorherigen Aufruf des gebothenen, zum ersten, andern und dritten Mahl, zuschlagen wolle.'

[79] Uffenbach, *Merkwürdige Reisen*, pp. 20–23, here p. 21: 'Es hat ihn [i.e. the altar] ein Brabanter, ein sehr berühmter und vortrefflicher Bildhauer, T. Quellinus, verfertiget, welcher sich öffters allhier aufgehalten, und in dieser Kirche bey zwölf unvergleichlich schöne und grosse Epitaphia von Marmor und Alabaster gemacht, die hier so schön zu sehen, und so merkwürdig sind, daß ich nicht glaube, daß man in einer Kirche in der Welt so viel schöne Epitaphia und Bildhauer-Arbeit so leicht beysammen finden werde.'

[80] I would like to thank Ian Maclean, Mona Garloff and Arthur der Weduwen for their thoughtful questions and remarks during discussion at the conference. I am especially grateful to Ian Maclean for reading an early draft of this article, and to Giles Mandelbrote for inspiring me to work on auctioning in Lübeck. The research for this article has been supported with an AHRC scholarship by the Scottish Graduate School for Arts and Humanities. Dominik Kuhn and Birgit Börngen from the Archiv der Hansestadt Lübeck provided invaluable comments and corrections. My deepest gratitude goes to Carolin Alff, who gave advice and support when it was most needed.

CHAPTER 11

Philosophie or *Commerce*? Classification Systems in Eighteenth-Century French Private Library Catalogues

Helwi Blom

On Friday 17 November 1713, after attending church and visiting a friend, Philippe de Gentil, Marquis of Langalerie, returned home to spend the rest of the day rearranging his bookshelves. At the time, Langalerie, a former high officer in the French army, lived in Kassel, since he had decided to enrol in the service of foreign rulers. In 1711, he had converted to Protestantism and embraced the fate of the Huguenot exiles. On this Friday, he rearranged the order of the titles on his bookshelves according to his new ideological convictions: the top four shelves were dedicated to books on Protestantism, below were the books he borrowed, then came history and profane books. Roman Catholic books were placed at the very bottom.[1] If contemporary bibliographers had seen this, Protestants as well as Catholics would probably have frowned in contempt at this intuitive and unconventional way of organising one's books.

Questions regarding the arrangement of book collections and the compilation of catalogues were the subject of growing attention and debate in seventeenth-century Europe. It was during this period that the art of describing and classifying books was increasingly recognised as a genuine scientific discipline, with its own specific methodological and theoretical framework.[2]

---

1   See the summary of the contents of the diary of Langalerie compiled by Lionel Laborie at pierre-marteau.com/wiki/index.php?title=Philippe_de_Gentil_de_Langallerie. The research described in this article was carried out in the context of the MEDIATE project (http://mediate18.nl/). This project has received funding from the European Research Council (ERC) under the European Union's Horizon 2020 research and innovation program under grant agreement No. 682022. The present article is a reworked version of my 'Philosophie ou Commerce? L'évolution des systèmes de classement bibliographique dans les catalogues de bibliothèques privées publiés en France au XVIIIe siècle', in Frédéric Barbier, István Monok and Andrea Seidler (eds.), *Les bibliothèques et l'économie des connaissances / Bibliotheken und die Ökonomie des Wissens 1450–1850* (Budapest: Magyar Tudományos Akadémia Könyvtár és Információs Központ, 2020), pp. 203–234.
2   See, among others, Sape van der Woude, *Een keurige wetenschap* (Deventer: Kluwer, 1967); Christiane Berkvens-Stevelinck, 'L'apport de Prosper Marchand au système des libraires de Paris', *De Gulden Passer* (1978), pp. 21–63, and Valérie Neveu, 'L'inscription de la classification

Around 1660, Louis Machon, a well-known French bibliographer and librarian, wrote a long and learned discourse on 'the order and method that should be followed to make and draw up the catalogue of a library'.[3] In it he reviewed all of the important publications on the subject, from the *Rosetum exercitiorum spiritualium et sacrarum meditationum* of Jean de Bruxelles (145?–1502) to Gabriel Naudé's *Advis pour dresser une bibliothèque* (1627), and from the *Bibliotheca universalis* and *Pandectarum sive partitionum universalium* (1545–1548) by Conrad Gessner to the *Bibliothecae Cordesianae catalogus* (1643). He concluded that not only did all of the classification and cataloguing systems present practical problems, but that they also lacked logic and theoretical justification. Machon ended his discussion by proposing a solution: a theoretically founded yet practically applicable new system of his own design.[4]

During the Age of Enlightenment, the issue of the relationship between library science and epistemology, between the classification of books and the classification of knowledge, gained new importance in the writings of philosophers and supporters of the ideology of the French Revolution, who sought to free themselves from the principles that underlay the political system of the *Ancien Régime*. This theme is at the heart of the entry entitled 'Catalogue' in the second volume of the famous *Encyclopédie*, published in 1752. After having noted, as Machon had done, that the diversity of existing systems seemed to underline the arbitrary nature of bibliographical classification, the printer-bookseller Michel-Antoine David (also known as David l'aîné, the Elder), who wrote the article, firmly expressed his conviction that it should be possible to design a truly reasonable and scientific taxonomy of books and book collections based on the figurative system of human knowledge presented at the beginning of the first volume of the *Encyclopédie*. By way of promising example, David described a system invented by Father Gabriel Girard (1677–1748) 'where we find an order that differs greatly from those we have known thus far ... Father Girard gives a philosophical account of the

---

bibliographique dans le champ des sciences (fin XVIIe–début XVIIIe s.)', HAL SHS (2010), shs.hal.science/halshs-00599276.

3 'l'ordre et méthode qu'il fault suivre pour faire et dresser le catalogue d'une bibliotheque'. Bordeaux, Bibliothèque municipale, ms 830: *Catalogue des livres de la bibliothèque de monseigneur Arnaud de Pontac, conseiller du Roy en ses conseils et premier président en son parlement de Bordeaux*, p. 5. See also Daspit de Saint-Amand (ed.), *Discours pour servir de règle ou d'advis aux bibliothécaires par Louis Machon. Publié et augmenté d'une notice sur Louis Machon et sur la bibliothèque du premier président Messire Arnaud de Pontac* (Bordeaux: Gounouilhou, 1883), p. 34.

4 See *Discours pour servir de règle*, pp. 56–76.

reasons which determined his choice of divisions and their hierarchy'.[5] The article closes with an invitation to the reader to take up the challenge.[6]

Was David the Elder's optimism justified? Would this recurring vision of a happy marriage between the philosophical approach to knowledge and collections on the one hand, and the practical management of libraries and their catalogues on the other, become a reality in eighteenth-century France? This article proposes to explore the question by studying the evolution of bibliographic taxonomy in French private library catalogues from this period.

The focus will be on one specific type of catalogue, namely catalogues of private collections that appeared in print. The printed private library catalogue is a phenomenon that experienced a remarkable uptake in the seventeenth and eighteenth centuries, not only in France, but also in several other countries in north-western Europe.[7] The proliferation of the genre is closely linked to developments in the book market and in particular to practices concerning public sales of books. It would however be a misconception to believe that all of the private library catalogues that came off the Dutch, English, Danish, German, French and other presses of the time were auction catalogues. This is an idea that is often suggested in studies of this type of catalogue, but, in reality, many of them did not appear in the context of a sale. Some of them served domestic purposes, while others were primarily published as a tribute to the owner and his collection.

In the case of book sales catalogues, the problem of the compatibility of a philosophical approach with the practical issues of cataloguing collections is all the more pressing since these catalogues had to take into account a number of criteria dictated by commercial logic. With regard to a catalogue of books for sale at the Frankfurt Book Fair, published by Georg Willer in 1592, Louis Machon had noted in his *Discours pour servir de règle ou d'advis aux*

---

5 'où il regne un ordre fort différent de ceux que l'on a connus jusqu'à présent ... M. l'abbé Girard y rend compte en Philosophe des raisons qui l'ont déterminé dans le choix & le rang de ses divisions'.
6 Michel-Antoine David, 'Catalogue', in Denis Diderot and Jean Le Rond, dit D'Alembert (eds.), *Encyclopédie, ou Dictionnaire raisonné des sciences, des arts et des métiers, par une société de gens de lettres*, vol. II (1751, i.e. 1752), pp. 759–766. The title of the Girard manuscript used by David was *Bibliotheque générale ou Essai de littérature universelle*. It was among the papers bequeathed by Girard to the printer-bookseller André-François Le Breton, but it is now considered lost.
7 For a recent overview of publications on this subject, see Helwi Blom, Rindert Jagersma and Juliette Reboul, 'Printed Private Library Catalogues as a Source for the History of Reading in Seventeenth- and Eighteenth-Century Europe', in Mary Hammond (ed.), *The Edinburgh History of Reading 1: Early and Modern Readers* (Edinburgh: Edinburgh University Press, 2020), pp. 249–269.

bibliothécaires that it was 'more like the catalogue of a bookseller who wants to sell his books by advertising them, than that of a library which one wants to organise with a catalogue'.[8]

1 Printed Private Library Catalogues from Early Modern France, a Bibliographic State-of-the-Art

Printed catalogues of private book collections have long served as sources for historians of the Enlightenment. When, more than a century ago, Daniel Mornet wrote his pioneering study on private libraries, he was seeking to measure the influence of the great authors of the Enlightenment by studying a corpus of 500 Parisian catalogues kept in the municipal library of Toulouse.[9] After Mornet, many others drew on this type of source to study the reading habits of French people in the seventeenth and eighteenth centuries and to analyse the penetration of 'enlightenment books' in private libraries of the time. The most important study, at least in scope, is that of Michel Marion, who examined no less than a thousand catalogues from the years 1700–1790, all of them found in the Bibliothèque nationale de France (BnF), in order to uncover the world of French book collectors of the Enlightenment.[10] Before him, the German scholar Friedhelm Beckmann had already worked on a corpus of some 800 catalogues kept at the same library.[11] Beckmann was mainly interested in the classification systems used in the catalogues, but he had also touched upon other questions, such as the typology of the book owners and the evolution of the contents of their libraries.

While these three studies represent a huge amount of work which makes it possible to chart the broad outlines of the forms and contents of eighteenth-century French catalogues and collections, they have serious limitations. For practical reasons, the researchers in question had to limit their analyses of the books listed in the catalogues to a small part of their initial corpus, that is 376 catalogues for Mornet, 586 for Marion, and 268 for Beckmann. All three

---

[8] 'plus tost le Catalogue d'un marchant Libraire qui veult vendre ses livres en les faisant conestre, que celuy d'une bibliothèque qu'on veult mettre en bon ordre avec son catalogue'. *Discours pour servir de règle*, pp. 44–45.

[9] Daniel Mornet, 'Les enseignements des bibliothèques privées (1750–1780)', *Revue d'histoire littéraire de la France*, 17 (1910), pp. 449–496.

[10] Michel Marion, *Collections et collectionneurs de livres au XVIIIe siècle* (Paris: H. Champion, 1999).

[11] Friedhelm Beckmann, *Französische Privatbibliotheken: Untersuchungen zu Literatursystematik und Buchbesitz im 18. Jahrhundert* (Frankfurt am Main: Buchhändler-Vereinigung, 1988).

made their selection on the basis of the number of items per catalogue and the presence of a classification structure facilitating thematic analysis. This means that certain types of catalogues were systematically neglected in their analyses.

A second problem consists of the fact that, unlike in the Netherlands, where a team of researchers has established an almost exhaustive descriptive inventory of all known book catalogues printed in the Dutch Republic between 1599 and 1800, the catalogues of private collections published in early modern France have not yet been the subject of a general inventory.[12] There have certainly been several initiatives to compile a census based on collections held in a number of French and American libraries, but it must be acknowledged that we have only a limited idea of the extent of the phenomenon in France, especially for the eighteenth and nineteenth centuries, and that we lack bibliographical tools sophisticated enough to allow a general analysis of the corpus.[13]

---

12 Bert van Selm, Hans Gruys, Henk W. de Kooker, *et al.* (eds.), *Dutch Book Sales Catalogues, 1599–1800*. (Leiden: Inter Document Company, 1990–), continued as Karel Bostoen, Otto Lankhorst, Alicia C. Montoya and Marieke van Delft (eds.), *Book Sales Catalogues Online – Book Auctioning in the Dutch Republic, ca. 1500–ca. 1800* (Leiden: Brill, 2015), http://primarysources.brillonline.com/browse/book-sales-catalogues-online. See also Hans Gruys and Henk W. de Kooker, *Guide to the Microfiche Collection 'Book Sales Catalogues of the Dutch Republic, 1599–1800* (Leiden: IDC Publishers, 1997–2005).

13 *Cf.* Christian Péligry, *Les catalogues de bibliothèques du XVIIe, XVIIIe et XIXe siècles, jusqu'en 1815: contribution à l'inventaire du fonds ancien de la Bibliothèque Municipale de Toulouse* (Toulouse: Bibliothèque Municipale, 1974). This bibliography contains around 730 entries listing private library catalogues as well as catalogues of institutional libraries published in different European countries, all held in the municipal library of Toulouse. See also Françoise Bléchet, *Les ventes publiques de livres en France, 1630–1750: répertoire des catalogues conservés à la Bibliothèque Nationale* (Oxford: The Voltaire Foundation, 1991). Bléchet gives an inventory of copies of 375 different French catalogues of private and institutional libraries conserved in the BnF. In spite of the title, the list also comprises catalogues that did not appear in the context of a sale. Michel Marion's *Collections et collectionneurs* includes a list of 1,097 names of French book collectors whose libraries were the object of a printed catalogue of which one can find a copy in the BnF, while Annie Charon's *Esprit des livres* (Paris: École nationale des chartes, 2015, elec.enc.sorbonne.fr/catalogevente) is a database offering metadata on 550 printed catalogues, private library catalogues as well as booksellers' catalogues, published between 1599 and 1810, mostly in France and in the Dutch Republic. The list is based on the collections of several Parisian libraries: the Bibliothèque Sainte Geneviève, the library of the Institut de France, the Bibliothèque de Fels of the Institut catholique de Paris, the library of the École des chartes, and the Bibliothèque Interuniversitaire de Santé. The database «*L'Esprit des livres*», *catalogues de ventes de bibliothèques conservés à Lyon et Grenoble* on the website of the Institut d'Histoire du Livre in Lyon, ihl.enssib.fr/bases-de-donnees/catalogue-de-vente-de-livres-anciens, records around 340 printed catalogues of private collections and booksellers' stocks from the years 1643–1815, of which copies are held in the municipal libraries of Lyon and Grenoble. There is also Michael North's *Printed Catalogues of French Book Auctions and Sales by Private Treaty, 1643–1830, in the Library of the Grolier Club* (New York: The Grolier Club, 2004) in which North describes 616 different French

The very rich chronological bibliography that Pierre Conlon has devoted to the literature of the Enlightenment has the merit of taking into account the holdings of provincial French libraries, but it only covers the period up to the French Revolution. Besides, it does not include all the collections in the French national library.[14] The Bibliothèque nationale de France holds thousands of copies of private library catalogues, but even at the present time it is not easy to identify them, because the general catalogue provides extremely concise descriptions and in many cases copies relating to a single edition have not been grouped together.

In order to fill this bibliographic gap, I am currently compiling a list of all known private library catalogues published in France between 1600 and 1830.[15] A handlist containing approximately 3,500 French private library catalogues has served as a starting point for the study of the evolution of the classification systems used in eighteenth-century private library catalogues, and forms the basis of the analysis presented below.

2 Catalogues, Classification Systems and the Development of the Second-Hand Book Market

Of the 3,500 French private library catalogues in my corpus, approximately 2,800 items date from the eighteenth century. Some 400 of these were produced during the first half of the century and another 2,400 during the second half of the century. The production curve of French private library catalogues clearly shows the growth of the genre from the 1740s onwards (see Figure 11.1).

---

private library catalogues from the Grolier Club collection. The checklist of French book sales catalogues from the period *ca.* 1630–*ca.* 1995 established by Gabriel Austin and presented at the Grolier Club in New York in 1995 has never been published, but Austin's archive with his notes on French sales catalogues can be consulted in the library of the Grolier Club. *Cf.* Gabriel Austin, 'Catalogues of French Booksales: A Handlist', *Papers of the Bibliographical Society of America*, 89 (1995), pp. 435–445.

14   *Cf.* Pierre Conlon, *Prélude au siècle des Lumières: répertoire chronologique de 1680 à 1715*, (6 vols.; Geneva: Droz, 1970–1975) and Pierre Conlon, *Le Siècle des Lumières: bibliographie chronologique*, (32 vols.; Geneva: Droz, 1983–2009). The European bibliography of private library catalogues and auction catalogues that Gerhard Loh is compiling currently consists of nine volumes, covering the years 1555–1741. *Cf.* Gerhard Loh, *Die europäischen Privatbibliotheken und Buchauktionen: ein Verzeichnis ihrer Kataloge* (Leipzig: s.n., 1997–).

15   This bibliography will be published in Brill's *Library of the Written Word* series, under the title *Printed Catalogues of Private Libraries Published in France during the Hand-press Era, a Bibliographical Survey*. BIBLIO (Bibliography of Individual Book and Library Inventories Online, 1665–1830), one of the two databases under construction within the MEDIATE project, will also incorporate basic metadata on a substantial corpus of French catalogues published between 1665 and 1830.

PHILOSOPHIE OR COMMERCE? 269

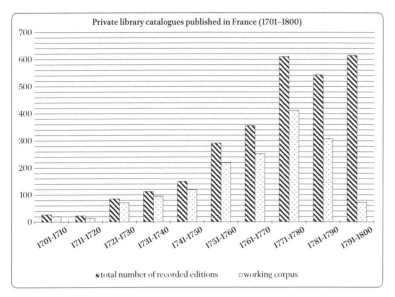

FIGURE 11.1   Private library catalogues published in France (1701–1800)

As it has not yet been possible to consult a copy of each catalogue on the list, I have based my research on a corpus of about 1,600 catalogues for which I have been able to gather sufficient information with regard to structure and classification systems (see Figure 11.1). Unfortunately, this means that catalogues from the period after 1789, which have received little attention so far, are underrepresented in my working corpus.

Within the corpus of selected catalogues, several different types of classification can be distinguished. In some cases, there is no apparent logic in the way the books are organised. Approximately one third of the catalogues use a system based mainly on formal criteria, such as classification by format, alphabetical order of author names or titles, classification by language, classification by genre (such as printed matter, manuscripts, pamphlets, 'Elzevirs', etc.), and an organising principle based on the order of the sale. This category of formally structured catalogues also includes catalogues that present a list of numbered multi-volume lots. These lists probably follow the order of the inventory drawn up by the notary in the context of the valuation of the possessor's movable goods. While it is not certain that all catalogues written in this 'inventory style' can be used to reconstruct the physical arrangement of the libraries in question, several do actually contain prefaces indicating that the compilers have used a handwritten inventory or that they have followed the order of the books on the shelves.[16]

---

16   See, for example, the 'Avis' in the *Catalogue des livres de la bibliothèque de feu Monseigneur Louis de La Vergne de Tressan* (Paris: Gabriel Martin, 1734), and the *Catalogue des livres de feue madame la comtesse de Verruë* (Paris: Gabriel Martin, 1737).

A number of catalogues (less than ten per cent of the corpus) combine a formal classification system with subject classification. Sometimes, thematic groupings of books can also be discerned in catalogues arranged by book format or by inventory number.[17] It is difficult to say whether this grouping is the result of choices made by those responsible for the inventory and the drafting of the catalogue, or whether it reflects the classification set up by the owner of the library himself.

A little more than half of the corpus consists of thematically arranged catalogues. While subject classification systems for books are as old as libraries themselves, in France, the beginning of the eighteenth century was an extremely important period in this respect. Around 1700, two Parisian booksellers, Prosper Marchand and Gabriel Martin, developed what would become known as the 'système des libraires de Paris', the Parisian booksellers' system. They proposed a classification scheme in five major subject classes: Theology, Jurisprudence, Arts & Sciences, Literature and History. Each subject class could be subdivided indefinitely to accommodate specific categories of books. Thanks to the lengthy and carefully composed catalogues published by bookseller Gabriel Martin from 1711 onwards, this systematic classification framework quickly became the model par excellence for bibliographical taxonomy.[18] The thematic catalogues of private libraries published in eighteenth-century France have a structural stability that is absent in catalogues from the seventeenth century.

Analysis of my corpus confirms the importance that book historians traditionally attribute to the Parisian booksellers' system, but also reveals exceptions that put it into perspective and thus downplay assertions such as those made by Michel Marion and Valérie Neveu, stating that the system was almost universally adopted in France, both by booksellers responsible for book sales

---

17   The copy of the *Catalogue d'une belle collection de tableaux, desseins, estampes, livres d'estampes et livres, du cabinet de M+++* (Paris: Joullain, 1774), held at the Austrian National Library (122262-A, digitised) is particularly interesting in this respect: in the section devoted to books, written in 'inventory style', an anonymous owner has pasted, in places where a change of category can be noted, small slips of paper cut out of another catalogue and bearing the subject titles of the five main classes of the bibliographical system used by Parisian booksellers.

18   The label 'Sciences & Arts' was introduced by Gabriel Martin in the *Bibliotheca Bultelliana* (1711) to replace the heading 'Philosophy', but like other features considered distinctive for the Parisian booksellers' system, it was not used systematically in catalogues published during the first quarter of the eighteenth century. On the origins of the system, see Neveu, 'L'inscription de la classification bibliographique'; Berkvens-Stevelinck, 'L'apport de Prosper Marchand', and idem, 'Prosper Marchand: remarques sur la *Bibliotheca Bultelliana*: lettre ouverte à Gabriel Martin, 1711', *Lias*, 17 (1990), pp. 91–107.

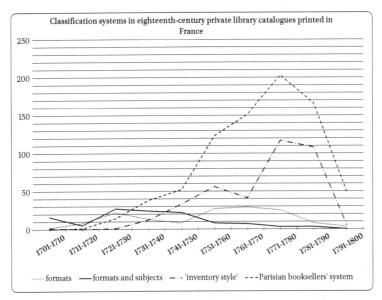

FIGURE 11.2   Classification systems in eighteenth-century private library catalogues printed in France

and by librarians and individual bibliophiles.[19] In fact, catalogues modelled on this system only represent half of the working corpus. Throughout the eighteenth century, other systems persisted, most notably classification by format and the 'inventory style' (see Figure 11.2). Alphabetical classification, on the other hand, which was very frequently used in booksellers' catalogues, was hardly ever used in eighteenth-century printed private library catalogues.[20]

Classification by format is a characteristic feature of catalogues printed in provincial centres such as Lille, Douai and Strasbourg, all cities located in border regions annexed by France in the second half of the seventeenth century. Of the 145 catalogues structured according to this principle, only eight were published in Paris. The structure of the Lille catalogues is very similar to that of the catalogues published in the Netherlands. On the other hand, the 'inventory style' is well represented in the corpus of Parisian catalogues of this period and even in the production of Gabriel Martin, generally considered the champion of thematic classification. I have recorded 123 catalogues bearing Martin's name, 118 of which appeared after the inauguration of the booksellers' system

---

19   Cf. Marion, *Collections et collectionneurs*, p. 73, and Valérie Neveu, 'Classer les livres selon le *Système figuré des connaissances humaines*: émergence et déclin des systèmes bibliographiques d'inspiration baconienne (1752–1812)', *Recherches sur Diderot et sur l'Encyclopédie*, 48 (2013), p. 208.

20   Cf. Claire Lesage, Ève Netchine et Véronique Sarrazin, *Catalogues de libraires 1473–1810* (Paris: BnF, 2006), p. 23.

in 1711. Only forty-five per cent of these follow the model of the five classes, while thirty-six per cent are written in the 'inventory style'. A closer look at the evolution of the production of these catalogues shows that it was around 1730, when his annual production of catalogues was growing, that Martin began to make increasing use of the 'inventory style'. He regularly apologised for this or justified it in the prefaces of his catalogues. For example, in the catalogue of the library of the Abbé Fleury (1756), Martin invoked a lack of time: 'The circumstances of an inventory, and the necessity of clearing the accommodation occupied by the library, did not allow for drawing up a methodical catalogue of the books'.[21] In other cases, he insisted on the small size of the collection or on its homogenous nature:

> the limited extent of Mr. d'Hermand's cabinet ... inhibiting us from giving his books any arrangement other than that which they had on the shelves, we were obliged to follow the order and numbers of the inventory. But we have made an effort to describe the titles with precision, and to indicate the authors and the editions.[22]

It would seem, therefore, that the boom in public book sales from the 1740s onwards not only led to an increase in the number of printed catalogues, but also to an impoverishment of their quality, at least as far as the production of a specialist such as Martin was concerned. The end of the 1760s saw the emergence of a new type of catalogue that also favoured the 'inventory style'. These were lists bearing the title 'note' or 'notice', an expression that accentuates the summary nature of this type of catalogue. These generally only listed the most interesting or valuable items in the collection, for which they provided all kinds of details that might appeal to a bibliophile's taste.[23] As Figure 11.3 shows, their appearance can also be linked to the expansion of the second-hand book market.

---

21   'Les circonstances d'un Inventaire, & la nécessité de vuider le logement qu'occupoit la Bibliothéque, n'ont pas permis de faire un Catalogue méthodique des Livres'. *Catalogue des livres de feu monsieur l'abbé de Fleury* (Paris: Gabriel Martin, 1756).

22   'le peu d'étenduë du Cabinet de M. d'Hermand ... ne nous ayant pas permis de donner à ses Livres d'autre arrangement que celui qu'ils avoient dans les tablettes, nous avons été obligez de suivre l'ordre et les N° de l'Inventaire. Mais nous nous sommes attachez à en exposer les Titres avec précision, & à en marquer les Auteurs & les Editions'. *Catalogue des livres de feu M. d'Hermand* (Paris: Gabriel Martin, 1739).

23   The non-exhaustive nature of the description of the collections advertised in these catalogues is sometimes underlined by a specification in the title stating that the catalogue presents the 'principaux articles' of the library in question. Interestingly, the titles of contemporary (satirical) catalogues of imaginary libraries reflected this development in the layout of private library catalogues. See Helwi Blom, 'Van *Inventaris* tot *Notitie*:

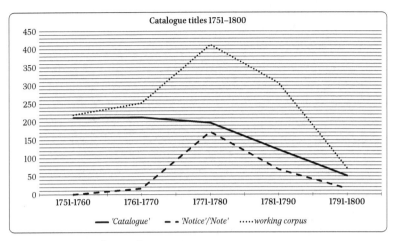

FIGURE 11.3   Catalogue titles 1751–1800

The analysis of the corpus thus leads us to suggest some nuances to the idea of a general diffusion of the Parisian booksellers' system in eighteenth-century France. Nevertheless, the research carried out by the MEDIATE team points to the fact that, compared to catalogues published in other European countries, French private library catalogues had an exceptional level of thematic organisation. In Dutch catalogues of the same period, classification by format and language was predominant, and if they provided some sort of subject classification, it seldom reached the level of standardisation and refinement achieved by French catalogues. The same applies to British catalogues. In addition to classification by format or language, sometimes in combination with classification by general subject matter, these often adopted a structure centred on the sales process, that is, the catalogue followed the order of the sessions. This is even the case for a number of catalogues compiled by the famous bookseller and auctioneer Samuel Paterson. When we compare the title pages of French sales catalogues with those of their British and Dutch equivalents, we see that, contrary to the latter, the French ones do not emphasise the commercial context of their publication. They note the date, time and address of the sale, but refrain from giving lengthy enumerations of items that might interest potential buyers, as well as from stating all kinds of practical details regarding the

---

ontwikkelingen in het genre van de imaginaire boekenlijst (*ca.* 1600–*ca.* 1800)', public lecture delivered at the occasion of the book launch of Anne-Pascale Pouey-Mounou and Paul J. Smith (eds.), *Early Modern Catalogues of Imaginary Books. A Scholarly Anthology* (Leiden: Brill, 2020), which took place in Leiden University Library, on 24 January 2020. The text and the slides can be found on my Academia page.

conditions of the sale. If these elements are already given, they are found in a notice inside the catalogue, as is the order of the sale.[24]

It is in fact thanks to the sophisticated nature of a good part of the private library catalogues published in France, that they were able to assume very diverse functions: as a commercial tool, a library management tool, a bibliographical reference tool, as a guide to the constitution of an ideal library, and as a tribute to a collection and its owner. French booksellers were well aware of this and the catalogue editors did not hesitate to boast about it when they thought it appropriate, as can be seen in the following statement in the catalogue of the collection of Denis-François Secousse (1755): 'This is not one of those common book catalogues, only intended to indicate the sale, and which become useless after it is over'.[25]

3   Bibliography and Philosophy, Two Conflicting Disciplines?

To what extent do these sophisticated thematically-arranged French catalogues reflect contemporary epistemological conceptions and discussions? To begin with Prosper Marchand and Gabriel Martin, the two booksellers who were responsible for the development of the Parisian booksellers' system, it is obvious that they attached great importance to a clear and well-reasoned order, but they did not justify the choices they made with arguments based on explicit philosophical reflection. However, the absence of reflection in the prefaces of the first catalogues designed according to the principles of the booksellers' system does not mean that the division of the catalogues into five classes, and the division of the classes into (multiple-level) sub-categories, was merely a matter of strictly formal and neutral logic. In fact, the system seems to refer to a hierarchical conception of knowledge, dependent on the order of precedence of the medieval university faculties (Theology, Law, Medicine and

---

24   In many cases, booksellers printed separate sheets announcing the date, the time and the order of the sale. These sheets were distributed and posted in the city where the sale took place.

25   'Ce n'est point ici un de ces Catalogues de Livres communs & ordinaires, uniquement destinés à en indiquer la Vente & qui restent sans utilité après qu'elle est terminée'. *Catalogue des livres de la bibliothèque de M. Secousse* (Paris: Barrois, 1755). This catalogue, which according to the author of the preface was based on a manuscript catalogue compiled by Secousse himself, is arranged according to the Parisian booksellers' system, but the five classes are presented in a slightly different order: Theology, Jurisprudence, History, *Belles-Lettres*, Sciences & Arts, the last category occupying only a very modest place in the collection as a whole. The text of the 'notice' was probably written by Secousse's brother and not by the bookseller Barrois himself, as Beckmann suggested.

the Arts), that was itself rooted in Christian epistemology: books of theology take up the first position, and within this class, editions of the Bible constitute the first category. In most catalogues, therefore, the first book mentioned is still the Bible. The class of theology is followed by two classes containing books belonging to the domain of the other main medieval faculties: Law and Medicine. A good part of the subjects belonging to the preparatory teaching provided by the Faculty of Arts is relayed at the end of the catalogue, in the classes of Humanities or *Belles-Lettres* and History.[26]

Despite the favourable reception of the first sales catalogues he had worked on, Prosper Marchand, who had been experimenting with the arrangement of catalogues from the beginning of his career, was not satisfied.[27] In 1709, before emigrating to the Dutch Republic, he published the catalogue of Joachim Faultrier's collection. This he organised according to principles explained in a preface entitled *Epitome systematis bibliographici*, in which he openly distanced himself from the five-class system and adopted an order that he considered more 'reasonable' and 'natural'. The system promulgated in this catalogue consists of three classes, namely Philosophy (*Scientia Humana*), Theology (*Scientia Divina*) and History (*Scientia Eventuum*). They were preceded by a preliminary class devoted to works of bibliography, and followed by an appendix containing dictionaries, miscellanea and other works on various subjects. Bibliography was thus the alpha and omega of this system based on a 'scientific' conception of book classification, in which there was no room for philosophical or ideological considerations concerning the pre-eminence of a particular discipline.[28] As for the position of theological books, Marchand observed in his *Remarques sur la Biblioteca Bultelliana* (1711) that 'it is only a question of arranging a library in the most convenient order that can be given to it, and not

---

26 For other hypotheses explaining the position of theology at the head of private library catalogues, see Valérie Neveu, 'La place de la Théologie dans les classifications bibliographiques françaises (XVIIe–XVIIIe s.)' (2009), shs.hal.science/halshs-00476355.

27 Marchand's working library contained, among other things, a copy of Louis Machon's treatise, which he had copied himself and provided with critical notes. Berkvens-Stevelinck, 'L'apport de Prosper Marchand', pp. 31–32.

28 *Cf. Catalogus librorum bibliothecæ domini Joachimi Faultrier* (Paris: Prosper Marchand and Jacques Quillau, 1709). On this catalogue, see Neveu, 'La place de la Théologie', and Ann-Marie Hansen, 'From private inventory to public catalogue. Prosper Marchand's *Catalogus librorum bibliothecae domini Joachimi Faultrier* and 'Epitome systematis bibliographici' (1709)', in Arthur der Weduwen, Andrew Pettegree and Graeme Kemp (eds.), *Book Trade Catalogues in Early Modern Europe* (Leiden: Brill, 2021), pp. 463–491.

of the respect that we must have for the Scriptures'.[29] This public revocation of the usual system did not, however, have any consequences for the cataloguing practices of his French colleagues, with whom he continued to maintain relations, at least for several years. Although the bibliographers of the time admired the *Epitome*, the Faultrier catalogue system was not reused in other printed catalogues.[30]

The '*système figuré de classification des connaissances humaines*' (the figurative classification system of human knowledge) published in 1751 in the first volume of the *Encyclopédie*, proposed a radical reorganisation of the tree of knowledge, based on the ideas of English philosopher Francis Bacon, who had classified the sciences according to the three faculties of human understanding: memory, reason and imagination.[31] French bookseller Michel-Antoine David urged his contemporaries to use this system, which gave only a subordinate, even dubious, place to theology, to develop a new, truly reasonable bibliographical taxonomy, which would leave nothing unclassified.[32] This suggested a neutral and 'scientific' approach, reminiscent of the one chosen by Prosper Marchand, but the tree of knowledge that was to serve as a model for the classifiers obviously represented a well-defined philosophical system. David the Elder also rejected the idea of the ideological arbitrariness of bibliographical classifications:

> The diversity of opinions on the order and divisions of a bibliographical system seems to prove that it is a rather arbitrary thing: however there must be one which really is in conformity with reason, and I think it is the one where subjects are arranged in the same order as the human mind has acquired knowledge of them; it is true that it takes a lot of philosophy to grasp this order and follow it. But I will not be afraid to say that the figurative system of human knowledge found at the beginning of the

---

29 'il ne s'agit icy que de disposer une *Bibliotheque* dans l'ordre le plus commode qu'on lui peut donner, et nullement du respect que nous devons avoir pour l'*Ecriture Ste*'. Berkvens-Stevelinck, 'Prosper Marchand: remarques sur la *Bibliotheca Bultelliana*', p. 96. See also Neveu, 'La place de la Théologie'.

30 *Cf.* Christiane Berkvens-Stevelinck, *Prosper Marchand, la vie et l'œuvre (1678–1756)* (Leiden: Brill, 1987), pp. 24–26.

31 In his *Systema bibliothecae collegii parisiensis Societatis Jesu* (1678), the Jesuit Jean Garnier, librarian at the Collège de Clermont, had already begun to develop, from the theory of the three faculties of the soul, a hierarchical classification system in four classes: theology (superior reason), philosophy (inferior reason), history (memory), and law or economics (social faculty). *Cf.* Neveu, 'L'inscription de la classification', pp. 2–5.

32 See, for example, Véronique Le Ru, 'De la science de Dieu à la superstition: un enchaînement de l'arbre encyclopédique qui donne à penser', *Recherches sur Diderot et sur l'Encyclopédie*, 40 (2006), pp. 67–76.

first Volume of this Book, can serve as an introduction and model for this work. Whomsoever will take the trouble to study it and compare it with the other systems, after comparing them with each other and observing their differences, will be able to push the divisions further, and to draw up a methodical plan or system, which will leave nothing indeterminate, and which will avoid the inconvenience of sometimes finding the same book in several different classes.[33]

Periodical articles and the dissertations written by members of the *Académies* testify to the fact that David's words were debated and his challenge was taken up by some librarians, but judging from the private library catalogues printed in the last decades of the eighteenth century, this appeal from a bookseller who had no expertise in the field of sales catalogues did not find an echo among his colleagues.[34] In the years following the publication of his article, Michel-Antoine David himself published two catalogues, but he followed the common classification system. My corpus contains only a handful of thematically organised catalogues which propose a classification that does not conform to the Parisian booksellers' system.[35]

Of all the editions I have seen, the catalogue of the collection of a certain Perrot, *maître des comptes*, published in 1776, is the first to present a completely new classification system, a peculiarity that the publishers did not fail to underscore on the title page and to discuss at length in the preface.[36]

---

33   'La diversité des opinions sur l'ordre & les divisions d'un système bibliographique, semble prouver que c'est une chose assez arbitraire: cependant il doit y en avoir un vraiment conforme à la raison, & je pense que c'est celui où les matieres sont rangées dans le même ordre que l'esprit humain en a acquis la connoissance; il est vrai qu'il faut beaucoup de philosophie pour saisir cet ordre & le suivre. Mais je ne craindrai point de dire que le système figuré des connoissances humaines que l'on trouve au commencement du premier Volume de cet Ouvrage, peut servir d'introduction & de modele à ce travail. Quiconque voudra prendre la peine de l'étudier & de le comparer aux autres systèmes, après les avoir comparés entr'eux & en avoir bien observé les différences, pourra pousser les divisions plus loin, & dresser un plan méthodique ou système, qui ne laissera plus rien d'indéterminé, & qui sauvera l'inconvénient de trouver quelquefois le même livre dans plusieurs classes différentes.' David, 'Catalogue'.

34   Regarding these initiatives, see the documentation gathered and discussed by Neveu, 'Classer les livres selon le *Système figuré des connaissances humaines*'.

35   The catalogues published by David are the *Catalogue des livres de feu M. Mandat, Maître des Requêtes* (1755), and the *Catalogue des livres de feu M. Maboul, maître des requêtes* (1758).

36   *Catalogue des livres et estampes de la bibliothèque de feu monsieur Perrot, maître des comptes; Disposé dans un Ordre différent de celui observé jusqu'à ce jour* (Paris: Gogué et Née de La Rochelle, 1776).

CATALOGUE

DES LIVRES ET ESTAMPES

DE LA BIBLIOTHEQUE

DE FEU

MONSIEUR PERROT,

MAITRE DES COMPTES;

Difposé dans un Ordre différent de celui obfervé jufqu'à ce jour.

Avec une Table des Auteurs.

La Vente fe fera en fa Maifon, rue & Ifle Saint-Louis, la premiere porte cochere au-deffus de la rue Regratiere, en entrant du côté du Pont-Rouge, le 22 Janvier 1776, & jours fuivans.

A PARIS;

Chez { GOGUÉ, Libraire, Quai des Auguftins, près le Pont Saint-Michel.
Et NÉE DE LA ROCHELLE, Libraire, même Quai.

M. DCC. LXXVI.

FIGURE 11.4   Catalogue Perrot 1776, Bibliothèque nationale de France, department of Littérature and Arts, Q-8300, title page

The initiative can probably be attributed to the younger of the two publishers, Jean-Baptiste Née de La Rochelle, who had become a bookseller in 1773. Since then, he had worked in association with his father-in-law, Jean-Baptiste Gogué. Née de La Rochelle had already contributed to some of the catalogues published by Gogué, but the Perrot catalogue was the first major sale which he could officially put to his name. In the catalogue's preface, the two editors stated that they were motivated by a desire to perfect bibliographical science by reforming a system that was respectable yet unsatisfactory from the point of view of logic.

This does not mean, however, that the classification system they presented was part of the reform project proposed by Michel-Antoine David. On the contrary, the first place of theology and especially of Catholic theology was consolidated. Firstly, to better distinguish Catholic theology from other religions, the catalogue introduced a new category: Orthodox Theology, which was put in parallel with the existing category of Heterodox Theologians. Secondly, by following Theology not with Jurisprudence but with Sciences & Arts, the catalogue established a direct link between theology on the one hand, and philosophy in its quality of the theology of the Ancients and the mother of sciences, on the other. Moreover, the authors insisted on the fact that they had not pushed their ideas, because they preferred clarity to the 'all the brilliance' of a philosophical system that would not be within the reach of the readers. The same concern to meet the expectations of a public accustomed to the five-class system had made them decide not to carry out their initial idea of reducing the number of main classes to three, namely Divine History, History of the Human Spirit, and History of Human Actions.[37]

This new system does not seem to have been received with any more enthusiasm than the appeal launched by David the Elder. The literary journals that announced the publication of the catalogue refrained from commenting on it, and it was not taken up by other booksellers. Its initiators themselves, who published several catalogues in the 1770s and 1780s, apparently did not want to repeat the experience. The bookseller René Merlin would later remark that 'in 1776, he [Née de La Rochelle] shook off the yoke with the classification of the beautiful library of M. Perrot, master of accounts. Unfortunately, he lacked the perseverance to continue the struggle, and he let himself fall back into the old

---

37   This rejected classification bears a strong resemblance to the one defined by Prosper Marchand in the Catalogue Faultrier (1709): *Scienta humana seu Philosophia, Scientia divina seu Theologia, Scientia eventuum seu Historia.*

way, frightened by the weight of habit. And perhaps he had not let his system mature enough'.[38]

It was not until the revolutionary period that a catalogue that met the wishes expressed by Michel-Antoine David was published in France. This was the catalogue of the collection of Honoré-Gabriel Riquetti (1749–1791), Count of Mirabeau, a member of the Constituent Assembly. The catalogue divides the books into three classes, modelled on the Baconian tri-partition of the faculties of human understanding, the class of *Belles-Lettres*, associated with imagination, the class of Sciences & Arts, associated with reason, and the class of History, associated with memory.[39] The first two traditional classes, Theology and Jurisprudence, which for some represented the pillars on which the *Ancien Régime* rested, were integrated into the Sciences & Arts category, itself copied on the model of the figurative system, and thus lost their predominant position.[40] In the process, the word 'theology' was replaced by the more neutral term 'religion'.

---

38 'en 1776, il [Née de La Rochelle] secoua le joug dans le classement de la belle bibliothèque de M. Perrot, maître des comptes. Malheureusement la persévérance lui manqua pour prolonger la lutte, et il se laissa retomber dans la vieille voie, effrayé par les résistances de la coutume. Peut-être aussi n'avait-il pas assez mûri son système'. *Cf.* the *Catalogue des livres composant la bibliothèque de feu M. Née de La Rochelle* (Paris: R. Merlin, 1839). Née de La Rochelle produced no less than sixty private library catalogues, some of them on his own, others in collaboration with colleagues.

39 *Catalogue des livres de la bibliothèque de feu M. Mirabeau l'aîné* (Paris: Rozet and Belin junior, 1791). The order of the three main categories differs from that used in the figurative system in the *Encyclopédie*: Imagination-Reason-Memory instead of Memory-Reason-Imagination. The class of *Belles-Lettres* that opens the catalogue contains the fewest items.

40 *Cf.* in this context also the curious preface of a catalogue of 1791–1792 presenting a collection of books from the fifteenth century which is said to have belonged to Father Maugérard: 'Nous savons que, si un jour on entreprend l'histoire des Français, au lieu de l'histoire des rois de France, on ne la fera jamais bien sans connoître de quoi les Français s'occupoient, et on ne le saura que dans des livres composés dans les siècles dont on écrira l'histoire; on y trouvera le principe de leur asservissement dans l'avilissement de leur esprit qu'on accabloit de futilités. On y remarquera que, lorsqu'un homme osoit s'écarter des opinions reçues, il ne manquait pas de sectateurs' (We know that, if one day someone should undertake to write the history of the French, instead of the history of the kings of France, one will not do it well without knowing what the French were occupied with, and this can only be found in books written in the centuries one is writing about; one will find there the principle of their enslavement in the debasement of their spirit which was overwhelmed with trivialities. One will see that, when a man dared to depart from received opinions, he did not lack followers). *Notice de livres rares,*

It is rather curious that, contrary to Née de La Rochelle and Gogué, the two politically-engaged booksellers responsible for the sale of Mirabeau's library and the publication of the printed catalogue, François II Belin and Benoît Rozet, did not seek to draw attention to this extraordinary classification. This might indicate that they were not the ones who designed it. This impression is reinforced by the fact that the preface referred to a project of Mirabeau's to create an annotated catalogue of his library. To this end, Mirabeau had already gathered a team of literary people who were to work on it:

> Mirabeau ... also wanted the Catalogue of his Library to be a work of literature and a bibliographical manual; several People of Letters were to work on it, each in the genre that concerned them; for him, his part was to guide and establish a kind of harmony between the different collaborators. He was already making the necessary preparations for this undertaking.[41]

Even if the authors of the preface said nothing specific about the inventor of the classification, it seems plausible that Mirabeau himself was the author. Valérie Neveu has put forward the tempting hypothesis that the idea

---

la plupart imprimés dans le quinzième siècle, dont la vente se fera ... le 16 janvier 1792 (Paris: Leclerc, s.d.).

41 'Mirabeau ... vouloit encore que le Catalogue de sa Bibliothèque fût tout ensemble un ouvrage de littérature et un manuel bibliographique; plusieurs Gens de Lettres devoient y travailler, chacun dans le genre qui l'auroit concerné; pour lui, son partage étoit de guider et d'établir une espèce d'harmonie entre les différens Collaborateurs. Déja même il s'occupoit des préparatifs nécessaires à cette entreprise'. See also a letter from the German composer Johann Friedrich Reichardt dated March 14, 1792, which contains a passage that seems to paraphrase part of the preface to the catalogue: 'J'ai su trop tard le jour de la vente de l'importante bibliothèque de Mirabeau. Il est remarquable que ... cet homme ... ait trouvé le temps de s'occuper de sa bibliothèque. Il voulait augmenter dans tous les domaines de la science celle qu'il avait héritée de son père, faire relier les plus belles éditions et ouvrir sa bibliothèque au public; il avait commencé de grands achats de livres et surveillait lui-même le classement et le catalogue'. (I heard too late about the date of the sale of Mirabeau's important library. It is remarkable that ... this man ... found the time to take care of his library. He wanted to increase in all fields of science the one he had inherited from his father, to have the most beautiful editions bound and to open his library to the public; he had begun large purchases of books and was himself overseeing the filing and cataloguing). Arthur Laquiante (ed.), *Un prussien en France en 1792 (Strasbourg-Lyon-Paris); lettres intimes de J.F. Reichardt* (Paris: Perrin et Cie, 1892), p. 286. Rozet had already published several private library catalogues before 1791, but all of these seem to have been organised according to the usual system of the five classes.

xvj TABLE
Polygraphes Italiens, page 96
Polygraphes Anglais, 97
Mélanges Littéraires et Dissertations variées, 98
Dialogues, 99

ÉPISTOLAIRES. ibid.
Épistolaires Grecs et Latins, ibid.
Épistolaires Français et Anglais, 101

SCIENCES ET ARTS.

PHILOSOPHIE.

Introduction et Histoire de la Philosophie, 103
Philosophes anciens, Grecs et Latins. ibid.
Philosophes modernes, Latins, Français et Anglais, 105

LOGIQUE. 107

MÉTAPHYSIQUE. ibid.
Traités généraux et Principes de Métaphysique, ibid.
Traités particuliers sur la Divinité, sur l'Origine du bien et du mal, 108
Traités particuliers sur l'Ame, sur son immortalité, etc. 109
Traités particuliers sur l'Esprit de l'Homme, sur son intelligence et ses facultés, ibid.
Traités singuliers de Métaphysique, concernant les Animaux, 111
Mélanges de Métaphysique, ibid.
Traités particuliers sur la Chiromancie, les Divinations, Augures, Songes, Enchantemens, Sortilèges, Magie, etc. 112

RELIGION.

RELIGION CATHOLIQUE. 113
Textes et Versions de l'Ecriture-Sainte, Bibles appellées Polyglottes, etc. ibid.
Concordes

FIGURE 11.5A Catalogue Mirabeau 1791, Bibliothèque nationale de France, Arsenal library, 8-H-25167, table of divisions

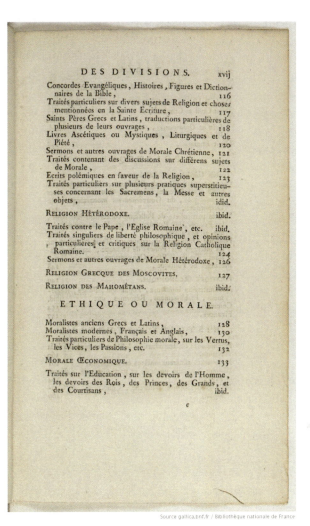

FIGURE 11.5B Catalogue Mirabeau 1791, Bibliothèque nationale de France, Arsenal library, 8-H-25167, table of divisions

of experimenting with Bacon's classification was suggested to Mirabeau by his friend Pierre-Jean-Georges Cabanis, who was familiar with the catalogue that diplomat and future American president Thomas Jefferson had drawn up according to the French model of the *Système figuré*.[42]

Another possibility that might be worth considering is that of a hypothetical influence of librarian and bibliographer Jean-Joseph Rive. Father Rive was obsessed with developing a bibliographical system 'in keeping with the most natural picture of the sciences and the arts'.[43] In 1774, he spoke of it in the following terms: 'I do not follow any known division … I am rectifying the genealogical depiction of the arts and sciences which is at the beginning of the *Encyclopédie*, and I criticise the arrangements of all French, Italian, German and Spanish catalogues. I have dreamt of this system for more than 20 years'.[44] At the time of his death, in October 1791, he had not yet published his plan, but his library was already arranged according to this unpublished system.[45] Rive and Mirabeau also knew each other. In 1789, Rive had strongly supported Mirabeau's candidacy for the election of the deputies of the *Sénéchaussée* of Aix-en-Provence to the General Assembly; according to Rive, before leaving for Versailles, Mirabeau had asked permission to come and see him to thank him for this support. It is possible that on that occasion Mirabeau took a look at the library and the catalogue of the learned abbot.[46] His contemporaries could have gotten an idea of Rive's ideal classification by leafing through the printed catalogue of the books of the famous singer Pierre de Jélyotte that Rive had compiled at the request of bookseller Jean-Claude Molini, even if Rive later accused the bookseller of having 'falsified' and 'corrupted' his system.[47]

---

42   Valérie Neveu, 'Classer les livres selon le *Système figuré des connaissances humaines*. La bibliographie en Révolution: une deuxième chance pour la classification encyclopédiste?', *Recherches sur Diderot et sur l'Encyclopédie*, 49 (2014), pp. 213–214. It should be noted, however, that the categories used in the Mirabeau catalogue are far from corresponding exactly to those of the Jefferson catalogue.

43   'conforme au tableau le plus naturel des sciences et des arts'. Letter dated 18–11–1786, quoted in François Moureau, 'L'abbé Rive ou l'homme-bibliothèque: une "physiologie" provençale', *Babel*, 6 (2002), pp. 105–125.

44   'Je ne suis aucune division connue … Je redresse le tableau généalogique des arts et des sciences qui est à la tête de l'*Encyclopédie*, et je critique l'arrangement de tous les catalogues français, italiens, allemands, espagnols … Je rêve à ce système depuis plus de 20 ans'. Moureau, 'L'abbé Rive'.

45   According to the compilers of the printed catalogue of his library (1793).

46   Jean-Joseph Rive, *Lettre des vénérables freres anti-politiques et de l'abbé Rive, présentée à MM. les commissaires du Roi* (Nosopolis [= Aix-en-Provence]: chez les Frères de la Miséricorde, [1791]).

47   [Jean-Joseph Rive], *Chronique littéraire des ouvrages imprimés et manuscrits de l'abbé Rive* (Éleutheropolis [= Aix-en Provence]: De l'imprimerie des Anti-Copet …, l'an 2^{ond} du nouveau siècle françois [1791]), p. 170. In the form in which it has been transmitted to

According to Valérie Neveu, the classification built on the tripartite division Bibliography – Sciences – Letters proposed around 1794 by the Marseille based librarian Claude-François Achard, who took hold of the manuscripts left by Jean-Joseph Rive, was invented by the late bibliographer.[48] If this is the case, our theory is not tenable, because Achard's system differed significantly from the one chosen for the sales catalogue of the Mirabeau collection, at least at the level of its main divisions.

In any case, neither of these two projects seems to have had an impact on printed (private) library catalogues. So far, I have identified only three other catalogues based on the classification used in the Mirabeau catalogue. The first, dating from 1793, was also issued by Benoît Rozet and presented the collection of the author Charles-Simon Favart. The bookseller Rozet had indeed enthusiastically embraced the revolutionary cause and he was eager to apply his ideals in the field of bibliography. In 1790, he had already written a treatise on the *True origin of ecclesiastical goods. Historical and curious fragments, containing the different ways in which the secular and regular clergy of France became enriched, accompanied by historical and critical notes*, and he was also the author of a *Familiar Conversation between a man of letters and a former bookseller, on the project to remove coats of arms and other marks of feudal ownership stamped on the binding from all the books in the National Library*.[49] He did not hesitate to ask the Committee of Public Instruction to finance the publication of this book.[50] The note to the reader of the Favart catalogue remains silent,

---

us, this catalogue, with the title *Catalogue des livres latins, françois, italiens, espagnols et anglois provenans du cabinet de M.J.*** * (Paris: J.C. Molini, 1783), presents an original, albeit unclear, classification into seven 'faculties': Theology, Jurisprudence, Philosophy, Medicine, Mathematics, Arts, and 'Facultés réunies', subdivided into chapters, sections, numbers and 'distinctions'.

48 See Claude-François Achard, *Cours élémentaire de bibliographie*, vol. 1 (Marseille: Joseph Achard Fils et Compagnie, 1806), p. 11, and Neveu, 'Classer les livres selon le *Système figuré*', 2014, p. 218.

49 *Cf.* Benoît Rozet, *Véritable origine des biens ecclésiastiques. Fragmens historiques et curieux, contenant les différentes voies par lesquelles le clergé séculier et régulier de France s'est enrichi, accompagnés de notes historiques et critiques* (Paris: Desenne, 1790), and idem, *Conversation familière entre un homme de lettres et un ancien libraire, sur le projet de supprimer les armoiries et autres marques de propriété féodale, empreintes sur la reliure de tous les livres de la Bibliothèque nationale* (S.l.: s.n., [1793–1794]).

50 *Cf.* James Guillaume (ed.), *Procès-verbaux du Comité d'instruction publique de la Convention nationale au Comité du Salut Public*, vol. IV (Paris: Imprimerie Nationale, 1901), p. 24. Rozet also seems to be the author of an anonymous dissertation dated around 1793–1794 pleading in favour of a system of classification suppressing the classes of Theology and Jurisprudence, these 'two parasitic branches [of the tree of knowledge, HB] which the spirit of the Revolution has dried up'. Text quoted in Neveu, 'Classer les livres selon le *Système figuré*', 2014, p. 216.

however, on the re-use of the bibliographical system of the sales catalogue of Mirabeau's library. I do not know of any other catalogues published by Rozet, who seems to have left the book trade towards the end of 1793.

The two other catalogues using the Baconian system as published in the Mirabeau catalogue also date from 1793.[51] Their appearance was the work of another bookseller won over to revolutionary doctrines, Philippe Denné, known as Denné the Elder. Like Rozet, he did not consider it necessary to comment on his choice of bibliographical system. As for the catalogue of Abbé Rive's collection, which also appeared in 1793, it was in a way the final nail in the coffin of the author of *La Chasse aux bibliographes et antiquaires malavisés* (1789). After his death, his library had been acquired by two freemasons from Marseille, Pierre Chauffard and Nicolas-Étienne Colomby, a former auctioneer, who had it catalogued by another member of one of the Marseille lodges, the secretary of the Academy of Marseille, Claude-François Achard. Achard did not use the particular system of the abbot, but instead followed the usual classification of what Rive called the 'bad catalogues of Paris'.[52] He apologised for this in the preface, explaining that at the time he compiled the catalogue, he did not have at his disposal the 'curious manuscripts' that the abbot had written on this 'interesting subject'.[53]

While the lack of interest in Mirabeau's classification system may have been due to the fact that he was disgraced shortly after his death, the apparent indifference of editors and publishers of private library catalogues to projects aiming at reforming the extant system is no less surprising. Indeed, during the revolutionary period and the *Directoire*, there was an extraordinary discrepancy between the abundance of ideas and discussions on renewing the French bibliographical system on the one hand, and the stability of the practices of the editors of printed catalogues on the other.[54]

---

51 These two catalogues were issued for sales that took place in April and July 1793.

52 See his letter to Joseph David, a bookseller in Aix-en-Provence, dated 16 July 1765: 'Tu es trop habitué à nos mauvais catalogues de Paris pour ne pas goûter l'ordre merveilleux de celui du comte de Bunaw' (You are too familiar with our bad Parisian catalogues, not to appreciate the marvellous order in the catalogue of the Count of Bunaw). Quoted in Moureau, 'L'abbé Rive'.

53 On this remark, which seems contradictory to the one in the *Cours de bibliographie* quoted above, and on Achard's negotiations with Rive's heirs, see Anna Delle Foglie and Francesca Manzari, *Riscoperta e riproduzione della miniatura in Francia nel Settecento. L'abbé Rive e l'"Essai sur l'art de vérifier l'âge des miniatures des manuscrits"* (Rome: Gangemi, 2016), pp. 76–78.

54 See Neveu, 'Classer les livres selon le *Système figuré*', 2014, pp. 214–220. *Cf.* also the articles written by Antoine Destutt de Tracy in the *Gazette nationale ou Moniteur universel* of 29 and 30 October 1797.

Among the catalogues of private collections published between 1794 and 1800, I have not found a single one that draws on the figurative system of knowledge or that proposes a new thematic classification. During these years, when the importance of theological and legal books in (the catalogues of) private libraries declined significantly, books were generally still classified according to the Parisian booksellers' system, even if this meant that the first two classes contained very few articles.[55] The Lyon bookseller Jean-François de Los-Rios was the exception that confirms the rule when he explained in one of his catalogues that the scarcity of books on theology and law had made him decide not to use the five-classes system. He did not, however, decide to use another subject classification, but he arranged the books according to the days of the sale.[56] In an essay on bibliography printed in 1790, abbé R. Duclos even appropriated the text describing Gabriel Girard's original system as it had appeared in the *Encyclopédie*'s article 'Catalogue', to give a philosophical foundation to the 'traditional' Parisian booksellers' system![57]

It should be noted, however, that at the level of the sub-divisions, the catalogues using the Parisian booksellers' system show quite significant variations. Over the course of the century, unprecedented headings such as 'new philosophers', 'education' or 'treatises of civil government' appeared, while others such as 'Italian stories' and 'Transylvania' disappeared.[58] The customary system thus attested, in its own way, to the changing perceptions, attitudes and interests of the contemporary public.

4 Conclusion

The evolution of the production of printed catalogues of private collections and that of the classification of the books they contain show that the wish of Louis Machon, Michel-Antoine David and others, to see the creation and general adoption of a truly 'philosophical' system of book classification, was not realised in eighteenth-century France, at least not in this important category

---

55 *Cf.* Beckmann, *Französische Privatbibliotheken*, pp. 79–83, and Marion, *Collections et collectionneurs*, pp. 135–140.

56 'Avis', in *Catalogue d'une riche collection des livres de la bibliotheque de feu son excellence M. le Marquis Sacchetti. et ceux de M. le Chevalier Wilmann* (Lyon: s.n., 1783).

57 [Abbé R. Duclos], *Dictionnaire bibliographique, historique et critique, des livres rares*, vol. 3 (Paris: Cailleau et fils, 1790), pp. 505–510.

58 See the overviews in Beckmann's *Französische Privatbibliotheken*.

of catalogues.[59] In this respect, the words of librarian Barthélemy Mercier de Saint-Léger, who in 1760 criticised the first draft of a catalogue inspired by the *Encyclopédie*'s figurative system, could be considered prophetic:

> A library catalogue is neither an Encyclopaedia nor a hierarchically organised tree of human knowledge; the main merit of a production of this nature consists in a distinction of Classes, divisions &c. so clear and palpable that it is immediately apparent in which Class & under which division one can find the book one is looking for; there is no need for metaphysical systems to determine the order of these divisions; Bibliography is independent of differing opinions as to how the human mind acquires its knowledge ... We have today ... an excellent bibliographical system, & I doubt whether the advantages to be gained from the most truly philosophical method can compensate for the inconvenience of abandoning the one in use.[60]

This seems to characterise the attitude of the editors and publishers of private library catalogues printed in France in the eighteenth century.

As for factors that could explain the failure of initiatives aimed at the imposition of a new order of ideas on the organisation of books in eighteenth-century France, I subscribe to Valérie Neveu's hypothesis that it is due to a fundamental incompatibility between two different visions of classification and the tasks

---

59   While serious efforts were made to introduce the Baconian system in public and institutional (school) libraries, most of these projects did not result in the publication of a real (printed) catalogue. See Neveu, 'Classer les livres selon le Système figuré', 2014, pp. 214–220.

60   'Un catalogue de Bibliothèque n'est ni une Encyclopédie, ni un arbre gradué des connoissances humaines; le principal mérite d'une production de cette nature consiste dans une distinction des Classes, divisions &c. si claire et si palpable qu'on voit sur le champ à quelle Classe & sous quelle division doit se trouver un Livre dont on a besoin; il est inutile d'avoir recours à des systêmes métaphysiques pour diriger l'ordre de ces divisions; la Bibliographie est indépendante des opinions différentes sur la manière dont l'esprit humain acquiert ses connoissances ... Nous avons aujourd'hui ... un excellent système bibliographique, & je doute que les avantages qu'on retireroit de la méthode la plus véritablement Philosophique, pussent entrer en compensation avec les désagrémens que l'on éprouveroit en abandonnant celle qui est en usage'. [Barthélemy Mercier], 'Suite des observations en forme d'une lettre sur l'essai sur un catalogue de bibliothèque &c.', *Journal encyclopédique*, VIII/2 (December 1760), pp. 131–132. The catalogue he criticised had been designed by the Abbé Montlinot, assistant librarian at the library of the collegiate church of Saint-Pierre in Lille. See Neveu, 'Classer les livres selon le *Système figuré des connaissances humaines*', 2013, pp. 214–215.

of bibliography, rather than to a 'conservative', or even reactionary attitude on the side of bibliographers. If projects aimed at developing a new classification system according to a philosophical method did not impact upon library catalogues printed in France in the Age of Enlightenment, it was probably because their abstract nature and the objective of applying a well-defined theory to variable collections, often consisting of a diverse mass of books of all times and genres, were obstacles to successful practical implementation. It seems plausible that is was precisely the flexibility of the Parisian booksellers' system, particularly at the sub-divisional level, that helped to ensure the longevity of this classification system.

With regard to printed private library catalogues, I believe that the commercial aspect of a large part of these catalogues should also be taken into account, in the sense that they were intended for a public of potential buyers. From this point of view, it was extremely important to accommodate readers by organising catalogues in a way that would help them find easily what they might be looking for. As the editors of the Perrot catalogue understood very well, making changes to a well-known classification system presented a risk. The book trade therefore preferred stability in classification practices to a bibliographical reform reflecting the progress of the Enlightenment.

CHAPTER 12

Sir Hans Sloane's Collection of Books and Manuscripts: an Enlightenment Library?

Alexandra Ortolja-Baird

Sir Hans Sloane is often presented as the embodiment of the Enlightenment and its concerns for rationalisation, classification and progress. A royal physician, Secretary and President of both the Royal Society and the Royal College of Physicians, and contributor to the *Philosophical Transactions*, Sloane was, as Arthur Macgregor has argued, an *éminence grise* of scientific society in early Enlightenment London.[1] Behind closed doors, Sloane, an omnivorous and prolific collector of books, manuscripts, objects of natural history, antiquities, fossils and much else, amassed a private cabinet which exceeded most others of the age in its size, diversity and scientific ambition. This encyclopaedic collection, its rigorous documentation, use by key figures in the history of scientific advancement, and contribution to the publication of one of the period's most important works of natural history, Sloane's own *Voyage to Jamaica*, set him apart as a figure who not only collected the world but sought to order, document and understand it.

However, the richness and diversity of Sloane's activities is a double-edged sword. As James Delbourgo has remarked, 'curators and scholars have differed over whether Sloane was a harbinger of the Enlightenment or the kind of figure the Enlightenment, in its dedication to systematic rational classification, had to sweep away'.[2] While some interpret Sloane's collecting practices as encapsulating the spirit of Enlightenment, others situate these same patterns firmly within the context of early modern cabinets of curiosities and their culture of opulence, excess, and social positioning.[3] This latter view was espoused by many of Sloane's contemporaries who mocked the unscientific virtuoso tastes

---

1 Arthur MacGregor, 'Sir Hans Sloane, *eminence grise* of early Enlightenment London', presentation transcript.
2 James Delbourgo, *Collecting the world: the life and curiosity of Hans Sloane* (London: Penguin Books, 2018), p. *xx*.
3 Roy Porter, *The Creation of the Modern World: The Untold Story of the British Enlightenment* (New York: Norton, 2000), p. 239.

underpinning his 'nicknackatory'.[4] In between these two polarised interpretations are those which view Sloane's collections and collecting practices as representative of the final transition from private cabinets to national museums, situating him somewhere in the passage from pre-modernity to modernity. Between his birth in 1660, the year of the Restoration, and his death in 1753, the year of the creation of The British Museum, Sir Hans Sloane witnessed significant societal change brought about by global expansion and imperialism, the growth of the book trade, the new ideas of the Enlightenment, changing views on sociability, and the rise of the public sphere, among many other developments. His collection duly reflected this amorphous, shifting landscape, blurring the boundaries of the Baroque and the Modern. This porousness is no less visible in his library. Bequeathed to the nation in 1753 along with the rest of his cabinet to become a foundation of The British Museum, Sloane's vast collection of books and manuscripts similarly traversed the characteristics of the courtly libraries of the seventeenth century and the public library culture that came to fruition in the late eighteenth century. It was, in many respects, both precursor and product of the Enlightenment.

There are many ways in which we might begin to untangle the interactions of Sloane's library with the Enlightenment. It would not take great effort, for instance, to locate the Enlightenment on the shelves of Sloane's library. Voltaire, Locke, Spinoza and other Enlightenment titans sat side by side with works on the newest scientific discoveries, economic theories and political treatises of the era. Yet, as in any good library, it would be just as easy to find the Renaissance, Classical Greece and Rome, and the Reformation on those same shelves. This chapter will consequently focus less on what Sloane collected and where it came from, and instead explore his practices of library organisation and formation within the context of late seventeenth- and early eighteenth-century English private library culture.[5] In so doing, it will reflect more broadly on how the ways in which collectors organised and arranged their books inform us about the shifting perceptions regarding the purposes of books and libraries. In the age of Enlightenment, when debates about the

---

4 See: Barbara M. Benedict, 'From Benefactor to Entrepreneur: Sloane's Literary Reputation 1685–1800', in Alison Walker, Arthur MacGregor and Michael Hunter (eds.), *From Books to Bezoars: Sir Hans Sloane and His Collections* (London: British Library, 2012), pp. 33–40.
5 For the contents of Sloane's library see: Giles Mandelbrote, 'Sloane and the preservation of printed ephemera', in Giles Mandelbrote and Barry Taylor (eds.), *Libraries Within the Library: The Origins of the British Library's Printed Collections* (London: British Library, 2009), pp. 146–170; Alison Walker, 'Collecting Knowledge: Annotated Material in the Library of Sir Hans Sloane', in Vera Keller, Ann-Marie Roos and Elizabeth Yale (eds.), *Archival Afterlives* (Leiden: Brill, 2019), pp. 222–240.

order of knowledge and the role of books and learning were at the fore, to what extent were private book collectors trying or even able to usher in this new thinking through their own libraries? And how did figures like Sloane interpret the interaction between libraries, books, and the Enlightenment? Moreover, is this engagement with Enlightenment ideas what defines an 'Enlightenment library'? Or are there other factors that determine this category, if it is truly a category at all? Through exploring Sloane's approaches to building, organising, and managing his library, which were shaped by both the genre of librarianship literature and the library practices of his peers, this chapter will offer four readings of the early Enlightenment library as a distinct entity, though one which manifested itself in many different shapes and forms.

1   What Is an 'Enlightenment' Library?

The important role played by libraries in the Enlightenment is unquestioned. Heralded as 'factories of Enlightenment', the 'workshop of the early Enlightenment both moderate and radical', and the 'material' of Enlightenment, late seventeenth- and eighteenth-century libraries have been viewed as paramount to the Enlightenment project: 'without Enlightenment there might still be libraries, but without libraries there can be no Enlightenment'.[6] Variously speaking of 'Libraries in the Enlightenment', 'Libraries of the Enlightenment', 'Enlightenment Libraries', 'Libraries during the Enlightenment', 'Libraries and the Enlightenment', and 'the Enlightenment in Libraries', among other incarnations of this pairing, scholarship to date has emphasised the unique connection between these two entities, exploring this relationship in diverse contexts ranging from private professional libraries, to university libraries, and Islamic and Oriental libraries, to name but a few.[7] Whether interpreting 'Enlightenment'

---

6 Respectively: K. A. Manley, 'Infidel Books and "Factories of the Enlightenment": Censorship and Surveillance in Subscription and Circulating Libraries in an Age of Revolutions, 1790–1850', *Book History*, vol. 19, 2016, pp. 169–196; Jonathan Israel, *Radical Enlightenment: Philosophy and the Making of Modernity 1650–1750* (Oxford: Oxford University Press, 2003), p. *vii.*; Chad Wellmon, *Organizing Enlightenment: Information Overload and the Invention of the Modern Research University* (Baltimore, MD: Johns Hopkins University Press, 2016); Wayne Bivens-Tatum, *Libraries and the Enlightenment* (Los Angeles: Library Juice Press, 2012), p. 45.

7 Gina Dahl, *Libraries and Enlightenment: Eighteenth-Century Norway and the Outer World* (Aarhus: Aarhus University Press, 2014); Bivens-Tatum, *Libraries and the Enlightenment*; Karen Baston, *Charles Areskine's Library: Lawyers and Their Books at the Dawn of the Scottish Enlightenment* (Leiden: Brill, 2016); Wellmon, *Organizing Enlightenment*; Alexander Bevilacqua, *The Republic of Arabic Letters: Islam and the European Enlightenment*, (Harvard: Harvard University Press, 2018).

as a form of periodisation; as a specific ideology embracing universality, reason and progress, and whose legacy still shapes modern libraries; or as a canon of books, this literature treats libraries and the Enlightenment as part of a continuous, cyclical feedback loop. However, what was it about these libraries that facilitated the foment of the Enlightenment? What makes them recognisable as tools of the Enlightenment, and how did they differ from the Renaissance or Baroque library? Which common threads can be found running through the dramatically different forms of libraries in this period (subscription libraries, circulating libraries, proprietary libraries, private libraries etc.)? Moreover, how did the Enlightenment manifest itself in these libraries?

Despite the universal acceptance of the library as a harbinger of Enlightenment, the interaction between libraries in the late seventeenth and eighteenth centuries and the Enlightenment as a phenomenon comprising a complex and diverse set of ideas, practices, sites, persons and objects has yet to be fully examined. Embedded in this issue are not only questions as to what defines the Enlightenment and how many Enlightenments we might speak of, but also early modern conceptual discussions regarding what constituted a library, and how we interpret them today. With such debates still ongoing, there is good reason to argue that the term 'Enlightenment Library' and its variations might be more reductive than useful. Yet, stepping away from concerns for classification and building upon scholarship from book history and Enlightenment studies, above all approaches examining history from below, we can use this device to map out some of the multifarious interactions between libraries and Enlightenment(s). The importance of dissecting the connections between books, their spatialization, and society writ large in this way, was famously underlined by Roger Chartier in his claims that no 'order of discourse' is separable from the contemporaneous 'order of books'.[8] Inverting Chartier's dictum, Garrett's claims that 'the order of books cannot be understood without reference to the order of discourse of which it is both a part and an expression', likewise illustrate the necessity of reinserting the library into its broader context.[9]

In her 2019 paper for the USTC History of the Book Conference, Alicia Montoya suggested a typology of ways in which we might frame the Enlightenment library, based upon her research within the MEDIATE project. It might refer to: 1.) period (early, high, late Enlightenment); 2.) owners (famous figures of the

---

8 Roger Chartier, *Forms and Meanings: Texts, Performances, and Audiences from Codex to Computer* (Philadelphia: University of Pennsylvania Press, 1995), p. 23.
9 Jeffrey Garrett, 'Redefining Order in the German Library, 1775–1825', *Eighteenth-Century Studies*, vol. 33, no. 1 (1999), p. 103.

Enlightenment); 3.) the composition of the collection (*bibliothèque choisie*); 4.) the knowledge organisation system used; 5.) its contents (subversive, radical, middlebrow); and 6.) its use.[10] It helpfully outlined the diversity of readings we might have of the Enlightenment in, of, and around the library, and vice versa, and the lenses through which we might interpret them. From this perspective, the reality that the *Bibliothèque du Roi* bore little resemblance to the private library of John Locke, or local German subscription libraries, only helps to recover the complexity of the library-Enlightenment dynamic. With this diversity in mind, I will use Sir Hans Sloane's Library to offer four additional ways of approaching the Enlightenment library in the late seventeenth and early eighteenth centuries, which take into consideration further social, cultural and epistemological dimensions of the Enlightenment:

1) The Enlightenment library was formed and evolved as a collaborative endeavour. This was not purely due to the expected reciprocity of exchange as part of the sociability of the Republic of Letters and the 'protocols of friendship', but was a practical solution intended to overcome issues of information overload and logistics such as geography, trade restrictions, and resource imbalances.[11] Additionally, this collaboration was often indirect as individuals built upon the efforts of peers by recycling and repurposing their bibliographic and library materials and approaches.

2) Digging down into the knowledge organisation system used in libraries, the Enlightenment library can be considered as a site of knowledge creation, not just a location where knowledge was ordered. This is evidenced by the widely varying projects of classification and organisation in individual libraries.

3) The Enlightenment library can be defined by the interaction between books and objects that took place within and beyond its walls. Although the *Wunderkammer* was no longer in its ascendancy, objects and books continued to be interpreted as relational and had not been strictly separated, as would occur in the libraries of the nineteenth century and continues to the present day.

---

10 Alicia Montoya, "What is an Enlightenment Library?" [conference presentation]. USTC History of the Book Conference: *Crisis or Enlightenment? Developments in the Book Trade (1650–1750)*, University of St Andrews, 20–22 June 2019.

11 Justin Champion, *Republican Learning: John Toland and the Crisis of Christian Culture, 1696–1722* (Manchester: Manchester University Press, 2003), p. 34.

4) Expanding on the category of library use, the Enlightenment Library can be read as conveying a clear concern for its purpose and legacy. With the growth of the public sphere and the shifting boundary between private and public, attitudes towards the library were similarly evolving.

There are, of course, many other ways in which we might interpret the Enlightenment library. Moreover, it is important to note that these elements were not necessarily unique to the Enlightenment, but were often a continuation or evolution of practices that were part of a longer trajectory of library history. Nonetheless, as the case of Hans Sloane will demonstrate, their co-occurrence can be read as characteristic of a specific turning point in the history of English private libraries.

2   Hans Sloane's Library and Library Catalogues

Sir Hans Sloane's library is estimated to have held 50,000 volumes of printed books, prints, drawings and manuscripts.[12] Few English contemporaries could boast such a prolific collection. The libraries of John Locke (3,500 volumes), John Evelyn (5,000 titles), Samuel Pepys (3,600 titles) and Robert Hooke (2,500 volumes), though large for the period, paled in comparison. Only the Harleian library – the product of multiple generations of Harleys – could match it in number of printed books. The diversity of Sloane's library was equally unparalleled. No discipline or genre went unrepresented: medicine, religion, history, the occult – all were present. Pouring over his shelves one would find fourteenth-century manuscripts of the *Canterbury Tales*, albums of prints and drawings by the likes of Dürer and Maria Sibylla Merian, *Horti Sicci*, contemporary medical advertisements, and theological dissertations, as well as books in languages ranging from classical Latin and Hebrew to Icelandic, Basque, Japanese and Algonquin.

The organisation of Sloane's library has understandably attracted less attention than these splendid contents. Nonetheless, the vital, though limited number of works on this topic have uncovered fascinating aspects of Sloane's information management system, such as his complex system of cataloguing, the interaction between his bibliographical materials and the composition

---

12 Alison Walker, 'The Library of Sir Hans Sloane (1660–1753): creating a catalogue of a dispersed library', Paper presented at *World Library and Information Congress*, Milan, 23–27 August 2009.

of his catalogues, the influence of his amanuenses on the cataloguing style, and the physical layout and organisation of his library.[13] Throughout his life, Sloane recorded his rich book and manuscript collection in a series of eight catalogues, now housed in the British Library. He had started this practice as early as 1685, shortly before he departed for Jamaica as the physician to the Governor of Jamaica, the 2nd Duke of Albemarle, when he used a small notebook to record the title, author, date and place of publication, format, and price of his books.[14] The entries in this inventory were grouped by format, starting with folios, but did not include pressmarks.

Sloane completed this original acquisition list after returning to London, and subsequently began to record his books in a series of library catalogues of folio sheets, complete with a separate author index. In these volumes Sloane included only bibliographic details, such as author, title, format, and place and date of publication of his books, as well as the newly created alphanumeric pressmarks, known as Sloane numbers (see Fig. 12.1). These codes indicated the format of the publication through the use of capital letters (folios) and lower-case letters (octavos and quartos), and they connected the catalogue entry to the physical location of the books in Sloane's home, which were shelved by format in running order within each letter group.[15] However, they were not recorded in the catalogues in any running order. Moreover, Sloane's books and manuscripts, catalogued together indiscriminately, were not organised by subject (with the exception of his catalogue of Latin medical material, addressed later), but rather in order of accession, either as they were acquired, or as Sloane or one

---

13 See: Amy Blakeway, 'The Library Catalogues of Sir Hans Sloane: Their Authors, Organization, and Functions', *Electronic British Library Journal* (2011), pp. 1–49; M.A.E. Nickson, 'Hans Sloane, book collector and cataloguer 1682–1698', *Electronic British Library Journal* (1988), pp. 52–89; Alison Walker, 'Lost in Plain Sight: Rediscovering the Library of Sir Hans Sloane', in Flavia Bruni and Andrew Pettegree (eds.), *Lost Books: Reconstructing the Print World of Pre-Industrial Europe* (Leiden: Brill, 2016), pp. 400–413; Walker, "Collecting Knowledge", pp. 222–240.

14 Blakeway, 'The Library Catalogues of Sir Hans Sloane', p. 4; British Library Sloane MS 3995.

15 BL Sloane MS 3972C and MS 3972B can be searched with reference to Sloane MS 3972D, which is the index of names, surnames, works, significant words and titles created by Sloane in 1694. This index is bound alphabetically in two volumes (A–K, L–Z) and references the page numbers in the catalogues; There is sadly no extant shelf-list documenting the arrangement of Sloane's library. Blakeway speculates that the document 'A Table shewing the Place of each Book in my Library wherein to be Noted, that the Books whose Numbers are accompanied with a Letter of the Alphabet and another Number (and which amount to 678) are Books added, since the last Adjustment thereof. 1693', which is sadly incomplete, was likely a plan of Sloane's library (Sloane MS 4019, f. 178.). See: Blakeway, 'The Library Catalogues of Sir Hans Sloane', p. 6; Walker, 'Lost in Plain Sight', p. 405.

of his amanuenses sat down to catalogue them in batches.[16] The catalogues contain extensive evidence suggesting that they were working documents which evolved and were altered in response to Sloane's growing collection: pressmarks are frequently struck through and replaced, sometimes twice or even three times; new object-type classmark categories are introduced, such as prints and oriental prints; and the insertion of new pressmark letters (which indicated the specific format of books) suggests that books were being housed in an ever increasing number of locations in Sloane's home in order to accommodate his fast-growing collection.

Sloane's library catalogues differ substantially from those recording other areas of his collection. His catalogues of natural and artificial objects like fossils, antiquities, and minerals mixed 'technical description and reported narrative', blending factual details like dates of acquisition and prices with discovery narratives and speculation on the provenance of objects.[17] While these documents applied empirical and experimental language to objects of circumstantial curiosity, Sloane's library catalogues were devoid of any such interpretative, observational or sensory-based record keeping. Though equally rich in detail, these catalogues recorded objects which had standardised characteristics: format, date of publication and author, none of which relied on personal perceptions of the book in question. This uniformity enabled Sloane to delegate the cataloguing of his books to a series of assistants, a trust which he did not extend to the other parts of his collection. Sloane's library and its organisation thus stand apart from the rest of his cabinet in their adherence to bibliographic convention and treatment of books as (mostly) replicable objects, rather than specimens, such as seeds, shoes or coins, which, although commonly occurring, were always unique. While Sloane's books were a fundamental part of his collection and were meant to interact with his objects, they were perceived as a distinct entity – a library – which was set apart in terms of its location, internal organisation, and function.

3 The Intellectual Origins of the Enlightenment Library

To understand the rationale behind Sloane's library practices, it is helpful to outline the early modern views on librarianship and library formation which

---

16   Sloane's books and manuscripts are no longer catalogued together. The pages listing manuscripts were removed by the British Museum Trustees to make a separate catalogue, BL Sloane MS 3972B.
17   Benedict, 'From Benefactor to Entrepreneur', p. 35.

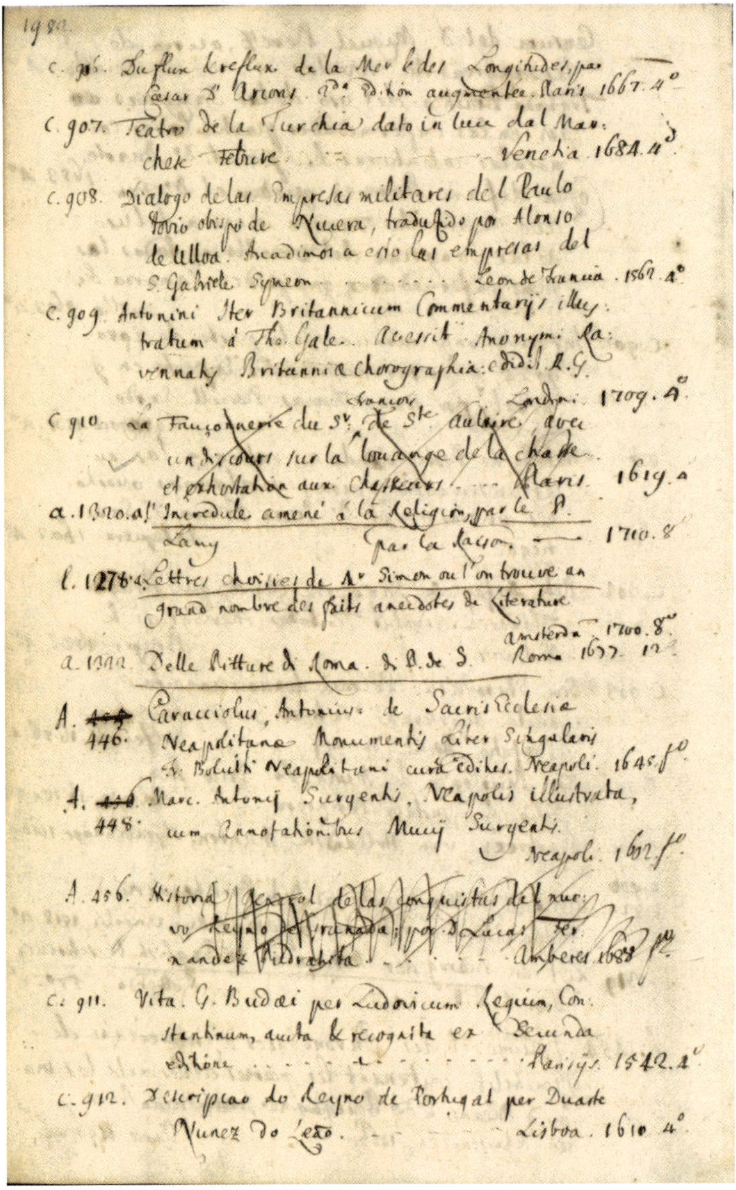

FIGURE 12.1   Two folios from Sloane's catalogue of books. Sloane MS 3972C, vol. 6, fols. 6v, 7r. British Library (Public Domain in most countries except the UK)

gh.199.200.   1983

a ~~1928~~   Traitté des maladies des Os par Jean Louys
         Petit.   Paris 1705 8°

a ~~1925~~   Traitté des Medicamens, & de la ma-
gh.6.   niere de s'en servir pour la guerison
   7.   des maladies suivant les experiences
         des medecins modernes avec les formules
         pour la Composition des Medicamens. Nouvel
         Editión. Par M.D. de Jaurey. M D.
         2. Tomes   Paris. 1722. 8°

a ~~1926~~   Nouveau traitté des Instrumens de
gh.10.   Chirurgie les plus utiles, & de plusieurs
   11.   nouvelles machines propres pour les
         maladies des Os par René Jacques
         Croissant de Garengot 2. Tomes   1723. 8°

A 457   Embaixada do Conde de Villar Mayor
         conduc'am da Rainha nostra Senno-
         ra &c. por Antonio Rodriguez da Cos-
         ta   Lisboa. 1694 f°

A 458   Ramillete de Epistolas y oraciones de S.
         Cathalina de Sena   Barcelona 1698 f°
         traduit par ordre du Card. Ximenes.

C.910   Vita do glorioso. S. Vicente Ferrer
         por Domingos Lopes Coelho   Lisboa 1713 4°

C.914   Historia de la vida del V. P. M. F.
         Juan de Vasconcellos por el R. P.
         Andres Ferrer de Valdecebro   Madrid 1668 4°

C.913   Rebellión de Ceylan y los progressos de
         su Conquista en el Govierno de Con-
         stantino de Saa y Noronna por Juan
         Rodriguez de Saa y Menestes   Lisboa. 1681 4°

c.?   Las Horas de Nostra Sennora.
Min.~~178~~ Chaque page ornée de marges gravées
  139.   taillées en bois   Lion de Francia. 1551 8°

P. ~~DXXV~~ Vetus Academia JesuChristi Iconibus,
P. CCCCLXXV Exemplis & ~~2a dicis~~ Documentis pris-
           corum Pietatis vere Doctorum Lyr.

foregrounded his experiences and understanding of libraries. After all, Enlightenment libraries, however we might choose to define them, did not arise in a vacuum. They were the culmination of centuries of practical librarianship, changing views on knowledge and its uses, and shifts in the social function of books and collecting. As such, we can situate them in a long trajectory of literature ruminating the nature of libraries and librarianship dating back to the classical era. These discussions on the nature of libraries, as well as the order of knowledge and ways of organising and managing information, had been renewed with the birth of the printing press and the growing availability of books, resulting in an early modern genre of writings too extensive and diverse to outline in any detail here. Notable examples include Conrad Gessner's *Bibliotheca Universalis* (1545) which popularised the concept of the universal library; the later sixteenth-century writings of Francesco Sacchini and Antonio Possevino (which advocated the need for the ruthless selection of a 'few good' books); Francis Bacon's criticism of libraries as repositories of archaic and uncritical knowledge; and Samuel Hartlib, Jan Amos Comenius, William Petty and Thomas Browne's views on the public purpose of libraries, connecting them to the advancement of knowledge and the reform of institutions of learning. By the formation of Sloane's library in the late seventeenth century, printed bibliographies and literature exploring the best ways of organising, furnishing and documenting a library were consequently commonplace, and many library owners actively engaged with this scholarship. We see this reflected in Sloane's library in myriad ways. Perhaps the most obvious is Sloane's possession of vast numbers of this literature. In addition to the majority of the abovementioned works, Sloane's catalogues list important publications such as John Dury's *Reformed Librarie-Keeper*, Louis Jacob's *Traité des plus belles Bibliothèques* and Frederik Rostgaard's *Projet d'une nouvelle méthode pour dresser le Catalogue d'une Bibliothèque selon les matières*. That many of his extant copies of such works are annotated, indicates that they were read, used and treated as functional works, if not by Sloane himself then by peers, assistants, or previous owners.

The most prominent work on libraries in Sloane's period was Gabriel Naudé's *Advis pour dresser une bibliothèque* (1627), later translated into English by John Evelyn as *Instructions Concerning the Erecting of a Library* (1661). Naudé's advice was based upon his own experience as the librarian to Henri de Mesme, President of the Parlement of Paris, and his work offered a host of advice on library economy and administration. Naudé broke new ground in asserting that the resources typically spent on library ornamentation should be directed instead towards providing a working study environment. He concerned himself with the logistics of library architecture and arrangement, warning readers of the dangers of damp, and the tempering effects of east-facing windows. He encouraged that books be arranged by subject, divided between theology, medicine, law, history, philosophy, mathematics and the humanities in order to allow readers to 'at pleasure discern the one from the other; draw, and separate them at his fantasie, without labour, without pains, without confusion'.[18] For similar reasons of expediency, he advocated the collecting of bibliographic materials which, he argued, would not only expedite the process of selecting books for libraries, but also serve to save precious space on the shelves. On a more fundamental level, Naudé offered a reconceptualization of the purpose of libraries. An advocate of Gessner's universal library, he argued that the value of books for subsequent generations could not be foreseen, and that all types of works, including heretical ones, should be collected. This linked to the most ground-breaking contribution of his work: his belief that the universal library served to benefit the public, not just collectors.

The significance of Naudé's treatise in the English context cannot be understated, though perhaps less for the true readership of the text than for the culture of reference to Naudé's hallowed precepts.[19] Although his treatise built on the work of other writers like Florian Trefler, and was directed at libraries much larger than any private collector would likely accumulate, it was Naudé who became the cultural reference point for English book collectors, who continued to cite the *Advis* for almost a century, in spite of growing numbers of works that reiterated Naudé's views, such as that of François de La Mothe le Vayer.[20] Sloane, for instance, purchased his copy of the French edition early in his collecting career, in 1696, almost 70 years after its first publication. The legacy of the *Advis* was further strengthened by the fact that John Evelyn, finding his translation 'so insufferably abus'd at the presse', made a concerted effort to supress the circulation of his English edition at home and abroad.[21] While it is debatable whether Naudé's *Advis* encapsulates the epitome of the Enlightenment library, his work did present a distinct and purposeful break with the Renaissance and Baroque traditions of library philosophy, and its popularity and legacy among

---

18   Quotation follows John Evelyn, *Instructions Concerning Erecting of a Library: Presented to My Lord The President De Mesme* (London: G. Bedle, and T. Collins, at the Middle-Temple Gate, and I. Crook in St. Pauls Church-yard, 1661), USTC 3071478, p. 75.

19   Sara Decoster, 'Gabriel Naudé entre bibliothèque docte et cabinet de curiosités', *Histoire et Civilisation du Livre: Revue Internationale*, VI (2010), pp. 255–277.

20   Florian Trefler, *Methodus exhibens per varios indices et classes subinde, quorumlibet librorum, cuiuslibet bibliothecae, brevem, facilem, imitabilem ordinationem* (Augsburg: Ulhard, 1560), USTC 675874; François de La Mothe le Vayer, 'Du moyen de dresser une Bibliotheque d'une centaine de livres seulement', *Œuvres*, vol. II. (Paris: Augustin Courbé, 1654), USTC 6164016.

21   G. Keynes, *John Evelyn: a study in bibliophily with a bibliography of his writings* (2nd ed., Oxford: Clarendon Press, 1968), p. 101.

collectors of the late seventeenth and early eighteenth centuries indicate that it resonated for diverse libraries in a period of transition. This echo sounds throughout the four readings of the Enlightenment library offered in the following sections. Although Naudé's treatise is not the impetus for choosing these characteristics, there are clear parallels between Sloane's library and Naudé's advice that highlight how changing views on librarianship began to manifest themselves in everyday library practices.

4 The Enlightenment Library as a Collaborative Endeavour

Enlightenment libraries grew out of a diverse set of influences, shared through informal channels of communication and personal exposure to working libraries.

Ann Blair's seminal work on early modern information management has revealed the extent of 'information overload' in the sixteenth and seventeenth centuries.[22] With the growing accessibility of books coupled with an increasing knowledge of the book market, book collectors had unprecedented possibilities to expand their libraries. However, this increasing demand, continuing well into the eighteenth century, could not always be met due to fluctuating restrictions of geography, trade, and conflict, among other factors, such as the cost of books, small print runs, censorship and confessional restrictions. As a consequence, book owners relied on networks of persons and bibliographic tools to procure the works they desired for their libraries. Booksellers, friends, traders and librarians formed a vital community behind the researching, locating, building and cataloguing of any library. The library practices of Hans Sloane demonstrate the dimensions of this collaborative climate. Alongside the libraries of The Royal Society, the Royal College of Physicians, and the Worshipful Society of Apothecaries, among other institutions, Sloane, like many contemporaries in early eighteenth-century London, could access the collections of friends and colleagues, either in person or through correspondence, to source and borrow books, examine catalogues, and generally soak up bibliographic and library information.

Much has been written on the circulation of books within early modern networks and their crucial role in library formation.[23] Sloane naturally participated

---

22 Ann Blair, *Too Much to Know: Managing Scholarly Information Before the Modern Age* (New Haven, CT: Yale University Press, 2011).
23 Recent examples include: Daniel Bellingradt, Paul Nelles, and Jeroen Salman (eds.), *Books in Motion in Early Modern Europe: Beyond Production, Circulation and Consumption* (Palgrave, 2017); Leah Knight, Micheline White, and Elizabeth Sauer, *Women's bookscapes in early modern Britain: Reading, ownership, circulation* (Ann Arbor: University of

in such fruitful exchange, however, it was not only the books themselves that changed hands. Sloane's correspondence indicates that he partook in a lively circulation of library catalogues, book auction catalogues, union catalogues, book lists and other more informal bibliographic records. These documents served a wide variety of library-building purposes: they were used to source information about new books; to compile lists of desiderata; to find out who or which institution might hold a particular book; and were even repurposed into catalogues for other collections. According to Naudé, such catalogues were necessary considering the 'brevity of our life and the multitude of things which we are now obliged to know', and he encouraged the discerning book collector to find:

> all the several Tables, Indexes, and Catalogues; and govern ones self by the greatest and most renowned Bibliotheques which were ever erected ... you must by no means omit, and neglect to cause to be transcrib'd all the Catalogues, not only of the great and most famous Libraries, whether ancient or modern, publike or private, with us, or amongst strangers; but also of the Studies and Cabinets, which for not being much knownn [sic], or visited, remain buried in perpetual silence.[24]

Collecting catalogues was not only expedient for the library owner, Naudé argued, but was a duty of the learned community. Such catalogues ensured that if collectors could not provide the book desired by a peer, they could at least direct them towards a copy held elsewhere.[25]

Hans Sloane's collection of over 800 printed sales catalogues, institutional library catalogues, manuscript library catalogues, and printed bibliographies testifies to the receptiveness of book collectors to Naudé's advice.[26] Moreover, their movements within his network communicate the extent to which they were perceived as vital library tools that ought to be shared among peers. Sloane received materials like the draft catalogue of the Sion library from its library keeper William Reading, and he himself sent Jacob Theodor Klein the newly printed catalogue of the Royal Society repository, and lent Samuel Pepys his

---

Michigan Press, 2018); M.R.M. Towsey and K.B. Roberts (eds.), *Before the Public Library: Reading, Community and Identity in the Atlantic World, 1650–1850* (Leiden: Brill, 2017).

24 Quotation follows Evelyn, *Instructions Concerning Erecting of a Library*, p. 13.
25 Ibid, p. 29.
26 Giles Mandelbrote, 'Sloane and the preservation of printed ephemera', in Giles Mandelbrote and Barry Taylor (eds.), *Libraries Within the Library: The Origins of the British Library's Printed Collections* (London: British Library, 2009), pp. 146–170.

copy of Nicolas Antonio's *Bibliotheca Hispana*.[27] Just as Naudé had intended, the catalogues that circulated within Sloane's network were treated as functional rather than dust-gathering works. Take, for instance, Edward Bernard and Humphrey Wanley's *Catalogi librorum manuscriptorum Angli et Hiberniae*, a copy of which Sloane sent to the Abbé Jean-Paul Bignon, royal librarian to Louis XIV of France.[28] An early union catalogue, Bernard and Wanley's compilation listed the manuscripts held in major English and Irish collections, and was frequently used as a finding and referencing tool for materials in private collections, Sloane's included.[29] Although the period was defined by the transnational correspondence of the Republic of Letters, in reality, geographical and political restrictions still greatly affected physical access to collections, and such catalogues consequently transported libraries across boundaries and to new audiences. As a library proxy, the catalogue enabled readers to access disparate and distant collections in terms of sourcing both physical books and bibliographic information. However, it relied on cooperation from library owners, readers and cataloguers alike. Projects like the *Catalogi librorum manuscriptorum Angli et Hiberniae*, which were intended to benefit readers and collectors, were dependent on individuals recognising this benefit, being willing to share their library contents, and encouraging their peers to do likewise.

Despite the enthusiasm of Sloane and his peers for Wanley's catalogue, at the height of Sloane's collecting, union catalogues were only in their infancy. In their absence, collectors often relied on the circulation of catalogue derivatives such as excerpted lists and thematic guides. Writing to John Locke in 1703, for instance, Sloane asked if he might borrow a work on the Montpellier garden, which he had found listed in a loose 'catalogue' among William Courten's papers.[30] Such lists acted as placeholders for catalogues proper and formed part of a much larger group of complementary paper reference tools commonly used by book collectors. Pepys, for instance, created painfully detailed additional lists of books pertaining to his professional interests and Hans Sloane interleaved his catalogues with alphabetical indices of pamphlets, tracts and handbills. These supplementary cataloguing tools were not only vital mediating documents which provided proxy-access to books and collections, but, as Sloane's letter to Locke demonstrates, were preserved and integrated into collectors'

---

27 BL Sloane MS. 4047, f. 148; BL Sloane MS 4068, f. 164; David McKitterick, *Catalogue of the Pepys Library at Magdalene College Cambridge* (Cambridge: D.S. Brewer, 1991), p. *xiv*.
28 BL Sloane MS 4069, f. 138.
29 BL Sloane MS 4049, f. 22.
30 To Sloane's disappointment, Locke owned no such work. John Locke and Esmond Samuel De Beer, *The Correspondence of John Locke in Eight Volumes* (Oxford: Clarendon Press, 1976), vol. 8, p. 199.

existing forms of information management. The collecting and subsequent repurposing of such existing bibliographic and book trade materials by collectors can thus also be interpreted as a collaborative venture. It was not just the circulation of catalogues that relied on a network of individuals, but their evolution and adaptation as well, as collectors actively built and expanded upon the bibliographic legwork of others to benefit their own libraries and often, in turn, recirculated these mediated materials. Sloane frequently repurposed these documents, such as the desiderata lists he compiled from his copies of the auction catalogue of Robert Hooke's library and the *Bibliotheca Hispana*.[31]

The most remarkable example of Sloane's adaptation of bibliographic works is his interleaved and annotated copy of *Lindenius Renovatus*, a published medical bibliography by Johannes Antonides van der Linden (Mercklin's edition, 1686), which he used to catalogue his Latin medical books. Sloane annotated the entries with pressmarks to record his own copies and used the interleaves to catalogue books that were not included in the printed edition. In addition to being an efficient means of cataloguing his books, Sloane had also intended to use his interleaved copy to publish an updated edition of *Lindenius*, as he saw this bibliographic revision as being 'extreamly useful for many purposes', though it never came to fruition.[32] Far from a unique practice, the interleaving and annotation of printed catalogues and bibliographies to record other collections can be dated back to Andrew Maunsell's first trade bibliography of English books in 1595.[33] By Sloane's day it had become an exceptionally common practice, with some catalogues, such as Thomas Hyde's *Catalogus impressorum librorum Bibliothecae Bodlejanae*, being repurposed by scores of private and institutional libraries, such as those of John Locke, most Oxbridge colleges, and the Bibliothèque Mazarine, among countless others.[34] As the next section will show, this collaborative format was one of many ways in which librarians

---

31 Blakeway, 'The Library Catalogues of Sir Hans Sloane', p. 16.

32 Hans Sloane, *A voyage to the islands Madera, Barbados, Nieves, S. Christophers and Jamaica* (London: s.n., 1707), pp. iii–iv.

33 Andrew Maunsell, *The first part of the Catalogue of English printed Bookes: which concerneth such matters of Diuinitie, as haue bin either written in our owne tongue, or translated out of anie other language, and have bin published ... Gathered into alphabet, etc. (The second parte ... which concerneth the sciences mathematicall, ... and also ... Phisick and Surgerie, etc.)* (London: Printed by Iohn VVindet [and James Roberts] for Andrew Maunsell, dwelling in Lothburie, 1595).

34 Bodleian Library, Locke 17.16; See also: Giles Mandelbrote, 'Personal owners of books', in G. Mandelbrote & K. Manley (eds.), *The Cambridge History of Libraries in Britain and Ireland* (Cambridge: Cambridge University Press, 2006), p. 187; Emmanuelle Chapron, 'Circulation et usages des catalogues de bibliothèques dans l'Europe du XVIIIe siècle', in Frédéric Barbier and Andrea De Pasquale (eds.), *Un'istituzione dei Lumi: la biblioteca.*

and collectors sought to bring order and navigation to idiosyncratic working collections.Bottom of Form

5   Order and Knowledge Production in the Enlightenment Library

Enlightenment libraries were as much sites of knowledge creation as of knowledge organisation. This knowledge was often working and embodied knowledge tailored to individual collections.

Reflecting on the Enlightenment spirit of classification, as epitomised by the works of Linnaeus, Réamur, Montesquieu, and the development of fields such as anatomy, law, and mineralogy, Robert Darnton has eloquently remarked on the role of 'booksellers and librarians ... to push that knowledge out to an eagerly waiting world. Booksellers purveyed that knowledge in the form of books, and librarians organized it onto bookshelves.'[35] However, the library itself was also a testing ground for explorations into order and classificatory systems, and librarians and book owners can be viewed as not only collectors, purveyors, and organisers of Enlightenment knowledge at a 'more modest level', but creators as well.[36] If, as Foucault claims, the seventeenth century was characterised by the transition from the desire for knowledge to new forms of knowledge construction (such as tables), then the library and its agents were undoubtedly at the forefront of this transformation.[37] As Garberson argues: 'library order, like Cartesian enumeration, Baconian tables, or Linnaean classification, delimits and orders a mass of dispersed information ... it is concentrated knowledge.'[38]

Order was perceived as central to the early Enlightenment library. Without it, Naudé had argued, a collection of books, regardless of its size or its contents, was no more a library than a vast heap of stones was a palace, until 'they be placed and put together according to rule, to make a perfect and accomplished structure.'[39] Even Claude Clément, whose treatise on libraries in many ways communicated the antithesis of Naudé's views in its focus on Baroque

---

Teoria, gestione e pratiche biblioteconomiche nell'Europa dei Lumi (Parma: Museo Bodoniano, 2013), pp. 29–49.

35 Robert Darnton, 'From Print Shop to Bookshelves: How Books Began the Journey to Enlightenment Libraries', in Alice Crawford (ed.), *The Meaning of the Library: A Cultural History* (Princeton and Oxford: Princeton University Press, 2017), pp. 91–2.
36 Ibid., p. 91.
37 Michel Foucault, *The Archaeology of Knowledge* (New York: Pantheon Books, 1972), p. 57.
38 Eric Garberson, 'Libraries, memory and the space of knowledge', *Journal of the History of Collections*, vol. 18, iss. 2 (2006), p. 124.
39 Quotation follows Evelyn, *Instructions Concerning Erecting of a Library*, p. 75.

ornamentation, had similarly underlined the necessity of order in making collections useful.[40] For many library theorists, catalogues were the root of this order. Naudé, for instance, encouraged producing two catalogues, one arranged by subject, the other by author, as a means of bringing order to the collection and making it navigable:

> two Catalogues of all the Books contained in the Library, in one whereof they should be so precisely dispos'd according to their several Matters and Faculties, that one may see & know in the twinkling of an eye, all the Authors which do meet there; and in the other, they should be faithfully ranged and reduced under an Alphabetical order of their Authours, as well to avoid the buying of them twice, as to know what are wanting, and satisfie a number of persons that are sometimes curious of reading all the works of certain Authors in particular.[41]

The combination of alphabetical and subject order was a longstanding cataloguing practice and served to accommodate both the general and specialist reader, respectively. Gessner had organised the *Bibliotheca Universalis* alphabetically by first name, indexed it by surname, and divided books under 21 categories in the accompanying *Pandects*. Likewise, La Croix du Maine and Du Verdier had arranged their bibliographies alphabetically by first name, to which were later added surname and subject indices.[42] Leibniz, too, had advocated complementing subject catalogues with alphabetical indices.[43] In spite of this tradition, however, the different forms of repurposed catalogues and bibliographic items outlined in the previous section indicate the diversity of approaches taken to information management in the Enlightenment library. Despite the uniform characteristics of printed materials, and the conventions of the librarianship tradition, there was little standardisation in the ways in which books were catalogued, grouped, and ordered by collectors, who had

---

40   Claudius Clemens, *Musei, sive Bibliothecæ tam privatæ quàm publicæ Extructio, Instructio, Cura, Usus. Libri IV. Accessit accurata description Regiæ Bibliothecæ S. Laurentij Escurialis* (Lyon: Jacobum Prost, 1635).
41   Quotation follows Evelyn, *Instructions Concerning Erecting of a Library*, p. 90.
42   François Grudé La Croix du Maine, *Premier Volume de La Bibliothèque du Sieur de La Croix du Maine* (Paris: Chez Abel l'Angelier, 1584); Antoine Du Verdier, *La Bibliothèque d'Antoine du Verdier Seigneur de Vauprivas* (Lyon: Par Barthelemy Honorat, 1585); François Grudé La Croix du Maine, Antoine Du Verdier and Jean-Antoine Rigoley de Juvigny, *Les bibliothèques françoises de La Croix-du-Maine et de Du Verdier* (Paris: Saillant & Nyon, 1772–1773).
43   See: G.W. Leibniz, Peter Remnant and Jonathan Bennett (eds.), *Leibniz: New Essays on Human Understanding* (Cambridge: Cambridge University Press, 1996).

their own collections, users, and purposes in mind when bringing order to their libraries. Hans Sloane, for instance, although producing both a catalogue and an alphabetical index of his books, contradicted much of the existing bibliographical literature by organising his catalogue by accession rather than subject or author, undoubtedly in an attempt to prevent altering or rewriting the catalogue to accommodate new additions to his library. John Locke, by contrast, used an interleaved copy of the author-alphabetical printed *Catalogus impressorum librorum Bibliothecae Bodlejanae*, to catalogue his books, to which he then added his own headings grouping titles by subjects. Different again, was the system of Samuel Pepys which included a "catalogue" arranged by shelf number, an alphabetical list by author, title, and topic, and an "appendix classica" or subject catalogue divided into 35 headings.

There was also little consistency in the level of bibliographic detail recorded within these catalogues. While Sloane generally documented all bibliographic information available, others, like Samuel Pepys, did not record the place or date of publication of their books, and frequently abbreviated titles and author names. Moreover, for those who integrated press- or shelf-marks into their library systems, these were similarly diverse. Come the seventeenth century, the assignment of letters to classes, as had been common to medieval libraries, had been largely abandoned in favour of varying alphanumeric and numeric schemes indicating the physical location of books. Sloane's alphanumeric pressmarks, for instance, indicated the location, as well as form, format or type of book or manuscript in question, while John Locke's fractional system allocated books of particular sizes to specific presses and shelves.[44]

Although often deviating from the advice offered by library theorists, these private collectors shared their view that catalogues were central to both representing and interpreting the contents of their libraries. What consequently tied these assorted library organisation practices together is the attempts made by their owners to bring coherence and order to working collections that were both private, in the sense that they reflected the means, interests and ambitions of an individual, and public, in that they were variously used by peers and colleagues. Their cataloguing systems were idiosyncratic and tailored to specific collections, and were not attempts to produce general systems of order or classification to be extended to other collections. However, their attempts to make specific collections navigable opened up space for new connections to be drawn. This is captured by Sloane's accession catalogue. While it was, on

---

44   Felicity Henderson and William Poole, 'The Library Lists of Francis Lodwick FRS (1619–1694): An Introduction to Sloane MSS. 855 and 859, and a Searchable Transcript', *Electronic British Library Journal* (2009), p. 3.

the one hand, a practical response to his expanding library, circumventing the issue of pre-emptive space-saving for new additions, as was the case for David Hume's catalogue, or the tiresome rewriting of catalogues as was preferred by Samuel Pepys, on the other, its openness and lack of adherence to existing taxonomies can be interpreted as indirectly contributing to the development and refinement of subject classification, as individuals using his books and objects were not bounded by existing disciplinary constraints, allowing them to reassess the links within the library and across the wider collection. By leaving his vast collections of books, naturalia, botanical samples, and rich, descriptive catalogue entries open to interpretation, Sloane facilitated epistemologically significant classificatory work: it is no secret that Linnaeus used Sloane's specimens in the creation of his new taxonomy.

The physical organisation of library shelves was similarly unbounded. Contrary to the advice of Naudé and others, Sloane and the majority of his peers, including Samuel Pepys, John Locke, Robert Hooke and Humphrey Wanley, organised their presses by book size or format, rather than by author or subject, making it simply impossible to browse the shelves for works of interest.[45] Format-based order disconnected from subject organisation was the result of the fast-growing collections of the seventeenth century, as it provided endless flexibility with which to accommodate expanding libraries.[46] However, the removal of subject and class order from shelves also prevented immediate visual and intellectual associations from being drawn between books, enabling readers to work across disciplinary boundaries. Moreover, the importance of memory within these systems indicates how collectors were themselves keepers of unique embodied knowledge derived from their extensive handling, use, and experience of their collections. It was impossible to look up a specific object within Sloane's catalogues easily and users would certainly not have found anything 'in the twinkling of an eye' as Naudé had so desired. Nonetheless, Sloane and his assistants would have had an extensive memory of where things were kept and where they were in the catalogue according to knowledge of when they entered the collection, which was to be exploited by readers and users of the collections. Of course, library owners and administrators had always had a privileged knowledge of their collections, however, it was during this period that they became integral parts of information management systems. Even Naudé had stressed that a library required a skilled and erudite

---

45   Naudé, *Advis*, p. 139.
46   P.S. Morrish, 'Baroque librarianship', in G. Mandelbrote & K. Manley (eds.), *The Cambridge History of Libraries in Britain and Ireland* (Cambridge: Cambridge University Press, 2006), p. 219.

librarian whose knowledge of both the world and the collection would help reveal its contents to the public. The importance of embodied knowledge is visible in the accounts of Sloane's home left by eminent persons and scholars, which reveal how individuals were given tours of Sloane's collection, but were not necessarily able to freely access the objects at their choosing.[47] To comprehend and use the collection fully, they required an interpreter of sorts, be it Sloane or one of his trusted assistants, who would guide them to the objects of their interest. The fact that Sloane never produced a printed catalogue of his library, or any other part of his cabinet for that matter, indicates that the catalogues were not a comprehensive guide to Sloane's collection that could act as a proxy beyond its walls, but were just one part of a wider knowledge system that also relied on Sloane as keeper. The centrality of human memory is echoed in Sloane's will. Concerned that the collection be exploited to its utmost, Sloane left his assistant James Empson the sum of forty guineas a year to:

> oversee and take care of my collection of rarities and curiosities, until they be fully disposed of; and to advise and assist my executors in the keeping, preserving and disposing of the same to most advantage.[48]

The library as a site of order and knowledge production which challenged the limits of existing taxonomies was partially a consequence of the lack of clear delineation between books and objects, and the need for these elements to interact freely, as the following section demonstrates.

6 Books and Objects in the Enlightenment Library

Enlightenment librarians made steps towards separating books and objects, but continued to perceive them as relational and complementary components in the pursuit of knowledge.

Naudé's *Advis* sought to counteract many of the extravagances of Baroque collecting culture as had characterised the grand courtly and princely libraries of the sixteenth and seventeenth centuries. Nowhere was this more apparent than in his claims that frugality must be practiced in library building and that the funds traditionally used for the ornamentation and decor of libraries ought

---

47 For more see: Alexandra Ortolja-Baird, "Chaos naturae et artis': imitation, innovation, and improvisation in the library of Sir Hans Sloane. Part 1", *Library & Information History*, 36 (2020), pp. 155–174.
48 *The Will of Sir Hans Sloane, Bart. Deceased*, vol. 1 (John Virtuoso, London, 1753), p. 15.

to be put towards furnishing the collection itself.[49] The lavish binding of books was to be abandoned (though it continued to be practiced by Samuel Pepys, John Evelyn, Martin Folkes, and others, in spite of Naudé's advice), as were the sumptuous gold and marble fittings on library walls and ceilings, the 'fragments of statues' which commonly adorned library shelves, and the iconography and murals as had been encouraged by library theorists like Claude Clément.[50] However, this reassessment did not banish objects from the library all together. Instead, Naudé stressed, libraries should be home to *instrumenta* rather than *ornamenta*, by which he meant those instruments and objects that supplemented or complemented book-based learning, as opposed to those which transformed the library into a space of curiosity. Among these acceptable items he included 'Mathematical Instruments, Globes, Mapps, Spheres, Pictures, Animals, Stones, and other curiosities as well Artificial as Natural, which are ordinarily collected from time to time, with very little expense', as well as balls of jasper, penknives, almanacks, clocks, pens and other practical workspace items.[51] It indicated a new way of thinking about and formalising the relationship between books and objects, and their purposes. Although books had featured prominently in early modern cabinets, interpreted as tools to be used in conjunction with the examination of curiosities, this dynamic was inverted in the early Enlightenment as select objects came to be seen as instruments to complement books. However, in spite of this inversion and the growing perception of the library as a standalone entity, its porousness to objects as tools for learning set it apart from later understandings of the library as a space for books only.

Naudé's advice penetrated the aesthetic of many Enlightenment libraries. Contemporary accounts of Sloane's home describe how his library rooms of floor to ceiling wall-presses also contained objects like natural history specimens and zoological items in spirit jars. Similar Naudéan interactions between books and objects were present in many English library spaces of the period: Globes, maps and armillary spheres adorned the libraries at Ham House, Winchester Cathedral, the Harley Collection, and the home of Samuel Pepys, among countless others.[52] However, there were also more subtle connections

---

49 Naudé, *Advis*, pp. 107–108.
50 For bindings see: Leona Rostenberg, *The Library of Robert Hooke: The Scientific Book Trade of Restoration England* (Santa Monica: Modoc Press, 1989), pp. 116–7; Keynes, *John Evelyn*, p. 24.
51 Quotation follows Evelyn, *Instructions Concerning Erecting of a Library*, p. 85.
52 See: Mark Purcell, *The Country House Library* (New York & London: Yale University Press, 2019), p. 157; Lucy Gwynn, '"A Paradise & Cabinet of Rarities": Thomas Browne, His Library, and Communities of Collecting in Seventeenth-Century Norfolk', in Annika

between books and objects in the Enlightenment library that can be situated within the wider transition in collecting culture away from the virtuoso tradition of collecting the world and towards approaches which sought to 'rationalize [the world], to place it in order through classification, thereby working towards the creation of an encyclopaedic resource for the improvement of knowledge'.[53] Such rationalisation required finding connections both within and beyond collections.

This process is visible in Sloane's cabinet, renowned for its blurred disciplinary boundaries yet clear classificatory spirit.[54] For Sloane, the natural and artificial worlds often overlapped and interacted in ways that we find curious today, for example in drawers containing objects that looked like one thing but were made of another, like a glass citron, or ears and eyes made from ivory. His intricate systems of cataloguing likewise demonstrate how he sought to find connections between objects, texts and descriptions both within his own collection and in relation to the wider world.[55] This overlap naturally extended to Sloane's books and manuscripts, which were integrated into a complex system of cross-references across Sloane's collection catalogues, which connected objects, and their descriptions with books, their contents, specific pages or sections within them and their physical location in his home. Other types of interactions were more conceptual. Many items in Sloane's collection – books of pressed plants (*Horti Sicci*), albums of prints, bound collections of paper samples, annotated and cross-referenced bibliographies – looked and felt like books, and were stored and catalogued alongside or among more conventional books, yet performed additional non-textual functions. While Naudé permitted objects to traverse the boundary of the library when classed as *instrumenta*, Sloane found nothing

---

Bautz and James Gregory (eds.), *Libraries, Books, and Collectors of Texts, 1600–1900* (New York: Routledge, 2018), pp. 43–53; David Adshead, '"A Noble Musaeum of Books": A View of the Interior of the Harleian Library at Wimpole Hall?', *Library History*, xviii (2002), pp. 191–206; Robert Latham and William Matthews (eds.), vol. 6 of *The Diary of Samuel Pepys: A New and Complete Transcription* (London: Bell, 1983), p. 252.

53   Alice Marples, 'Creating and keeping a national treasure: the changing uses of Hans Sloane's collection in the eighteenth century', in Toby Burrows and Cynthia Johnston (eds.), *Collecting the Past: British Collectors and their Collections From the 18th to the 20th Centuries* (London: Routledge, 2018), p. 9.

54   Paul Nelles, 'Libraries, books and learning, from Bacon to the Enlightenment', in G. Mandelbrote & K. Manley (eds.), *The Cambridge History of Libraries in Britain and Ireland* (Cambridge: Cambridge University Press, 2006), pp. 33–4.

55   Kim Sloan and Julianne Nyhan, 'Enlightenment architectures: The reconstruction of Sir Hans Sloane's cabinets of 'Miscellanies'', *Journal of the History of Collections*, 2020. doi.org/10.1093/jhc/fhaa034.

uncomfortable about items which traversed the very line between book and object being central to the library collection.

In this interstitial space they were neither the curiosities of earlier cabinets, nor the reclassified object types of the modern museum. That this attitude was symptomatic of the early Enlightenment library is highlighted by the differing understanding of order and the relationship between books and objects espoused by the early British Museum trustees. At the founding of the museum, it was agreed that the individual collections of Sloane, Cotton and Harley would be kept separate, however, this posed significant difficulties with the creation of distinct museum departments. The fate of Sloane's Jamaican volumes of *Horti Sicci* captures this struggle. In spite of the importance of these working tools for natural history studies, concerns that the Department of Natural Curiosities would end up looking more like a library than a museum, resulted in their relocation to the Department of Printed Books and Manuscripts, a department completely atomised from non-standard book objects (see Fig. 12.2).[56] Although these volumes had originally been housed in Sloane's library, their formal detachment from the natural history collection due to their form alone, indicated how the divide between books and objects had become strict and uncrossable and how the interactions between the various components of Sloane's collection were severed by the increasing division and codification of modern fields and disciplines.[57] However, as the final section will show, this difference in attitude was not only due to the formalisation of the disciplines but also to fundamentally incompatible understandings of the purpose of libraries.

7 The Purpose and Legacy of the Enlightenment Library

Enlightenment libraries, even when private, were public- and often future-oriented.

This chapter initially explored the idea of the Enlightenment library as a collaborative venture. Yet, we might also interpret the Enlightenment library as an unfinished project: an endeavour that owners knew would evolve with time, input, and resources, and which would potentially outgrow and outlive them as collectors. This interpretation of the library as an ongoing project stemmed from evolving ideas regarding its meaning and purpose in society. While the private Renaissance library had frequently sought to display wealth and status,

---

56   Edwin D Rose, 'Natural history collections and the book: Hans Sloane's *A Voyage to Jamaica* (1707–1725) and his Jamaican plants', *Journal of the History of Collections*, vol. 30, iss. 1 (2018), pp. 15–33.
57   See: Delbourgo, *Collecting the World*, p. xix.

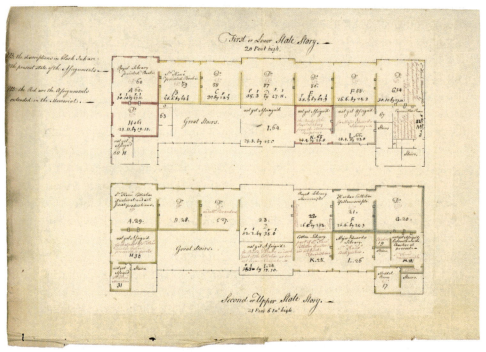

FIGURE 12.2 Floorplan showing the arrangement of the foundational collections of the British Museum and the separation of Hans Sloane's books and manuscripts from the other objects in his collection. BMCA, (uncatalogued, Flitcroft and Brazier Plans of Montague House 1740–1779)
© THE TRUSTEES OF THE BRITISH MUSEUM

its early Enlightenment counterpart placed the public benefit at its core, albeit in varying interpretations. In so doing, it reclaimed the library as a site of learning – an outlook that had been lost in the sixteenth century as the increasing accessibility and democratisation of books had prompted collectors to turn to other luxury goods to symbolise their standing.[58]

Naudé had presented a forward-looking interpretation of the role of libraries as universal collections. Libraries served the public benefit not only as repositories of potentially useful future knowledge but also as accessible sites to be used by the immediate learned 'public' community in the pursuit of this same knowledge. By placing the advancement of science and the activity of scholars at the heart of the library, rather than social prestige, Naudé fundamentally

---

58   Andrew Pettegree, 'The Renaissance Library and the Challenge of Print' in Alice Crawford (ed.), *The Meaning of the Library: A Cultural History* (Princeton and Oxford: Princeton University Press, 2017), pp. 75–6.

opposed the outlook of the cabinet of curiosity and the courtly library, and ushered in new thinking regarding the purpose of collections.[59] Sloane followed Naudé in acknowledging that one could not anticipate the usefulness of a book for future generations and although he did not explicitly refer to his library as a universal library, he communicated sentiments suggesting that his collection was intended to serve the public benefit.[60] This is perhaps best articulated by his ambitions for its legacy, which attest to his understanding of the inherent and yet to be discovered scientific and public value of his unclassified objects. In his will, Sloane desired that his collection be purchased by the nation for £20,000, in order to ensure that the collection remained open not just to the 'curious' or learned community, but to 'all persons'.[61] For this to be possible, however, it was paramount that the collection of 'all my library of books, drawings, manuscripts, prints, medals and coins, antient and modern, antiquities, seals, &c. cameas and intaglios, &c. precious stones, agates, jaspers, &c. vessels, &c. of agate and jasper, &c. chrystals, mathematical instruments, drawings and pictures', remain intact:[62]

> Now desiring very much that these things tending many ways to the manifestation of the glory of God, the confutation of atheism and its consequences, the use and improvement of physic, and other arts and sciences, and benefit of mankind, may remain together and not be separated, and that chiefly in and about the city of London, where I have acquired most of my estates, and where they may by the great confluence of people be of most use.[63]

However, preservation as a coherent whole did not mean that the collection should be frozen in time, as had been the case for Samuel Pepys' library, conserved to the present day in its original form and order in Magdalene College, Cambridge. Beyond his initial request that the collection be kept together, Sloane left its subsequent order and development to the trustees of the British Museum, who were free to add to, or rearrange it, in ways that they interpreted as beneficial to mankind and which glorified God. And, so they did: already in

---

59 Naudé, *Advis*, pp. 115–116.
60 For more see: Alexandra Ortolja-Baird, "Chaos naturae et artis': imitation, innovation, and improvisation in the library of Sir Hans Sloane. Part 2", *Library & Information History*, 37 (2021), pp. 49–69.
61 *The Will of Sir Hans Sloane, Bart. Deceased*, vol. 1 (John Virtuoso, London, 1753), pp. 28–9.
62 Ibid, p. 19.
63 Ibid, p. 3.

1755 Sloane's library was assessed to be in a state of disorder and it was decided that it should be rearranged by subject, and that the corresponding catalogues and pressmarks should be duly altered to reflect this.[64] Sloane's relinquishing of control over the future of his collection as a set of interconnected, relational objects, is testament to his perception of the public role of his museum and his convictions regarding the universal library: he could not anticipate the future uses of his collection, the ways in which his objects would be classified and reclassified, or the knowledge that they would possibly help create.

Sloane might have been unique in leaving his collections and their order to the nation, however, the ambition of preserving one's library for the public stretched back for centuries.[65] What separated these earlier attempts from those of Sloane's period, broadly speaking, was the rationale behind this public legacy. While the desire for posthumous admiration and esteem often underpinned the public orientation of pre-Enlightenment libraries, the Enlightenment library was driven by an understanding that private collections were, to a large degree, public collections. At his death in 1753, Sloane's collection was already described in *The Gentleman's Magazine* as 'perhaps the most magnificent private, if not publick, collection upon earth'.[66] Moreover, it was understood that these private-public libraries should continue to serve this purpose beyond the possession of their owners and their collecting habits. Even those collections, like that of Edward Harley, which did not end up as public endowments, were underpinned by this same rationale and understanding of the role of the library.[67]

However, Sloane's bequest and its subsequent treatment also marked the point at which the public ambitions of the universal library were being overtaken by new visions of both the public and the library. As Jonathan Israel has argued, 'around 1750, the diversification of knowledge and the proliferation of publications outstripped what even the most zealous individual bibliophile could acquire, and the ideal of the "universal" library fell into desuetude except for large institutional collections'.[68] This is not to say that the Enlightenment

---

64 P.R. Harris, *A History of The British Museum Library* (London: The British Library, 1998), p. 3.
65 See: Pettegree, 'The Renaissance Library', pp. 72–4.
66 Benedict, 'From Benefactor to Entrepreneur', p. 39.
67 Harley had considered the future of the Harley library 'as an independent endowment' before eventually leaving it to his widow Henrietta Cavendish Harley. The collection was later sold to the nation in 1753. See: David McKitterick, 'Wantonness and Use: Ambitions for research libraries in early eighteenth-century England', in R.G.W. Anderson, M.L. Caygill, A.G. MacGregor and L. Syson (eds.), *Enlightening the British: Knowledge, Discovery and the Museum in the Eighteenth Century* (London: British Museum, 2004), p. 40.
68 Israel, *Radical Enlightenment*, p. 13.

library neatly reached its telos in the modern public library and the Public Libraries Act of 1850. Despite the commonplace rhetoric of the public good and the benefit of the universal library at the heart of Enlightenment library, early Enlightenment understandings of the public and the public good were variously conceived, frequently plural, and often highly restrictive.[69] As it turned out, Sloane's 'learned and curious' public – those who were permitted to use, not just observe the collection – was further refined by the British Museum Trustees in 1753 as 'the learned and those of polite behaviour and superior degree'.[70]

8 Conclusion: Whither the 'Enlightenment Library'?

The Enlightenment may have been made by ideas, and communicated through books, but it also played out in, and was shaped by, specific sites. Salons, universities, coffee houses, academies, libraries – all were part of the intricate tapestry of Enlightenment. As a means of interrogating how the library was interwoven in this tapestry, this chapter has briefly outlined four characteristics of Sir Hans Sloane's library. This exercise is not intended as an attempt at a definition or classification of this term, but rather aims to provide additional points of entry for the study of English private libraries in the late seventeenth and early eighteenth centuries. Although the Enlightenment library was undoubtedly as diverse in form as the Enlightenment itself, we can – cautiously – find commonalities in the understandings of the purpose, development, and functioning of the library that underpinned these varied forms. The elements of Sloane's library explored here – its collaborative nature; its order and capacity for knowledge creation; its receptiveness to objects; and its public and future-oriented purpose – are just four of many avenues that could have been taken to investigate the relationship between his collecting and collection of books and the Enlightenment. Although less obvious in their connection than aspects such as the types of books and authors on his shelves, they nonetheless link to fundamental developments associated with the Enlightenment: the library's collaborative origins and public, future-oriented purpose

---

69 See: Joanna Innes, 'Libraries in context: social, cultural and intellectual background', in G. Mandelbrote & K. Manley (eds.), *The Cambridge History of Libraries in Britain and Ireland* (Cambridge: Cambridge University Press, 2006), pp. 285–300.
70 Cited in Marjorie L. Caygill, 'From Private Collection to Public Museum: The Sloane collection at Chelsea and the British Museum in Montagu House', in R.G.W. Anderson, M.L. Caygill, A.G. MacGregor and L. Syson (eds.), *Enlightening the British: Knowledge, Discovery and the Museum in the Eighteenth Century* (London: British Museum, 2004), p. 19.

can be attributed to the rise and evolution of the public sphere, changing views on the nature, spaces, and value of sociability, and the dynamics of the Enlightenment book trade; its receptiveness to *instrumenta* over *ornamenta* ties into the Enlightenment's commodity culture and criticism thereof, while the hybridity of objects and books reflects the period's shifting taxonomical boundaries; and its role in knowledge creation is indicative of the new sites and forms of Enlightenment learning. Taken together, these elements present a library that was highly responsive to the pulse of Enlightenment, but which, at the same time, consciously provided both literal and figurative space in which the Enlightenment could evolve.

Index

Aberdeen 212
Abraham a Sancta Clara 143, 158
Academies 73–5, 77, 79, 82–5, 91, 95, 277, 286, 317. *See also* Accademia della Crusca
Accademia della Crusca 78–9, 89
Achard, Claude-François 285–6
advertisements 4, 6–15, 17, 19–20, 48*n*, 125, 144, 148–9, 157, 160, 176, 232–6, 257, 266, 295
Advis pour dresser une bibliothèque 264, 300–1, 310
Aix-en-Provence 147, 284, 286*n*
Aldrovandi, Ulisse 98
Alembert, Jean le Rond d' 122
almanacs 4, 7, 15, 48, 52–4, 66, 129, 219, 311
Alzugaray, Josef de 124
Americas 106–7, 109, 124, 126, 198, 224. *See also* New Granada; New Spain; Peru
Amsterdam 4–9, 11, 13–15, 19, 100, 141–4, 164, 167, 169, 172, 177, 180, 210, 213, 229, 231, 233, 236–7, 242–3
Ancona 76, 78, 90
Anisson-Dupéron, Étienne-Alexandre 168
Anisson-Duperron, collection 167–8
Antonio, Nicolas 304
Antwerp 143, 223
Arbuthnot, Alexander 236–7
Arizon, Joseph de 117, 120
auctions 220, 223, 225, 227–9, 233–5, 238–262. *See also* catalogues, auction
Augsburg 127–9, 131–2, 143, 154
Austria 129–33, 138, 149*n*, 155
Austria, Juan José de 26
authorities 6, 9, 21–3, 43, 71, 78, 95–6, 98, 105, 129, 133–4, 145–7, 159, 165, 179, 181–4, 232, 236, 246, 251, 257, 262
Avignon 173, 175–6
Ayllón, Juan de 117–20

Bachaumont, Louis Petit de 180
Bacon, Francis 222, 230, 276
Bamberg 140
Barberini, Francesco 98
Barcelona 21–2, 26, 29–30, 32–4, 36–40, 42
Barret, Jean-Marie 172

Basel 128*n*, 177
Bavaria 129, 131, 149*n*
Belin, François II 281
Bencard, Johann Caspar 132
Berlin 54, 57, 63, 127, 128*n*, 130, 134–5
Bernard, Edward 304
Beza, Theodore 198, 203
Biblia Sacra (German) 139–40
Biblia Sacra Polyglotta 221, 227, 230
Bibliotheca Universalis 264, 300, 307
Bibliothèque du Roi 164, 294
Bibliothèque Mazarine 305
Bignon, Jean-Paul 304
bindings 41, 55*n*, 109, 151, 197, 203, 222, 285, 311
Blankaart, Steven 15–7
Böckmann, Peter 250
Bodleian Library 215, 221, 226, 305, 308
Boeckholt, Joannes 233
Bohemia 129–33, 135, 137–42, 145–6, 148, 150–1, 153–4, 158–60. *See also* Czech Republic
Böhm, Michel 229
Bologna 75–6, 78–9, 81–4, 86, 92, 97, 99, 101–2, 104
Bonarelli, Prospero 76
book fairs 38, 49, 127–30, 132–5, 137–8, 140, 142–3, 146–50, 152, 159–60, 213, 265. *See also* catalogues, fair
Book Sales Catalogues Online 217, 267
bookbinders 161, 197, 227, 241, 243, 245, 248
books, second-hand 11, 114–6, 119, 125, 158, 200, 207–8, 229, 268–274
booksellers 3, 4–5, 8–15, 17, 19–20, 29–30, 32–4, 36–41, 76–7, 78*n*, 81, 106, 108, 116, 127–160, 161, 164–9, 172, 176, 179, 182–5, 200–1, 208, 212–3, 217, 218, 228–9, 232–6, 238, 241, 243, 245, 247, 250–1, 253, 257–8, 260, 262, 264, 266, 270–1, 273–4, 276–7, 279, 281, 284–7, 289, 302, 306. *See also* catalogues, trade
bookshops 11, 13, 15, 20, 37, 39, 180, 129, 132, 134–5, 137, 148, 150–2, 155, 158–9, 179, 182, 235, 256. *See also* print shops
Bornat, Claudi 34
Bornemann, Johan Adolph 220

Bothall, Abraham   17
Boubers, Charles-Louis de   172
Boubers, Jean-Louis de   172
Boudot, Jean   183–4
Boulay, François   184
Bourgelat, Claude   179, 183
Boyle, Robert   223–4
Brandenburg   57, 59
Bratislava   137
Breitenau, Christoph Gensch von   238, 257–9
British Isles   56, 100, 176, 210, 212–3, 220, 223, 225, 229, 236–7. *See also* England; Ireland; Scotland
British Museum   291, 313–5, 317
Brno   137, 143–4
broadsheets   4, 46, 48, 52–4, 66–7, 218, 234, 260
Brochmand, Rasmus Hansen   225–6, 230–3
Broenner, Henri-Louis   176
Browne, Thomas   300
Browning, Mercy   13
Brussels   172
Bruxelles, Jean de   264
Bruyning, Joseph   13–14
Bruyset, Jean-Marie   162, 176, 181
Buchanan, George   222, 225, 236

Cabanis, Pierre-Jean-Georges   284
cabinets of curiosities   78, 290–1, 294, 297, 303, 310–3, 315–6
Cadiz   108, 120, 123–4
Calvin, John   193, 198, 201, 203–5, 207
Cambridge   197, 212, 215, 231
Capizucchi, Raimondo   97
Cartagena (Colombia)   107, 117, 123–4
Cartwright, Thomas   206–7
Cassini, Giovanni Domenico   82–3, 85, 92
Cassube, Christian   235
Casteleyn, Abraham   7
Castelli, Benedetto   82, 103–4
Castile   27, 37
catalogues   11, 114, 161–4, 177, 179, 201, 213, 222, 240, 257, 262, 263–5, 303–5, 307–10, 312, 316
    auction   164, 213–4, 216–20, 223–5, 227–9, 231–2, 235–7, 239, 243, 245–6, 248, 251, 257–8, 260, 265, 273–4, 279, 285–6, 303, 305
    fair   48, 52, 54, 157, 213, 216, 265

library   109–11, 210, 221, 226, 258–9, 265–289, 295–300, 302–5
trade   139, 142–5, 155–60, 164–5, 176, 201, 216, 235, 266, 267*n*, 271, 275
Catalonia   21–43
Cavalieri, Bonaventura   82–3, 85–6
censors   71, 95, 97, 105, 107, 117, 121, 126, 166, 172, 246
censorship   71, 84, 95–6, 98, 105, 106–9, 117, 119–21, 124, 126, 130, 134, 143, 145–8, 154, 158–9. *See also* Inquisition
Cervera (Catalonia)   40–1
Chambeau, Louis   175
Chambre syndicale de Paris   166–7
Charles III, Duke of Bourbon   41–2
Charles IX, King of France   166
Charles V, Emperor   36
Chetham, Humphrey   192–3, 195–6, 200–3, 206–9
Choiseul, Étienne de   181–2
Cicero   22, 34–6, 39
classification   210, 258, 263–289, 290–7, 300, 306–9, 312
Clément, Claude   306, 311
collectors   74, 78, 80, 87, 89, 125, 164, 212, 214–5, 217, 221–3, 226, 231–3, 235, 237, 239, 251, 253, 258, 266, 290–2, 301–9, 313–4
Cologne   128*n*, 143, 154, 163, 176
Colombia. *See* New Granada
Comenius, Jan Amos   142, 158, 300
Congreve, William   212
Copenhagen   210, 217, 220, 223, 225–7, 234, 242–3. *See also* Denmark
Cospi, Ferdinando, Marquis of   78–9, 81, 92–3, 96, 99, 104
Czech Republic   138. *See also* Bohemia; Prague

Danube (river)   132
Dati, Carlo Roberto   89–90, 93, 103–4
David, Michel-Antoine   264–5, 276–7, 279–80, 287
Delaroche, Aimé   184
Della Bella, Stefano   100
Denmark   56, 212, 214–5, 217, 221–3, 225–8, 230–1, 234, 236. *See also* Copenhagen; Scandinavia
Denné, Philippe   286
Diodati, Elia, jurist   72

INDEX   321

Direction de la Librairie   162, 164, 166
Dombes   183–4
Dordrecht   11, 14
Dordrecht, Synod of   224
Douai   271
Dozza brothers, publishing firm   76, 77n, 79–81, 104
Dresden   57, 149, 154, 239
Du Verdier, Antoine   307
Dublin   212, 222. *See also* Ireland
Dunkirk   172
Duplain, Joseph   179
Dury, John   300
Dutch Republic   3–20, 56, 163, 210, 212, 214–7, 221–4, 226, 229–31, 267, 275

Edinburgh   175, 177, 212, 222, 236–7
Egmont, Jacobus II van   15
Elzevier, publishing firm   73, 225, 236
Encyclopédie   122, 179, 264, 276, 280n, 284, 287–8
Endter, Wolfgang Moritz   131, 133
England   42, 208, 189–209, 210, 212–7, 220–1, 223–32, 235–7, 290–318
Enlightenment   46, 65–6, 124, 128, 160, 179, 181, 255, 264, 266, 268, 289, 290–5, 300–2, 306–7, 310–4, 316–8
Erasmus, Desiderius   21, 34, 36, 39
Evelyn, John   295, 300–1, 311

false imprints   138, 141–2, 144, 161–85, 236
Faucheux, Claude-André   179–80
Fenner, Rest   13
Ferdinand II, Holy Roman Emperor   153
Ferroni, Clemente   77
Figueró, Rafael   33, 38
Fleury, Claude   122
Florence   77, 79–80, 96, 101–2, 104
France   56, 161–85, 210, 215, 263–89, 304
Francke, August Hermann   238
François I, King of France   164, 166
Frankfurt   128n, 129, 137–8, 142, 150, 152, 154, 159, 176–7, 213, 265
Frederick II, King of Denmark   215
Frederick II, King of Prussia   181
Frederick III, King of Denmark   210
French Revolution   264, 268, 280, 285–6
Fritsch, Caspar   229
Fritsch, Thomas   130, 132

Fuochi, Guglielmo   95–9
Furly, Benjamin   228–233
Furly, Benjohan   229

Galilei, Cosimo   93, 102
Galilei, Galileo   71–5, 80, 82, 85–93, 96, 98, 102, 105
Ganeau, Etienne   184
Ganeau, Louis   184
Gelabert, Martí   33–4
Geneva   177, 180, 182
Germany. *See* Holy Roman Empire
Gersdorff, Joachim   210
Gessner, Conrad   264, 300–1, 307
Girard, Gabriel   264–5, 287
Girard, Jean-Baptiste   146–7
Girona   38–40
Giunti, publishing firm   80
Glasgow   212
Gleditsch, Johann Friedrich   132
Godfrey, Garrett   197
Gogué, Jean-Baptiste   279, 281
González y Avendaño, Francisco   113–7, 119
Gosse, Pierre Jr   176
Gotha   143, 238
Göttingen   54
Gottsched, Johann Christoph   53–4, 62, 255
Götze, Georg Heinrich   238, 242, 259
Green, Anne   226
Green, Johann Nicolaus   256, 258, 260
Grimaldi, Lorenzo   82, 85
Grimaldi, Francesco Maria   83
Gröbel, Ulrich   149
guilds   5–7, 15, 32, 36–40, 239–46, 248, 251, 260, 262
Guillemot, Mathieu   169
Gutierrez de Piñerez, Juan   21–3
Guttmann, Christian Gottlieb   57, 60, 62

Haarlem   7, 9, 11, 229
Halle   54, 58–9, 128n, 143, 239
Hamburg   54, 128n, 130, 154, 235–6, 245, 250, 255, 258
Hardy, bookseller   168
Harleian Library   295, 311, 313, 316
Harley, Edward   316
Hartlib, Samuel   300
Heck, Joseph   149, 152
Heinsius, Johann Samuel   146, 149

Hémery, Joseph d'   168, 181–3
Heyn, Johann   57–64
Hoffmann, Ferdinand   146–7
Hoffmann, Johann   131, 144
Höger, Matthias Adam   140
Holm, Petrus   227–8, 230–1, 233
Holy Roman Empire   46, 48, 51–4, 56, 64–66, 128–31, 138, 160, 238–262
Hönn, Georg Paul   249
Hooke, Robert   295, 305, 309
Huguetan, Jean Antoine   102

index   87–8, 107–8, 114, 122, 126, 145, 165–9, 180, 240, 245–6, 248, 251, 257, 302. *See also* inquisition
inquisition   34, 74, 77*n*, 78*n*, 84, 90, 92, 94–100, 105, 106–9, 113–4, 117, 122–3, 126. *See also* censorship; index
inventories   30, 39, 103, 106, 108–9, 116–7, 217, 247, 260, 269–72, 296
Ireland   212, 225. *See also* Dublin
Italy   56, 71–105, 210

Jacob, Louis   300
Jamaica   296
Jefferson, Thomas   284
Jena   54, 57–8, 128*n*, 143, 227, 239
Jolly, widow of Jean Francois   13, 15
journals   15, 17, 20, 46–7, 49–56, 60, 63–7, 213, 277
journals: *Acta Eruditorum*   51
  Collectanea Medico-physica   15
  Giornale de' Letterati   51
  Journal de Trévoux   184
  Journal des savants   51, 184
  Philosophical Transactions   51, 290

Kaliningrad   3
Kant, Immanuel   53
Kepler, Johannes   96
Kindermann, Eberhard Christian   57
Knutzen, Martin   53–4, 60, 62
Köneken, Jasper   242–50, 253–4
Koniáš, Antonín   145
Königsberg. *See* Kaliningrad
Krems   132

La Croix du Maine, François Grudé   307
La Mothe le Vayer, François de   301

Lacavalleria, Antoni   38
Laet, Johannes de   223–5, 231–3
Lancashire   189, 191–2, 195, 207
Langalerie, Philippe de Gentil, Marquis of   263
Lausanne   177
legislation   22, 97, 99, 109, 133, 166, 168, 239–43, 249–51, 262
Lehmann, Georg   132–3, 135, 137, 139–40, 142, 144
Leibniz, Gottfried Wilhelm   158, 307
Leiden   11, 223, 225
Leipzig   51, 53–4, 62, 127–32, 137–8, 143, 146–7, 149–50, 152, 154, 159, 176, 239, 251, 255
Lequien, Gerardus Jr   15
Lerche, Cornelius Pedersen   220
Liberós, Esteve   32
librarians   89, 93, 164, 210, 264, 271, 277, 284–5, 288, 300, 302, 304–6, 310
libraries
  design   296, 300, 314
  private   108, 113, 121, 125, 164, 217, 236, 263–289, 291, 293–5, 317
  public   164, 195, 201, 203, 291, 316–7
Liège   172
Lille   172, 271
Lincolnshire   189, 191–2, 194, 204, 208
Linden, Johannes Antonides van der   305
Linnaeus, Carl   306, 309
Linz   132
Littlebury, Robert   200–1, 208
Lloris, Joan Dimas   22, 30
Lochner, Paul   131, 147–9, 160
Locke, John   212, 229, 291, 294–5, 304–5, 308–9
London   4, 13–14, 51, 164, 172, 176–8, 180–1, 197, 200–1, 203, 210, 212–3, 215, 221–7, 231, 234–7, 290, 296, 302, 315
Löscher, Valentin Ernst   255–6
Los-Rios, Jean-François de   287
Louis Auguste de Bourbon, Duke of Maine   183
Louis XIII, King of France   77, 166
Louise Bénédicte de Bourbon, Duchesse of Maine   183
Low Countries. *See* Dutch Republic
Lübeck   238–262
Lund   227
Lyon   161–2, 166–7, 172–3, 175–6, 179–84, 287

Macerata 76, 90
Machon, Louis 264–5, 287
Malesherbes, Chrétien Guillaume de Lamoignon de 167, 181–3
Malvasia, Cornelio 81–2, 85, 92
Manchester 192, 195, 200–1
Mangoldt, Gregor 149, 152, 160
Manolessi, Carlo 75–82, 85–6, 88–90, 92–7, 99–104
manuscripts 48, 74, 166, 181–3, 257, 269, 285–6, 290–1, 295–6, 304, 312, 315
Manzini, Carlo Antonio 82, 84–5
Manzini, Giovanni Battista 77
Marchand, Jean-Henri 172
Marchand, Prosper 270, 274–6
Maria Theresia, Empress 130, 145–6, 151, 154
Marseille 285–6
Marteau, Pierre 163
Martin, Gabriel 270–2, 274
Mataró (Catalonia) 21, 26, 34, 36
Maunsell, Andrew 305
Mayer, Johann Caspar 149, 160
Mayer, Johann Friedrich 245
Mazà, Nicolau 32
Medici, Cosimo III de', Grand Duke 91
Medici, Ferdinando II de', Grand Duke 80, 90–1, 101
Medici, House of 73, 75, 78, 80, 85–6, 88, 90–92, 94, 99, 101, 103–4
Medici, Leopoldo de', Prince 74–5, 78–80, 87–90, 92–3, 96, 99–101
Medici, Mattias de' 87
Meibom, Marcus 210
Mersenne, Marin 73
Mexico City 109–10, 113
Mexico. *See* New Spain
Middelburg 11, 14, 210
Milton, John 122, 222–3
Mir, Gaspar 29
Mirabeau, Honoré-Gabriel Riquetti comte de 280–6
Modena 82
Monath, Peter Conrad 132–3, 142
Montalbani, Ovidio 83–4, 95–6, 98
Montanari, Geminiano 82
Montesquieu, Charles-Louis de Secondat baron de 122, 161–2, 306
Montpellier 166, 304
Mullem, Johann Conrad 149

Nassau, Albertine Agnes van 217
Naudé, Gabriel 264, 300–4, 306–7, 309–12, 314–5
Nebrija, Antonio de 22, 32–4, 36, 39
Née de La Rochelle, Jean-Baptiste 279, 281
Netherlands. *See* Dutch Republic
Neuchâtel 177
New Granada 106–7, 109, 117–125
New Spain 106–117, 125
newspapers 4, 6–8, 17, 19, 46, 50, 63–4, 66, 132, 135, 144, 148, 219, 229, 232–6, 257
Newton, Isaac 59, 120–21, 124–5
Nicolai, Friedrich 127
Nuremberg 127–129, 131–5, 137–44, 148–52, 154, 159–60

Olomouc 137
Olot (Catalonia) 21, 26, 38
Oprechte Haarlemsche Courant 7–9, 229, 234
Oxford 212, 215, 221, 225–6, 228, 231, 237

Palatine War of Succession 134
Palm, Carl Joseph Freiherr von 258
pamphlets 4, 19–20, 46, 48–9, 52–5, 57, 59–60, 64–7, 96, 145, 147, 182, 218–9, 224, 245, 269, 304
Panckoucke, Charles-Joseph 179–80
paper 30, 37, 38n, 151–2, 161, 170, 172, 175, 212, 312
Paris 51, 90, 143, 165–9, 172–3, 175, 177–8, 181–2, 184–5, 237, 270–1, 286, 300
Parma 83
Paterson, Samuel 273
Paulmy, Marquis de 164
Peace of Roskilde 212
Pellerel, Gaspar 120
Pepys, Samuel 295, 303–4, 308–9, 311, 315
Pérez de Soto, Melchor 113
Perrot, collector 277–9, 289
Peru 107, 124
Petersen, Johann Wilhelm 236, 241
Petersen, Johanna Eleonora 241
Petty, William 300
Philadelphia 175
Philip II, King of Spain 107
Philip V, King of Spain 23, 39–40
Planella, Miquel 33
Posa, Pere 29–30

Possevino, Antonio   300
Potsdam   135
Pozzo, Cassiano dal   89
Prague   129, 131–8, 140–155, 157–160
Preßburg. *See* Bratislava
Preti, Vincenzo   97
print shops   30, 36–41, 142, 151*n*, 155, 165–6, 168, 172, 175, 179, 181, 183–5, 200. *See also* bookshops
print, price of   7–8, 26, 34–5, 37, 41, 51, 53, 55, 94, 100–2, 144, 155, 157, 160, 212, 218, 229, 249, 251, 296–7
printers   23, 29, 32–4, 36, 38–9, 76–7, 78*n*, 80, 99, 149, 161, 163–7, 169, 172–3, 175–81, 183–5, 197, 212, 218, 229, 234–6, 241, 256, 258, 260, 264
privileges   26, 36, 38–40, 96, 98, 107, 133–4, 137–8, 140, 145, 147, 150–9, 162, 164–9, 172, 176, 178, 183–4, 241, 243, 249–51, 260
Prussia   56, 181
publishers   3, 11, 15, 73, 75–6, 77*n*, 79–81, 85–6, 92–4, 96, 102, 104, 127–30, 132–5, 140–4, 146, 154, 157–9, 213, 218, 236, 250, 260, 277, 279, 286, 288

Raynal, Guillaume Thomas François   180
Reading, William   303
Réamur, René Antoine Ferchault de   306
Regensburg   132, 258*n*
Regnault, Geoffroy   179–80
Réguilliat, Jean-Baptiste   176
Republic of Letters   95, 104–5, 240–1, 251, 253–60, 290, 304
Rey, Marc-Michel   169, 172
Riccioli, Giovanni Battista   83, 98
Rigollet, François   182–3
Rinaldini, Carlo   75, 89–93, 101–3
Rive, Jean-Joseph   284–6
Rodríguez Sandoval, Ignacio   116–7
Rome   51, 73, 87, 90, 96–8, 100, 175, 237
Rosembach, Joan   29, 32
Rosenmüller, Sophia Johann   149, 155, 156*n*
Rostgaard, Frederik   300
Roth-Scholtz, Friedrich   141–2
Rothwell, John   200–1
Rotterdam   11, 17, 19, 22, 177, 223, 229, 231
Rouen   166
Rousseau, Jean Jacques   172, 176*n*
Rovirola, Rafael de   32

Rüdiger, Johann Andreas   134–5
Rüdiger, Johann Friedrich   127, 129–30, 132, 134–160
Rüdiger, Johann Michael   134
Russia   56

Sacchini, Francesco   300
Saillant, Charles   181–2
Saint-Léger, Barthélemy Mercier de   288
Salmasius, Claude   222
Salzburg   131, 143
Scaliger, Josephus   223
Scandinavia   241. *See also* Denmark; Sweden
Scavenius, Peder Lauridsen   210, 212
Schouten, Anthony   233
Schultze, Gottfried   235
Scotland   212*n*, 224–5
Scott, Robert   234
Seelen, Johann Heinrich von   255–261
Selden, John   222, 225–6, 228, 231, 236
Seville   108
Shaftesbury, Anthony Ashley Cooper, 3rd Earl of   229
Sloane, Hans   290–318
Société typographique de Neuchâtel   172, 179
Spada, Bernardino   88
Spada, Virgilio   87–8
Spain   26, 106–7, 109, 121, 210
Sporck, Franz Anton Graf von   139, 141–2
St. Petersburg   56–7
Starck, Carpar Heinrich   245–6
Stationers' Company   212
Stöter, Burchard   250
Strasbourg   271
Stuttgart   143
Sweden   210, 227–8. *See also* Scandinavia
Swiss Confederation   131, 163

Tebaldini, Niccolò   76, 77*n*, 80
Tebano, Artemisio. *See* Malvasia, Cornelio
Temple, William   216, 233
ten Hoorn, Jan   15, 17
The Hague   8, 11, 176, 180, 210
Thirty Years' War   83, 90, 239
Thomas, Thomas   197
Thou, Jacques Auguste de   258
Torricelli, Evangelista   85
Torti, Invenzio   95

INDEX

Trefler, Florian 301
Trent, Council of 205
Trévoux 183–5
Trigge, Francis 192–9, 203, 205, 208
Trinxer, Joan 30
Turmeda, Anselm 27

Uffenbach, Zacharias Conrad von 238–9, 241–2, 253, 257–8, 262
Ulfeldt, Laurids 210, 212
Ulm 132, 143
universities 3, 5, 7, 82–3, 85, 95, 99, 102, 197, 218, 241, 256, 274
University of: Angers 215
    Barcelona 39
    Bologna 82, 86
    Cambridge 197
    Cervera 39–40
    Copenhagen 225
    Girona 39
    Heidelberg 134
    Helmstedt 239
    Jena 57
    Lleida 39
    Lund 227
    Macerata 90
    Oxford 194, 215, 221
    Paris 73, 166
    Pisa 75, 91, 93, 102–3
    Prague 146, 152–4
    del Rosario 120
    Uppsala 227
Ussher, James 222
Utrecht 11, 14, 17, 233

Valladares, Gavino de 42
Vasari, Giorgio 79–81, 88
Veith, Philipp Jakob 132
Velde, Jacob van de 14

Verhoeve, Johannes 235
vernacular print 7, 13, 15, 32, 57, 73, 94, 113, 117, 120, 129, 138, 143, 158, 177, 200–1, 203, 210, 212–4, 216–7, 220, 224, 226, 230, 232–5, 237
Vernet, Antoni 29
Vialon, Claude-André 179–80
Vic (Catalonia) 25, 36, 40
Vienna 128n, 132–3, 137–8, 140, 144
Vives, Lluís 22
Vivian, Peter Paul 144
Viviani, Francesco 93
Viviani, Vincenzo 74–5, 88–9, 91–4, 96, 99–101, 104
Voltaire (François-Marie Arouet) 147, 180, 182–3, 291

Walder, Daniel 132
Walther, Conrad Georg 148–9, 154–5, 160
Walton, Brian 221–2, 226–7, 230
Wanley, Humphrey 304, 309
War of the Spanish Succession 25, 39
Weidmann, George 130, 176
Wessel, Johann 248–50
West India Company, Dutch 223–4
Wiedeburg, Johann Bernhard 57, 60, 62, 64
Willer, Georg 257, 265
Willers, Christian Heinrich 257
Winchelsey, Robert 189
Witt, Cornelis de 214–6, 225
Witt, Johan de 214–6, 225
Wittenberg 239
Worshipful Society of Apothecaries 302
Würzburg 141
Wussin, Kaspar Zacharias 152, 160

Zedler, Johann Heinrich 249
Zieger, Clara Susanna 135, 152n
Zieger, Johann 135, 137, 139–41